THE LAW AND GOVERNANCE OF MINING AND MINERALS

This book explores a disciplinary matrix for the study of the law and governance concerning mining and minerals from a global perspective. The book considers the key challenges of achieving the goals of Agenda 2030 and the transition to low-carbon circular economies. The perspective encompasses the multi-faceted and highly complex interaction of multiple fields of international law and policy, soft law and standards, domestic laws and regulations as well as local levels of ordering of social relations.

What emerges is a largely neglected, unsystematised and under-theorised field of study which lies at the intersection of the global economy, environmental sustainability, human rights and social equity. But it also underlies the many loopholes to address at all levels, most notably at the local level – land and land holders, artisanal miners, ecosystems, local economies, local linkages and development. The book calls for a truly cosmopolitan academic discipline to be built and identifies challenges to do so. It also sets a research agenda for further studies in this fast-changing field.

Global Energy Law and Policy: Volume 3

Global Energy Law and Policy

Series Editors
Peter D Cameron
Pieter Bekker
Volker Roeben

Energy policy and energy law are undergoing rapid global transformation, characterised by the push in favour of decarbonisation. The 2015 Sustainable Development Goals and the 2015 Paris Agreement on international climate action have forged a consensus for a pathway to a universal just transition towards a low-carbon economy for all states and all societies.

This series publishes conceptual work that help academics, legal practitioners and decision-makers to make sense of these transformational changes. The perspective of the series is global. It welcomes contributions on international law, regional law (for example, from the EU, US and ASEAN regions), and the domestic law of all states with emphasis on comparative works that identify horizontal trends, and including transnational law. The series' scope is comprehensive, embracing both public and commercial law on energy in all forms and sources and throughout the energy life-cycle from extraction, production, operation, consumption and waste management/decommissioning. The series is a forum for innovative interdisciplinary work that uses the insights of cognate disciplines to achieve a better understanding of energy law and policy in the 21st century.

Recent titles in this series:

Decarbonisation and the Energy Industry
edited by Tade Oyewumni, Penelope Crossley, Frédéric Gilles Sourgens and Kim Talus

The Global Energy Transition: Law, Policy and Economics
for Energy in the 21st Century
edited by Peter D Cameron, Xiaoyi Mu and Volker Roeben

The Law and Governance
of Mining and Minerals

A Global Perspective

Ana Elizabeth Bastida

·HART·
OXFORD · LONDON · NEW YORK · NEW DELHI · SYDNEY

HART PUBLISHING

Bloomsbury Publishing Plc

Kemp House, Chawley Park, Cumnor Hill, Oxford, OX2 9PH, UK

1385 Broadway, New York, NY 10018, USA

29 Earlsfort Terrace, Dublin 2, Ireland

HART PUBLISHING, the Hart/Stag logo, BLOOMSBURY and the Diana logo are
trademarks of Bloomsbury Publishing Plc

First published in Great Britain 2020

First published in hardback, 2020
Paperback edition, 2022

Copyright © Ana Elizabeth Bastida 2020

Ana Elizabeth Bastida has asserted her right under the Copyright, Designs and Patents
Act 1988 to be identified as Author of this work.

All rights reserved. No part of this publication may be reproduced or transmitted in any form or by
any means, electronic or mechanical, including photocopying, recording, or any information
storage or retrieval system, without prior permission in writing from the publishers.

While every care has been taken to ensure the accuracy of this work, no responsibility for loss or
damage occasioned to any person acting or refraining from action as a result of any statement in it
can be accepted by the authors, editors or publishers.

All UK Government legislation and other public sector information used in the work is Crown
Copyright ©. All House of Lords and House of Commons information used in the work is
Parliamentary Copyright ©. This information is reused under the terms of the Open Government
Licence v3.0 (http://www. nationalarchives.gov.uk/doc/open-government-licence/version/3) except
where otherwise stated.

All Eur-lex material used in the work is © European
Union, http://eur-lex.europa.eu/, 1998–2022.

A catalogue record for this book is available from the British Library.

Library of Congress Cataloging-in-Publication Data

Names: Bastida, Ana Elizabeth, author.

Title: The law and governance of mining and minerals : a global perspective / Ana Elizabeth Bastida.

Description: Oxford, UK ; New York, NY : Hart Publishing, an imprint of
Bloomsbury Publishing, 2020. | Series: Global energy law and policy;
volume 3 | Includes bibliographical references and index.

Identifiers: LCCN 2020036724 (print) | LCCN 2020036725 (ebook) |
ISBN 9781849463454 (hardback) | ISBN 9781509942589 (paperback) |
ISBN 9781782255680 (Epub) | ISBN 9781782255673 (pdf)

Subjects: LCSH: Mining law. | Mineral industries—Law and legislation.

Classification: LCC K3904 .B375 2020 (print) | LCC K3904 (ebook) | DDC 343.07/7—dc23

LC record available at https://lccn.loc.gov/2020036724

LC ebook record available at https://lccn.loc.gov/2020036725

ISBN: HB: 978-1-84946-345-4
PB: 978-1-50994-258-9
ePDF: 978-1-78225-567-3
ePub: 978-1-78225-568-0

Typeset by Compuscript Ltd, Shannon

To find out more about our authors and books visit www.hartpublishing.co.uk. Here you will find
extracts, author information, details of forthcoming events and the option to sign up for our newsletters.

For Ana, Diana, Lucía and Tiago

PREFACE AND ACKNOWLEDGEMENTS

'Minerals and metals', or 'subsoil resources' or 'strategic resources', are called as such from the perspective of sites of extraction. They are known as 'raw materials', 'commodities' or 'critical substances' from the point of view of global markets; 'commercial assets' from the perspective of investors; or 'commons', 'fruits of nature' or 'natural heritage' from perspectives that place emphasis on the value of nature; and 'recycled materials' and 'recovered inputs' as they enter the circular economy. The many ways of naming the very same phenomenon provide a glimpse into the challenges of systematisation of this area of enquiry.

The study of mining law – *stricto sensu* the rules and procedures to obtain mineral rights; *lato sensu* the multi-layered framework relevant to mining as an activity – has so far been mostly circumscribed to domestic legal systems and generally limited to national boundaries. It has not yet broadened systematically to encompass the international, transnational, regional, national and local levels of normative orderings of social relations concerning mining and minerals – what I call the law and governance of mining and minerals or 'mineral law' *latissimo sensu*. Unlike energy law, which has been subject of academic enquiry and shifted from its domestic law locus to the field of international and transnational law studies, attention to this area has increased exponentially in recent years, but this has remained scattered, and international perspectives are only now starting to engage with the literature and framings on mining law as typically developed at domestic levels.

To build the law and governance of mining and minerals 'as an academic discipline' requires overcoming the challenges of *definition*; of scope and breadth of the *subject matter*; of understandings on its *normative* guidance and its implications, and of much needed *diversity* in knowledge-making. It is only through a truly cosmopolitan community of practice that more textured understandings of governance from global to local levels can be achieved. A diverse community has an important role in shaping academic framings, practice and mindsets and contributes in shifting from a focus on *extractives* towards their role in *transformative* outcomes for sustainable futures and the just resource transition.

The need for a global ethical framework to understand and regulate mining and minerals has become even more visible in the last few months, as the paramount role of minerals in the energy transition, the weaknesses of global supply chains, and the acceleration of trends concerning automation and digitalisation of mining operations and ethical investment have come to the fore.

viii *Preface and Acknowledgements*

This all happens at a time when governments face great pressure to rebuild post-pandemic economies and public finances and resource rich countries are questioning anachronistic legal and tax structures for the sector, and how they benefit from their resource endowment.

In writing this book, I have greatly benefited from the wealth of knowledge, wisdom and diverse perspectives of many colleagues and friends, particularly from the space, academic environment and exposure to a global community of practice provided by CEPMLP at the University of Dundee. Particularly thanks go to Peter Cameron for strongly supporting this publication, and to Volker Roeben for reading my draft manuscript and encouraging the whole process of writing to its final completion. Many thanks to my colleague Ms Janeth Warden-Fernandez and to the School of Social Sciences' Executive team for continuing support; and to Pieter Bekker, Phillip Crowson, Sergei Vinogradov, Antonio Pedro and Magnus Ericsson, as well as Hugo Vivot, Marcela Flores, Diego Murguía and Adriano Trindade for either sharing knowledge and commenting on pieces of my work, or providing me with invaluable material and insights. My late father was a great source of knowledge on mining and minerals. The late Thomas Wälde was a source of knowledge on the global energy and resources industries and of inspiration on the vision of diversifying communities of practice. PhD, LLM, MSc and MBA candidates have for many years engaged with new questions and diverse perspectives to the open collaborative space proposed in my classes, with particular thanks to Hamidou Drame, Jaqueline Terrel, María Sol Iriart, Jamil Hijazi, Kwabena Mensah, Hugo Ossandon and Fiorella Romero for helping me to review and collect new material. I am solely responsible for any potential errors and inaccuracies.

I am very grateful to the Rocky Mountain Mineral Law Foundation and the excellent Frances Hartogh for supporting me with funding under their grants scheme to cover research assistance, and to Liliana Lerchundi for reviewing and editing many drafts of my manuscript. A special word of thanks to Roberta Bassi and her team with Hart Publishing for strong and patient support.

Above all, thanks to my family and friends. To Ana, for her unique wisdom and constant encouragement; to Leandro, for very insightful discussions on my draft manuscript and being so supportive, and to Gabriela, Claudia, Lili, Silvina, Silvana and Lynne for continuing encouragement. The book is dedicated to Ana, Diana, Lucía and Tiago.

CONTENTS

Preface and Acknowledgements.. vii
Abbreviations and Acronyms... xiii
Table of Cases xvii
Table of Instruments.. xix

1. **Understanding the Law of Mining and Minerals from a Global Perspective** 1
   I.   The Argument of this Book 5
   II. Mineral Law from a Global Perspective: A Cosmopolitan View............ 7
        A.   The International Level.. 11
        B.   The Transnational Level.. 13
        C.   The Regional Level 15
        D.   States.. 17
        E.   The Local Level 19
   III. Mineral Law in International Scholarship.............................. 20
   IV. Law and the Governance of Mining and Minerals................ 25
   V.   The Purpose of this Book.. 26
   VI. The Structure of this Book.. 27

2. **Mining and Minerals, Actors and Governance from a Global Perspective**.. 28
   I.   Minerals: 'The Third Kingdom of Nature' 28
   II.   Minerals in Global Production Networks 30
   III. The Question of Minerals' 'Criticality' or 'Strategic' Status.... 32
   IV.   Mining: 'The Science, Technique and Business of Mineral Discovery and Extraction' 33
         A.   Mining Processes.. 34
         B.   Environmental, Social and Governance Impacts of Mining........ 34
         C.   The Lifecycle of Industrial Mining................................ 36
              i.   From Surveys to a Proven Ore Reserve.................... 36
              ii. From Site Construction to Extraction:
                   Mining Investment Decision 38
         D.   The Capital-Intensive Nature and Risk Profile of Industrial Mining.. 39
   V.   The Structure of the Mining Industry 41
   VI.   Actors and Governance.. 43
   VII. Mining, Development and the Role of Law under International Policy and 'Scripts' 44

x *Contents*

3. Mining and Minerals in International Law and Policy **52**
    I.   Jurisdictional Basis for Controlling Resources:
        The Principle of Territorial Sovereignty..52
    II.   International Law: From Coordination to Cooperation.........................53
    III. The Principle of Permanent Sovereignty Over
        Natural Resources 55
    IV. The Environment, Natural Resources
        and Sustainable Development 62
        A.   1972 Stockholm United Nations Conference on the
             Human Environment 62
        B.   The 1987 Brundtland Report..65
        C.   The 1992 Rio Declaration and Agenda 21 68
        D.   2002 Johannesburg Declaration and Plan of Implementation........71
        E.   2012 Rio+20...76
        F.   Agenda 2030 and the SDGs...78
        G.   The Paris Agreement and Other Multilateral
             Environmental Agreements 81
    V.   Law, Sustainable Resources Management
        and the Paradigm of Sustainability...83
        A.   The Status of Sustainable Development under
             International Law..84
        B.   The Core Constitutive Elements of
             Sustainable Development 86
        C.   Integrated Decision-Making Processes for Sustainable
             Resource Management..88

**4. Mining and Minerals in Fields of International
Law and Governance** **92**
    I.   Mining and Minerals in International Economic Law 93
        A.   Mining and Minerals under WTO Law..95
        B.   Mining under International Investment Law 96
           i.   The 'Treatification' of International Investment Law 96
           ii.   Investment Standards and International
                Mining Disputes...98
           iii. A 'Global Regime Governing Investment' 102
           iv. Investment Treaties and the Question of Policy Space.........103
    II.   Mining and Minerals in International
        Human Rights Law 105
        A.   The Human Rights System 105
        B.   Human Rights and Resource Development 106
    III. Mining and Anti-Corruption Instruments...110
    IV. The Responsibility of Transnational
        Corporations and Business Enterprises 112

Contents xi

V. Transnational Mining and Minerals Standards
and Governance 112
    A.   Standards Set by Intergovernmental Organisations....................113
    B.   Intergovernmental Initiatives
        with Accountability Mechanisms 115
    C.   Multi-Stakeholder Governance...116
    D.   Corporate Self-Regulation...118

**5. Mining and Minerals Regimes in the
Global Commons.. 123**
  I. Extent of Territorial Sovereignty Over Maritime Zones.....................124
  II. Mining Regimes in the Global Commons..126
    A.   The Seabed Mining Regime..127
        i.   Common Heritage of Mankind...128
        ii. The Mining Code 130
        iii. The Enterprise and the 'Parallel System'.................................131
        iv. The Regime for Prospecting, Exploring
            and Mining in the Area 132
    B.   The Question of Banning Mining in Antarctica............................134
    C.   Exploring the Moon and Other Celestial Bodies 135

**6. Mining Law Regimes at the Level of Nation-States
(and their Interface with Local Levels) 138**
  I. Ownership and Jurisdiction Over Minerals in Situ...............................140
    A.   The Landownership Doctrine 141
    B.   The *Regalian* and Domanial Doctrines...144
        i.   The *Regalian* Doctrine 144
        ii. The Domanial Doctrine 145
    C.   The *Res Nullius* Doctrine 148
    D.   Interpreting States' Duties to Manage Resources 149
  II. Typologies and Functions of Mining Law Regimes 150
    A.   Possessory, Licensing and Contractual Systems............................152
        i.   Background – 'The Free Mining'
            Tradition – Possessory Systems...152
        ii. Licensing 154
        iii. Contractual Regimes 156
    B.   Open Access, Bidding and Discretionary
        Processes of Allocation 160
  III. The Interface with Land Rights 161
  IV. The Principle of 'National Interest' or
     'Public Purpose' in Mining and Minerals 163
  V. From *Thin* Tenure Regimes to *Thick* Regulation....................................164
  VI. Mineral Law 'As Interfaces' 167
    A.   The Transition from Exploration to Exploitation Rights..............169

xii   *Contents*

	B.	The Multi-Faceted Nature of the Title and Permitting Process......170
	C.	The Mineral Rights–Land Nexus: Spatial Planning 172
	D.	The Processes of Consultation and Consent...................................173
	E.	Administrative Processes and the Rule of Law...............................174
	F.	Administrative Processes and Transparency Standards...............175
VII.		Redefining the Disciplinary Matrix of Mineral Law for Sustainability...176

7. The Law and Governance of Mining and Minerals from a Global Perspective: 'An Overarching Vision' 178

  I. Conclusions..179

  II. A Research Agenda 182

Selected Bibliography *184*

Index *197*

ABBREVIATIONS AND ACRONYMS

AIPN	Association of International Petroleum Negotiators
ALSF	African Legal Support Facility
AMLA	Africa Mining Legislation Atlas
AMV	Africa Mining Vision
ARM	Alliance for Responsible Mining
ASEAN	Association of Southeast Asian Nations
ASM	Artisanal and Small-Scale Mining
BIT	Bilateral Investment Treaty
CEPMLP	Centre for Energy, Petroleum, Mineral Law and Policy, University of Dundee, UK
CERDS	Charter of Economic Rights and Duties of States
CIMVAL	Code for the Valuation of Mineral Properties
CMV	Country Mining Visions
COMESA	Common Market for Eastern and Southern Africa
COP	Conference of the Parties
CS	Continental Shelf
DRC	Democratic Republic of the Congo
EC	European Commission
ECLAC	Economic Commission for Latin America and the Caribbean
ECOWAS	Economic Community of West African States
EEZ	Exclusive Economic Zone
EIA	Environmental Impact Assessment
EITI	Extractive Industries Transparency Initiative

xiv *Abbreviations and Acronyms*

ESS	Environmental and Social Standards (World Bank)
EU	European Union
FET	Fair and Equitable Treatment
GA	United Nations General Assembly (alternatively UNGA)
GATS	General Agreement on Trade in Services
GATT	General Agreements on Tariffs and Trade
IBRD	International Bank for Reconstruction and Development
IBA	International Bar Association
ICGLR	International Conference on the Great Lakes Region
ICJ	International Court of Justice
ICMM	International Council for Mining and Metals
ICSID	International Convention on the Settlement of Investment Disputes between States and Nationals of Other States
IFC	International Finance Corporation
IGF	Intergovernmental Forum on Mining, Minerals, Metals and Sustainable Development
ILA	International Law Association
ILM	International Legal Materials
IMF	International Monetary Fund
IRMA	Initiative for Responsible Mining Assurance
IRP	International Resource Panel
IRR	Internal Rate of Return
IUCN	International Union for Conservation of Nature
JENRL	Journal of Energy and Natural Resources Law
JORC	Joint Ore Reserves Committee
KPCS	Kimberley Process Certification Scheme
MCEP	Mining Certification Evaluation Project
MFN	Most–Favoured Nation
MIGA	Multilateral Investment Guarantee

Abbreviations and Acronyms xv

NAFTA	North American Free Trade Agreement
NIEO	New International Economic Order
OAS	Organisation of American States
OECD	Organisation for Economic Co-operation and Development
OEIGWG	Open-ended Intergovernmental Working Group on Transnational Corporations and Other Business Enterprises with Respect to Human Rights
PNAS	Proceedings of the National Academy of Sciences of the USA
PSONR	Permanent Sovereignty over Natural Resources
RIAA	Reports of International Arbitral Awards
RMMLF	Rocky Mountain Mineral Law Foundation
SCM	Southern Common Market (MERCOSUR or MERCOSUL in their Spanish and Portuguese acronyms, respectively)
SDGs	Sustainable Development Goals
STRADE	Strategic Dialogue on Sustainable Raw Materials for Europe
TCFD	Task Force on Climate-related Financial Disclosures
TRIMS	Agreement on Trade-Related Investment Measures
TSM	Towards Sustainable Mining
UK	United Kingdom of Great Britain
UNCITRAL	United Nations Commission on International Trade Law
UNCLOS	United Nations Convention on the Law of the Sea
UNCTAD	United Nations Conference on Trade and Development
UNDP	United Nations Development Programme
UNEA	United Nations Environment Assembly
UNECA	United Nations Economic Commission for Africa
UNECE	UN Economic Commission for Europe
UNEP	United Nations Environment Programme
UNFCCC	United Nations Framework Convention on Climate Change
UNGA	United Nations General Assembly (alternatively GA)

xvi   *Abbreviations and Acronyms*

UNGP	UN Guiding Principles on Business and Human Rights
UNTS	UN Treaty System
US	United States of America
USMCA	United States–Mexico–Canada Agreement
WAEMU	West African Economic and Monetary Union
WAOML	World Association of Mining Lawyers
WCED	World Commission on Environment and Development
WSSD	World Summit on Sustainable Development
WTO	World Trade Organization
WWF	World Wide Fund for Nature

TABLE OF CASES

International Court of Justice

Gabčíkovo–Nagymaros Project (Hungary v Slovakia), Judgment,
ICJ Reports 1997, 78 84–85
Gabčíkovo–Nagymaros Project (Hungary v Slovakia), Separate Opinion
of Judge Weeramantry, 85 84
*Armed Activities on the Territory of the Congo (Democratic Republic
of the Congo v Uganda)*, Judgment, ICJ Reports 2005, 168................................61
Pulp Mills on the River Uruguay (Argentina v Uruguay), Judgment,
ICJ Reports 2010, 14 84

International Arbitral Tribunals

Island of Palmas Case (or Miangas) (*United States of America v
The Netherlands*), Award of the Tribunal, The Hague, 4 April 1928,
II RIAA 829 52
Trail Smelter Case (*United States v Canada*), 16 April 1938 and
11 March 1941, RIIA III 1905..69
*Iron Rhine ('Ijzeren Rijn') Railway between the Kingdom of Belgium and the
Kingdom of the Netherlands*, Decision of 24 May 2005, RIAA XXVII,
35–125, para 59..84

ICSID

Carnegie Minerals Limited v Republic of The Gambia, ICSID no ARB/09/19,
Award..99
Gold Reserve Inc v Bolivarian Republic of Venezuela, ICSID Case No
ARB(AF)/09/1, Award..101
*Quiroborax SA, Non Metallic Minerals S and Allan Fosk Kaplún
v Plurinational State of Bolivia*, ICSID Case no ARB/06/2, Award...................99

UNCITRAL

Glamis Gold, Ltd v United States of America, UNCITRAL. Awarded
8 June 2009 100

xviii   *Table of Cases*

Inter-American Court of Human Rights

Kichwa Indigenous People of Sarayaku v Ecuador, Judgment (Merits and
  Reparations). Inter-American Court of Human Rights, 27 June 2012 109
*Saramaka People v Suriname, Judgment (Preliminary Objections, Merits,
  Reparations and Costs)*, Inter-American Court of Human Rights, 28
  November 2007, Series C No 172... 108–09

WTO Appellate Body

China – Measures Related to the Exportation of Various Raw Materials
  (China – Raw Materials), Report of the WTO Appellate Body
  (30 January 2012) WT/DS394/AB/R, WT/DS395/ABR and
  WT/DS398/AB/R...96
Shrimp/Turtle Case, WTO, 6 November 1998, 38 ILM121 (1999),
  para129, at no 107 84

Municipal Courts

England

Consett Iron Co Ltd v Clavering Trustees [1935] 2 KB 42.......................................164

India

Reliance Industries Limited v Reliance Natural Resources Limited [2010],
  Insc 374 (7 May 2010), Supreme Court of Justice of India.............................149

South Africa

De Beers Consolidated Mines Ltd v Ataqua Mining (Pty) Ltd and Others (3215/06)
  [2007] ZAFSHC 74 (13 December 2007)...147

TABLE OF INSTRUMENTS

Treaties and Other International Acts

1941   Atlantic Charter, Declaration of Principles issued by the President of the United States and the Prime Minister of the United Kingdom, 14 August 1941 93

1945   Statute of the International Court of Justice, 33 UNTS 993........................11

1945   United Nations Charter 53, 55, 105

1948   GA Resolution A/RES/217A (III). Universal Declaration of Human Rights. Adopted at its 183th plenary meeting, 10 December 1948 105

1950   European Convention for the Protection of Human Rights and Fundamental Freedoms, 4 November 1950, 213 UNTS 221............................106

1966   International Convention on the Settlement of Investment Disputes between States and Nationals of Other States (ICSID), Washington DC, World Bank...98

1966   GA Resolution. International Covenant on Civil and Political Rights. Adopted on 19 December 1966. 999 UNTS 172...................................105

1966   GA Resolution 2200A (XXI). International Covenant on Economic, Social and Cultural Rights. Adopted on 16 December 1966. 999 UNTS 3.. 105, 107

1969   American Convention on Human Rights, 22 November 1969, 1144 UNTS 144 106

1971   Convention on Wetlands of International Importance especially as Waterfowl Habitat. Concluded at Ramsar, Iran, on 2 February 1971. 996 UNTS 245 82

1972   Convention for the Protection of the World Cultural and Natural Heritage. Adopted by the General Conference of the United Nations Educational, Scientific and Cultural Organization at its 17th session, Paris, 16 November 1972. 1037 UNTS 151...82

1978   Vienna Convention on Succession of States in respect of Treaties (Vienna, 23 August 1978 and entered into force on 6 November 1996). 1946 UNTS 3 60

1979   Agreement Governing the Activities of States on the Moon and Other Celestial Bodies (Moon Treaty) (signed on 18 December 1979 and entered into force on 11 July 1984 under Secretary-General of the United Nations (Depositary))...136

xx   *Table of Instruments*

1979   Convention on the Conservation of Migratory Species of Wild
Animals (with appendices). Concluded in Bonn on 23 June 1979,
1651 UNTS 333; 1 82

1981   African Charter on Human and Peoples' Rights, 27 June 1981,
1520 UNTS 217 .... 61, 106

1982   United Nations Convention on the Law of the Sea,
10 December 1982, 21 ILM1261 (1982) (in force as of
16 November 1994 ....60, 124, 127, 131

1983   Vienna Convention on Succession of States in respect of State
Property, Archives and Debts (Vienna, 8 April 1983, not yet in force).
See Official Records of the United Nations Conference on Succession
of States in Respect of State Property, Archives and Debts, II
(UN publication, sales no E 94, vol 6) 60

1989   Convention (No 169) Concerning Indigenous and Tribal Peoples
in Independent Countries. Adopted by the General Conference
of the International Labour Organisation at its 76th session,
Geneva, 27 June 1989, 1650 UNTS 383..107

1992   Convention on Biological Diversity, 5 June 1992,
31 ILM818 (1992).. 68–69

1992   Framework Convention on Climate Change, 9 May 1992,
31 ILM849 (1992)..68

1994   Convention to Combat Desertification in Countries Experiencing
Serious Drought and/or Desertification Particularly in Africa,
17 June 1994, 33 ILM 1328 (1994)..82

1994   General Agreement on Tariffs and Trade [adopted on
15 April 1994 and entered into force on 1 January 1995]
1869 UNTS 299 93–97

1994   General Agreement on Trade in Services (adopted under
GATT on 15 April 1994 and entered into force on 1 January 1995),
1869 UNTS 183; ILM 1167 (1994)... 95, 97

1994   Agreement on Trade-Related Aspects of Intellectual Property
(adopted on 15 April 1994 and entered into force in 1995) 95

1994   Agreement on Trade-Related Investment Measures (adopted
in 1994 and entered into force in 1995 under the WTO) 97

1998   Protocol to the 1979 Convention on Long-Range Transboundary
Air Pollution on Heavy Metals, Aarhus, 24 June 1998,
2237 UNTS 4 69

2001   DOHA WTO Ministerial 2001: Ministerial Declaration,
WT/MIN(01)/DEC/1, 20 November 2001. Adopted on
14 November 2001 72

2002   Monterrey Consensus of the International Conference on
Financing for Development. Adopted on 22 March 2002 in
Monterrey, Mexico (updated at Doha, Qatar in 2008 and at
Addis Ababa in 2015) 72

Table of Instruments xxi

2003   GA Resolution 58/4, 31 October 2003. United Nations Convention
against Corruption. Entered into force on 14 December 2005 in accordance
with article 68(1), 2349 UNTS 41 111
2015   United Nations Framework Convention on Climate Change (UNFCCC),
Paris Agreement – Decision 1/CP.21 – Report of the Conference of the Parties
on its twenty-first session, held in Paris from 30 November to13 December
2015 Addendum Part Two: Action taken by the Conference of the Parties at
its Twenty-First Session...10
2018   Regional Agreement on Access to Information, Public Participation
and Justice in Environmental Matters in Latin America and the Caribbean)
adopted at Escazú, Costa Rica, on 4 March 2018, opened for signature on
27 September 2018 16

United Nations

1972   Declaration of the United Nations Conference on the
Human Environment (Stockholm), 16 June 1972 (1972)
11 ILM 1416.. 62–66, 68–70, 88
1992   Rio Declaration on the Environment and Development,
13 June 1992, 31 ILM 874 (1992) 68–71, 86–87
1992   Agenda 21, 13 June 1992, UN Doc. A/CONF. 151/26 (1992) 68–72, 86
1992   Statement of Principles for a Global Consensus on the
Management, Conservation and Sustainable Development
of all Types of Forests, 13 June 1992, 31 ILM 881 (1992) 68
2002   Johannesburg Declaration on Sustainable Development,
also known as the Earth Summit 2002 (adopted by the World
Summit on Sustainable Development (WSSD) in
September 2002)... 71–72, 79, 87–88

General Assembly Resolutions

1950   GA Resolution 421 (V). Draft International Covenant on Human
Rights and Measures of Implementation: Future Work of the
Commission on Human Rights. Adopted at its 317th plenary meeting,
4 December 1950..55
1952   GA Resolution 523 (VI). Integrated Economic Development and
Commercial Agreements. Adopted at its 360th plenary meeting,
12 January 1952 55–56
1952   GA Resolution 623 (VII). Financing of Economic Development
through the Establishment of Fair and Equitable International Prices for
Primary Commodities and through the Execution of National Programmes
of Integrated Economic Development. Adopted at its 411th plenary
meeting, 21 December 1952 55

xxii   *Table of Instruments*

1952   GA Resolution 626 (VII). Right to Exploit Freely Natural Wealth
and Resources. Adopted at its 411th plenary meeting,
21 December 1952...55
1958   GA Resolution 1314 (XIII). Recommendations Concerning
International Respect for the Right of Peoples and Nations to
Self–Determination. Adopted at its 788th plenary meeting,
12 December 1958...55
1960   GA Resolution 1514 (XV). Declaration on the Granting of
Independence to Colonial Countries and Peoples (adopted at its
947th plenary meeting, 14 December 1960) 55
1960   GA Resolution 1515 (XV). Concerted Action for Economic
Development of Economically Less Developed Countries. Adopted
at its 948th plenary meeting, 15 December 1960...55
1962   GA Resolution 1803 (XVII). Permanent Sovereignty over
Natural Resources. Adopted at its 1194th plenary meeting,
14 December 1962..55–57, 99, 180
1962   GA Resolution 1831 (XVII). Economic Development and the
Conservation of Nature. Adopted in its 1197th plenary meeting,
18 December 1962...63
1966   GA Resolution 2158 (XXI). Permanent Sovereignty over
Natural Resources (adopted at its 1478th plenary meeting,
25 November 1966)...61
1968   GA Resolution 2398 (XXIII). Problems of the Human Environment.
Adopted at its 1733th plenary meeting, 3 December 1968.................................62
1969   GA Resolution 2581 (XXIV). United Nations Conference on the
Human Environment. Adopted at its 1834th plenary meeting.
15 December 1969...62
1970   GA Resolution 2692 (XXV). Permanent Sovereignty over Natural
Resources of Developing Countries and Expansion of Domestic Sources
of Accumulation for Economic Development (adopted at its 1926th
plenary meeting, 11 December 1970) 61
1974   GA 3201 (S–VI), Declaration on the Establishment of a New
International Economic Order. Adopted at its 2229th plenary meeting,
1 May 1974, A/RES/S-6/3201 56
1974   GA Resolution 3281 (XXIX) Charter of Economic Rights and
Duties of States. 29th session, agenda item 48, 12 December 1974,
A/RES/29/3281 56
1974   GA Resolution 3326 (XXIX), 16 December 1974 64
1982   GA Resolution 37/7. World Charter for Nature. Adopted
28 October 1982 64
1983   Draft UN Code of Conduct on Transnational Corporations,
May 1983, 23 ILM 626..57
1992   Draft UN Code of Conduct for Transnational Corporations............ 57, 113
1993   GA Resolution 48/121. World Conference on Human Rights.
Adopted at its 85th plenary meeting, 20 December 1993................................105

Table of Instruments xxiii

1993   Vienna Declaration (adopted at the World Conference on Human
Rights on 25 June 1993 and endorsed by GA Resolution 48/121 in its
85th plenary meeting, 20 December 1993)...105
2007   GA Resolution 61/295. Declaration on the Rights of Indigenous
Peoples. Adopted at 61st session, 107th plenary meeting on
13 September 2007 108
2012   GA Resolution 66/288, The Future We Want (Rio + 20) (adopted
by the General Assembly on 27 July 2012, endorsing the Outcome
Document of the United Nations Conference on Sustainable
Development held in Rio de Janeiro on 20–22 June 2012
(A/RES/66/288))...10, 69, 76–79, 87
2015   GA Resolution A/RES/70/1, Transforming Our World:
the 2030 Agenda for Sustainable Development, Sustainable
Development Goals (SDGs). 25 September 2015 .... 10, 76
2015   GA Resolution 69/313. Addis Ababa Action Agenda of the
Third International Conference on Financing for Development,
27 July 2015 76
2015   GA Resolution 69/283. Sendai Framework for Disaster Risk
Reduction 2015–2030, 3 June 2015 (approved at the Third UN World
Conference on Disaster Risk Reduction held in Sendai, Japan,
18 March 2015; updated and succeeded the earlier Hyogo Framework
for Action 2005–2015: Building the Resilience of Nations and
Communities to Disasters) 76
2017   GA Resolution on Work of the Statistical Commission pertaining
to the 2030 Agenda for Sustainable Development (A/RES/71/313)
on 6 July 2017 78
2018   GA Resolution 73/165. Declaration of Rights of Peasants and
Other People Working in Rural Areas. Adopted at 73rd session,
17 December 2018..109

ECOSOC

2017   UN, Economic and Social Council, Committee on Economic,
Social and Cultural Rights. General comment No. 24 (2017) on State
obligations under the International Covenant on Economic,
Social and Cultural Rights in the context of business activities,
E/C.12/GC/24, 10 August 2017 .... 105, 110

ILO

1977   ILO (International Labour Organisation) Tripartite Declaration
of Principles Concerning Multinational Enterprises and Social Policy,
amended in 2000, 2006 and 2017...115

xxiv   *Table of Instruments*

1998   ILO Declaration on Fundamental Principles and Rights at Work
(adopted at its 86th session in Geneva on 18 June 1998 and Annex
revised on 15 June 2010) 115

Security Council

2000   UN Security Council Resolution 1291. Adopted at its 4104th
meeting, 24 February 2000 60
2000   UN Security Council Resolution 1304. Adopted by the Security
Council at its 4159thmeeting, 16 June 2000 60

UN Environment Assembly

2019   UN Environment Assembly Resolution 4/19 Mineral Resource
Governance. Adopted on 15 March 2019 at Fourth session
Nairobi, 11–15 March 2019 (UNEP/EA.4/Res.19) 1, 79, 81, 88

UNEP

1980   World Conservation Strategy, IUCN, UNEP AND WWF 65

UNESCO

1948   UNESCO. Memorandum by the Department of Exact and
Natural Sciences, The Scientific Conference on Resource Conservation
and Utilisation. NS/UNR/1, 10 November 1948...62
2017   Operational Guidelines for the Implementation of the World
Heritage Convention. United Nations Educational, Scientific and
Cultural Organisation. Intergovernmental Committee for the Protection
of the World Cultural and Natural Heritage.WHC. 17/01 12 July 2017 82

UN Human Rights Bodies

2003   Draft Norms on the Responsibilities of Transnational Corporations
and Other Business Enterprises with regard to Human Rights.
Sub-Commission on the Promotion and Protection of *Human* Rights.
UN Doc E/CN.4/Sub.2/2003/12/Rev 2. 55th session, Geneva, 2003 113
2005   Office of the High Commissioner on Human Rights, Human Rights
and Transnational Corporations and other Business Enterprises, Human
Rights Resolution 2005/69, E/CN.4/RES/2005/69, 20 April 2005.................114

Table of Instruments xxv

2008   UN Human Rights Council, Protect, respect and remedy:
a framework for business and human rights: report of the Special
Representative of the Secretary–General on the Issue of Human
Rights and Transnational Corporations and Other Business
Enterprises, John Ruggie, 7 April 2008, A/HRC/8/5,¶ 36 .... 104, 110, 114
2011   UN Human Rights Council. 17/4 Human Rights and Transnational
Corporations and other Business Enterprises. A/HRC/RES/17/4.
Adopted at its 33rd meeting, 16 June 2011 .... 110, 114
2014   UN Human Rights Council. Resolution 26/9 Elaboration of an
international legally binding instrument on transnational corporations
and other business enterprises with respect to human rights.
A/HRC/26/L.22/Rev.1. Adopted at its 26th session, 26 June 2014 112

Specialised agencies and related bodies

World Bank, IFC and IMF

1944   Articles of Agreement of the International Monetary Fund
(adopted at the United Nations Monetary and Financial Conference,
Bretton Woods, New Hampshire, 22 July 1944. Entered into force
on 27 December 1945) 54, 93
1944   Articles of Agreement of the International Bank for Reconstruction
and Development (adopted at the United Nations Monetary and
Financial Conference, Bretton Woods, New Hampshire, 22 July 1944.
Entered into force on 27 December 1945. Amended on
17 December 1965, 16 February 1989 and 27 June 2012) 54, 93
2012   IFC's Sustainability Framework (including the Environmental
and Social Performance Standards) 116
2018   World Bank's Environmental and Social Framework
(including Environmental and Social Standards) 116

Regional Organisations

African Commission on Human and Peoples' Rights

2012   ACHPR/Res.224 (LI) 2012: Resolution on a Human Rights–Based
Approach to Natural Resources Governance. Adopted in Banjul at
its 51st Ordinary Session, 2 May 2012 16

African Union

2009   Africa Mining Vision 15, 49, 77, 167

xxvi *Table of Instruments*

ECOWAS

2009 Directive No C/DIR3/05/09 on the Harmonization of Guiding
Principles and Policies in the Mining Sector dated 27 May 2009....................16
2011 Regional Mineral Development Policy, Industry and Mines
Directorate, Mine Division, May 2011 16
2019 Model Mining and Minerals Development Act, June 2019 .... 16, 173

ICGLR

2006 International Conference on the Great Lakes Region Protocol
against the Illegal Exploitation of Natural Resources,
30 November 2006 60–61

WAEMU

2000 Common Mining Code, Additional Act 01/2000 130–31
2003 Regulation No 18/2003/CM/WAEMU dated 23 December 2003
relating to the Mining Code 15

OECD

1976 Declaration on International Investment and Multinational
Enterprises, recommending the observance of the OECD Guidelines
for Multinational Enterprises (adopted on 21 June 1976 and reviewed
to date in 1979, 1984, 1991, 2000 and 2011)... 115–16
2006 Recommendation of the Council on Bribery and Officially
Supported Export Credits, OECD/LEGAL/3048 (adopted on
14 December 2006) 111
2006 Risk Awareness Tool for Multinational Enterprises in Weak
Governance Zones 116
2009 Recommendation on Tax Measures for Further Combating
Bribery of Foreign Public Officials in International Business
Transactions (released 25 May 2009) 111
2009 Recommendation for Further Combating Bribery of Foreign
Public Officials in International Business Transactions (released
9 December 2009) 111
2015 Recommendation on Public Procurement..111
2016 Due Diligence Guidance for Responsible Supply Chains
of Minerals from Conflict-Affected and High-Risk Areas:
Third Edition..61, 115–16
2017 Due Diligence Guidance for Meaningful Stakeholder Engagement
in the Extractive Sector 116
2018 Due Diligence Guidance for Responsible Business Conduct 115–116

1

Understanding the Law of Mining and Minerals from a Global Perspective

A global perspective on specific legal disciplines entails shaping a vision of 'what a genuinely cosmopolitan discipline of law must become', 'an overarching vision that understands the diversity of legal phenomena and the underlying challenges of the age (such as poverty, sustainable development and climate change) and what they mean for each discipline'.

William Twining[1]

The shift to low carbon economies is likely to be materially intensive, and entail a shift from hydrocarbons to metals.[2] Minerals and metals are also at the heart of the Fourth Revolution. From the Stone Age to the Iron Age and on to the Bronze Age and through the Industrial Revolution, minerals and technology have been the basis for breakthroughs that have shaped the nature of life and lifestyles.[3] Minerals are

---

[1] W Twining, 'The Implications of "Globalisation" for Law as a Discipline' in A Halpin and V Roeben (eds), *Theorising the Global Legal Order* (Oxford, Hart Publishing, 2009) 39. See also W Twining, *Legal Jurisprudence: Understanding Law from a Global Perspective* (Cambridge, Cambridge University Press, 2009).

[2] UN Environment Assembly Resolution 4/19 Mineral Resource Governance. Adopted on 15 March 2019 at Fourth session Nairobi, 11–15 March 2019 (UNEP/EA.4/Res.19) ('Noting that clean technologies, highly dependent on metals and minerals, are important for combating climate change issues', and pointing at the findings and recommendations of the International Resource Panel (IRP), 'Mineral Resource Governance in the 21st Century: Gearing extractive industries towards sustainable development' (2020). E Ayuk, AM Pedro and P Ekins (lead authors), A Report of the International Resource Panel. United Nations Environment Programme (Nairobi, 2020) and IRP, 'Global Resources Outlook 2019: Natural Resources for the Future We Want' (2019). See T Addison, 'Climate Change and the Extractives Sector' in T Addison and A Roe (eds), *Extractive Industries. The Management of Resources as a Driver of Sustainable Development* (Oxford, Oxford University Press, 2018) 463; B Sovacool, S Ali, M Bazilian, B Radley, B Nemery, J Okatz and D Mulvaney, 'Sustainable minerals and metals for a low-carbon future' (2020) 367 *Science* 6473, 30; D Humphreys, 'The mining and energy "paradox"' (2018) *Mining Journal* (online, 27 February 2018) (observing that 'The transition to the low carbon economy is a transition from hydrocarbons to metals – the metals required to produce solar panels, wind turbines and battery systems'). See also SH Ali, D Giurco, N Arndt, E Nickless, G Brown, A Demetriades, R Durrheim, MA Enriquez, J Kinnaird, A Littleboy, LD Meinert, R Oberhänsli, J Salem, R Schodde, G Schneider, O Vidal and N Yakovleva, 'Mineral supply for sustainable development requires resource governance' (2017) 543 *Nature* 367. D Arrobas, K Hund, M McCormick, J Ningthoujam and J Drexhage, *The Growing Role of Minerals and Metals for a Low Carbon Future* (Washington DC, World Bank Group, 2017).

[3] Giorgio Agricola, in his famous treatise on mining and metallurgy dating back to 1556, observed that mining is at least as ancient as agriculture as no man 'ever tilled a field without implements'.

2 *Understanding the Law of Mining and Minerals from a Global Perspective*

basically core inputs for components of most products fabricated, traded and used in the global economy. Thus, from the point of view of the organisation of the global economy, the mining industry, including the artisanal and small-scale mining (ASM) segment, represents 'the beginning of the beginning', the very first stage of the circuit of production and of the web of global production networks.[4] Such fact provides a glimpse of the true value of metals as the material foundation of the entire society over thousands of years.[5]

Minerals and metals are scattered unevenly in the Earth's crust. Because of the essential contribution of minerals and the economic opportunities created by mining, from a historical perspective mining has been considered as being intrinsically linked to development. Indeed, some countries have managed to capitalise upon mineral wealth to spur business and other economic activities.[6] But in many others, particularly middle and low-income countries, the opportunities have dissipated partly due to the 'enclave' nature of large projects – their links with global rather than with local economies, the volatility of mineral prices,[7] the environmental and social impacts of projects and, in certain contexts, their potential to trigger complex political dynamics that can undermine governance and lead to conflict.[8]

Minerals, 'the third kingdom of nature', are then both at the centre of an industry that is global by nature and of the core global challenges of our age. They are hailed as part of the solution to build the infrastructure required to deal with climate change – 'the most systemic threat to humankind'[9] – and for technological innovation. If managed well, mining – the process of extracting minerals from the

---

G Agricola, *De Re Metallica* in H Hoover and L Hoover, trans, 1st edn from the 1st 1556 Latin edn (New York, Dover Publications Inc, 1950) xxvi.

[4] P Dicken, *Global Shift. Mapping the Changing Contours of the World Economy*, 7th edn (London, Sage, 2015) 396.

[5] On the economic, technical and political importance of metals and minerals throughout Western history, see E Staley, *Raw Materials in Peace and War* (New York, Council on Foreign Relations, 1937); CK Leith, *World Minerals and World Politics: A factual study of minerals in their political and international relations* (New York: McGraw-Hill Book Co, 1931; SD Krasner, *Defending the National Interest: Raw Materials Investment and U.S. Foreign Policy* (Princeton, New Jersey, Princeton University Press, 1978); JD Bernal, *Science in History* (MIT Press, 1970); AE Eckes, *United States and the Global Struggle for Minerals* (Austin, University of Texas Press, 1979); CW Sames, *Die Zukunft der Metalle* (Frankfurt, 1974); DSL Cardwell, *Turning Points in Western Technogy: a Study of Technology, Science and History* (New York, Science History Publications, 1972).

[6] M Ericsson and O Löf, 'Mining's Contribution to Low- and Middle-Income Economies' in T Addison and A Roe (eds), *Extractive Industries. The Management of Resources as a Driver of Sustainable Development* (Oxford, Oxford University Press, 2018) 51–70, 63 and 69.

[7] This is particularly acute in the case of minor metals – most of those needed for the energy transition – as their market is a 'buyers' market' which has shown to respond dynamically to shortages by technological change, efficiency or substitution. See S Renner and F Wellmer, 'Volatility drivers on the metal market and exposure of producing countries' (2019) *Mineral Economics*, available at https://doi.org/10.1007/s13563-019-00200-8.

[8] IRP, *Mineral Resource Governance in the 21st Century* (2020).

[9] UN Secretary General, 'Secretary-General's press encounter on climate change', 29 March 2018, available at www.un.org/sg/en/content/sg/press-encounter/2018-03-29/secretary-generals-press-encounter-climate-change-qa.

Understanding the Law of Mining and Minerals from a Global Perspective 3

Earth's crust – can contribute very significantly to broader–based development and poverty eradication. On the contrary, it has been stressed that increased levels of extraction at ever lower grades threat to compound the problem of ecosystems' loss and of imbalance of the systems that sustain the very stability and resilience of Earth, local communities' disruption and inequity in global and local allocation of resources. Networks of actors are calling for a paradigm shift in the way minerals are produced, sourced and used in end products; indeed, there is a growing demand in some circles for a progressive phasing out from extraction with increased reuse, recycling and circular economy models.[10]

In historical terms, the search for minerals has long driven conquest and global patterns of investment and trade. For centuries, minerals have been part and parcel of land and territories in sovereignty claims, which have been considered primarily in the context of changes in territorial control or disputes.[11] Mining and minerals started to receive attention under international law and policy in the context of the global architecture emerging from the network of institutions established in the post-war period. They have been identified as an object of early claims over natural resources in pursuit of exercising economic self–determination and control by peoples of developing countries; conceptualised as the 'common heritage of mankind' and similar formulations when lying in the international seabed and other areas beyond national jurisdictions; and included most recently in global action plans to advance sustainable development. At the same time, developments in a number of fields of law, particularly those relating to international investment, trade, economics and finance, environment and human rights, and anti-corruption, have been redefining the contours of the internal space of nation-states in the exercise of their sovereign powers for regulating and allocating rights over minerals within their jurisdictions.[12] Each of these fields is embedded in different normative values that might result in framing minerals as commercial assets, commodities, raw materials, 'commons', fruits of nature or natural heritage, and in endowing the land where they lie as having special cultural and spiritual significance.[13]

At the level of nation-states, the definition of ownership, as well as the rules and conditions for governing and regulating mineral resources, are dealt with under

---

[10] The circular economy is already happening, with 40% of copper and 40% of steel and 30% of aluminium, lead and zinc being produced by recycled products. See J Korinek, 'Trade restrictions on minerals and metals' (2019) 32 *Mineral Economics* 176.

[11] See the argument concerning land and sovereignty claims in L Cotula, 'Land, Property and Sovereignty in International Law' (2017) 25 *Cardozo Journal of International and Comparative Law* 219.

[12] See L Cotula, 'The New Enclosures? Polanyi, international investment law and the global land rush' (2013) 34 *Third World Quarterly* 9, 1605–29 (using Polanyi's 'double movement' framework to understand the competing role of law in both facilitating land commodification and in restoring social embeddedness by recognising non-commercial relations and values on land through human rights law). See also L Cotula, 'Land, Property and Sovereignty' (2017); and R Barnes, *Property Rights and Natural Resources* (Oxford, Hart Publishing, 2009) (pointing at how colliding legal and socio-political values underlying legal regimes shape property rights).

[13] Cotula (n 11) 225.

4   *Understanding the Law of Mining and Minerals from a Global Perspective*

mining laws. At its most basic, mining law *stricto sensu* is associated to mineral tenure regimes; it defines the rules and procedures to acquire mineral rights as well as the relevant rights and obligations of the parties involved.[14] At their core, mining law regimes usually establish a nexus between three forms of ownership and property rights or entitlements: (i) primary ownership on minerals over the subsoil; (ii) property rights (or rights with proprietary characteristics) to explore and extract minerals (and rights over minerals themselves, once extracted); and (iii) the interface with the surface rights owners and holders to land, as well as entitlements to water and other natural resources. They also set the procedures for the allocation of those entitlements, and corresponding rights and obligations. The overarching principle of mining law has typically been public purpose or national interest, providing the grounds for 'accessing' territories, resources and land.[15] The design of mining law regimes historically intended to reconcile the interests of the public authority and of the miner, while establishing precedence of mining over other land uses.

The overall legal framework of mining and minerals at national levels (mining law *sensu lato*), usually comprises the multi-layered framework governing mineral resources' development and the relationships between the state, the miners and surface rights holders, local communities as well as other actors involved in the activity, and the regulatory procedures to obtain permission from different administrative agencies to operate, often at lower government levels. It also encompasses, more broadly, a whole range of contracts and those areas of law which have implications in the various aspects of mineral investment and development, financing, infrastructure, taxation, competition, planning and management.[16]

Being among the most ancient economic activities, mining law regimes are deeply embedded in laws and customs going back thousands of years. Their function has typically been to lay down rules for providing access or permission to miners to extract minerals, favouring mining over other land uses, and they have existed ever since there have been 'structures of public government, economic interest in minerals and technical ability to extract them'.[17] As in the fields of the law of energy and natural resources, systems of private property law have influenced the development of principles of mining law regimes in Western jurisdictions.[18] Furthermore, the concept of mines as *iura regalia*, and the ancient customs of 'free mining' dating

---

[14] See ch 6.

[15] AA Debrah, H Mtegha and F Cawood, 'Social licence to operate and the granting of mineral rights in sub-Saharan Africa: Exploring tensions between communities, governments and multinational mining companies' (2018) 56 *Resources Policy* 95 (the authors highlight the conversion of 'real' land ownership to 'access' through surface and user rights by virtue of the separation of minerals from land ownership). See further ch 6.

[16] See ch 6.

[17] T Wälde, 'Mineral Development Legislation: Result and Instrument of Mineral Development Planning' (1988) 12 *Natural Resources Forum* 2, 175.

[18] A McHarg, B Barton, A Bradbrook and L Godden, 'Property and the Law in Energy and Natural Resources' in A McHarg, B Barton, A Bradbrook and L Godden (eds), *Property and the Law in Energy and Natural Resources* (Oxford, Oxford University Press, 2010) 1; H Mostert, *Mineral Law: Principles and Policies in Perspective* (Cape Town, Juta, 2012).

back to medieval Europe have had a significant, and often ongoing, impact.[19] These systems have been the subject of wide diffusion with processes of colonisation and borrowing. In many cases, these systems have coexisted over time or have preceded systems crystallising a greater role of the nation-state or set straight within administrative law, which are dominant in most countries.[20] These have typically been a small but crucial piece of the 'legal infrastructure' set to facilitate the extractives industries.[21]

I. The Argument of this Book

The study of mining law has so far been mostly circumscribed to domestic legal systems and generally limited to national boundaries. It has not yet broadened systematically to encompass the international, transnational, regional, national and local levels of normative orderings of social relations concerning mining and minerals – what I call the law and governance of mining and minerals, or 'mineral law' when referring to mining law *latissimo sensu*. Unlike energy law, which has been the subject of academic enquiry and shifted from its domestic law locus to the field of international and transnational law studies,[22] attention to this area

[19] B Barton, 'The History of Mining Law in the US, Canada, New Zealand and Australia, and the Right of Free Entry' in E Bastida, T Wälde and J Warden-Fernandez (eds), *International and Comparative Mineral Law and Policy: Trends and Prospects* (The Hague, Kluwer Law International, 2005) 644.

[20] ibid. See also L Godden, 'Governing Common Resources: Environmental Markets and Property in Water' in McHarg, Barton, Bradbrook and Godden, *Property and the Law* (2010) 413, 414.

[21] D Szablowski and B Campbell, 'Struggles over extractive governance: Power, discourse, violence, and legality' (2019) 6 *The Extractive Industries and Society* 3, 635–41.

[22] A Bradbrook, 'Energy Law as an Academic Discipline' (1996) 14 *Journal of Energy and Natural Resources Law* 2, 193; T Wälde, 'International Energy Law – An Introduction to Modern Concepts, Context, Policy, and Players' in JP Schneider and C Theobald (eds), *Handbuch zum Recht der Energiewirtschaft* (München, Verlag C.H.Beck, 2003) 1129; A Wawryk, 'International Energy Law: An Emerging Academic Discipline' in P Babie and P Leadbeter, *Law as Change: Engaging with the Life and Scholarship of Adrian Bradbrook* (The University of Adelaide: University of Adelaide Press, 2014) 223–56, available at www.adelaide.edu.au/press/system/files/media/documents/2019-04/uap-law-change-ebook.pdf; Peter Cameron, *International Energy Investment Law: The Pursuit of Stability* (Oxford, Oxford University Press, 2010); RJ Heffron, A Rønne, JP Tomain, A Bradbrook and K Talus, 'A treatise for energy law' (2018) 11 The Journal of World Energy Law & Business 1, 34–48; S Schill, 'The Rule of Law and the Division of Labour Between National and International Law: The Case of International Energy Relations' in M Kanetake and A Nollkaemper (eds), *The Rule of Law at the National and International Levels. Contestations and Deference* (Oxford, Hart Publishing, 2018); K Talus (ed), *Research Handbook on International Energy Law* (Cheltenham and Northampton, Edward Elgar Publishing, 2014); MJ Pereira Rolim, *Reconciling Energy, the Environment and Sustainable Development: The Role of Law and Regulation* (Alphen aan den Rijn, The Netherlands, Kluwer Law International, 2019); M Roggenkamp, L Barrera-Hernandez, D Zillman and I del Guayo (eds), *Energy Networks and the Law. Innovative Solutions in Changing Markets* (Oxford, Oxford University Press, 2012); B Barton, C Redgwell, A Rønne and D Zillman (eds), *Energy Security. Managing Risk in a Dynamic Legal and Regulatory Environment* (Oxford, Oxford University Press, 2004). On EU Energy Law, see P Cameron (ed), *Legal aspects of EU energy regulation: implementing the new directives on electricity and gas across Europe* (Oxford, Oxford University Press, 2005); V Roeben, *Towards a European Energy Union: European Energy Strategy in International Law* (Cambridge, Cambridge University Press, 2018); K Talus,

6 Understanding the Law of Mining and Minerals from a Global Perspective

has increased exponentially in recent years, but this has remained scattered, and international perspectives are only now starting to engage with the literature and framings on mining law as typically developed at domestic levels.

A first challenge in any attempt of systematisation of the discipline is encountered by the many ways of naming the very same phenomenon – 'minerals and metals'; or 'subsoil resources' or 'strategic resources' from the point of view of the sites of extraction; or 'sustainable production and consumption' initiatives; or 'raw materials', 'commodities' or 'critical substances' from the point of view of global markets; 'value chains'; or 'responsible sourcing' initiatives. They are also seen as 'commercial assets' from the perspective of investors; or 'commons', 'fruits of nature' or 'natural heritage' from perspectives that place emphasis on the value of nature. Furthermore, the land where they lie can be considered as accessory to mineral rights and interests in traditional patterns of mineral tenure, or as endowed of special cultural, spiritual and economic significance if viewed from the standpoint of indigenous peoples, peasant communities or rural women.

A second challenge is found, then, in the scope and breadth of the subject matter. The study of 'mining' or 'mineral' or 'subsoil' law has usually been undertaken in resource-rich countries at domestic levels and scholarship has usually focused on the analysis of statutory acts and precedents, and their relationship with other statutory and regulatory instruments, notably those concerning investment and the environment. From a global perspective, this comprises a crucial level of relations and legal ordering on mining and minerals – but not the only one.

This book calls for adopting a global perspective to the study of the law and governance of mining and minerals 'as an academic discipline',[23] and makes two closely connected claims. The first one advances that a global perspective will further our understanding of the breadth and the interdependence of the international, transnational, regional, national and local levels of normative orderings of social relations concerning mining and minerals – and of the countless networks of actors at all these levels. The second one posits that a global perspective implies engaging with sustainable development and sustainability as an objective of the global community and as a 'conceptual matrix' for integrating environmental sustainability and social and economic equity into decisions about economic projects at all levels, while it heightens awareness of the diversity of beliefs and value systems.

The expanded understanding derived from these two closely intertwined analytical and normative claims allows grasping the function that mining laws and contracts at domestic levels have typically assumed 'as interfaces' between national law and the international legal architecture governing international mineral

---

EU Energy Law and Policy: a Critical Account (Oxford, Oxford University Press, 2013); M Roggenkamp, C Redgwell, A Ronne and I del Guayo (eds), *Energy Law in Europe. National, EU and International Regulation*, 3rd edn (Oxford, Oxford University Press, 2016).

[23] Bradbrook, 'Energy Law as an Academic Discipline' (1996).

markets and investment, and their common underpinnings in the concept of the 'rule of law' as guiding 'the exercise of public authority'.[24,25] At the same time, it enables us to critically engage with the many loopholes and the inherent contradictions underlying current fragmented systems of decision-making. Furthermore, it promotes imagining a vision of interconnected and overall more textured and cosmopolitan decision-making processes for sustainable resources management.

Such a vision seeks to capture the complexity of the normative phenomena and the diversity of sources, and critically entails recalibrating law and governance to ensure that the coherence and integration of disparate regimes is consistent with the changing paradigm of the value of nature and resources, mainstreaming human rights, transparency and accountability, and science-based, informed and systemic decisions, in the context of a more interconnected planet conscious of its boundaries and of the just transition towards low-carbon futures. It also provides an opening for the debate and contestation needed for advancing scholarship, starting with a clarification on the scope of this area of enquiry. The matrix in Figure 1.1 below synthesises the constituent legal and normative basis of the law and governance of mining and minerals from a global perspective.

II. Mineral Law from a Global Perspective: A Cosmopolitan View

The study of mineral law has so far been confined mostly to the realm of domestic legal systems. This approach seems far too narrow in today's world, in the face of a broad range of variegated reasons that distinguish the present scenario. The first reason is defined by the very nature of the industry, particularly of the energy and metal segments, with the far-ranging geographical expansion of exploration and

---

[24] Schill, 'The Rule of Law and the Division of Labour' (2018) (arguing that many areas of social relations in this globalised and interconnected world are governed by an amalgamation of both national and international law – so the lines between national and international law and the exercise of public authority at national and international levels have become increasingly blurred; that the relationship between national and international law can otherwise be considered as of 'division of labour' which is reflected through 'interfaces'; and that these, in turn, have a very significant function in the operationalisation of the rule of law in global governance. The author frames energy relations around this argument).

[25] Schill refers to Kanetake in defining 'interfaces' as 'the points where the actors, norms and procedures belonging to respective [international and national] legal orders connect and interact with one another'. See M Kanetake, 'The Interfaces between the National and International Rule of Law: A Framework Paper' in M Kanetake and A Nollkaemper (eds), *The Rule of Law at the National and International Levels. Contestations and Deference* (Oxford, Hart Publishing, 2018). Kanetake argues that the opportunities for interaction have been furthered by the overlapping 'subject-matter' between national and international law. She understands 'subject-matter' as the scenarios, factual or legal, justifying legal regulation – the 'subject-matter of the 'rule of law' [being] the exercise of authority by institutions in a society'.

8 *Understanding the Law of Mining and Minerals from a Global Perspective*

Figure 1.1 Disciplinary Matrix

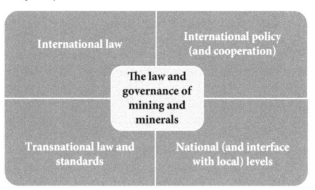

Source: Own elaboration.

extraction, the use of its products across a global value chain and the uneven presence of minerals in the Earth's crust. Second, there is the participation of a wide range of actors and networks (and evolving thinking on their responsibilities) even in a changing global context marked by contestation about globalisation (which entails, in a narrow sense, economic liberalisation[26] and, in a broad sense, processes expanding and intensifying interconnectedness and the interdependence of human activity and human relations, where the sovereign state has been lying at the crossroads of a range of regimes and organisations managing different areas of transnational activity).[27] Third, the transmission of law across boundaries[28] and increased interconnections between international law and domestic law and subnational levels of legal ordering (and their interface with transnational standards) within the constrained space of national boundaries is noteworthy. A single social situation might not be subject to national law only, but to a complex and diverse legal and normative landscape operating at supra-national, national and local scales, as well as transnational standards. These might create different legal realities along different criteria to determine the relevant details of the activity to be regulated.[29] Fourth, a changing ethics of the underlying value of minerals and nature and their role in realising the common goals of global, national and local communities has gained momentum. This is all set amidst convoluted global and local scenarios of profound political, economic, social and

---

[26] E Merino Blanco and J Razzaque, *Globalisation and Natural Resources Law: Challenges, Key Issues and Perspectives* (Cheltenham and Northampton, Edward Elgar Publishing, 2011) 8 and 33 and ss.
[27] Twining, 'Globalisation' (2009) 40. D Held, *Cosmopolitanism: Ideals and Realities* (Cambridge, Polity Press, 2010) 29–30. See also The World Commission on Environment and Development, *Our Common Future* (Oxford, Oxford University Press, 1987) chs 2 and 3.
[28] A Halpin and V Roeben, 'Introduction' in Halpin and Roeben (n 1) 1.
[29] This phenomenon has been observed by the socio-legal literature and termed as 'interlegality'. B de Sousa Santos, 'Law: A Map of Misreading. Toward a Postmodern Conception of Law' (1987) 14 *Journal of Law and Society* 3, 287–88; D Szablowski, *Transnational Law and Local Struggles: Mining, Communities and the World Bank* (London, Bloomsbury Publishing, 2007) 292. Twining, 'Globalisation' (n 1) 47.

Mineral Law from a Global Perspective: A Cosmopolitan View 9

ecological crisis,[30] which will require strengthened international cooperation as the way forward.

I argue that a broader view is required to capture the range of legal and normative phenomena on mining and minerals from a global perspective. That requires an understanding of all geographical levels of relations and legal ordering concerning rules and procedures in order to access, use and manage minerals (and the rights and obligations derived therefrom).[31] These entail implied decisions on distribution of derived wealth.[32]

Recalibrating our vision of the law from the vantage point of different levels of social relations and normative ordering serves as an analytical tool, shedding some light on the growing complexity of law in this subject.

From such a vantage point, mineral law should be understood as normatively plural because a diversity of forms of law and normative phenomena that interact at different levels can be discerned. In other words, when looking at the normative phenomena considering the broad range of actors active in mining and minerals – or affected by mining operations – including not only the host state, but also mining companies and investors and their home states, landowners, landholders and local communities, as well as minerals users and their home states, one can observe that traditional sources of law at every level (from municipal law to supra-state law, both international and regional, and forms of soft law) coalesce with a growing and disparate range of non-state norms comprising transnational private regulation, transnational multi-stakeholder governance, customary law and emerging forms of community agreements.

This broadening view for understanding the law applicable to mining and minerals crucially engages with sustainability and sustainable development, as a common normative objective of the global community and as an analytical framework for integrating environmental sustainability and social and economic equity into decisions about economic projects across all levels. Whereas sustainable development began as a concept pertaining to international policy making in a compromise between developed and developing countries,[33] it has certainly been recognised as an objective by

---

[30] 'Mega-trends' which are transforming the global landscape and the dynamics of international relations include the rapid growth of the world population, their urbanisation and ageing, the increase of income and of a 'global middle class' at the same time than growing disparity of income and wealth and widespread social inequality – a phenomena that encompasses industrialised countries – and immigration flows; the expansion of technology and digitalisation; the emergence of a global multipolar order which is moving eastwards and would include China, India and Indonesia, apart from the US and Brazil. Climate warming is having an impact on global temperature, the rise of sea levels and water cycles, as well as accelerated biodiversity losses. These all determine the shape of the industry and its regulation. MinPol, 'Global Raw Materials', Report of the project Towards a World Forum on Raw Materials (December 2017).

[31] I will use the term 'access' throughout the text, but will reflect on it in the light of the sustainability paradigm in ch 6.

[32] W Twining, 'Diffusion of Law: A Global Perspective' (2004) 36 *The Journal of Legal Pluralism and Unofficial Law* 1, 11–12. Merino Blanco and Razzaque, *Globalisation and Natural Resources Law* (2011) 8.

[33] The World Commission on Environment and Development, *Our Common Future* (1987) legal annex; see ch 3.

10   *Understanding the Law of Mining and Minerals from a Global Perspective*

a wide range of legal instruments and most of its constituent principles are a part of the corpus of the existing international legal obligations of nation-states.[34] Agenda 2030 and the Sustainable Development Goals (SDGs) comprise goals and targets that are universally relevant to all the global community, developing and developed countries alike, and call to all actors to share responsibility for their achievement. The call for global collective action to eradicate poverty, change unsustainable patterns of consumption and production and rapidly transition towards low-carbon economies as embraced in Agenda 2030 and the SDGs[35] and the Paris Agreement on Climate Change,[36] within planetary boundaries, has enormous implications for mining and for the use and full appreciation of the value of minerals.

Sustainable development entails a governance system that shapes behaviour and promotes integrated decision-making processes that bring together all actors to cooperate in achieving commonly agreed goals. Such decision-making processes must be well-informed and supported by holistic and coherent legal and regulatory frameworks (thus capturing the multiplicity of spheres of legal ordering impinging on minerals development and mainstreaming human rights) at all levels. Thus, law is shaped and, in turn, plays a fundamental role in shaping governance. An ethics of mining and minerals will demand a value shift from resource exploitation to resource stewardship, and from resources to commons.

William Twining has challenged lawyers to engage in shaping a vision of 'what a genuinely cosmopolitan discipline of law must become', in ways that consider all levels of relations and legal ordering. Thus, a global perspective on specific legal disciplines entails shaping 'an overarching vision that understands the diversity of legal phenomena and the underlying challenges of the age (such as poverty, sustainable development and climate change) and what they mean for each discipline'.[37] Patrick Glenn, in turn, defines 'cosmopolitan legal orders' as

> ones which are aware both of their own limits or jurisdiction restrictions, and of their immediate priorities.[38] At the same time, they are able to work, where appropriate, in cosmopolitan fashion with multiple sources of law and multiple forms of belief … Cosmopolitan legal orders are characterised by some measure of openness.[39]

---

[34] See International Law Association (ILA) New Delhi Declaration of Principles of International Law Relating to Sustainable Development. Adopted at the 70th Conference of the ILA, held in New Delhi, India, 2–6 April 2002. MC Cordonier Segger and A Khalfan, *Sustainable Development Law Principles, Practices, and Prospects* (Oxford, Oxford University Press, 2004).

[35] United Nations General Assembly Resolution 66/288 adopted on 27 July 2012, The Future We Want (endorsing the Outcome Document of the United Nations Conference on Sustainable Development held in Rio de Janeiro on 20–22 June 2012 (A/RES/66/288). United Nations General Assembly Resolution 70/1 adopted on 25 September 2015, Transforming Our World: The 2030 Agenda for Sustainable Development.

[36] United Nations Framework Convention on Climate Change (UNFCCC), Paris Agreement, Decision 1/CP.21, Report of the Conference of the Parties on its twenty-first session, held in Paris from 30 November to 13 December 2015 Addendum Part two: Action taken by the Conference of the Parties at its twenty-first session.

[37] Twining, 'Globalisation' (n 1) 39. See also Twining, *Legal Jurisprudence* (2009).

[38] HP Glenn, 'Cosmopolitan Legal Orders' in Halpin and Roeben (n 1) 25–26.

[39] ibid 28.

Mineral Law from a Global Perspective: A Cosmopolitan View 11

What lies at the heart of these forms of cosmopolitanism is 'the moral duty each of us would owe to all of the rest of us'.[40] He emphasises that 'to resist closure', cosmopolitan legal thought must look *backwards* (to be reminded of its own 'normative justification'), look *forward* (to continue being cosmopolitan) and look *around* (to be nurtured by multiple sources of law and beliefs, to engage in conversation, with the experiences and beliefs of others).[41]

To structure the analysis in this monograph, I will explore the following geographical levels of relations and legal ordering concerning minerals access and management (and their diversity), which seem to interpenetrate each other, in the points below.

A. The International Level

Article 38(1) of the Statute of the International Court of Justice (ICJ) identifies as sources of international law: (i) treaties between states; (ii) international custom derived from a widespread and consistent practice of states accepted as law; (iii) general principles of law; and (iv) judicial decisions and teachings of the 'most highly qualified publicists' as subsidiary means for determining rules of law.[42] An important normative phenomenon, characteristic of international environmental and resources diplomacy and the law-making processes concerning economic matters, has been the rise and rapid development of soft law instruments.[43] While not formally binding, they entail 'strong moral obligations'[44] and carry political-legal significance, serving as guides of international and domestic policies and as precursors to the development of binding law.[45] 'Soft law' encompasses a range of instruments which include UN General Assembly resolutions and multilateral declarations, codes of conduct, guidelines and recommendations from international organisations and others.

Treaties are a main source of law used by states to govern conduct between states, and the most frequently used to create multilateral rules concerning the environment. Parties to a treaty are bound to it and must observe it in good faith pursuant to the customary principle of '*pacta sunt servanda*'. They cannot invoke provisions of internal law to justify failure to performing obligations under a treaty.[46]

---

[40] ibid. See also Held, *Cosmopolitanism* (2010).

[41] ibid 33–34.

[42] Statute of the International Court of Justice, 33 UNTS 993.

[43] See P Birnie, A Boyle and C Redgwell, *International Law and the Environment*, 3rd edn (Oxford, Oxford University Press, 2009) 31–37.

[44] C Dalupan, 'Mining and Sustainable Development: Insights from International Law' in E Bastida, T Wälde and J Warden-Fernández (eds), *International and Comparative Mineral Law and Policy* (The Hague, Kluwer Law International, 2005) 149–69.

[45] P Malanczuk, *Akehurst's Modern Introduction to International Law*, 7th edn (London and New York, Routledge, 1997) 245.

[46] Arts 26 and 27, Vienna Convention on the Law of Treaties. Done at Vienna on 23 May 1969. Entered into force on 27 January 1980. UNTS 1155, 331.

12 Understanding the Law of Mining and Minerals from a Global Perspective

An expansive look at social relations concerning access to, and the extraction and management of, minerals will allow us to understand how they occur at different geographical levels and are subject to distinct bodies of normative and legal ordering.[47] There is even what Twining calls a 'galactic' dimension to the regulation of minerals exploration and development, brought about by the Outer Space Treaty and the Moon Agreement, and also by emerging municipal laws legislating on exploring and mining space resources which are currently subject to debate. Minerals in the international deep seabed are subject to a specific resource regime under the UN Convention on the Law of the Sea (UNCLOS) that defines them as 'the common heritage of mankind'. Meanwhile, since 1991, mining in Antarctica has been under a moratorium that shelved the stillborn Convention on the Regulation of Antarctic Mineral Resource Activities of 1988.

Apart from the international law regimes applicable to mining and minerals in areas beyond national jurisdictions, these have scantly been considered under international law. They have been the object of attention of international law and policy through the development of the principle of Permanent Sovereignty over Natural Resources (PSONR) in the context of the New International Economic Order (NIEO), and most recently through investigation and action addressing the connection between armed conflict and natural resources;[48] and through their inclusion in Agenda 2030 and the Sustainable Development Goals (SDGs) embraced by the global community.[49] There is no convention regulating mining and minerals governance, but there exists a growing set of standards and a range of calls for scaling up international cooperation.[50] A growing number of UN specialised agencies (at international and regional levels) and international bodies with competence in environmental and economic affairs as well as voluntary partnership forums have begun to engage in agendas on mining and minerals governance. Meanwhile, international and regional financial and development banks and organisations, such as the World Bank, have issued policy documents guiding technical assistance programmes for sectoral institutional and legal reform in developing countries, which have been very influential in steering the content and direction of law and policy reform in the mining and minerals sector in many middle- and low-income countries.[51]

---

[47] W Twining, 'Globalisation and Legal Scholarship', Montesquieu Lecture, LAPA (Princeton University, 2009) 5.

[48] This monograph will not deal with this aspect at length. See D Dam-de Jong, *International Law and Governance of Natural Resources in Conflict and Post-Conflict Situations* (Cambridge, Cambridge University Press, 2015); D Dam-de Jong, 'The Role of Informal Normative Processes in Improving Governance Over Natural Resources in Conflict-torn States' (2015) 7 *The Hague Journal on the Rule of Law* 2, 219–41.

[49] See ch 3.

[50] See ch 3. See D Humphreys, AE Bastida and A Hermann, 'Platforms for Strategic Dialogues on Mining and Minerals: A possible way forward', STRADE Strategic Dialogue on Sustainable Raw Materials for Europe (STRADE) EU Horizon 2020 Project; European Policy Brief No 4/2017.

[51] The policy models and narratives ('scripts') disseminated by international financial and development organisations have been called 'global scripts'. See an illustration of the concept and its

Nation-states hold the sovereign right to regulate their natural resources within their jurisdictions and are bound under international law – most prominently under the international treaties they might be part of, to a constellation of obligations that either: (i) impinge on standards of treatment of foreign investment and trade; (ii) qualify the places, manner and extent of extraction; (iii) protect a range of human rights that might be affected by resource extraction; or (iv) engage in the struggle against corruption. States might also agree on standards and terms of management of transboundary mineral resources, such as the Mining Integration Treaty between Argentina and Chile governing mining in the Andean border zones of those countries.

B. The Transnational Level

Transnational law was famously defined by Jessup in 1956 as 'all law which regulates actions or events that transcend national frontiers' comprising 'Both public and private international law ... as are other rules which do not wholly fit into such standard categories'.[52] It received full impetus with globalisation, and the multiplication of transnational phenomena beyond the binary of international and national law.

On one hand, transnational law manifests as forms of legal regulation regarding transnational corporations and cross-border business transactions.[53] When carried out by transnational corporations, mining transactions generally involve a web of firms that are established in and operate in different jurisdictions. International investment and commercial arbitration lawyers commonly use terms such as 'transnational law' and 'new *lex mercatoria*' to refer to non-national or supra-national legal rules or principles used by arbitration tribunals in the reasoning of disputes settlement.[54] Investor–state arbitration mechanisms within interstate systems or international commercial arbitration schemes established by professional networks are forms of transnational phenomena. In the mining and petroleum sector, transnational contracts were the distinctive arrangement for structuring access to extractive resources in the developing world before the advent of bilateral investment treaties.

On the other hand, transnational regulatory phenomena have manifested in a shift in ordering through classical government authority to governing through processes in which the state exercises authority alongside many other actors, what

---

contextualisation in J Gillespie, 'Developing a framework for understanding the localisation of global scripts in East Asia' in Halpin and Roeben (n 1) 209–31.

[52] PC Jessup, *Transnational Law* (New Haven, Yale University Press, 1956).

[53] P Zumbansen, 'Transnational Law, Evolving', King's College London Dickson Poon School of Law, Legal Studies Research Paper Series: Paper No 2014–29, 8.

[54] K Noussiaa, 'Transnational Law and Arbitration' in K Noussiaa, *Confidentiality in International Commercial Arbitration* (Berlin, Springer, 2010) 145.

has been captured by political science by the term 'governance'.[55] The development of norms outside the nation-state is an expression of social networks operating transnationally, bringing together regulators, business and civil society actors in arenas transcending nation-states.[56] They can start within nation-states or in transnational spheres.[57]

Globalisation has heightened the gaps in governance of: (i) the global business firms, particularly when they operate projects having high impact on local environments, communities and economies as mining does, in countries that might be in the process of, but have yet to develop, fully functional regulatory structures (and institutional investors); or (ii) complex supply chains in which firms source minerals as inputs for their products, particularly from places where demand for minerals is a driver of local conflict. Transnational private norms have emerged to coordinate and regulate the conduct of private firms by setting standards to their operations or global supply chains and by establishing mechanisms for certifying or recognising compliance with those standards. These norms might be drafted by companies themselves in traditional forms of self-regulation, or by international organisations, or in multi-stakeholder forums. In the mining and minerals sector, these norms emerged as the types of instances that have been described by Szablowski as 'highly influential elements of the legal infrastructure' underpinning the global order.[58]

These transnational norms raise key points of contention from a range of perspectives, beginning with the very question of what law is, which has long been posed by the socio-legal school of legal pluralists, and following with the crucial issue of their democratic deficits.[59] Countering a rather extended view on regulatory 'empty spaces' at host state level, it has been argued that these deterritorialised transnational norms are juxtaposed over domestic governance structures and set 'rules without rights'.[60] Another point of contention revolves around the question of whether transnational law is building a new regime of substantive law composed of rules that apply directly across national borders (that point at convergence or transnational unification in regulation), or whether they have a predominantly procedural and coordinating function in articulating substantive rules of state and other regimes 'to serve transnational networks'.[61]

Another important legal phenomenon in the transnational space is constituted by norms of extra-territorial application whereby a state exercises its legal power beyond its territorial boundaries.[62]

---

[55] Szablowski, *Transnational Law and Local Struggle* (2007) 4–6.

[56] R Cotterrell, 'What is Transnational Law?' (2012) 37 *Law & Social Inquiry* 2. The author specifically refers to 'transnational networks of community'.

[57] T Halliday and G Schaffer, 'Transnational Legal Orders' in T Halliday and G Schaffer (eds), *Transnational Legal Orders* (Cambridge, Cambridge University Press, 2015) 19.

[58] Szablowski (n 29) 7.

[59] Szablowski (n 29) 6.

[60] T Bartley, *Rules without Rights: Land, Labor, and Private Authority in the Global Economy* (Oxford, Oxford University Press, 2018).

[61] R Cotterrell, 'What is Transnational Law?' (2012) 37 *Law & Social Inquiry* 2.

[62] AJ Colangelo, 'What Is Extraterritorial Jurisdiction' (2014) 99 *Cornell Law Review* 1303. See ch 4.II.E.i.

C. The Regional Level

At the regional and subregional levels, there is a range of legal phenomena governing, and policy instruments guiding, specific aspects for accessing and managing mineral resources, apart from regional investment and trade treaties and business forums. As an example, in Africa,[63] the Africa Mining Vision (AMV) adopted by the heads of states of the African Union in February 2009 set a pathway for minerals development in the continent. This was Africa's homegrown response for dealing with the bleak divergence between enormous mineral wealth and stark poverty that profoundly affect the continent,[64] adopting a diametrically opposing view from the World Bank's 1992 Strategy for African Mining, which put the focus on the role of mining in generating tax and foreign currency and influenced a generation of mining codes across the continent. The AMV is perhaps the first regional policy framework that looks beyond the mining sector and places mining in the context of broader development plans at the local, national and regional levels. It calls for integrating mineral policy into development policy in a more consistent manner, building economic and social connections for promoting industrialisation and diversifying economies to catalyse structural economic transformations.[65] The AMV is being mainstreamed at the domestic levels through the Country Mining Visions Guidebook ('CMV Guidebook'), which provides guidelines in an effort to ensure that the AMV key tenets find expression in national mineral policy, legal and regulatory frameworks as well as to align mining with other national policies through multi-stakeholder participation processes. The CMV Guidebook has set in motion a new generation of development-oriented mining laws that break away from unsuitable categorisations built around colonial legal heritage.[66] At the subregional level, the West African Economic and Monetary Union (WAEMU) has enacted a Mining Code,[67] while the Economic Community of

---

[63] See extensive and in-depth analysis of law and regulation in the mining and oil and gas industries across the continent in D Olawuyi, *Extractive Industries Law in Africa* (Cham, Switzerland, Springer Nature AG, 2018).

[64] African Union, *Africa Mining Vision*, February 2009. United Nations Economic Commission for Africa (UNECA) (2011) 'Minerals and Africa's Development – The International Study Group Report on Africa's Mineral Regimes' 9.

[65] UNECA (ibid) ch 8. See also A Pedro, 'The Africa Mining Vision (AMV) as a Model for Natural Resources Governance in Africa', a paper submitted following a presentation at the International Forum Governing Natural Resources for Africa's Development organised by the North–South Institute, 9 and 10 May 2013; K Busia and C Akong, 'The African Mining Vision: Perspectives on Mineral Resource Development in Africa' (2017) 8 *Journal of Sustainable Development Law & Policy, Afe Babalola University* 146.

[66] NV Nwogu, 'Mining at the Crossroads of Law and Development: A Comparative Review of Labor-Related Local Content Provisions in Africa's Mining Laws through the Prism of Automation' (2019) 28 *Washington International Law Journal* 139 (contesting the iterations of 'mining codes' drawn in H Besada and P Martin, 'Mining codes in Africa: emergence of a 'fourth' generation?' (2015) 28 *Cambridge Review of International Affairs* 263, and suggesting that 'this generation of mining laws focuses on domestic development').

[67] WAEMU Regulation No 18/2003/CM/WAEMU dated 23 December 2003 relating to the Mining Code.

West African States (ECOWAS) has adopted a range of instruments which include the Model Mining and Minerals Development Act of 2019.[68] In 2012, the African Commission on Human and Peoples' Rights notably adopted the Resolution on a Human Rights-Based Approach to Natural Resources Governance.[69]

In Latin America, there are no regional instruments defining strategies for the sector, but rather distinguishable patterns of legal and normative phenomena, and ongoing dialogues at continental, and subregional levels. The Economic Commission for Latin America and the Caribbean (ECLAC) is consolidating visions and lines of work about the governance of natural resources in the region around the cornerstone concepts of equality, environmental sustainability, productive linkages and the rights of peoples and communities.[70] The standardisation of mining law regimes that occurred across the region in the 1990s as part of the focus of the time on establishing enabling environments for private investment, was contested by a handful of countries in the subsequent decade, with Bolivia and Ecuador putting in place laws and contracts that implemented alternative pathways to development in what was, until not too long ago, a wider regional trend.[71] On the regional convention on human rights, the Inter-American Court has interpreted specific aspects of rules and procedures applicable to minerals access and management. The Escazú Agreement, adopted at Escazú, Costa Rica, on 4 March 2018, currently opened for signature, aims at guaranteeing 'the full and effective implementation of the rights of access to environmental information, public participation in the environmental decision-making process and access to justice in environmental matters' and a safe environment for environmental human rights defenders, laying out the basis to enhance natural resources' governance in the region.[72] Many transition countries that have undergone a transition from socialist to market economies have also shown over time discernible patterns of legal reform (liberalisation, democratisation and decentralisation) with important changes in the structuring of mining laws.

In the EU, the Raw Materials Initiative established in 2008 a three-pronged strategy to deal with access to 'raw materials': (i) promoting mining regionally;

---

[68] ECOWAS Directive No C/DIR3/05/09 on the Harmonization of Guiding Principles and Policies in the Mining Sector dated 27 May 2009; ECOWAS Regional Mineral Development Policy, Industry and Mines Directorate, Mine Division, May 2011; ECOWAS Model Mining and Minerals Development Act, June 2019.

[69] ACHPR/Res.224 (LI) 2012: Resolution on a Human Rights–Based Approach to Natural Resources Governance. Adopted in Banjul at its 51st Ordinary Session, 2 May 2012.

[70] R Sánchez, 'Introducción' in R Sánchez (ed), *La bonanza de los recursos naturales para el desarrollo: dilemas de gobernanza*, ECLAC Books, no 157 (LC/PUB.2019/13-P) (Santiago, Economic Commission for Latin America and the Caribbean (ECLAC) 2019) 19–27.

[71] AE Bastida and L Bustos, 'Towards Regimes for Sustainable Mineral Resources Management. Constitutional Reform, Law and Judicial Precedents in Latin America' (2017) 9 *International Development Policy (Revue Internationale de Politique de Développement)* 235. See further ch 6.

[72] The Escazú Agreement (Regional Agreement on Access to Information, Public Participation and Justice in Environmental Matters in Latin America and the Caribbean) adopted at Escazú, Costa Rica, on 4 March 2018, opened for signature on 27 September 2018.

Mineral Law from a Global Perspective: A Cosmopolitan View   17

(ii) calling for 'resource diplomacy' to ensure reliable, undistorted and rules-based access to minerals; and (iii) supporting substitution and recycling. Standards on access are evolving under the concept of 'responsible sourcing'. Most recently, the European Battery Alliance affirmed that batteries development and production is crucial for the transition to low-carbon economies and restated the importance of 'securing access to raw materials for the EU economy'.[73] Relying on 'new impetus' derived from the European Innovation Partnership on Raw Materials, it observed it is based on '(1) sustainable sourcing of raw materials from global markets: (2) sustainable domestic raw materials production; and (3) resource efficiency and supply of secondary raw materials'. It builds on a renewed EU industrial policy strategy emphasising the importance of raw materials, especially critical raw materials, for competitive value chains, and is further expanded and complemented by the European Green Deal and the Circular Economy Action Plan of 2020. A series of Directives increasingly qualifies cooperation approaches with third countries under partnership arrangements and in ways to advance policy coherence, while others regulate minerals development internally. Beyond regional boundaries, distinctions about legal and normative approaches to mining law and governance have drawn around other criteria (eg, OECD v non-OECD countries; Global South v Global North, etc).

D. States

States as sovereigns hold authority to govern on ownership and management of minerals within their territories. Depending on their constitutional structures, subnational levels of government might hold powers to regulate minerals access and management (including powers of taxation), whereas municipalities might hold powers to decide on land use planning that might enter into conflict with minerals development. At state level, broad patterns of mining law regimes can be drawn along legal traditions and historical patterns of diffusion, with the caveat put forward by Scott that 'systems of mining law are not easily classified into distinct national or theoretical types'; most of these systems are very old and they have survived because they have been adapted to changing circumstances.[74] Many of them show the persistence of 'first come, first served' approaches while others have shown a steady evolution towards administrative type of regimes and contracts.

A perspective on the evolution of law and policy in the sector in the post-war order shows that contending archetypes of market and regulation have swayed between competing development models, influenced in turn, or characterised by,

---

[73] Brussels, 13.9.2017 COM(2017) 479 final.

[74] A Scott, *The Evolution of Resource Property Rights* (Oxford, Oxford University Press, 2008). As other regimes of natural resources law and property law more generally, mineral tenure regimes have proved to be remarkably adaptable. See also McHarg, Barton, Bradbrook and Godden (n 18) 7.

18 *Understanding the Law of Mining and Minerals from a Global Perspective*

changing bargaining powers, changing attitudes to foreign investment and policy priorities, and changing societal attitudes to mining and the use of resources (and the influence of international actors). Variations in minerals demand and the cyclical nature of mineral prices have provided the occasional political space for promoting policy reform.[75] In this monograph, I will refer mostly to broad types of legal phenomena in middle- and low-income countries influenced by reforms steered by international governmental organisations; and industrialised economies embedded in democratic structures of governance.

In Western countries, *thin* forms of tenure or property regimes have often evolved towards *thicker* 'subsystems' of administrative law and regulations governing or regulating mining as public interest in a wide range of values (eg, the environment, the value of nature, respect for human rights, climate action) might grow. Some of these 'subsystems' develop to crystallise commitments under international treaties ratified by states or constitutional reforms and operationalised in environmental regulation and regimes of public consultation, consultation to indigenous communities, transparent bidding processes or public procurement. Low- and middle-income countries that have gone through processes of reform driven by international organisations to liberalise their mining regimes and which are generally perceived as highly risky for business, the crafting of tenure systems and contracts, as well as the interconnected nature of obligations under investment treaties has been highly influenced by the grammar of investment risks and rewards. Court decisions across many jurisdictions are interpreting mining codes within the context of the broader charts of rights and duties (often bridging in through their arguments across international, local and customary normative phenomena).

Some nation-states issue *minerals policies* to guide actions within their territories and internationally to influence the supply of minerals on their economies.[76] The national interest in minerals as 'raw materials' derives from their status as inputs to national industries and value chains. Minerals policies are part and parcel of economic policies and might establish a framework based on analysis of minerals consumption of primary and secondary production (obtained through recycling), imports and exports. They are usually composed of actions on foreign affairs diplomacy on trade (to secure access to raw materials) and development, international cooperation, domestic minerals planning and promotion of research and technology.[77] The preparation of 'critical minerals lists' is constituent of minerals policies actions.[78] Actions to promote resource efficiency to shift

---

[75] AE Bastida, 'Mining Law in the Context of Development' in P Andrews-Speed (ed), *International Competition for Resources: The Role of Law, State and Markets* (Dundee, Dundee University Press, 2008) 101–36.

[76] G Tiess, 'The Concept of a Minerals Policy' in G Tiess, *General and International Mineral Policy* (Verlag/Wien, Springer, 2011).

[77] ibid. On EU raw materials' policy, see above C in this section.

[78] See ch 2.III below.

Mineral Law from a Global Perspective: A Cosmopolitan View   19

towards a circular economy are expected to become a key component of integrated minerals policy frameworks.[79]

E. The Local Level

Broadly speaking, the local level of legal and normative ordering, comprising the rich universe of landowners, landholders, and indigenous and local communities, as well as local artisanal and small-scale miners, has typically been absent of granular regulation and agreements. The recognition of local peoples' rights under international and domestic legal systems, and their emergence as key stakeholders, are partly driving a 'contractual turn' for the enforcement of corporate duties towards those affected by the extractive industries.[80] Broadly speaking, they are also permeating into the very same structures of mining law through legal reform or judicial interpretation, in the form of consultation and consent processes, requirements for entering into contracts,[81] local equity or customary landholders or communities' entitlements to mineral rights,[82] and the crystallisation of corporate duties towards local communities,[83] adaptations in impact assessments[84] and, generally, obtaining the 'social licence to operate'.[85] While not clear in all contexts, the dawn of a new phase on the mediation with local communities in the law of energy and natural resources is being observed, shifting the traditional focus

---

[79] D Murguía and G Tiess, 'D7.1. Report on relevant business and policy issues for Europe pertinent to Critical Raw Materials (CRMs). SCRREEN Project Deliverable, Dreistetten, 2017. On the EU policies, see above C in this section.

[80] J Gathii and IT Odumosu-Ayanu, 'The Turn to Contractual Responsibility in the Global Extractive Industry' (2015) 1 *Business and Human Rights Journal* 69 (arguing for the potential role of contracts in natural resources, including community development agreements, in enforcing corporate obligations towards those affected by business, and that investors, as governments, are trustees, extractive resources having to be mobilised for the benefit of societies).

[81] KE Dupuy, 'Community Development Requirements in Mining Laws' (2014) 1 *Extractive Industries and Society* 200; KD Bruckner, 'Community Development Agreements in Mining Projects' (2016) 44 *Denver Journal of International Law and Policy* 413; C Nwapi, 'Legal and Institutional Frameworks for Community Development Agreements in the Mining Sector in Africa' (2017) 4 *Extractive Industries and Society* 202; RJ Heffron, L Downes, OM Ramírez Rodríguez and D McCauley, 'The Emergence of the "Social Licence to Operate" in the Extractive Industries?', *Resources Policy* (2018), available at https://doi.org/10.1016/j.resourpol.2018.09.012; C O'Faircheallaigh, 'Community Development Agreements in the Mining Industry: An Emerging Global Phenomenon' (2013) 44 *Community Development* 222.

[82] See ch 6.

[83] J Otto, 'How Do We Legislate for Improved Community Development?' in T Addison and A Roe (eds), *Extractive Industries. The Management of Resources as a Driver of Sustainable Development* (Oxford, Oxford University Press, 2018) 673–94.

[84] L Barrera-Hernández, B Barton, L Godden, AR Lucas and A Rønne, 'Introduction' in L Barrera-Hernández, B Barton, L Godden, AR Lucas and A Rønne (eds), *Sharing the Costs and Benefits of Energy and Resource Activity. Legal Change and Impact on Communities* (Oxford, Oxford University Press, 2016) 1–2.

[85] D Smith, 'Social Licence to Operate in the Unconventional Oil and Gas Development Sector. The Colorado Experience' in Barrera-Hernández, Barton, Godden, Lucas and Rønne, *Sharing the Costs* (2016).

20 *Understanding the Law of Mining and Minerals from a Global Perspective*

on compensation and liability to a deeper understanding of costs for communities and a wider range of benefit-sharing mechanisms, public participation and collaborative governance schemes,[86] bringing in resources law at the interface with human rights and environmental law.

Many ASM activities occur 'extralegally', where they align with local customs and land tenure traditions but actually operate outside the boundaries of the nation-state's legal frameworks and mining laws.[87] There is increased attention to the integration and recognition of these customary practices as well as of local contexts, as a more effective way forward for strategies which are embedded in miners' views and oriented to support them in processes of formalisation.[88] Research in recent years has also broadened the definitions of ASM and stressed the important contribution that minerals mined and consumed locally (what have been called 'development' minerals) can have to local economies.[89] More broadly, the focus on local content and local and regional development and industrialisation strategies across a wide range of jurisdictions highlight the policy concerns on building and strengthening local linkages.[90] In all cases, the widening circle of actors is setting dialogue and collaboration at the centre of emerging approaches to ordering social relationships in mining and minerals.

III. Mineral Law in International Scholarship

International scholarship has begun to pay attention to mineral law,[91] a long-neglected area of enquiry, while there is an important and growing body of literature on natural resources law more generally that is pertinent to the analysis of a range

---

[86] ibid.

[87] S Siegel and MM Veiga, 'Artisanal and small-scale mining as an extralegal economy: De Soto and the redefinition of "formalization"' (2009) 34 *Resources Policy* 52.

[88] G Hilson, A Hilson, R Maconachie, J McQuilken and H Goumandakoye, *Artisanal and small-scale mining (ASM) in sub-Saharan Africa: Re-conceptualizing formalization and 'illegal' activity* (2017) 83 *Geoforum* 80; Intergovernmental Forum on Mining, Minerals, Metals and Sustainable Development (IGF), 'IGF Guidance for Governments: Managing artisanal and small-scale mining' (Winnipeg, IISD, 2017).

[89] DM Franks, L Pakoun and C Ngonze, *Development Minerals: Transforming a Neglected Sector in Africa, the Caribbean and the Pacific* (Brussels, United Nations Development Programme, 2016); C Akong, 'Reframing matter: Towards a material-discursive framework for Africa's minerals' (2020) 7 *Extractive Industries and Society*; C Afeku and AA Debrah, 'Policy convergence on development minerals in Africa: A study of Ghana's regulatory frameworks', (2020) 7 *Extractive Industries and Society*; A Lebdioui, 'Uncovering the high value of neglected minerals: "Development Minerals" as inputs for industrial development in North Africa' (2020) 7 *Extractive Industries and Society*.

[90] Africa Mining Vision, 2009. See also OECD Mining Regions project at oecd.org/cfe/regional-policy/mining-regions-project.htm. See further ch 6.

[91] Bastida, Wälde and Warden–Fernandez (n 19) (reviewing the state-of-the-art of evolving international law, transnational standards and comparative regimes of mineral law, and enquiring on progress and obstacles towards sustainability in the sector, in 62 chapters written by established and emerging academics, industry experts and practitioners); reviewed by G Kuhne (2008) 72 *Rabels Zeitschrift für ausländisches und internationales Privatrecht / The Rabel Journal of Comparative and International*

Mineral Law in International Scholarship 21

of issues and trends.[92] The international literature has long focused on aspects of the foreign investment regime and on the evolution of the principle of PSONR, investment regimes, state mining agreements[93] and international arbitration,[94] adding to a number of comparative law studies and practitioner guides.[95] The lion's share of attention has been for international law regimes applicable to mining and

Private Law 209). The book builds on extensive scholarly work by the late professor Wälde in this field published in articles over many years, a few of them cited in the Bibliography of this monograph; TL Field, *State Governance of Mining, Development and Sustainability* (Cheltenham and Northampton, Edward Elgar Publishing, 2019) (exploring the conflicting narratives on the role of the state in both promoting mining development and protecting the environment, and how they manifest in mining laws, taxation and the interface with the environment, and how the law could transform within a post-development, post-extractivism lens); J Otto and J Cordes, *The Regulation of Mineral Enterprises: A Global Perspective on Economics, Law and Policy* (Colorado, RMMLF, 2002) (providing an interdisciplinary introduction to the main systems of mineral tenure, contracts, regulation and taxation in the industry); D Olawuyi, *Extractive Industries Law in Africa* (Cham, Switzerland AG, Springer Nature, 2018) (offering a comprehensive and multi-jurisdictional perspective on the law and institutions of extractive industries in the continent, emphasising the need for their systemic and coherent examination); J Vildósola Fuenzalida, *El dominio minero y el sistema concesional en América Latina y el Caribe* (Caracas, OLAMI/ECLAC, 1999) (providing what is, to my knowledge, the most extensive study available today on the origins of ownership and mineral tenure regimes under Roman law and European law, as sources of Latin American mining regimes, which are also reviewed); A Vergara Blanco, *Principios y sistema de derecho minero. Estudio histórico y dogmático* (Santiago de Chile, Editorial Jurídica de Chile, 1992) (a thoroughly researched, systematised and authoritative study of historical sources of mining law as basis of current principles and systems of mining law); E Liedholm-Johnson, 'Mineral Rights: Legal Systems Governing Exploration and Exploitation' (2010) Institutionen för infrastruktur, Fastighetsteknik (Stockholm, Kungliga Tekniska högskolan), to name a few. See also the excellent and continuing publications and scholarly work of the Rocky Mountain Mineral Law Foundation based in the US, which has expanded its focus and internationalised.

[92] N Schrijver, *Sovereignty over Natural Resources. Balancing Rights and Duties* (Cambridge, Cambridge University Press, 1997); Barnes, *Property Rights and Natural Resources* (2009); L Cotula, *Human Rights, Natural Resource and Investment Law in a Globalised World. Shades of Grey in the Shadow of the Law* (London, Routledge, 2012); E Morgera and K Kulovesi, *Research Handbook on International Law and Natural Resources* (Cheltenham and Northampton, Edward Elgar Publishing, 2016); Merino Blanco and Razzaque (n 26); J Gilbert, *Human Rights and Natural Resources* (Oxford, Oxford University Press, 2018) (adopting a rights-based perspective to natural resources law); J Faundez and C Tan, *Natural Resources and Sustainable Development* (Cheltenham and Northampton, Edward Elgar Publishing, 2017); S Alam, JH Bhuiyan and J Razzaque (eds), *International Natural Resources Law, Investment and Sustainability* (London, Routledge, 2017). See also the excellent work of the ILA Committee on the Role of International Law in Sustainable Natural Resource Management for Development, established in 2012 (which has notably begun examining the international rules and practices of sustainable management of 'mineral commodities' and has anticipated work on precious metals, see report of ILA, Sydney Conference (2018) Role of International Law in Sustainable Natural Resource Management for Development, section III.1 with I Espa and M Oehl, 'Rules and Practices of International Law for the Sustainable Management of Mineral Commodities, including Nickel, Copper, Bauxite and Rare Earths' 5–11); and of the series edited by the Academic Advisory Group of the International Bar Association (IBA)'s Section on Energy and Environment, Natural Resources and Infrastructure Law (SEERIL) published by Oxford University Press on a biannual basis.

[93] See, eg, D Barberis, *Negotiating Mining Agreements: Past, Present and Future Trends* (London, Kluwer Law International, 1998).

[94] H Burnett and LA Bret, *Arbitration of International Mining Disputes: Law and Practice* (Oxford International Arbitration Series) (Oxford, Oxford University Press, 2017).

[95] eg Getting the Deal Through; International Comparative Legal Guides, Mining Laws and Regulations; The Mining Law Review.

minerals in areas beyond national jurisdictions (the oceans, Antarctica and outer space) that, while not framed as 'mining law', certainly fulfil the function of typical mining laws in the narrower sense of the term.[96]

Mining law scholarship has logically developed in resource-producing countries. In a large number of these nations, the study of the legal framework applicable to mining focuses on the traditional sources of law at the domestic level: the national mining code, cases and doctrinal studies, with references to the applicable investment regime and environmental regulation, and at varying degrees, it is beginning to engage with international developments. Theoretical work depends naturally on each jurisdiction. In the EU, until not very long ago, mining law had become a long-forgotten discipline – either a chapter in administrative law or natural resources law or hidden behind other terminology such as 'raw materials' or the current 'energy sources' or 'new forms of energy' or 'commodity law'. In many countries, comprehensive materials to study the subject have not been developed. In any case, and as a general observation, there is scant scholarly connection between this body of work and the international literature.

Nevertheless, in recent years, different lines of enquiry are beginning to shine a new light on national and subnational law and governance of mining and minerals even though, broadly speaking, they have not engaged with, or have paid little attention to, mining law scholarship and conceptual frameworks. The first of these threads of enquiry comes hand in hand with scholarship on the 'resource curse' paradox developed over the last two decades, especially in the fields of economics and political science, which has observed an inverse correlation between resource wealth and development outcomes, and propounded that it originates from corruption and poor quality governance, or from gaps in governance. The international community has embraced this line of thought, positing that the quality of governance and institutions is crucial in preventing or counteracting the resource curse.[97] For a long time, the main focus of attention has been on the role of external and overarching interventions, such as the Extractive Industries Transparency Initiative (EITI) and other international standards (eg, on responsible sourcing) to improve the quality of governance and fill in gaps. More recent studies have begun to focus on localising the resource curse discourse within particular territories[98] or industries, particularly oil territories, and on interrogating about the extent to which international standards can and actually do articulate with national laws and policies.[99] In the same direction, an emerging line of enquiry is beginning

---

[96] See ch 5.

[97] M Busse and S Groning, 'The Resource Curse Revisited: Governance and Natural Resources' (2013) 154 *Public Choice* 1.

[98] E Wilson and J van Alstine, 'Localising Transparency: Exploring EITI's Contribution to Sustainable Development' (International Institute for Environment and Development, 2014) 22.

[99] J Pott, M Wenban-Smith, L Turley and M Lynch, 'Standards and the Extractive Economy', State of Sustainability Initiatives Review (IGF/IISD 2018).

Mineral Law in International Scholarship 23

to trace the extent to which mining laws uphold transparency in order to explore the role of broader frameworks in supporting civic space.[100] These developments cohere with the evolution of the EITI Standard from reporting resource revenue to expanding reporting to mineral licensing and contractual arrangements, and more recently to promoting systematic disclosure to embed transparency in governance and management systems.[101]

A more critical line of enquiry from socio-legal and political economic perspectives argue for the inherent contradictions entailed in the introduction of governance innovations through, for example, negotiated agreements and performance standards to stimulate outcomes at local levels within the persistent patterns of mineral tenure and legal infrastructures used to facilitate the activity, which result in regulatory stalemate and further devolution of responsibilities to private parties.[102] Another line of work arrives to similar conclusions from analysis of mining codes and their interface with broader constitutional structures and international commitments, as well as evolving legal and regulatory regimes for managing extraction and the use of mineral resources more generally. These studies venture that legal regimes for this sector suffer from deficits of constitutionality and coherence[103] – and, more broadly, from deficits of design[104] – as they have

---

[100] Civil Society reports include Open Contracting Partnership and NRGI, 'Open Contracting for Oil, Gas and Mineral Rights: Shining a Light on Good Practice' (June 2018); L Caripis, 'Combatting Corruption in Mining Approvals: Assessing the Risks in 18 Resource-Rich Countries' (Mining for Sustainable Development Programme, Transparency International Australia, 2017).

[101] See EITI, 'Systematic Disclosure. Mainstreaming the EITI', available at eiti.org/systematic-disclosure.

[102] B Campbell and MC Prémont, 'What Is Behind the Search for Social Acceptability of Mining Projects? Political Economy and Legal Perspectives on Canadian Mineral Extraction' (2017) 30 *Mineral Economics* 171–80. D Szablowski and B Campbell, 'Struggles over Extractive Governance: Power, Discourse, Violence and Legality' (2019) 6 *The Extractive Industries and Society* 635 (a review of literature on the resource curse and institutional change, which emphasise path dependencies and the continuity of extractives' structure through governance changes, and similar findings from the literature on extractivism). See also Szablowski (n 29) (the author focuses on the development of transnational regulation in extractive sites as a result of globalising forces and on the resulting redistribution of legal authority between public and private actors). B Campbell (ed), *Mining in Africa. Regulation and Development* (London, Pluto Press, 2009) (this text draws attention, from a political economy perspective, to the role of mining codes in broad processes of legal and institutional reform in the sector). See also from the same author: 'New Rules of the Game: The World Bank's Role in the Construction of New Normative Frameworks for States, Markets and Social Exclusion' (2000) 21 *Canadian Journal of Development Studies* 7; and (editor) *Regulating Mining in Africa: For Whose Benefit?* Discussion Paper 26 (Uppsala, Nordiska Afrikainstitutet, 2004). For a law and development perspective on mining codes, see Bastida, 'Mining Law' (2008) 101.

[103] H Santaella Quintero, '*Un territorio y tres modelos de gestión: análisis de la necesidad de armonizar y constitucionalizar las competencias urbanísticas, ambientales y mineras sobre el territorio*' in JC Henao and S Díaz Ángel (eds), *Minería y desarrollo. Tomo V: Historia y gobierno del territorio minero* (Bogotá, Universidad Externado de Colombia, 2016) 175–226.

[104] Bastida and Bustos, 'Towards Regimes for Sustainable Mineral Resources Management'(2017). See also AA Debrah, H Mtegha and F Cawood, 'Social licence to operate and the granting of mineral rights in sub-Saharan Africa: Exploring tensions between communities, governments and multinational mining companies' (2018) 56 *Resources Policy* 95. Mostert, *Mineral Law* (2012).

24 Understanding the Law of Mining and Minerals from a Global Perspective

not been structured from the vantage point of local contexts. In other words, it is posited that mining laws and institutions must transform themselves to work for sustainability. Finally, a range of studies are beginning to examine mining codes from a distributional justice perspective, critical theories of development, transition theories as extractivism and from political ecology framings,[105] and ecological law.[106] These enquiries coalesce in calls for the constitutionalisation and democratisation of mining law and even advance on their decolonisation. Another rich line of scholarship has, in turn, analysed investment treaties and transnational contracts, and explored the extent to which commitments to foreign investors under such agreements (or to investors more generally under national resource regimes) can undermine other public policy goals relating to sustainable development.[107]

These disconnected strands of scholarship implicitly point at the fact that theoretical framings to critically engage with mining and mineral law are now emerging and that there are scant analytical framings that fully capture the growing complexity of the law and governance of mining and minerals and the interactions between different levels and spheres of legal and normative ordering. To begin reconstructing the disciplinary matrix for studying the law and governance of mining and minerals, I use an analytical toolbox consisting of: (i) a global perspective inasmuch as it provides a lens that expands on understanding the problem, actors, sources and patterns of legal and normative order at different levels and the relationship between them, and promotes its engagement with the global challenges of our age (such as sustainable development, climate action and the eradication of poverty); and (ii) the 'conceptual matrix' of sustainable development, as it provides a basis for supporting an understanding of the interface between those levels and the different spheres of normative ordering, and of processes for bringing together actors with divergent interests in order to achieve common objectives.

---

[105] TL Field, *State Governance of Mining, Development and Sustainability*; B Meyersfeld, 'Empty Promises and the Myth of Mining: Does Mining Lead to Pro-Poor Development?' (2017) 2 *Business and Human Rights Journal* 31; X Sierra Camargo, *Derecho, desarrollo y extractivismo: la disputa por el oro en Colombia en un contexto de colonialidad global*, Tesis de Doctorado, Universidad del Rosario (2019). Svampa observes that socio-environmental struggles in Latin America have paved the way for an 'eco-territorial turn' – conflating the intersections between indigenous communitarian and environmental discourses, as well as ecofeminist perspectives – which build common frames of collective action around the commons, food sovereignty, environmental justice and '*buen vivir*'. M Svampa, 'Commodities Consensus: Neoextractivism and Enclosure of the Commons in Latin America' (2015) 114 *The South Atlantic Quarterly* 69.

[106] C Sbert Carlsson, 'Mining from the Lens of Ecological Law: Obstacles and Opportunities for Re-formation' (Faculty of Law, University of Ottawa, 2019); C Sbert, 'Re-Imagining Mining: The *Earth Charter* as a Guide for Ecological Mining Reform' (2015) 6 *IUCNAEL EJournal* 66.

[107] L Cotula, 'Reconciling Regulatory Stability and Evolution of Environmental Standards in Investment Contracts: Towards a Rethink of Stabilization Clauses' (2008) 1 *The Journal of World Energy Law & Business* 158; L Cotula, *Human Rights* (2012); K Tienhaara, *The Expropriation of Environmental Governance: Protecting Foreign Investors at the Expense of Public Policy* (Cambridge, Cambridge University Press, 2009).

IV. Law and the Governance of Mining and Minerals

'Governance' is an ambiguous term, meaning different things to different constituencies.[108] The governance of the minerals resources' sector is characterised by complex processes involving actors (governmental and non-governmental, private actors, civil society, landholders, traditional communities), rules (both formal and informal), structures and relationships, which take place at different levels and take into consideration varying temporal boundaries.[109] Global, regional, national and local patterns of social dynamics involving individuals and institutions shape the decision-making processes in the minerals resources sector.[110] These processes define how power and authority are exercised, how decisions are taken (including questions on who takes decisions and on the basis of which information) and how citizens and affected parties participate.[111]

In political science, in seeking to identify an analytical tool that can be used for the observation of social dynamics at different levels by different societies at different times, Marc Hufty has defined governance as 'decision-making processes that take place whenever collective stakes lead to competition and cooperation'. He distinguishes this scientific, analytical definition, from the normative dimensions encountered in literature and thinking on global governance as steered towards the solution of cooperation problems. In this regard, he points at the remarkable definition of governance as

> the sum of the many ways individuals and institutions, public and private, manage their common affairs … [as] a continuing process through which conflicting or diverse interests may be accommodated and co–operative action may be taken … [including] formal institutions and regimes empowered to enforce compliance, as well as informal arrangements that people and institutions either have agreed to or perceive to be in their interest.[112]

This definition underlines a procedural approach to bring a wide range of actors that include non-state and informal ones into multi-level decision-making processes. Hufty draws a distinction between these and the definition of 'good governance', which emerged in World Bank documents in the 1990s with connotations as a

---

[108] M Hufty, 'Governance: Exploring Four Approaches and Their Relevance to Research' in U Wiesmann and H Hurni (eds), *Research for Sustainable Development: Foundations, Experiences, and Perspectives.* Perspectives of the Swiss National Centre of Competence in Research (NCCR) North–South, University of Bern, vol 6 (Bern, Switzerland: Geographica Bernensia, 2011).

[109] See A Pedro, ET Ayuk, C Bodouroglou, B Milligan, P Ekins and B Oberle, 'Towards a sustainable development licence to operate for the extractive sector' (2017) 30 *Mineral Economics* 153.

[110] ibid.

[111] cf P Martin, B Boer and L Slobodian (eds), 'Framework for Assessing and Improving Law for Sustainability A Legal Component of a Natural Resource Governance Framework' (IUCN, 2016) (referencing IUCN WCC Resolution 3.012).

[112] Hufty, 'Governance' (2011), quoting the definition of the Commission on Global Governance in 1995 (in I Carlsson, S Ramphal, A Alatas and H Dahlgren, *Our Global Neighbourhood: The Report of the Commission on Global Governance* (Oxford, Oxford University Press, 1995)).

political tool of transformation. He also identifies a fourth approach: that one of 'modern governance', which has come to denominate the phenomenon of diffusion of power from the central state towards international, regional, subnational and local units, and networks of interdependent actors, characteristic of globalisation, which we have highlighted when addressing the normative phenomena which have emerged at the transnational level.

Governance serves to steer[113] processes through rules and mechanisms that guide the exercise of authority, the behaviour of parties, the protection of nature and human rights as well as the establishment of the institutional setting, towards the sustainable management and stewardship of natural resources for the common interest.[114] Law is vital to equitable and effective governance.[115] It establishes the substantive rules, the institutions and processes of decision-making, and the mechanisms for accountability and dispute resolution.[116]

V. The Purpose of this Book

This book aims to explore a disciplinary matrix for the study of the law and governance of mining and minerals that cuts across the different geographical levels, diversity of sources and patterns of legal phenomena, and normatively engages with sustainable development: one of the underlying challenges of our age. In doing so, it seeks to connect mining law regimes, which have typically been confined to domestic and local processes, not only with the global economy, global developments on their regulation and the global sustainability challenges, but also, crucially, with the local level of legal and normative ordering.

The book offers a *perspective* to connect the levels of legal and normative ordering concerning mining and minerals as a contribution to this emerging field of study and enquiry. But it neither intends to cover all aspects nor deal with every topic exhaustively. It focuses mostly on developments in Western jurisdictions.

Shaping a 'cosmopolitan' vision is, by definition, a collective enterprise. The book ultimately aims to contribute to growing dialogues and more granular studies to advance our understanding on the role and function of the law and governance of mining and minerals beyond the traditional forms and structures if it is meant to work towards transformative outcomes and attaining a sustainable and equitable future.

---

[113] E Cussianovich, 'La gobernanza de los recursos naturales desde la mirada de los ciudadanos' in R Sánchez (ed), La bonanza de los recursos naturales para el desarrollo: dilemas de gobernanza, ECLAC Books, no 157 (LC/PUB.2019/13-P) (Santiago, Economic Commission for Latin America and the Caribbean (ECLAC) 2019) 257–76.

[114] S Kumra, 'La gobernanza de los recursos naturales y su vínculo con los objetivos de desarrollo sostenible' in Sánchez, La bonanza de los recursos naturales para el desarrollo (2019) 164–65.

[115] Martin, Boer and Slobodian, Framework (2016) 1.

[116] ibid.

VI. The Structure of this Book

This chapter sets the scene and framing to explore the law and governance of mining and minerals from a global perspective. Chapter two seeks to provide an understanding of the mining and minerals industry, actors and institutions engaged in policy formulation from a global perspective, as well as introduce the evolving framing of mining and its linkages with development in the formulation of policy and narratives ('scripts') at international level, and the role of law in such contexts, to provide a broad overview of aspects to be analysed in more detail in the following two chapters.

Chapter three reviews the concept of territorial sovereignty, tracing the evolution of the principle of PSONR from its origins in the ideas on a NIEO to its place within the global framework for sustainable development. It focuses on the concept of sustainable development and its key constituent principles, and on key concepts of mining and minerals emerging from soft law instruments. Chapter four turns our attention to key fields of international law relevant to mining and minerals and to transnational standards that are emerging to coordinate and regulate activities beyond national borders and will point to extra-territorial norms. Chapter five looks at international resource regimes in areas beyond national jurisdictions that govern the global commons, eg, the deep seabed, outer space and the moratorium on Antarctica.

Chapter six examines core concepts of mining law regimes at national levels. It provides general categorisations of the basic concepts of ownership in situ, processes for allocating mineral rights, and of approaches to the interface between mineral rights and land tenure, as well as the overarching principle of national and public interest. It also delves into aspects of legal and regulatory design lying at the interface of tenure regimes with fields of law that widen the actors and criteria to consider in decision-making processes. This chapter paints a broad picture of typical features of mining law but, not least for reasons of space, cannot cover the topics exhaustively or replace specific analyses. It focuses on the typical pattern of mining law regimes of industrial mining while it observes general trends relevant to ASM.

Chapter seven concludes by consolidating the findings and exploring 'an overarching vision' for the study of the law and governance of mining and minerals from a global perspective. It also proposes a research agenda for future studies.

2

Mining and Minerals, Actors and Governance from a Global Perspective

Understanding the law and governance of mining and minerals and its evolving nature from a global perspective requires a preliminary and broad comprehension of the facts and problems, as well as of the actors involved in, and affected by, this sector. This chapter will provide a high-level introduction, beginning with a definition of minerals and their place in global production networks, and followed by a definition of mining, its processes, defining features, lifecycle, impacts and risks, and its interface with developmental outcomes. It will look at the industry structure and at the wide constellation of actors holding a diverse range of interests in the sector. Finally, it will provide an overview of the stages in the evolution of international mineral policy towards developing countries – which enshrine distinctive functions for law and contractual arrangements. Through the schematic exploration of these stages, it will introduce a range of institutions acting in the global sphere and participating in the formulation of policy and initiatives in mining and minerals – and shaping over time interpretations of the relationship between mining and development.

I. Minerals: 'The Third Kingdom of Nature'

From time immemorial, minerals and technology have been the basis for breakthroughs that have shaped the nature of life and lifestyles.[1] Much is said today about the essential role of minerals and metals in the Fourth Revolution and in the shift towards low-carbon economies.[2] Bauxite (as a constituent of aluminium), cobalt, copper, iron ore, lead, lithium, nickel, manganese, the platinum group of metals, rare earth metals, silver, steel, titanium and zinc are basic inputs required

---

[1] G Agricola, *De Re Metallica* in H Hoover and L Hoover, trans, 1st edn from the 1st 1556 Latin edn (New York, Dover Publications Inc, 1950) xxvi.

[2] O Vidal, B Goffé and N Arndt, 'Metals for a Low-Carbon Society' (2013) 6 *Nature Geoscience*, 894–96; SH Ali, D Giurco, N Arndt, E Nickless, G Brown, A Demetriades, R Durrheim, MA Enriquez, J Kinnaird, A Littleboy, LD Meinert, R Oberhänsli, J Salem, R Schodde, G Schneider, O Vidal and N Yakovleva, 'Mineral Supply for Sustainable Development Requires Resource Governance' (2017) 543 *Nature* 367. D Arrobas, K Hund, M McCormick, J Ningthoujam and J Drexhage, *The Growing Role of Minerals and Metals for a Low Carbon Future* (Washington DC, World Bank, 2017).

for building wind, solar and energy battery technologies.[3] Virtually all the elements of the periodic table are involved as material compositions of emerging technologies, in contrast to the Stone Age, the Iron Age or the Bronze Age, which revolved around a single metal or alloy.[4] So, elements which had received little attention are now being required in 'unprecedented quantities' for the artefacts of advanced technology.[5] These might be produced by a handful of countries, recovered mainly as by-products and not recycled in meaningful volumes following their use.[6]

Demand for most minerals and metals is 'derived-driven': It is driven by their physical and chemical properties, and their use as inputs to materials for consumer and industrial goods.[7] Copper, for example, is an excellent electricity conductor, so is used extensively in wires. Rare metals used in smartphones are precisely what allow them to be 'smarter', ie, smaller, faster and more powerful.[8] Notably among precious metals, the case of gold is somehow different. Since prehistoric times, it has served as currency and store of value because of its scarcity, beauty and durability.[9] Phillip Crowson notes that gold 'continues to exert a mystical allure for mankind, seemingly embedded deep in the human psyche'.[10]

Minerals have commonly been defined as naturally occurring, inorganic substances with a distinctive chemical formula and ordered structure.[11] Economists draw a distinction between *resources* (ie the presence of minerals in the Earth, which might be amenable to exploitation with currently available technology) and *reserves* (ie those resources that have been measured with more precision and might be economically extracted).[12] Their definition as 'raw materials', 'commodities', 'commercial assets', 'strategic' or 'critical' resources', 'natural capital', as part of 'geoheritage' and 'geodiversity',[13] or 'commons' situate minerals in varying disciplinary, political, economic, ecological and legal framings, assigning them different values.[14]

---

[3] Ali, Giurco, Arndt, Nickless, Brown, Demetriades, Durrheim, Enriquez, Kinnaird, Littleboy, Meinert, Oberhänsli, Salem, Schodde, Schneider, Vidal and Yakovleva, 'Mineral Supply' (2017); Arrobas, Hund, McCormick, Ningthoujam and Drexhage, *Growing Role of Minerals and Metals* (2017).

[4] AL Gulley, NT Nassar and S Xun, 'China, the United States, and competition for resources that enable emerging technologies' (2018) 115 *PNAS* 4111.

[5] ibid.

[6] ibid.

[7] P Crowson, *Mining Unearthed. The Definitive Book on how Economic and Political Influences Shape the Global Mining Industry* (London, Aspermont, 2008) 47.

[8] D Abraham, *The Elements of Power. Gadgets, Guns, and the Struggle for a Sustainable Future in the Rare Metal Age* (New Haven and London, Yale University Press, 2015) 2–3.

[9] P Crowson, *Inside Mining. The Economics of the Supply and Demand of Minerals and Metals* (London, Mining Journal Books Limited, 1998) 58.

[10] ibid 59.

[11] There are over 5,500 mineral species. New minerals are approved by the Commission on New Minerals, Nomenclature and Classification of the International Mineralogical Association.

[12] Crowson, *Inside Mining* (1998) 62 and 65.

[13] J Brilha, M Gray, DI Pereira and P Pereira, 'Geodiversity: An integrative review as a contribution to the sustainable management of the whole of nature' (2018) 86 *Environmental Science & Policy* 19.

[14] B Fornillo, '¿Commodities, bienes naturales o Recursos Naturales Estratégicos? La importancia de un nombre' (2014) *Revista Nueva Sociedad* 252.

30 *Mining and Minerals, Actors and Governance from a Global Perspective*

The mining industry is characterised by the sheer diversity of its products. Common classifications distinguish between *energy minerals* (coal, oil and gas, uranium); *metallic minerals* (ferrous metals, ie iron ore, niobium, tantalum and titanium; precious metals, ie gold, silver and platinum; base metals, ie bauxite, cobalt, copper, lead, magnesium, nickel and zinc; alkali metals, ie sodium, potassium and lithium, the lightest metal; and rare earths); and *non-metallic minerals* (construction materials, ie sand and gravel; industrial minerals, as bentonite, kaolin, salt, potash and silica; and precious stones, ie diamonds and gems).[15] Within metallic minerals, further distinctions can be drawn between *major* metals (eg aluminium, copper, zinc, or tin), *minor* metals (which most often occur as by-products with the major metals) and *coupled elements* (which always occur together due to their chemical composition, like rare earths or the platinum group elements).[16]

II. Minerals in Global Production Networks

From the point of view of the organisation of the global economy, the mining industry represents 'the beginning of the beginning': the very first stage of the production circuit and of the web of global production networks.[17] Mineral extraction, processing, refining, trading and consumption involves a range of activities and actors including firms, workers and customers from geographically dispersed areas.[18] However, the business models of companies are changing and two sets of trends are visible: on the one hand, further vertical integration from exploitation to refining to trading; and, on the other, a move towards fragmentation of the exploration and exploitation business, with large companies entering into strategic alliances with junior exploration companies.[19]

The volume of minerals used in an economy is associated with higher levels of economic development. Lower income economies mostly have low demands for raw materials, except for minerals used domestically such as construction materials, where deposits are usually located in relative proximity to towns and cities.[20] As economies develop, urbanise and industrialise, they undergo periods of

---

[15] See, eg, UNCTAD, 'World Investment Report: Transnational Corporations, Extractive Industries and Development' (UN, 2007) and more recent classifications in N Arndt, S Kesler and C Ganino, *Metals and Society. An Introduction to Economic Geology* (Verlag Berlin Heidelberg, Springer Mineralogy, Springer International Publishing, 2015).

[16] S Renner and F Wellmer, 'Volatility drivers on the metal market and exposure of producing countries' (2019) *Mineral Economics*, available at https://doi.org/10.1007/s13563-019-00200-8.

[17] P Dicken, *Global Shift. Mapping the Changing Contours of the World Economy*, 7th edn (London, Sage, 2015) 396.

[18] Dicken, *Global Shift* (2015) 397. OECD Trade and Agriculture Directorate Trade Committee – Working Party of the Trade Committee, 'The Mining Global Value Chain and the Impact of Embodied Services', TAD/TC/WP(2018)27/FINAL 18 December 2019.

[19] UNCTAD, 'World Investment Report' (2007) 112–13.

[20] These are being referred to as 'development minerals'; see section V below.

Minerals in Global Production Networks 31

intensive resources use to build up the infrastructure of higher income economies and the demands of growing middle classes.[21] Mineral use in highly industrialised economies tends to stabilise and slow down. At the same time, emerging economies account for the fastest growth in global mineral use today, predominantly in China, India and the ASEAN economies.[22]

Minerals demand has historically been met with deposits close to where they were to be consumed. In Europe, the demand for coal and iron ore required by the Industrial Revolution was met with deposits in England, Scotland, France, Spain and Germany, among others. By the 1850s, more than 50 per cent of global mineral production occurred in Europe (a share that has fallen below five per cent today).[23] China is now the world's largest mineral producer: its domestic production supplies the demands of the manufacturing industries, a growing middle class and infrastructure building. Over the years, the easiest to mine, and most accessible deposits have been depleted[24] or have become off-limits due to environmental regulation and land-use planning. Minerals are unevenly distributed in the Earth's crust and some minerals are found in concentrations that make their extraction feasible only in certain parts of the globe. For mining companies, the decision to mine abroad may be deemed the most cost-effective option, or may otherwise be prompted by higher ore grades or types of minerals; or be inherent to the business models of companies.[25]

In many countries, the bulk of mineral production is geared to exportation instead of the domestic market, and in a few of them mining provides a major source of export revenues. High-income countries, notably Australia, Canada, Chile, Russia and the US, or higher-middle-income countries, such as Brazil, China and South Africa, dominate mineral production, whereas countries with higher levels of export dependence are predominantly low- or lower-middle-income countries.[26]

While the bulk of mining activity occurs onshore, marine mining has long taken place on shallow (less than 50m) shores in many countries, concentrating mainly on aggregates (eg, in many European countries, China, and the Pacific Island states) and also on diamonds (Namibia and South Africa), tin (Indonesia),

---

[21] Crowson (n 9) 10.

[22] D Humphreys, *The Remaking of the Mining Industry* (New York, Palgrave Macmillan, 2015); D Humphreys, 'The mining industry after the boom', Presentation to the XIV Mining Seminar, CEPMLP, Dundee, 5–6 April 2017.

[23] C Hinde and M Farooki, 'Promoting Investor Interest in the EU Mining Sector', STRADE (Report), 28 March 2018, 14.

[24] See ch 7.

[25] Hinde and Farooki, 'Promoting Investor Interest' (2018).

[26] A Roe and S Dodd, 'Dependence on extractive industries in lower income countries. The Statistical Tendencies' in T Addison and A Roe (eds), *Extractive Industries. The Management of Resources as a Driver of Sustainable Development* (Oxford, Oxford University Press, 2018) 35. International Council for Mining and Metals, 'The Role of Mining in National Economies', 2nd edn (2014) and 3rd edn (2016).

magnesium, salt, sulphur, gold, and heavy minerals. It has been noted that pressure on land-based resources might trigger further marine mining, particularly on the deep seabed, as technology develops, although there are growing concerns about the environmental impact of deep seabed mining, which might influence decisions about its development.[27] Meanwhile, the further expansion of mining to 'new frontiers' under international jurisdiction resurfaces from time to time alongside cycles of high mineral prices, perceptions over resource scarcity, advances in technology and business prospects, as illustrated most recently with the increased interest, investment and emerging regulatory responses in space mineral resources exploration.[28]

Metals (eg copper, iron, tin and lead) are recyclable and can be melted and recast for other uses. Already 40 per cent of copper, 40 per cent of steel and 30 per cent of aluminium, lead and zinc are produced using recycled products.[29] It is widely agreed that strong efforts should be made to promote the recycling of products containing minerals – the most sustainable option for meeting minerals demand, fully consistent with SDG 12, and the most energy-efficient. This entails promoting product design for such purposes.[30] In the future, states that currently drive demand (eg China and the EU) will likely transition from being global consumers of ore, to becoming suppliers of recycled materials.[31]

III. The Question of Minerals' 'Criticality' or 'Strategic' Status

From a strategic viewpoint, large industrial states (US, EU, Japan, Korea, India) have focused part of their foreign policy on securing the supply of so-called 'critical minerals'. Each jurisdiction has developed its own methodology to determine which minerals are considered critical in accordance with their priorities, and industrial countries regularly publish lists of minerals within this range. In general, 'criticality' is defined by their economic significance for the industrial sector and

---

[27] E Baker, F Gaill, A Karageorgis, G Lamarche, B Narayanaswamy, J Parr, C Raharimananirina, R Santos and R Sharma, 'Offshore Mining Industries' in United Nations, Division for Ocean Affairs and the Law of the Sea, Office of Legal Affairs (ed), *The First Global Integrated Marine Assessment: World Ocean Assessment* I (Cambridge, Cambridge University Press, 2014) 363–78.

[28] See ch 5.

[29] J Korinek, 'Trade restrictions on minerals and metals' (2019) 32 *Mineral Economics* 176. MA Reuter, C Hudson, A van Schaik, K Heiskanen, C Meskers, C Hagelüken, 'Metal Recycling: Opportunities, Limits, Infrastructure, A Report of the Working Group on the Global Metal Flows to the International Resource Panel' (UNEP, 2013). The authors call for a shift 'from material-centric to product-centric approaches' to promote recycling.

[30] ibid.

[31] C Durant, 'A Tale of Two Markets – The Future for Copper and Aluminum Recycling', CRU Conference: Metals in the Future, 20 March 2018.

a high risk of supply due to geological or geopolitical factors, business policies, among others.[32] Minor elements valuable for their use in high technology prevail in the current criticality paradigm.[33]

The typology distinguishing between 'critical' and 'strategic' minerals was drawn by industrial countries over the war period based on the perceived need of ensuring supply and reserves in times of scarcity or war, but remained to reflect the extent of dependency on external supply sources and the importance of some minerals. A mineral might be considered *strategic* whenever its importance for the development of a country, or third countries, determines the convenience of applying a policy or restrictions and reserves, even though current demands are met.[34] The classification is crucial to understand the role of minerals in tensions over trade policies.

IV. Mining: 'The Science, Technique and Business of Mineral Discovery and Extraction'

Mining has been defined as 'the science, technique and business of mineral discovery and exploitation'[35] and as 'a process that begins with the exploration for and the discovery of mineral deposits and continues through ore extraction and processing to the closure and remediation of worked-out sites'.[36] Mines produce ore, which usually requires some treatment, ranging from only sorting and washing, such as in the case of coal, to more complex processing so as to be transformed into final saleable products.[37] Dependence on depletable assets and the scale of projects in relation to host economies are defining features of the mining sector, as an economic activity.[38]

---

[32] European Commission, 'Report on Critical Raw Materials for the EU – Report of the Ad hoc Working Group on defining critical raw materials', May 2014.

[33] S Hayes and E McCullough, 'Critical minerals: A review of elemental trends in comprehensive criticality studies' (December 2018) 59 *Resources Policy* 192. In the EU, these have been defined as 'those which display a particularly high risk of supply shortage in the next 10 years and which are particularly important for the value chain. The supply risk is linked to the concentration of production in a handful of countries, and the low political-economic stability of some of the suppliers. This risk is in many cases compounded by low substitutability and low recycling rates'. Communication from the Commission to the European Parliament, the Council, the European Economic and Social Committee and the Committee of the Regions Tackling the Challenges in Commodity Markets and on Raw Materials/* COM/2011/0025 final (4.1) (updated in 2014 and 2017).

[34] It has been suggested that a mineral might be considered 'strategic' due to its value and use in the functioning of production systems or the Green economy or 'post-development'; and due to certain conditions inherent to its availability, which include its scarcity, uneven distribution and the fact they cannot be substituted. Fornillo, '¿*Commodities?*' (2014).

[35] US Bureau of Mines, *Dictionary of Mining, Mineral, and Related Terms* (1968).

[36] UNEP, 'Mining – Facts, Figures and Environment' (2000) 23 *Industry and Environment* 4.

[37] Crowson (n 9) 61.

[38] P Crowson, 'The Resource Curse: A Modern Myth?' in JP Richards (ed), *Mining, Society and a Sustainable World* (Berlin, Springer-Verlag, 2009) 4.

34 *Mining and Minerals, Actors and Governance from a Global Perspective*

Mining is usually associated with large operations conducted by transnational companies. But the industry structure is rather diverse and includes the 'low-tech, labour-intensive mineral extraction and processing' ASM segment.[39] It is estimated that around 20 per cent of the global gold and diamond supply, as well as 80 per cent of the global sapphire supply, comes from ASM.[40]

A. Mining Processes

Apart from the range of minerals that define it, the industry is also characterised by the variety of deposits and processes used. *Underground* mining, where the excavation is driven from below the Earth's surface, was historically the predominant extraction process and prevails in some contexts for ASM. *Surface* mining, where the excavation is entirely open, is the principal process today in industrial mining, used in about 84 per cent of metallic mines. Other processes include *solution* mining, where ores in deep deposits, usually salt and potash, but sometimes uranium, are dissolved and 'pumped up' to the surface; and *water-based mining*, where dredging is used for minerals lying in riverbeds and coastal waters. Advances in technology have made it possible to rework old mine waste dumps[41] and tailings. Alluvial mining predominates in some contexts for ASM.

B. Environmental, Social and Governance Impacts of Mining[42]

Mining has grown exponentially with growing global demand over the last few decades. Ore grades have systematically been falling, and due to the shift from underground to open-pit mining, higher volumes of waste rock are being moved to produce the same amounts of commodity.[43] For this reason, the mining of large open-pit mines has become a large generator of excavation material. Mining and metals are among the largest generators of waste, including tailings[44] (some have described it as essentially

---

[39] G Hilson and R Maconachie (2020) *Geoforum* (May) 125.

[40] IGF, 'Global Trends in Artisanal and Small-Scale Mining (ASM): A Review of Key Numbers and Issues' (Winnipeg, IISD, 2018).

[41] Crowson (n 7), 8–11.

[42] I will refer to macro-economic impacts captured under the 'resource curse' theory in section VII below. For the impact of volatility of prices particularly of minor metals, see Renner and Wellmer, 'Volatility drivers' (2019). This is one of the problems in the mining industry that have been identified as in need of global action – at least through more dedicated research in D Humphreys, AE Bastida and A Hermann, 'Platforms for Strategic Dialogues on Mining and Minerals: A possible way forward', STRADE Strategic Dialogue on Sustainable Raw Materials for Europe (STRADE) EU Horizon 2020 Project; European Policy Brief No 4/2017.

[43] G Mudd, 'The Environmental Sustainability of Mining in Australia: Key Mega-Trends and Looming Constraints' (2010) 35 *Resources Policy* 98.

[44] World Economic Forum, 'Mining and Metals in a Sustainable World 2050' (September 2015) 22.

a 'waste management industry'). An important trend is the rapid growth of techno-logical innovation to promote productivity and the safety of operations, and to reduce costs, which includes the automation of vehicles and mobile mining machinery. It has been estimated that these innovations will ultimately reduce operational-type jobs but create other jobs requiring skills in data processing and analysis.[45]

Mining can disrupt ecosystems, place stress on water, land and biodiversity, and impact on other natural resources.[46] The extent of impacts are determined by the mineral extracted, the type, scale and geological characteristics of deposits (deter-mining the method of operation, the ore grade, the ecosystems and social context, and the processes and substances used in beneficiation).[47] Poorly managed sites pose the greatest challenges for surface and groundwater pollution from acidic mine water and chemicals used in metal extraction, whereas soil contamination and dust emissions and risks can extend following closure of these sites through acid mine drainage and tailing dam failures.[48] The principal threat of environmen-tal disaster in mining is indeed constituted by tailing dam leakages or collapse.[49] Mining is an intensive water user and as companies expand operations in search of feasible deposits, they are moving towards more remote and arid regions, some-thing that might exacerbate water scarcity.[50] Mining is also an intensive energy user. Climate change requires operations to adapt to higher temperatures, changes in sea levels and weather events, and at the same time each and every stage of the lifecycle of a mine is exposed to physical damage and breakdowns.[51]

Mining can have enormous impacts on local communities, human rights and the social fabric of local societies if not anticipated and managed. Impacts can start with inflows of workers and contractors that can be socially disruptive and trigger alcoholism, prostitution, gambling and violence. The landing of a mine in local territories can disrupt the culture and traditional social structures and increase gender inequality (as a result of unequal access to jobs) as well as increase internal

---

[45] A Cosbey, H Mann, N Maennling, P Toledano, J Geipel and M Dietrich Brauch, 'Mining a Mirage? Reassessing the Shared-Value Paradigm in Light of the Technological Advances in the Mining Sector' (IIED and CCSI, 2016).

[46] For a global overview of the impacts of resource extraction, see IRP (2019), 'Global Resources Outlook 2019: Natural Resources for the Future We Want'. B Oberle, S Bringezu, S Hatfield-Dodds, S Hellweg, H Schandl and J Clement (lead authors), 'A Report of the International Resource Panel. United Nations Environment Programme' (Nairobi, 2019).

[47] J Potts, M Wenban-Smith, L Turley and M Lynch, 'State of Sustainability Initiatives Review. Standards and the Extractive Economy, Intergovernmental Forum on Mining, Minerals, Metals and Sustainable Development' (2018).

[48] UNDP and UN Environment, 'Managing Mining for Sustainable Development: A Sourcebook' (Bangkok, United Nations Development Programme, 2018).

[49] C Roche, K Thygesen and E Baker (eds), 'Mine Tailings Storage: Safety Is No Accident. A UNEP Rapid Response Assessment' (United Nations Environment Programme and GRID-Arendal, 2017).

[50] P Toledano and C Rourda, 'Leveraging Mining Investments in Water Infrastructure for Broad Economic Development: Models, Opportunities and Challenges', CCSI Policy Paper (March 2014).

[51] T Addison, 'Climate Change and the Extractives Sector' in Addison and Roe (eds), *Extractive Industries* (2018) 469.

economic inequality and living costs (due to higher wages earned by a very small segment of the population, often outsiders). Practices of resettlement impact on poverty, social cohesion and the cultural heritage of local communities. These impacts are compounded when projects affect indigenous and rural communities and are obviously exacerbated by irresponsible practices. As in the case of oil and gas, and as other economic activities that generate large money inflows, the sector has shown vulnerabilities to corruption, which hinder the potential role that the sector can have for developmental outcomes. These are all *potential* impacts; they are neither universal nor inevitable, and require responsibility in anticipating risks and adopting management measures.

In certain instances, mining, as well as oil and gas projects, have triggered political dynamics that lead to weakening governance and severe conflict. Mining has also been associated with wars and criminal networks that use minerals to fund their activities. The informality that generally characterises ASM operations has been linked to compounded social and environmental impacts, particularly with regard to child labour, poor health and working conditions, environmental degradation (generally associated with the use of mercury), use of minerals to financing conflict and connections with armed groups, and consequent human rights abuses.[52]

C. The Lifecycle of Industrial Mining

Mining consists basically of a series of sequential stages that begin with reconnaissance, prospecting, exploration and the discovery of mineral deposits and continue through ore extraction and processing to the closure and remediation of worked-out sites'.[53] Each successive stage (from exploration to exploitation) typically involves more time and expenditure, and less land than the previous stage. Moreover, discovery risk declines as activity moves from one of these phases to the next.[54] The incorporation of closure and post-closure phases has entailed a significant shift in thinking about the mine lifecycle. It is obvious to say that today mines have to be closed and land reclaimed.

i. From Surveys to a Proven Ore Reserve

For centuries, prospecting consisted of direct visual identification of mineralisation in the surface and that was the start of mining throughout history. Eggert evokes the skills and resources of prospectors of the time in the US, who were

---

[52] UNITAR and UN Environment, 'Handbook for Developing National ASGM Formalization Strategies within National Action Plans' (Geneva, 2018) 17–18.

[53] UNEP, 'Mining – Facts, Figures and Environment' (2000) 23 *Industry and Environment* 4.

[54] R Eggert, *Metallic Mineral Exploration: An Economic Analysis* (Washington DC, Resources for the Future, 1987).

'typically equipped with only an intuitive understanding of geologic science, and little more than grubstake and a pack animal, [and] relied on [their] keen eye for surface mineralisation'.[55] When exposed, small, but relatively high-grade deposits were the norm, the time span between the beginning of prospecting and the commencement of production was often quite short, ranging from three to four years.[56] With the invention of core drilling in the nineteenth century, exploration has been moving away from direct visual discovery to systematic, scientific identification of deposits concealed below the Earth's surface. Improved geophysical, geochemical and geological tools revolutionised mineral exploration in the postwar period.[57]

The identification of a proven mineral reserve today is preceded by a costly and long programme that requires advancing from regional geological surveying through prospecting, exploration and evaluation.[58] The common view is that most deposits that are located close to the surface and can easily be targeted have already been found. The odds of discovering a mine are calculated at the ratio of '1 in 10,000 mineral occurrences (no drilling and no calculated mineral resources or reserves) ... and 1 in 1,000 deposits (meaning a discovery with drill indicated resource and/or reserve estimates)'.[59] The 10,000:1 odds determine that regional surveys are generally carried out by national geological surveys, often supported by international cooperation projects.[60] New discoveries require advancing and testing geoscientific ideas creatively, which entails significant skills, technology, costs, time and 'tolerance of risk'.[61] This task differs from oil and gas exploration where costs are extremely high but the odds of finding mineralisation of potential economic value following successful indication from remote sensing (and the odds that those findings will then progress to confirmation of actual economic value) are also high. Investment recovery is also much faster in the oil and gas industry than in the hard rock minerals industry, a situation that ultimately affects value and the length of exposure to political and economic changes.[62]

In industrial operations, a feasibility study is the basis for the decision to mine, which also comprises environmental and social impact assessments and the evaluation of the commercial viability of the project (eg, whether water supply is sufficient; the extent of infrastructure and transportation costs; the assessment of environmental and social factors).[63]

---

[55] ibid.
[56] ibid.
[57] ibid.
[58] K Haddow, 'Should Mineral Rights for Hard-Rock Minerals Be Awarded by Tender?' (2014) 32 *Journal of Energy & Natural Resources Law* 337.
[59] ibid 338.
[60] ibid 339.
[61] ibid.
[62] This heightens arguments for supporting and expanding geological mapping and research. See ch 6.VI.
[63] See Crowson, *Mining Unearthed* (2008) 117.

Table 2.1, borrowed from the materials developed by Paul Schlauch and Glen Ireland for a learning module, draws 'the anatomy of a mining project', synthesising the typical stages, timing and costs, as well as the usual players, involved in the progression from greenfield exploration to a discovery and preparation of a feasibility study, to construction and operations, to closure and reclamation in medium and large mining projects. The key phases of the mining lifecycle, particularly the one leading to the identification of a proven ore reserve, have crucial implications for business models and for the design of regulatory regimes in the sector.[64]

ii. From Site Construction to Extraction: Mining Investment Decision

Whenever there is a decision to mine, the next stage is the construction and development of the mine site and infrastructure. Exploitation, or mining production, consists of the extraction of ore from the mine and the preparation of run-of-mine materials for mineral processing. These materials might undergo further conversion, smelting or refining to provide usable industrial materials.

Each stage entails a decision as to whether to move on to the next one. The mining investment decision ultimately weighs risks and rewards. It consists of the evaluation of the commercial prospects and potential profitability of a project and of an assessment of risks. It has been said that geology and topography influence the shape and choice of mining methods whereas economics determines the viability of the project, and investors will strive to maximise value by designing the mine with the optimum production method, output capacity and capital costs

Table 2.1 Anatomy of a mining project – greenfield exploration to reclamation

Activity	Duration	Cost	Players
Greenfield exploration	1–3 years	€250,000–1 million	Juniors and small groups
Exploration to prefeasibility	2–4 years	€1 million–10 million	Mid tiers, juniors and small groups
Feasibility	2–4 years	€10 million–100 million	Mid tiers and majors
Permitting	1–3 years	€10 million–100 million	Mid tiers and majors
Construction	1.5–2 years	€500 million–5 billion	Majors
Operations	10–50 years		Majors
Closing and reclamation	3 years to perpetuity	€10 million–100 million	Majors

Source: P Schlauch and G Ireland, Materials from International Mining Transactions and Agreements module (CEPMLP, 2017).

[64] See ch 6.

for building, operating and closing the mine.[65] While capital costs relate to the size of the project, operating costs for extracting a unit of mineral are a function of the mining method and can be lower in large-scale projects due to economies of scale. For lower-grade deposits, even slight increases in operating costs can render the projects uneconomic.[66] The 'go ahead' decision is based on the viability of the project, assessed on its internal rate of return (IRR).[67]

The investment decision is informed by 'internal' and 'external' elements. Investors design risk management strategies to deal with internal elements such as the choice of equipment, processing techniques and the management team. External elements are beyond their control and relate to third parties or factors in the global economy such as international mineral prices, financial markets and, from that optic, may include tenure and permitting processes. Elements considered as 'unexpected' or 'unpredictable' in the investment decision process raise the level of risk associated with a project and lead to requiring a higher rate of return (to offset the higher risk), extracting higher-grade ore only for faster returns, or outright withdrawing from the project.[68]

The investment decision is subject to the requirements of 'bankability'.[69] Once the investment has been made and the mine site has been built, the financial value of the mine will be maximised by reaching commercial production and operating at full capacity without delay – yet it will risk being eroded with delays in commencing production, limits on production, and increases in operating costs or higher perceived risks. The financial value of a mine is calculated by quantifying the stream of revenue from future production and subtracting the costs, taking into consideration 'the time value of money'. The growth of mine automation entails important implications for increased productivity and for risk management, and it has been observed that it may significantly shorten the lifecycle of mines. The implications of all these business models and decisions for the design of public policies in resource-rich countries are just now beginning to be accounted for more systematically.

D. The Capital-Intensive Nature and Risk Profile of Industrial Mining

Mining large projects is fundamentally capital-intensive; economies of scale can be significant, and infrastructure requirements can be enormous in comparison to many other industries. Large projects often connect remote sites to markets and

---

[65] Hinde and Farooki (n 23).

[66] ibid.

[67] ibid 16.

[68] ibid.

[69] R Pritchard, 'Safeguards for Foreign Investment in Mining' in AE Bastida, T Wäld and J Warden–Fernandez (eds), *International and Comparative Mineral Law and Policy: Trends and Prospects*, (The Hague, Kluwer Law International, 2005) 73–97.

to do so investors embark on infrastructure undertakings such as the construction of roads, railways and even ports. The extent, rigour and cost of pre-production activities in mineral resource development are far in excess of those required for the development of many other industries.[70]

Risk is a defining feature of the mining industry. The total risk in mineral resource development is in most cases considerably higher than in other industries, particularly because of geological risk, ie, the uncertainty surrounding the results of exploration. Exploration expenditure constitutes the high-risk element of any project although it generally amounts to only a small part of total project costs, as in most cases the expenditure is made without yielding a viable deposit. An underlying concern in the industry is the decreasing efforts placed on grassroots exploration, which has a crucial role in generating new discoveries.[71]

Geological, technical, financial and economic risks are spread throughout the life of the project, extending to the uncertainties raised by the usual obstacles of raising funds for the development of the project, and further escalating with the volatility of mineral prices, material substitution and shifting trends in mineral markets during the operational phase, to name just a few.

In the classic mining investment literature, political risk is said to be one of the most feared by investors. Political risk refers to actions or inactions of governments on the terms and conditions of the investment and also to changes in the rules of the game. This risk ranges from expropriation to changes in the fiscal and regulatory terms.

Mining investment in industrial-scale projects requires pre-production capital investment to be recovered over a long time, which entails great risk exposure as the investor becomes 'hostage' to host state powers of regulation and taxation.[72] Financial investors often perceive higher risks for adverse government action in developing countries. Legal instruments for investment protection include investment agreements, international commercial and investment arbitration, state contracts with explicit government assurances, stabilisation clauses, mechanisms of contractual adaptation and insurance schemes offered by international institutions (eg, the Multilateral Investment Guarantee Agency (MIGA)) serve to manage this category of non-commercial risks and 'change the risk–reward balance to encourage investment'.[73] They also have a function in strengthening the 'rule of law' entailing respect to individual rights against the state – in other words, predictability of legal rules and respect for acquired rights.[74]

---

[70] R Bosson and B Varon, *The Mining Industry and the Developing Countries* (The World Bank, Oxford University Press, 1977) 8.

[71] Hinde and Farooki (n 23) 12.

[72] TW Wälde, 'Renegotiating acquired rights in the oil and gas industries: Industry and political cycles meet the rule of law' (2008) 1 *Journal of World Energy Law & Business* 57.

[73] ibid. See also ch 4.I.B.

[74] ibid (suggesting that 'Bringing the "rule of law" to such arrangements means to transform them from political understandings subject to the discretion of the host state to contractual promises that can be made effective under a legal system and enforcement procedure outside host state control and therefore credible and more suitable to be the basis for large-scale, initial capital investment').

In recent years, obtaining the so-called 'social licence to operate' has become one of the most significant challenges to investment. The characteristics of the mining industry and their concomitant implications in terms of risk and risk-management techniques for a long time have been mainly couched in the predominant literature from an *investment* perspective. Key UN Resolutions, important reports, and many threads of literature and practice are shining a new light on the need for understanding and devising responses to risks posed by mining from the point of view of the environment, water,[75] human rights,[76] communities, governance,[77] local, regional and national economies,[78] and faced to risks of conflict recurrence;[79] for internalising the costs of extraction and then moving away from a 'risk management' focus to a working method that places collaboration at its heart.[80] Yet this still falls short of becoming streamlined into current business models and into widespread practice.[81]

V. The Structure of the Mining Industry

Unlike the oil and gas industry, there are a variety of companies in the mining industry, ranging from miners and cooperatives to national players, state-owned and transnational enterprises. The large transnational mining companies that have long dominated the business were for many years mostly from the EU and US (and later from Canada and Australia) and most recently from China. They operate in a wide range of countries, all the while selecting exploration and project targets on a 'global' basis and selling their products in regional and/or global markets. These types of companies particularly seek 'world class deposits' or aim to partner with, or source exploration projects from, junior exploration

---

[75] A Humphrey, *IWRM-tested national law and policies: towards catchment-based management of water resources during the life cycle of large-scale mining sites* (University of Dundee, PhD thesis, 2018).

[76] UN Guiding Principles on Business and Human Rights, Principle 17, Commentary: 'Human rights due diligence can be included within broader enterprise risk management systems, provided that it goes beyond simply identifying and managing material risks to the company itself, *to include risks to rights-holders*' (emphasis added).

[77] Extractive Industries Review, 'Striking a Better Balance. The World Bank Group and Extractive Industries. The Final Report of the Extractive Industries Review' (December 2003). 'Governance should be strengthened until it is able to withstand the risks of developing major extractions.'

[78] For example, by strengthening planning and revenue management vis-à-vis fluctuations in mineral prices and along the life of a mine, taking into account vital public policy considerations.

[79] V Roy, 'Stabilize, rebuild, prevent?: An overview of post-conflict resource management tools' (2017) 4 *The Extractive Industries and Society* 227.

[80] B Harvey and S Bice, 'Social Impact Assessment, Social Development Programmes and Social Licence to Operate: Tensions and Contradictions in Intent and Practice in the Extractive Sector' (2014) 32 *Impact Assessment and Project Appraisal* 327. Also, A Hodge, 'Towards Contribution Analysis' in Addison and Roe (n 26) 369–94.

[81] Eg, on social models, see D Kemp and JR Owen, 'Community Relations and Mining: Core to Business But Not "Core Business"' (2013) 38 *Resources Policy* 523. JR Owen and D Kemp, 'Social Licence and Mining: A Critical Perspective' (2012) 38 *Resources Policy* 29.

42 *Mining and Minerals, Actors and Governance from a Global Perspective*

companies. Juniors, typically Canadian or Australian enterprises, also operate on a regional or global basis and are very dynamic in mineral exploration. They are in the business of discovering deposits and will seek to either negotiate a deal with a larger company once a discovery has been made or acquire a controlling interest in the operating mine.[82]

Another group of transnational companies has entered into mining to secure the supply of minerals for their own businesses and, thus, have a vertically integrated structure. Apart from aluminium producer Alcoa and steelmakers such as ArcelorMittal Steel, companies such as Mitsubishi own a number of mining operations in order to supply their high-value manufactured products. Tianqi Lithium Global is also pursuing a strategy of vertical integration. Chemical companies such as Albermarle operate across the supply chain in the lithium industry and, at the heart of the energy transition underway, more technology companies and car-makers are deliberately seeking to secure the supply of minerals in the face of the boom sparked by electric vehicle batteries. Commodity trading firms like Glencore have become major participators in the industry and smelters are buying minority stakes in mining assets.

Unlike the oil and gas business, very few state-owned companies remained in the West after the sweeping trend towards privatisation and liberalisation in the 1990s.[83] The few remaining, such as Codelco in Chile and LKAB in Sweden, generally concentrate their production in just a few minerals and, over time, their business has expanded to other minerals. Debswana Diamond Company is owned in equal shares by the Government of Botswana and the De Beers Group, having extended its business to trading. The Government of Botswana also holds a 15 per cent equity in the De Beers Group, whose business has expanded across the whole supply chain of the diamond industry. State ownership is increasing again with the growth of China's internationalisation and its domestic production, albeit still relatively on a low level.[84]

Medium-sized companies and national players typically operate several small- to medium-sized deposits, in one or more than one country. They mostly work in locally and regionally traded minerals, particularly industrial minerals.

ASM has been defined as a 'low tech, labour intensive mineral processing and excavation activity'.[85] It is an umbrella term comprising a range of practices from individual miners operating alone, to groups of miners using machinery, and

---

[82] Streaming and royalty companies have emerged most recently as a financing vehicle. They receive metals and royalty fee payments from mining operations without shareholding equity (eg, Franco Nevada and Wheaton Precious Metals).

[83] Raw Materials Group, 'Overview of State Ownership in the Global Minerals Industry. Long Term Trends and Future, Extractive Industries for Development Series #20' (Washington, The World Bank, May 2011).

[84] M Ericsson and O Löf, 'China in African mining – present situation and future trends', presentation at China Mining, Tianjin, 18 October 2018.

[85] G Hilson, 'Small-scale mining, poverty and economic development in sub-Saharan Africa: An overview' (2009) 34 *Resources Policy* 1.

is used in contrast to medium-scale mining and large-scale mining, which are associated with industrial operations and operate with greater access to resources such as mechanisation and geological information.[86]

ASM has been characterised by 'complex labour hierarchies, unique forms of production and informal systems of assistance, all of which have evolved, for the most part, in an environment devoid of regulation and formal support'.[87] ASM miners often belong to local and rural communities; their activities might conflict with large-scale mining over the same mineral deposits.[88] ASM miners frequently frame their activities within local customs and land tenure traditions. The literature and policy documents have further distinguished between ASM that operate '*extra-legally*' (neither considered nor prohibited under formal legal frameworks);[89] legally; illegally; formally; informally; or illicitly and as part and parcel of criminal networks.[90] The usual view on small and artisanal miners has been that they concentrate mostly in producing high-unit-value products which are commercialised in complex supply chains. But this view is expanding to also encompass 'the minerals and materials that are mined, processed, manufactured and used mainly domestically in industries such as construction, manufacturing, infrastructure, craftsmanship and agriculture' – which have been called 'development minerals'.[91] It usually denotes both artisanal mining and small-scale mining operations and their trading chains moving minerals up to export points[92] (value and supply chains being generally more complex and opaque than for large-scale mining due to the size and multiple actors involved).

VI. Actors and Governance

So far, the description of the global industry has provided a glimpse into the myriad of stakeholders involved at different levels. To some extent, mining laws usually aim to balance the diverging interests of the various actors involved in the business: the miners themselves; those holding rights over the surface land; and the nation-states in which mining takes place. The circle of stakeholders, however, expands

---

[86] N Eslava, 'Successful implementation of conflict mineral certification and due diligence schemes and the European Union's role: lessons learned for responsible mineral supply', STRADE Project, May 2018.

[87] Hilson, 'Small-scale mining' (2009) 5.

[88] Eslava, 'Successful implementation' (2018).

[89] S Siegel and MM Veiga, 'Artisanal and small-scale mining as an extralegal economy: De Soto and the redefinition of "formalization"' (2009) 34 *Resources Policy* 51.

[90] UNITAR and UN Environment, 'Handbook for Developing National ASGM Formalization Strategies' (2018) 17–18.

[91] Mosi-oa-Tunya Declaration on Artisanal and Small-scale Mining, Quarrying and Development adopted at the International Conference on Artisanal and Small-scale Mining and Quarrying held in Livingstone, Zambia, 11–13 September 2018 (affirming the recommendation of the ACP–EU Development Minerals Programme on adopting and role of 'Development Minerals').

[92] ibid.

exponentially depending on the minerals involved; on whether they are traded and used locally, regionally or globally; on whether illegal mining or networks might be involved; and on whether the projects will attract transnational companies.

To begin with, the 'state' in its internal sphere encompasses the organs with power to administer, legislate and adjudicate, as well as a wide configuration of jurisdictional levels, from national to subnational, and of government agencies with competencies in the various aspects of licencing formalities required for the sector to operate, also including state-owned companies.

The 'miner', in turn, is not usually a single entity either. A transnational company is composed of shareholders and might be backed by a larger set of investors. If registered at stock exchanges, they may be subject to a set of specific regulations. They usually use project assets as security to lenders to obtain financing. The 'investor' may be at the forefront of responsible practices or at the very back end, entering into the business for speculative purposes. The 'miner' may be a state-owned enterprise from another country, a small or medium-sized local company, or an artisanal miner working for her or his livelihood. They might source products and services domestically or from global suppliers. Furthermore, those holding rights over the surface land may be large economic groups or small landholders, indigenous or communities, or customary landholders.

The 'state', moreover, might be part of regional or subregional economic communities and be bound by commitments as a party to international treaties. Mining companies and private investors might be members of chambers of mines and business organisations, and local landholders and communities might relate to larger networks of civil society organisations.

A broader set of stakeholders also includes the home countries of investors as well as of industries that use minerals as inputs to their products, traders and financiers, and international governmental organisations (the World Bank, regional banks, UN agencies), many of which have significant influence in policy design and implementation. Each of these actors has distinct interests and strives to achieve different objectives at diverse spatial and temporal scales in contexts marked by distinctive social, cultural, political, economic and environmental circumstances.[93]

VII. Mining, Development and the Role of Law under International Policy and 'Scripts'

This section explores the evolving framing of mining and its linkages with development in the formulation of policy and narratives ('scripts') at international level, to provide a broad overview of themes that will be analysed in more detail in the next

---

[93] A Pedro, ET Ayuk, C Bodouroglou, B Milligan, P Ekins and B Oberle, 'Towards a sustainable development licence to operate for the extractive sector' (2017) 30 *Mineral Economics* 153, 157. See also L Gerber and J Warden-Fernandez, 'The institutional framework for access to mineral resources' (POLINARES Working Paper no 56, December 2012) 2.

two chapters. In many developing countries – a disparate set of countries that comprise many of those producing minerals today, or containing large prospective or actual reserves – changing views on development and the role of law are often supported in changing agendas and practices of international development agencies, which can act as powerful drivers of legislative and institutional change. This link between domestic mining law, international investment regimes, reform processes driven by international organisations and the global economy has been further framed in scholarship from a 'law and development' perspective – 'a field that exists at the intersection of law, economics and the practices of states and development agencies'.[94]

Otto and Cordes discern distinctive periods in the evolution of international policy applied to mining investment in developing countries, each encompassing a role for law and a view of the world embedded in economic theories and developmental models.[95] In the colonial/imperial period, the main motivation for investment was 'access to supplies rather than economic development' of the countries and locations where operations took place – the very same concept of economic development had not yet emerged. They note that while European powers had for centuries embarked in ventures for localising and appropriating precious metals, the impetus for the internationalisation of production of other mineral commodities was triggered by the demands of the industrial revolution. In the first period of expansion of international investment in the late nineteenth century, small European and North American companies spread across the territories that were held as colonies or the countries that had obtained their independence earlier that century, most usually using concession agreements as a vehicle to facilitate access and to establish terms and conditions for investment,[96] or otherwise by acquiring mineral rights granted under the liberal tenure regimes of the time.

Commonly used in the petroleum sector, the traditional concession agreements were effectively 'self-constituted charters' lacking the fundamental terms for regulating the relationship between the parties on an equal and just footing,[97] creating 'economic, political and legal enclaves within host territories'.[98]

---

[94] D Trubek and A Santos, 'Introduction: The Third Moment in Law and Development and the Emergence of a New Critical Practice' in D Trubek and A Santos (eds), *The New Law and Development: A Critical Appraisal* (Cambridge, Cambridge University Press, 2006). On the legal framework for mining from a law and development perspective, see AE Bastida, 'Mining Law in the Context of Development' in P Andrews-Speed (ed), *International Competition for Resources: The Role of Law, State and Markets* (Dundee, Dundee University Press, 2008) 101–36. See also NV Nwogu, 'Mining at the Crossroads of Law and Development: A Comparative Review of Labor-Related Local Content Provisions in Africa's Mining Laws through the Prism of Automation' (2019) 28 *Washington International Law Journal* 137.

[95] J Otto and J Cordes, *The Regulation of Mineral Enterprises: A Global Perspective on Economics, Law and Policy* (Colorado, RMMLF, 2002) 32–34.

[96] ibid.

[97] Y Al-Saman, 'Evolution of the Contractual Relationship between Saudi Arabia and Aramco' (1994) 12 *Journal of Energy & Natural Resources Law* 257.

[98] Otto and Cordes, *The Regulation of Mineral Enterprises* (2002) 1–33; Y Omorogbe and P Oniemola, 'Property Rights in Oil and Gas under Domanial Regimes' in A McHarg, B Barton, A Bradbrook and L Godden (eds), *Property and the Law in Energy and Natural Resources* (Oxford, Oxford University Press, 2010) 125.

46 Mining and Minerals, Actors and Governance from a Global Perspective

The 'theoretical cornerstone of the concession' was that of proprietary rights and corresponding rights of control vested in a foreign oil company.[99] They typically granted exclusive rights to explore and exploit resources over extensive areas for long periods of time with no renegotiation clauses, royalties being the main financial obligation of the concessionaire.[100]

The second wave of international expansion responded to the booming mineral demand in the post-war period, higher production costs in 'core mining regions' and advances in transportation technology.[101] Concession agreements were again the favoured vehicle of protection of foreign direct investment.[102] As this period drew to a close, the mining industry in Africa, Asia and Latin America was dominated by private companies from industrialised countries. Projects most usually operated as economic, political and legal 'enclaves' in territories without forging any linkages with local communities and the local economies.[103]

In the subsequent period in the evolution of international mineral policy, the balance shifted towards developing countries, with an expanding circle of newly independent countries entering the then young UN. The UN Centre on Transnational Corporations, and other specialised agencies, were established within the UN to provide, among other functions, technical cooperation in mining and petroleum legislation.[104] Based on a leading role for the state as regulator and entrepreneur, emphasis was placed on regulating foreign investment and in negotiating agreements favourable to national interests, mining being considered as a vehicle for development. In the early years of the post-war order, and following the decolonisation movement, across the 1960s and 1970s, the UN General Assembly Resolutions on Permanent Sovereignty over Natural Resources were instrumental in framing stronger powers of control by the state, and influenced the wording of a new generation of mining laws and mining agreements, with a turn towards the use of risk and service contracts, joint ventures and forms of concessions with strengthened administrative powers, which became a preferred arrangement across the developing world to regulate international foreign investment in those years.

Throughout the 1980s and 1990s, in the context of global economic and financial liberalisation, policy prescriptions of international organisations, notably the

---

[99] P Cameron, *Property Rights and Sovereign Rights: The Case of North Sea Oil* (London, Academic Press, 1983) 11.

[100] Otto and Cordes (n 95) quoting Maniruzzaman, 'The New Generation of Energy and Natural Resource Development Agreements: Some Reflections' (1993) 11 *Journal of Energy & Natural Resources Law* 207.

[101] ibid.

[102] ibid.

[103] R Auty, 'Mining enclave to economic catalyst: large mineral projects in developing countries' (2006) 13 *Brown Journal of World Affairs* 135–45.

[104] N Beredjick, 'Technical cooperation in response to the evolving situation of the international petroleum industry' in N Beredjick and T Wälde (eds), *Petroleum Investment Policies in Developing Countries* (London, Graham & Trotman, 1988) 1.

Mining, Development and the Role of Law   47

World Bank, exerted tremendous influence in the massive processes of sectoral institutional and legal reform implemented through technical assistance programmes.[105] These aimed to establish environments to attract investment in order to generate tax revenue and foreign currency. This applied particularly to low- and middle-income economies, which emerged highly indebted following the economic crises of the time.[106] The Strategy for African Mining (1992) recommended the implementation of competitive terms and conditions and private sector-led strategies to succeed in the competition with other jurisdictions for new high-risk capital from foreign investors. A Mining Strategy for Latin America and the Caribbean (1996) suggested that a main challenge ahead for the region consisted of deepening and sustaining reform, which required the establishment of clear and effective legal frameworks for private sector-led industry.[107] The advice was for the introduction of mining laws based on models that would allocate mineral rights upon the principle of 'first come, first served', and would strengthen security of tenure and the entitlements of mineral rights holders; and, whenever in place, for agreements that would strengthen investment protection, notably through stabilisation clauses and recourse to international arbitration. The advice was also for the privatisation of state-owned enterprises.[108]

It is noteworthy that until the 1990s transnational mining contracts were the prime instrument acting 'as interfaces' with the global economy, foreign direct investment and resource projects in the developing world. The use of these types of arrangements notably decreased over the implementation of the market reforms of the 1990s, which saw trends towards streamlined mining laws, extensive reform of investment law and ratification of Bilateral Investment Treaties. Still, mining agreements entered between governments and investors and set out either in a model agreement or negotiated in ad hoc agreements have been used in countries where the mining law is considered insufficient to govern and regulate large-scale mining projects.[109] Their function has been to supplement or substitute the general mining law in order to specify regulations,

---

[105] The World Bank had by then shifted its focus away from project financing to providing financial and technical support for establishing the conditions for private sector participation and privatisation of state-owned assets.

[106] E Dietsche, 'Diversifying Mineral Economies: Conceptualising the Debate on Building Linkages' (2014) 27 *Mineral Economics* 89.

[107] The World Bank, Industry and Energy Division – Mining Unit, 'Strategy for African Mining', Africa Technical Department Series, World Bank Technical Paper No 181 (1992). The World Bank, Industry and Mining Division – Industry and Energy Department, 'A Mining Strategy for Latin America and the Caribbean', World Bank Technical Paper No 345 (1996).

[108] Bastida, 'Mining Law in the Context of Development' (2008).

[109] Many countries influenced by the French legal tradition in the development of their legal institutions have adopted mining codes that set forth the granting of administrative concessions by the state, as well as the main provisions of mining agreements ('*convention minière*' or '*convention d'établissement*') to establish specific terms, conditions and safeguards for investment in large projects. In countries influenced by the English legal tradition, the mining title issued under a Mining Act has commonly been supplemented by an agreement with the Minister or equivalent officer in government, often formalised through a law. Mining laws usually refer to this type of agreement in the text. T Wälde, 'Third World Mineral Investment Policies in the Late 1980s: From Restriction Back to Business' (1988) 3 *Mineral Processing and Extractive Metallurgy Review* 121.

48   *Mining and Minerals, Actors and Governance from a Global Perspective*

as a way of overcoming uncertainties by filling in gaps and ambiguous provisions in the mining code, or to provide specific safeguards to foreign investment as recourse to international arbitration, tax stabilisation, government support in accessing land, and less often, regulatory stabilisation and tax relief, thus facilitating the approval of processes, reducing risks and providing remedies against the state in the case of breach or expropriation. Such agreements often address regulatory aspects related to the infrastructure required for a complex project. They often customise rights and obligations of the mineral rights-holder as security of tenure and the 'right to mine', and exceptions to mineral tenure terms under the mining act (such as extended duration or size), or specific terms and guarantees applicable to foreign investment.[110]

Under the rationale of these reform processes, law has a fundamental role in creating a climate of stability and predictability to provide the conditions for business activity, reducing business and political uncertainty, and buttressing the institutions of well-functioning markets, guaranteeing property rights, enabling contract enforcement and protecting against arbitrary government power.[111] In a second phase of reform processes, the promotion of the rule of law in development assistance was championed as a main component of good governance and institutions, seen as the pathway to economic growth. The focus on good governance and institutions was further reinforced to counter the 'resource curse'.[112]

This concept of the rule of law underscores the practice of investment protection through bilateral and multilateral treaties, which expanded exponentially from the late 1980s and which, at its core, establishes 'a unilateral right of foreign investors to arbitrate against host state governments on the basis of a limited set of 'investment disciplines'.[113] This concept of the rule of law is also crystallised in contracts between host states and investors, stabilisation clauses or agreements and property rights, and guarantees established under mining legislation which, for some, become internationalised through submission of claims to international arbitration. Mining laws and contracts would play a critical role in promoting the rule of law. This architecture would serve to facilitate access to, and connect, local remote sites with the global economy.[114]

---

[110] ibid 132–33.

[111] The World Bank, Industry and Energy Division – Mining Unit, Strategy for African Mining – Africa Technical Department Series, World Bank Technical Paper No 181 (Washington DC, The World Bank, 1992).

[112] In more recent years the World Bank has engaged with initiatives to promote local value and diversification, community benefits and low-carbon economies, and furthered its support to transparency initiatives. The Bank's Legal Vice-Presidency also steered the Africa Mining Legislation Atlas (AMLA) project, implemented in partnership with the African Development Bank's African Legal Support Facility (ALSF) and the African Union Commission in coordination with a network of African Universities. AMLA widens the methodologies used for reform processes by focusing on comparative analysis of legislation across the continent, adopting a 'responsive' rather than a 'prescriptive' approach. See AMLA: a-mla.org/about/about.

[113] TW Wälde, 'Renegotiating acquired rights in the oil and gas industries: Industry and political cycles meet the rule of law' (2008) 1 *Journal of World Energy Law & Business* 55, 57.

[114] For a critical political economy perspective see B Campbell, 'New Rules of the Game: The World Bank's Role in the Construction of New Normative Frameworks for States, Markets and Social

Mining, Development and the Role of Law   49

In the 2000s, emphasis expanded to efforts on avoiding the 'resource curse'. The 'resource curse' theory (a term coined by Auty) is based on the observation of an inverse correlation between extractive industries and development.[115] A first set of explanations put forward was based on economic phenomena such as the Dutch disease while a second set of explanations focused on the workings of the political economy, eg, incentives to politicians to seek private gain at the expense of the public interest, 'rentier states' relying on resource rent rather than on taxation.[116] The debate has evolved over time from an emphasis on the causes of the curse to a focus on governance and institutions that might eventually be a 'cure' to the resource curse. To calibrate mining in terms of development, those who support rent-seeking explanations have argued for the need to introduce policy interventions (often externally) to enhance the quality of institutions in resource-producing countries.[117] This debate has been very influential in devising the engagement and policy guidance of intergovernmental organisations for low- and middle-income countries. It has also guided the mandate of a range of organisations emerging over this period and engaging in advice and knowledge-sharing on resource governance,[118] with an initial focus on transparency. Transnational contracts, the terms of which, for a long time, remained confidential and inaccessible to civil society, were placed under intense scrutiny because of the underlying asymmetries of information and power, the constraints on the sovereign powers of states to regulate, and the democratic and legitimacy deficits often found at their roots.

From around the late 2000s, greater emphasis has been placed on building linkages between the resources sector and other economic sectors to promote economic diversification and industrialisation, notably reflected in the Africa Mining Vision and the preparatory work led by the UN Economic Commission for Africa (UNECA).[119,120] More recent studies show a link between mining and

---

Exclusion' (2000) 21 *Canadian Journal of Development Studies* 7; and B Campbell (ed), 'Regulating Mining in Africa: For Whose Benefit?', Discussion Paper 26 (Uppsala, Nordiska Afrikainstitutet, 2004).

[115] R Auty, *Sustaining Development in Mineral Economies: The Resource Curse Thesis* (London, Routledge, 1993); JD Sachs and A Warner, 'Natural Resource Abundance and Economic Growth', National Bureau of Economic Research Working Paper 5398 (1995).

[116] P Stevens and E Dietsche. 'Resource curse: An analysis of causes, experiences and possible ways forward' (2008) 36 *Energy Policy* 56.

[117] ibid.

[118] See ch 3.

[119] In reviewing the literature in this area, Dietsche stresses the question is not new. In the 1950s, structural economists had advocated for diversification based on the observation that primary products are exposed to declining terms of trade. Dietsche, 'Diversifying Mineral Economies' (2014).

[120] See a review of the literature on this topic in Dietsche (n 106). See also AE Bastida, 'From *Extractive* to *Transformative* Industries: Paths for Linkages and Diversification for Resource-Driven Development', Review Paper of Special Issue; AE Bastida and M Ericsson (eds), Can Mining Be a Catalyst to Diversifying Economies? (2014) 27 *Mineral Economics* 73. See Di Boscio and Humphreys, 'Mining and Regional Economic Development' in AE Bastida, T Wälde, J Warden-Fernandez (eds), International and Comparative Mineral Law and Policy: Trends and Prospects (The Hague, Kluwer Law International, 2005) 589–604 (noting that local and regional economic development does not occur automatically, but assertive policy directions are needed. In their absence, the opportunity for mining regions to maximise the relatively strong monetary contributions from mining to build the basis for a diversified and sustainable economic structure might be missed).

50 *Mining and Minerals, Actors and Governance from a Global Perspective*

increased economic contributions in medium and particularly low-income economies as manifested in statistics over the 1996 to 2016 period.[121]

Two further, more recent, trends can be observed in the relationship between
mining and development in the post-2015 development agenda. The first trend
focuses on achieving the Sustainable Development Goals (SDGs) under Agenda
2030 and has placed a great deal of attention to local participation and local development outcomes as well as on working towards systemic governance integration
for achieving the SDGs, whereas the second relates to the unprecedented challenges posed by the global energy shift adopted under the Paris Agreement.[122]
IGF, the International Resource Panel, UN Environment, UNDP, NRGI and other
organisations are contributing substantial research to this complex and challenging development agenda.[123]

Many voices in the industry are calling for radical new pathways for mining if
the industry is to meet the multiple pressures and challenges it faces: water scarcity; energy and fuel resources use, as well as deposits that might be smaller, deeper
and lower grade;[124] and the turn to sustainability. These conflate with increasing
and more assertive demands for higher rents, state participation or control by
nationals. Industry leaders are suggesting that industry should pioneer new business models and could become service providers to investors,[125] or to national
mining enterprises;[126] partner with customers and suppliers for the circular
economy;[127] or partner in radically different schemes of metals leasing as alternatives to ownership to enable cross-value chains,[128] or with downstream companies
and manufacturers for recycling;[129] or otherwise constrain their business to some
countries where they can operate safely and responsibly or become more regional
or specialised in scope.[130]

The great development potential of the ASM segment has been widely recognised. Formalisation of the ASM sector, tending to its integration into the formal
economic, social and regulatory system, is emerging as recommended policy
pathway.[131] In Africa, this is being framed within more comprehensive approaches

---

[121] M Ericsson and O Löf, 'Mining's Contribution to Low- and Middle-Income Economies' in Addison
and Roe (n 26) 51–70, 63 and 69. See also M Ericsson and O Löf, 'Mining's contribution to national
economies between 1996 and 2016' (2019) 32 *Mineral Economics* 223.

[122] See ch 3.

[123] See ch 3.

[124] D Upton, 'The Way We Mine Must Fundamentally Change' *Australia's Mining Monthly* (25 March
2019) quoting Ewan Sellers, in a presentation at Australia's Future of Mining 2019 conference: 'Radical
new ways to mine are needed if the industry is to meet the challenge of multiple pressures threatening
the industry's viability'.

[125] N Hume, 'Big miners need to reinvent themselves, says Rio Tinto CEO' *Financial Times*
(29 October 2018).

[126] D Humphreys, 'Mining: the next chapter' (2019) *Mining Journal*.

[127] See World Economic Forum, 'Mining & Metals in a Sustainable World 2050' (September 2015) 29.

[128] ibid 20.

[129] ibid 29.

[130] Humphreys, 'Mining: The Next Chapter' (2019).

[131] UNITAR and UN Environment (n 52) 17–18.

to rural livelihoods, with numerous studies showing the extent to which families engage both in mining and agriculture (often funding smallholder activities with income generated by ASM). Formalisation is also gaining attention with studies showing the links between the growth of ASM and poverty and structural adjustment, and pointing at the scant focus of sectoral policy to this segment of activities.[132] In connection with the 'minerals and materials that are mined, processed, manufactured and used mainly domestically in industries such as construction, manufacturing, infrastructure, craftsmanship and agriculture', the recommendation of referring to them as 'development minerals' is based on 'their exceptional contribution to local, domestic and regional economies and potential for structural transformation of developing nations'.[133]

This chapter has provided a glimpse into the relevance of minerals in the global economy and a broad introduction to the mining industry, the stages of mining projects, and the impacts, risks and potential developmental outcomes of mining. Mining law regimes, as rules and processes predominantly established under domestic legal systems, typically consider how to balance the equation of diverging interests between domestic actors. But the range of actors involved and affected by the industry is much broader and diverse, interacting at multiple levels and sites and constituting the larger processes of decision-making in mining and minerals, from a global perspective. The chapter also begun to explore the evolving framing of mining and its links with development in the formulation of policy and narratives at international level, and the role of law in those contexts, to provide a broad overview of themes that will be analysed in more detail in the next two chapters. These will focus on mining and minerals under international law and policy documents, and in fields of international law and transnational governance.

---

[132] G Hilson, A Hilson, R Maconachie, J McQuilken and H Goumandakoye, 'Artisanal and small-scale mining (ASM) in Sub-Saharan Africa: re-conceptualizing formalization and "illegal" activity' (2017) 83 *Geoforum* 80.

[133] Mosi-oa-Tunya Declaration on Artisanal and Small-scale Mining, Quarrying and Development adopted at the International Conference on Artisanal and Small-scale Mining and Quarrying held in Livingstone, Zambia, 11–13 September 2018.

3

Mining and Minerals in International Law and Policy

This chapter will begin by defining the principle of territorial sovereignty; the *grundnorm* underlying the jurisdictional basis of states for controlling natural resources within the confines of their territories. It will review the principle of Permanent Sovereignty of Natural Resources (PSONR) and the treatment of mining and minerals under the key international instruments formulating environmental policy and shaping the concept of sustainable development. It will also enquire into the elements and legal nature of sustainable development.

I. Jurisdictional Basis for Controlling Resources: The Principle of Territorial Sovereignty

By virtue of the cornerstone principle of territorial sovereignty, each state has jurisdiction for controlling resources located within their own boundaries. Sovereignty represents 'the basic constitutional doctrine of the law of nations, which governs a community consisting primarily of states having a uniform legal personality'.[1] Sovereignty and territory are key concepts of public international law. They define essential attributes of a state, the primary subject of international law.[2]

The famous pronouncement of Max Huber, the sole arbitrator in the *Island of Palmas* (*Miangas*) case (*United States v The Netherlands*) implicitly distinguished between an internal and an external dimension of territorial sovereignty.[3] In its external dimension, regarding relations between states, the judgment expressed that sovereignty 'signifies independence' and entails the right of a state to exercise within the portion of the globe that is its territory, the functions of a state to the exclusion of any other. It denotes 'the principle of the exclusive competence of

---

[1] J Crawford, *Brownlie's Principles of Public International Law*, 9th edn (Oxford, Oxford University Press, 2019) 431.

[2] AE Bastida, A Ifesi, S Mahmud, J Ross and T Wälde, 'Cross-Border Unitization and Joint Development Agreements: An International Law Perspective' (2007) 29 *Houston Journal of International Law* 355.

[3] *Island of Palmas* case (or *Miangas*) (*United States v Netherlands*), Award (4th April 1928), II RIAA 829.

the state with regard to its own territory'.[4] The internal dimension of sovereignty refers to the inner expression of independence and puts the emphasis on exclusive jurisdiction.[5]

A state owns (*dominium*) and exercises control (*imperium*) over a territory, including the natural resources within its boundaries.[6] Jurisdiction denotes the powers a state exercises over persons, property or events within their territories, including legislative, adjudicative and enforcement powers over natural resources situated therein.[7] By virtue of the exercise of sovereign powers and its prerogatives, a state will determine whether and how mineral resources are allocated, how they are controlled, how they are used and how revenue and benefits are distributed.

II. International Law: From Coordination to Cooperation

The concept of sovereignty has implicitly framed claims over minerals under international law for a very long time. For centuries, minerals have been in the backdrop of land and territories in sovereignty claims, which have been considered primarily in the context of changes in territorial control, colonialism and disputes.[8] As a nation-state asserted sovereignty claims over a territory, new (often colonial) authorities would exercise their sovereign powers to regulate and to allocate property rights for mineral exploration and extraction.[9]

The process of globalisation, which was triggered by the design of a new global architecture and the creation of a network of institutions in the aftermath of the Second World War,[10] set the context for the evolution of the key constitutive international law aspects of the law and governance of mining and minerals. On the one hand, the United Nations (UN), founded in 1945 upon the principle of the sovereign equality of states, self-determination and human rights,[11] provided the basis for the process of decolonisation that kicked off in the late 1940s; thus, UN membership composition expanded over time to include the newly independent

---

[4] ibid.

[5] J Viñuales, 'The Resource Curse: A Legal Perspective' (2011) 17 *Global Governance: A Review of Multilateralism and International Organizations* 197.

[6] V Barral, 'National Sovereignty over Natural Resources: Environmental Challenges and Sustainable Development', in E Morgera and K Kulovesi (eds), *Research Handbook on International Law and Natural Resources* (Cheltenham, Edward Elgar Publishing, 2016) 3–25.

[7] A Orakhelashvili, *Akehurst's Modern Introduction to International Law*, 8th edn (London and New York, Routledge, 2019) 10.1.

[8] See the argument built in connection with land by L Cotula, 'Land, Property and Sovereignty in International Law' (2017) 25 *Cardozo Journal of International and Comparative Law* 219.

[9] ibid.

[10] D Held, A McGew, D Goldblatt and J Perraton, *Global Transformations. Politics, Economics and Culture* (Cambridge, Polity Press, 1999) 425.

[11] UN Charter, Art 1.

54 *Mining and Minerals in International Law and Policy*

countries. On the other hand, the World Bank and the International Monetary Fund (IMF), founded in 1944 under the Bretton Woods Agreement between the allied countries[12] to oversee the currency exchange system, consequently laid the foundations for global trade and investment. From thereon, international law has undergone a process of substantial change, transitioning from a system of coexistence and coordination of international relations between mainly European states on specific matters as diplomatic relations and war to a universal system of cooperation in various fields and including subjects of international law other than states, notably intergovernmental organisations,[13] increasing global economic and political interdependence and the need to address problems that can no longer be properly dealt with within a national framework.[14]

More recent years have witnessed continuous challenges to multilateralism, which coalesce with those raised by technology and climate change in the context of an emerging multipolar global order. Calls place emphasis on the need of adapting and reforming existing international organisations, enhancing multilateral processes and strengthening accountability of actors to reflect plural agreements sharing goals and commitments.[15]

In the context of the above-mentioned transition of the international legal order, minerals and mining began to be subject of attention under international law and international documents emerging from the UN *aegis*: first, through the establishment of the principle of PSONR; second, through the development of a legal regime applicable to minerals and mining in areas beyond national jurisdiction, notably over the international seabed, and the concept of 'common heritage of mankind'; third, through investigation and action addressing the connection between armed conflict and natural resources; and fourth, through the inclusion of mining and minerals in global action plans to advance sustainable development.

This chapter reviews key aspects of the evolving normative body relevant to mining and minerals under international law. First, it traces the evolution of the principle of PSONR from its origins in the ideas on a New International Economic Order (NIEO) to its place within the global framework for sustainable development. It then focuses on the emergence of international environmental law and the concept of sustainable development under UN instruments, examining their treatment of mining and minerals.

---

[12] See Articles of Agreement of the IMF; Articles of Agreement of the International Bank for Reconstruction and Development. The Bank is formed by 189 states, with voting powers allocated at the time of membership and thereafter in accordance to their capital subscriptions.

[13] See P Bekker, *The Legal Position of Intergovernmental Organizations* (Dordrecht, Martinus Nijhoff Publishers, 1994); P Malanczuk, *Akehurst's Modern Introduction to International Law*, 7th edn (London and New York, Routledge, 1997) 7.

[14] Malanczuk, *Akehurst* (1997) 7 and 33.

[15] N Woods, A Betts, J Prantl and D Sridhar, 'Transforming Global Governance for the 21st Century', UNDP Human Development Report Office Occasional Paper 2013/09; Chief E Anyaoku, 'The End of Multilateralism: Whither Global Governance?' (2004) 93 *The Round Table* 193.

III. The Principle of Permanent Sovereignty Over Natural Resources

The principle of PSONR adopted by the UN General Assembly (UNGA or GA) in Resolution 1803 (XVII) in 1962 acknowledges that 'The right of peoples and nations to permanent sovereignty over their natural wealth and resources must be exercised in the interest of their national development and of the well-being of the people of the State concerned'.[16] It draws on a series of UNGA resolutions and documents developed progressively from the early 1950s.[17] On the one hand, it is grounded on the principle of the self-determination of peoples consecrated in the UN Charter (Articles 1 and 55) and in common Article 1.2. of the International Covenant on Civil and Political Rights and the International Covenant on Economic, Social and Cultural Rights. Self-determination is a cardinal principle of human rights law, ie, the right of peoples to freely use and exploit their natural wealth being inherent to their sovereignty and having not only a political but also an economic dimension.[18] On the other hand, the principle reflects the line of work of the General Assembly on supporting and financing the economic development of the then so-called 'under-developed' countries.[19] The very first GA Resolution 523 (VI) of 12 January 1952 in this last thread of work shows the search for a compromise in international trade between the contending interests of resource owners and mineral markets by calling for measures for an adequate production and the equitable international distribution of raw materials and for the regulation of prices in the face of inflationary pressures brought about by an increase in the demand for raw materials, all the while taking into account

> that the under-developed countries have the right to determine freely the use of their natural resources and that they must utilise such resources in order to be in a

---

[16] GA Resolution 1803 (XVII). Permanent sovereignty over natural resources. Adopted at its 1194th plenary meeting, 14 December 1962 (Principle 1).

[17] N Schrijver, 'Fifty Years Permanent Sovereignty over Natural Resources. The 1962 UN Declaration as the *Opinio Iuris Communis*' in M Bungenberg and S Hobe (eds), *Permanent Sovereignty Over Natural Resources* (Cham, Springer, 2015) 15.

[18] GA Resolution 421 (V). Draft International Covenant on Human Rights and Measures of Implementation: Future Work of the Commission on Human Rights. Adopted at its 317th plenary meeting, 4 December 1950; GA Resolution 626 (VII). Right to Exploit Freely Natural Wealth and Resources. Adopted at its 411th plenary meeting, 21 December 1952; GA Resolution 1314 (XIII). Recommendations Concerning International Respect for the Right of Peoples and Nations to Self-Determination. Adopted at its 788th plenary meeting, 12 December 1958; GA Resolution 1514 (XV). Declaration on the Granting of Independence to Colonial Countries and Peoples. Adopted at its 947th plenary session, 14 December 1960.

[19] GA Resolution 523 (VI). Integrated Economic Development and Commercial Agreements. Adopted at its 360th plenary meeting, 12 January 1952; GA Resolution 623 (VII). Financing of Economic Development through the Establishment of Fair and Equitable International Prices for Primary Commodities and through the Execution of National Programmes of Integrated Economic Development. Adopted at its 411th plenary meeting, 21 December 1952; GA Resolution 1515 (XV). Concerted Action for Economic Development of Economically Less Developed Countries. Adopted at its 948th plenary meeting, 15 December 1960.

56   *Mining and Minerals in International Law and Policy*

better position to further the realisation of their plans of economic development in accordance with their national interests, and to further the expansion of the world economy.[20]

The context for the emergence of these Resolutions was of strong assertion of national sovereignty in the developing world as a reaction to the existing situation and to the imbalances of power that had featured prominently in international relations. This was the era of the decolonisation movement and the emergent view that the dominance of Western countries (their organisation, institutions and legal systems) prevented developing countries from moving forward in domestic development and tended to favour the position of transnational corporations over domestic priorities.[21] The principle commenced as a political claim posed by the developing countries and the new ex-colonies, who demanded recognition of their right to participate in the development of their natural resources and the benefits accruing from their exploitation.[22] As an extension of the struggle for political independence from former colonial powers, the objective of achieving economic independence became a top priority. Mining was intended to provide financial resources for development, and this was considered a 'springboard for industrialisation'. The belief that minerals were a special finite resource, the exploitation of which should be carefully controlled and optimised, engendered the perception of scarcity, which coupled with high mineral prices, made a battle for control inevitable and contributed to the contemporary profitability of public investment in mining.[23]

Resolution 1803 proclaiming the principle of PSONR was the cornerstone of the Declaration on the Establishment of a New International Economic Order (NIEO) and the Charter of Economic Rights and Duties of States (CERDS), both adopted by the General Assembly in 1974.[24] The Declaration on the Establishment

---

[20] GA Resolution 523 (VI). Integrated economic development and commercial agreements. Adopted at its 360th plenary meeting, 12 January 1952.

[21] T Wälde, 'A Requiem for the "New International Economic Order". The Rise and Fall of Paradigms in International Economic Law' in N Al-Nauimi and R Meese (eds), *International Legal Issues Arising under the United Nations Decade of International Law* (The Hague; Boston, Martinus Nijhoff Publishers, 1995) 1209–48.

[22] It was introduced in the GA on the initiative of Latin American countries, especially Chile, in the early 1950s, and was meant to express the widespread perception of inequitable distribution of benefits and wealth, vis-à-vis the United States. N Schrijver, *Sovereignty over Natural Resources. Balancing Rights and Duties* (Cambridge, Cambridge University Press, 1997) 36.

[23] Adams has called this the 'era of conflict for control', beginning in the mid-1960s and extending until about 1980. The author notes: 'these trends were not confined to developing countries. For example, there was a period of confiscatory taxation in British Columbia where the effective tax on profits exceeded 100%'. R Adams, 'Restructuring of the World Metals Industry: Implications for the Future' in Department of Technical Cooperation for Development, 'Prospects for Mining to the Year 2000 – Proceedings of the Seminar on Prospects for the Mining Industry to the Year 2000, New York, 1989' (New York, United Nations, 1992) 35–39.

[24] GA 3201 (S–VI), Declaration on the Establishment of a New International Economic Order; Adopted at its 2229th plenary meeting, 1 May 1974. A/RES/S–6/3201; GA Resolution 3281 (XXIX) Charter of Economic Rights and Duties of States. Twenty-ninth session Agenda item 48, 12 December 1974. A/RES/29/3281. The CERDS was an initiative of President Echeverría of Mexico, to remove 'economic cooperation from the realm of good will and rooting it in the field of law by transferring

The Principle of Permanent Sovereignty Over Natural Resources 57

of a NIEO was founded, among other principles, on the sovereign equality of states, the self-determination of all peoples, territorial integrity, the recognition of the right of every country to adopt the economic and social system that it deems convenient for its own development and the full permanent sovereignty of every state over its natural resources and all economic activities. The NIEO placed major responsibilities on the state for the promotion of the economic, social and cultural development of its people. The CERDS acknowledged 'the sovereign and inalienable right [of every state] to choose its economic system, as well as its political, social and cultural systems in accordance with the will of its people' (Article 1) and the right to 'freely exercise full permanent sovereignty, including possession, use and disposal, over its wealth, natural resources and economic activities' (Article 2.1). Article 2.2 asserts that every state is entitled to 'regulate and exercise authority over foreign investment within its national jurisdiction in accordance with its laws and regulations and in conformity with its national objectives and priorities'; 'regulate and supervise the activities of transnational corporations within its national jurisdiction'; and 'nationalize, expropriate or transfer ownership of foreign property, in which case appropriate compensation should be paid by the State adopting such measures'. An initiative related to the regulation and supervision of the activities of transnational corporations was the development of the Draft UN Code of Conduct for Transnational Corporations, which aimed to maximise the contribution of transnational corporations to development and minimising their negative impacts.[25]

Resolution 1803 contains a Declaration of eight principles that articulate all main areas of the law applicable to mining and minerals as developed at that time, including foreign investment law and aspects of trade, technology, development and international cooperation, around a search for balancing the competing interests of host and home countries and transnational corporations. Its starting point is the above-mentioned basic principle in accordance to which peoples and nations must exercise their right to permanent sovereignty over their natural wealth and resources in the interest of their national development and of the people of the state concerned (Principle 1). From that it follows that their exploration, development and disposition must be subject to the rules and conditions freely established by the relevant peoples and nations for their authorisation, restriction or prohibition (Principle 2); that, whenever authorisation is granted, the capital imported and earnings on that capital are subject to the provisions of such authorisation, as well as national and international law (Principle 3); and

---

consecrated principles of solidarity among men to the sphere of relations among nations.' See K Hossain, 'Introduction' in K Hossain (ed), *Legal Aspects of the New International Economic Order* (London, Frances Pinter Publishers Ltd, 1980) 4–5.

[25] Draft United Nations Code of Conduct on Transnational Corporations, May 1983, 23 ILM 626. The Intergovernmental Working Group on a Code of Conduct began negotiations at UNCTC at the first session that took place on 10–15 January 1977. The Draft was shelved in 1992. See K Sauvant, 'The Negotiations of the United Nations Code of Conduct on Transnational Corporations Experience and Lessons Learned' (2015) 16 *The Journal of World Investment & Trade* 11, 38 and 55.

58 *Mining and Minerals in International Law and Policy*

that foreign investment agreements shall be observed in good faith (Principle 8). The rules applicable to nationalisation, expropriation or requisitioning reflect a search for balance between the interests of host states and investors in as much as this is limited to grounds of public utility that override national or foreign private interests and upon the payment of compensation pursuant to the relevant national legislation and international law. Domestic jurisdiction must be exhausted in case of controversy although dispute settlement through arbitration or international adjudication should proceed upon agreement among states and other parties concerned (Principle 4). The Declaration places emphasis on the mutual respect of states based on their sovereign equality and of international organisations for the free exercise of the sovereignty of peoples and nations over their natural wealth and resources, stressing that this should permeate into the different forms of international cooperation, be it public or private investment, the exchange of goods and services and scientific information, or technical assistance (Principles 6, 5, 7, 8).

At the core of the PSONR principle was the recognition of the effective power of a state to control and dispose of its natural wealth and resources for the benefit of its own people.[26] The principle was initially invoked by newly independent countries and was sought to fulfil a protective function, acting against potential encroachments to their economic sovereignty resulting from claims to contractual or property rights by other states – often former colonial powers – and foreign enterprises.[27] Whereas capital exporting countries have characteristically argued for the application of classic principles of international law, notably *pacta sunt servanda*, capital-importing countries began to advocate for principles and concepts emerging at that time and which included *clausula rebus sic stantibus*, the duty to cooperate for development, the right to development and 'common but differentiated responsibilities' in international environmental law, as well as the common heritage of mankind in the law of the sea and outer space.[28]

The principle was invoked as an overriding principle to invalidate and restructure existing arrangements regarded as incompatible with sovereign interests (thereby grounding the nationalisation, expropriation and transfer of ownership of foreign property) and to develop new forms of arrangements for state control.[29] Thus, states began to exercise control over mineral resources by means of instruments ranging from outright nationalisation[30] to the creation of state

---

[26] K Hossain, 'Introduction' in K Hossain and SR Chowdhury, *Permanent Sovereignty Over Natural Resources in International Law. Principle and Practice* (London, Frances Pinter Publishers, 1980) xiii.

[27] Schrijver, *Sovereignty over Natural Resources* (1997) 171. N Schrijver, 'Self-determination of peoples and sovereignty over natural wealth and resources' in United Nations Human Rights Office of the High Commissioner, 'Realizing the Right to Development. Essays in Commemoration of 25 Years of the United Nations Declaration on the Right to Development', United Nations Publication HR/PUB/12/4 (New York and Geneva, 2013) 95–102.

[28] Schrijver, *Sovereignty* (1997) 171.

[29] Hossain, 'Introduction' (1980).

[30] Full nationalisation of foreign copper companies whose capital was transferred to the state-owned copper corporation (Spanish acronym: Codelco) in Chile, and of Cerro de Pasco Corporation in Peru

The Principle of Permanent Sovereignty Over Natural Resources   59

enterprises,[31] partnering with the private sector through joint ventures providing for major state equity at the development stage[32] and adopting, on the one hand, comprehensive mineral development agreements concluded between governments and transnational mining companies (including the renegotiation of existing agreements)[33] and, on the other, agreements restricting the rights of the foreign company to dispose freely of the extracted resources.[34] Whereas government equity holdings were insignificant in the early 1950s, they amounted to nearly half the metallic mineral production capacity in developing countries by the mid-1980s.[35]

Another way to exercise control was through the replacement of traditional concessionary regimes by statutes regulating foreign investment. Brown considers the 1969 Zambian Act as the starting point of a new generation of mining laws in Africa.[36] The Zambian Act was part and parcel of a more extensive programme of reform that included the acquisition by the state of most of the shares of Anglo American's copper holdings. The 1967 Botswanan Act, the 1979 Tanzanian Act, the 1981 Malawian Act, a few statutes of South Pacific and Caribbean countries, as well as the OK Tedi Agreement ratified by the Parliament in Port Moresby and part of the Statute Law of Papua Nueva Guinea, were all aimed towards regulating foreign investment in large-scale projects according to what was described by Brown as a new philosophy in mineral projects development.

(1974) are notable examples. In the Democratic Republic of Congo (formerly Zaire), the properties of Union Minière du Haut Katanga were nationalised in 1967, to form the SME Gecamines.

[31] Large SMEs created at the time in Latin America include COMIBOL in Bolivia, CVRD in Brazil, Mineroperú in Perú, ECOMIN in Colombia and the Consejo Siderúrgico Nacional in Venezuela, and Codelco in Chile. Pertamina was created in Indonesia.

[32] As in Botswana, Guinea, Liberia, Papua New Guinea and Sierra Leone. In Jamaica, agreements signed with foreign bauxite and alumina companies in 1976–1978 included provisions for the nationalisation of mining lands and for the establishment of joint enterprises, with the Government holding from 6–51% of the assets. UNCTAD, 'Management of Commodity Resources in the Context of Sustainable Development: Governance Issues for the Mineral Sector', UNCTAD/ITCD/ COM/3 (18 February 1997).

[33] For reviews of literature on the subject see T Wälde, 'Lifting the Veil from Transnational Mineral Contracts. A Review of Recent Literature' (1977) 1 *Natural Resources Forum* 166, to understand the form and substance of such emerging forms of mining agreements. From the same author, see also 'Third World Mineral Development: Recent Issues and Literature' (1984) 2 *Journal of Energy and Natural Resources Law* 282, and 'Permanent Sovereignty over Natural Resources: Recent Developments in the Minerals Sector' (1983) 7 *Natural Resources Forum* 239; AFM Maniruzzaman, 'The New Generation of Energy and Natural Resource Development Agreements: Some Reflections' (1993) 11 *Journal of Energy and Natural Resources Law* 207.

[34] S Asante and A Stockmayer, 'Evolution of development contracts: the issue of effective control' in United Nations, *Legal and Institutional Arrangements in Minerals Development* (London, Mining Journal Books, 1982) 57.

[35] M Radetzki, *State Mineral Enterprises: An Investigation into their Impact on International Mineral Markets* (Washington, Resources for the Future, 1985).

[36] This generation included (then) Zaire (1967), Tchad (1970), Mali (1970), Rwanda (1971), Senegal (1972), Burundi (1971), Nigeria (1976), Zambia (1969), Sudan (1972), Sierra Leone and Botswana (1976), as well as Uganda, Ethiopia, Ghana, and beyond the continent, Indonesia and Sri Lanka. R Brown, 'New Mining Codes: Salient Features' (Commonwealth Secretariat, 1986).

60   *Mining and Minerals in International Law and Policy*

The principle of PSONR was substantially embraced across the domestic legal systems of many developing countries. In general terms, a reaction against traditional international economic law, with its emphasis on protecting foreign investment, paved the way to a new international legal system based on planning and restricting business activities and foreign investment.[37] Legal reform in domestic legal institutions was aimed at constraining the market, weakening the institutions of private property and developing new legal forms endowing the state with enhanced power over land and natural resources, with public law becoming the basic law of economic and business activity. Salacuse affirms that law was thought of as a tool for economic and social engineering to bring about desired economic and social change.[38]

The attitudes and concerns underlying the NIEO are also evident in the legal regime for deep seabed mining debated in the third United Nations Conference on the Law of the Sea from 1973 to 1982. This declared that 'the seabed and ocean floor and subsoil thereof, beyond the limits of national jurisdiction' and its resources are the 'common heritage of mankind'.[39] This was called a 'laboratory' for testing the ideas emerging from the NIEO agenda.[40]

The principle of PSONR has been reaffirmed in subsequent GA Resolutions and international instruments.[41] In the context of the illegal exploitation of natural resources, UN Security Council Resolutions called for holding the International Conference on the Great Lakes Region.[42] Held in 2006, it culminated with the adoption of the Pact on Security, Stability and Development for the Great Lakes Region, which contemplated a range of protocols which included the Protocol Against the Illegal Exploitation of Natural Resources. States agreed thereby to set up regional rules and mechanisms 'for combating the illegal exploitation of natural resources which constitute a violation of the states' right of permanent sovereignty over their natural resources and which represent a serious source of insecurity, instability, tension and conflicts'.[43]

---

[37] J Salacuse, 'From Developing Countries to Emerging Markets: A Changing Role for Law in the Third World' (1999) 33 *The International Lawyer* 880.

[38] ibid.

[39] United Nations Convention on the Law of the Sea, 10 December 1982, in force from 16 November 1994, (1982) 21 *ILM* 1261. See ch 5.

[40] F Paolillo, 'The Future Legal Regime of Seabed Resources and the New International Economic Order: Some Issues' in K Hossain (ed), *Legal Aspects of the New International Economic Order* (London, Frances Pinter Publishers Ltd, 1980) 165–66.

[41] See eg, Vienna Convention on Succession of States in respect of Treaties. Vienna, 23 August 1978. Entered into force on 6 November 1996. United Nations, Treaty Series, vol 1946, 3; Vienna Convention on Succession of States in respect of State Property, Archives and Debts 1983. Vienna, 8 April 1983. Not yet in force.

[42] UN Security Council Resolution 1291. Adopted at its 4104th meeting, 24 February 2000 and UN Security Council Resolution 1304. Adopted by the Security Council at its 4159th meeting, 16 June 2000. See further D Dam-de Jong, *International Law and Governance of Natural Resources in Conflict and Post-Conflict Situations* (Cambridge, Cambridge University Press, 2015).

[43] Article 9. The same Article stated that activities 'bearing on natural resources must scrupulously respect the permanent sovereignty of each state over its natural resources and comply with harmonized national legislation as well as the principles of transparency, responsibility, equity, and respect for the environment and human settlements'; ending impunity in the illegal exploitation of natural resources

The Principle of Permanent Sovereignty Over Natural Resources   61

The circle of subjects of PSONR was initially vested either in 'peoples and nations' or 'underdeveloped' countries as the principle was intended to assert the self-determination of peoples and of those countries.[44] It was thus initially linked to human rights and it has been acknowledged as such through its inclusion in the two international human rights covenants of 1966.[45] As the process of decolonisation advanced, the circle moved on to include 'developing countries', by articulating their grievances against home states and foreign companies, and later embraced 'all states'.[46] The essence of the principle is the territorial sovereignty of states over their resources and their entitlement to such use within the limits of international law. In the end, this very essence has achieved the status of a principle of customary international law.[47]

The next section will examine into the place of mining and minerals in the key UN instruments shaping the concept of sustainable development. To do so, it will engage with aspects of the development of international environmental law and policy, 'one of the most remarkable exercises in international lawmaking, comparable only to the law of human rights and international trade law in the scale and form it has taken', focusing on concerns relevant to the conservation and management of natural resources and the concept of sustainable development.[48]

---

through national and international legal means; and adopting 'a regional certification mechanism for the exploitation, monitoring and verification of natural resources within the Great Lakes Region'. Pact on Security, Stability and Development for the Great Lakes Region adopted at the International Conference on the Great Lakes Region (ICGLR), Nairobi, 15 December 2006. See further the Lusaka Declaration of the ICGLR Special Summit to Fight Illegal Exploitation of Natural Resources in the Great Lakes Region adopted in Lusaka on 15 December 2010 (approving six tools to curb illegal exploitation of natural resources; endorsing the OECD Due Diligence Guidance for Responsible Supply Chains of Minerals from Conflict Affected and High Risk areas 'as crosscutting to the Regional Initiative on the Fight against Illegal Exploitation of Natural Resources' and calling upon companies sourcing minerals from the Region to comply with them).

[44] Schrijver (n 22) 8.

[45] Article 1.2 of both the International Covenant on Civil and Political Rights and the International Covenant on Economic, Social and Cultural Rights are drafted in identical terms: 'All peoples may, for their own ends, freely dispose of their natural wealth and resources without prejudice to any obligations arising out of international economic co-operation, based upon the principle of mutual benefit, and international law. In no case may a people be deprived of its own means of subsistence'. See also African Charter on Human and Peoples' Rights (Art 21). Adopted on 27 June 1981, 21 ILM 58 (1982), entered into force 21 October 1986. See ch 4.

[46] Schrijver (n 22) 8. GA Resolution 2158 (XXI). Permanent sovereignty over natural resources. Adopted at its 1478th plenary meeting, 25 November 1966; GA Resolution 2692 (XXV). Permanent sovereignty over natural resources of developing countries and expansion of domestic sources of accumulation for economic development. Adopted at its 1926th plenary meeting, 11 December 1970.

[47] International Court of Justice (ICJ) in its judgment of 19 December 2005 in the case concerning Armed Activities in the Territory of the Congo (*Democratic Republic of the Congo v Uganda*). See S Hobe, 'Evolution of the Principle on Permanent Sovereignty Over Natural Resources: From Soft Law to a Customary Law Principle?' in M Bungenberg and S Hobe (eds), *Permanent Sovereignty Over Natural Resources* (Cham, Springer, 2015) 11.

[48] P Birnie, A Boyle and C Redgwell, *International Law and the Environment*, 3rd edn (Oxford, Oxford University Press, 2009) 1.

62 *Mining and Minerals in International Law and Policy*

IV. The Environment, Natural Resources and Sustainable Development

A. 1972 Stockholm United Nations Conference on the Human Environment

Concerns about the conservation and effective management of natural resources were discussed between two United Nations units in the late 1940s. In effect, the UN Economic and Social Council (ECOSOC) held the Scientific Conference on Resource Conservation and Utilisation in 1947,[49] upon a proposal that the US had raised in 1945, bringing to the attention of the Council the importance of conserving resources for safeguarding peace.[50] It aimed at providing effective tools for avoiding the wasteful use of resources and enhancing their effective management. The focus of this conference on efficient resource utilisation for industrial purposes contrasted with the emphasis on the environment and resource protection that would drive another conference convened jointly by the UN Educational, Scientific and Cultural Organisation (UNESCO) and the International Union for the Protection of Nature (IUPN, later the International Union for the Conservation of Nature (IUCN)) (founded in 1948) and held in 1949.[51] The contending views put forward in these conferences would set a pattern of varying emphases on resources, nature and the environment for years to come.

The UN Conference on the Human Environment (UNCHE) convened in 1972 and reflected on a first common view of the way forward in dealing with the challenge of preserving and enhancing the human environment.[52] The Conference

---

[49] UN ECOSOC, 'Scientific Conference on Resource Conservation and Utilization', *Yearbook of the United Nations, 1946–1947* (New York, 1947) 491–92.

[50] Noting the letter dated 4 September 1946 in which a representative of the US Government highlighted that 'The real or exaggerated fear of resource shortages and declining standards of living has in the past involved nations in warfare. Every member of the United Nations is deeply interested in preventing a recurrence of that fear and of those consequences. Conservation can become a major basis of peace' Letter from President Truman to US representative on Economic and Social Council, 4 September 1946.

[51] UNESCO and IUPN, International Technical Conference on the Protection of Nature, Lake Success, NY, US, 22–29 August 1949 (Paris, UNESCO) 1949. See T Dueling, Visions for the Postwar World: the UN and UNESCO 1949 Conferences on Resources and Nature, and the Origins of Environmentalism' (2014) 101 *Journal of American History* 44.

[52] GA Resolution 2398 (XXIII). Problems of the Human Environment. Adopted at its 1733th plenary meeting, 3 December 1968, deciding to convene in 1972 a United Nations Conference on the Human Environment, considering among other reasons the need to 'provide a framework for comprehensive consideration within the United Nations of the problems of the human environment in order to focus the attention of Governments and public opinion on the importance and urgency of this question and also to identify those aspects of it that can only or best be solved through international co-operation and agreement'. GA Resolution 2581 (XXIV). United Nations Conference on the Human Environment. Adopted at its 1834th plenary meeting. 15 December 1969, affirming that 'it should be the main purpose of the Conference to serve as a practical means to encourage, and to provide guidelines for, action by Governments and international organizations designed to protect and improve the human environment and to remedy and prevent its impairment, by means of international co-operation, bearing in

The Environment, Natural Resources and Sustainable Development   63

resulted in a series of initiatives, including a Declaration comprising 26 principles and an Action Plan for the future.[53] Principle 1 of the Stockholm Declaration articulated the right of humankind to 'adequate conditions of life, in an environment of a quality that permits a life of dignity and well-being' as well as 'a solemn responsibility to protect and improve the environment for present and future generations'. The Declaration also contained a series of rather policy-oriented principles, of which Principles 8 to 13 emphasise the correlation between development and environment, calling for an integrated and coordinated approach to development planning.[54] This call for an integrated approach echoed the debate that had been evolving over those years. GA Resolution 1831 (XVII), Economic development and the conservation of nature, adopted in 1962, had endorsed a decision taken by UNESCO and recommended, particularly to developing countries, taking early action for the preservation of 'natural resources, flora and fauna', 'simultaneously with economic development', by adopting effective domestic legislation aimed at eliminating wasteful exploitation 'of soil, rivers and flora and fauna' while taking action towards preventing natural resources pollution, protecting landscapes and promoting education at all levels and 'associating all interested ministerial departments in this effort to protect flora and fauna'.[55]

UNCHE became the point of departure for the development of international environmental treaties, which reached a plain multilateral character aimed at protecting the environmental commons and services of each country that contributes to global benefits, and established the UN Environment Programme (UNEP) to strengthen environmental management within the UN system and facilitate the negotiation of multilateral environmental agreements.

It is important to recall that these developments occurred against the backdrop of perceptions of resource scarcity. The prevailing view among mainstream economists such as Barnett and Morse, who claimed that knowledge, equipment and economic institutions could prevent quantitative diminishing returns, had been challenged by the influential Limits to Growth report published by the Club of Rome in 1972. This report contained alarming predictions on the

---

mind the particular importance of enabling developing countries to forestall the occurrence of such problems'.

[53] Declaration of the United Nations Conference on the Human Environment (Stockholm), 16 June 1972 (1972) 11 ILM 1416.

[54] Principle 13 states that 'In order to achieve a more rational management of resources and thus to improve the environment, States should adopt an integrated and co-ordinated approach to their development planning so as to ensure that development is compatible with the need to protect and improve environment for the benefit of their population'.

[55] GA Resolution 1831 (XVII). Economic Development and the Conservation of Nature. Adopted in its 1197th plenary meeting, 18 December 1962. '*Considering* that natural resources, flora and fauna may be of considerable importance to the further economic development of countries and of benefit to their populations, *Conscious* of the extent to which the economic development of the developing countries may jeopardize their natural resources and their flora and fauna, which in some cases may be irreplaceable if such development takes place without due attention to their conservation and restoration …'.

64 *Mining and Minerals in International Law and Policy*

state of the environment and the long-term consequences of the degradation of life-supporting environmental assets. It also warned that the world was exhausting its natural resources, particularly minerals. Scarcity of minerals and arable land were considered as limiting growth.[56]

Against this backdrop, one can observe at least three main threads of concerns that related to mining and minerals in the documents of the time. A first thread is visualised in the Stockholm Declaration and Action Plan, as well as in the 1982 World Charter for Nature,[57] all of which specifically stipulated principles for the conservation and management of non-renewable resources. Principle 5 of the Stockholm Declaration called for using the 'non-renewables resources of the earth in such a way as to guard against the danger of their future exhaustion and to ensure that benefits from such employment are shared by all mankind'. Recommendation 56 of the Stockholm Action Plan advised the Secretary General on adopting mechanisms for information exchange, aiming to systematise, disseminate and improve accessibility to information regarding the environmental conditions of mine sites, their impacts and likely courses of action, with a view to devising criteria for planning and management that would identify limits to mining ('where certain kinds of mining should be limited, where reclamation costs would be particularly high, or where other problems would arise'), on the one hand, and to assisting developing countries with information on technology that could prevent impacts, on the other.[58] Recommendation 75 turned its attention to supporting international cooperation on radioactive waste, including problems related to mining and tailings.[59] The World Charter for Nature, in turn, stated that 'non-renewable resources which are consumed as they are used shall be exploited with restraint, taking into account their abundance, the rational possibilities of converting them for consumption, and the compatibility of their exploitation with the functioning of natural systems'.[60]

A second thread of concerns visible in some GA Resolutions links irrational and wasteful exploitation of natural resources to a threat in the exercise of PSONR.[61] The NIEO Declaration highlights 'the necessity for all states to put an end to the waste of natural resources, including food products'. GA Resolution 3326 (XXIX) expresses that 'irrational and wasteful exploitation and consumption of natural resources represent a threat to developing countries in the exercise of their permanent sovereignty over natural resources'. The third thread concerns the Stockholm Declaration's acknowledgement of the connection between

---

[56] R Auty and R Mikesell, *Sustainable Development in Mineral Economies* (Oxford, Clarendon Press, 1998).

[57] GA Resolution 37/7. World Charter for Nature. Adopted 28 October 1982.

[58] Report of the United Nations Conference on the Human Environment, Stockholm, 5–16 June 1972, Ch II, Action Plan for the Human Environment.

[59] ibid.

[60] GA Resolution 37/7. World Charter for Nature, Article 10(d).

[61] As observed by Schrijver (n 22).

environmental management and 'stability of prices and adequate earnings for primary commodities and raw materials' as 'economic factors as well as ecological processes must be taken into account', a point particularly relevant for developing countries (Principle 10). This relates to a more general concern for placing limits on the impairment of the human environment in order to achieve sound economic and social development, which is present in the 1972 Stockholm Declaration in an embryonic form.[62]

Dalupan remarks on the foundational character of the Stockholm Declaration and Action Plan, as well as the World Charter for Nature, for the development of international environmental law and their significance for mining and minerals, inasmuch as they recognise the value of non-renewable resources and extend on aspects related to their 'development, management and consumption'.[63] She stresses the Stockholm Declaration proposes two complementary aspects of 'sustainable use of mineral resources', the first one related to the management of the *resource itself*, which can be extended through recycling, and the second one pointing at the *benefits* derived from their use, which should be shared and expanded to drive other productive uses.[64]

B. The 1987 Brundtland Report

The term 'sustainable development' was used for the first time in the 'World Conservation Strategy', a report published by IUCN, UNEP and WWF in 1980.[65] The Strategy promoted a focused approach to managing living resources and regarded conservation and development as mutually dependent. The concept of sustainable development was initially focused on the *sustainable use of the resource*, rather than on economic development, and hence it was a principle of conservation.[66]

---

[62] Principle 8: 'Economic and social development is essential for ensuring a favourable living and working environment for man and for creating conditions on earth that are necessary for the improvement of the quality of life'.

[63] C Dalupan, 'Mining and Sustainable Development: Insights from International Law' in E Bastida, T Wälde and J Warden-Fernández (eds), *International and Comparative Mineral Law and Policy* (The Hague, Kluwer Law International, 2005) 161.

[64] ibid 167.

[65] IUCN, UNEP and WWF, *World Conservation Strategy: Living Resource Conservation for Sustainable Development* (1980). It says that 'For development to be sustainable, it must take account of social and ecological factors, as well as economic ones; of the living and non-living resource base; and of the long-term as well as the short-term advantages and disadvantages of alternative actions'.

[66] MCW Pinto, 'The Legal Context: Concepts, Principles, Standards and Institutions' in F Weiss, E Denters and P de Waart, *International Economic Law with a Human Face* (The Hague, Kluwer Law International, 1998) 16. N Schrijver, 'Development – The Neglected Dimension in the Evolution of the International Law of Sustainable Development' in *Seminar International Law and Sustainable Development: Principle and Practice* (Amsterdam, 29 November–1 December 2001) 6; The World Commission on Environment and Development, *Our Common Future* (Oxford, Oxford University Press, 1988).

66 *Mining and Minerals in International Law and Policy*

'Our Common Future' (the Brundtland Report), adopted by the World Commission on Environment and Development (WCED) in 1987, brought together separate strands of critical views on the negative consequences of development activities that by then had been the subject of contention for a long time. The Brundtland Report criticised the fundamental disconnection between environment and development, which was already present in the Stockholm Declaration, albeit in imprecise terms.[67] It broadened the concept of sustainability beyond environmental and conservation concerns, by acknowledging the contemporary critique of the concept of economic growth as applied separately from what should be the very essential ends of development: social equity, embracing the fulfilment of basic health and educational needs and participatory democracy.[68] The Brundtland Report called for overcoming the fragmented vision that saw development and the environment as separate and forging a new approach to development. It observed that:

> In most countries, environmental policies are directed at the symptoms of harmful growth; these policies have brought progress and rewards and must be continued and strengthened. But that will not be enough. What is required is a *new approach* in which all nations aim at a type of development that integrates production with resource conservation and enhancement, and that links both to the provision for all of an adequate livelihood base and equitable access to resources.[69]

Under the Brundtland Report, the concept of sustainable development provides a framework for that new approach, with a view that environmental policies and development strategies are integrated 'to ensure that [development] meets the *needs* of the present *without compromising* the ability of future generations to meet their own needs'.[70] It holds two central concepts: on the one hand, is an emphasis on *needs*, particularly those of the most vulnerable, which deserve overriding priority; on the other, it posits that there are *limits* to development 'imposed by the state of technology and social organisation on the environment's ability to meet present and future needs'.[71] It also implies an expanded time horizon for development. In a broad sense, the concept brings forward an ethical appraisal of the purpose and processes of development.[72] It is a pathway by which each member of society is called on to expand their sphere of cooperation towards achieving that common goal.[73]

---

[67] ibid.

[68] *See* J Harris, T Wise, K Gallagher and N Goodwin, *A Survey of Sustainable Development Social and Economic Dimensions* (Washington, Island Press, 2001).

[69] WCED, *Our Common Future* (1988) para 47 (emphasis added).

[70] ibid, ch 2, para 1 (emphasis added).

[71] ibid (emphasis added).

[72] JR Walsh, '*El ambiente y el paradigma de la sustentabilidad*' in JR Walsh and ME Di Paola (eds), *Ambiente, Derecho y Sustentabilidad* (Buenos Aires, La Ley, 2000) 1–66.

[73] 'We do not offer a detailed blueprint for action, but instead a pathway by which the peoples of the world may enlarge their spheres of cooperation' (WCED (n 66), introductory paragraphs).

The Environment, Natural Resources and Sustainable Development   67

Mining and minerals again underpin many of the themes elaborated in the Brundtland Report. A first theme can be traced back to the concerns of the NIEO amidst observations on changing attitudes to opening up to foreign investment. When pointing at the 'interlocking crises' that international economic relationships pose for overexploiting the environmental resource base in many developing countries, the Report directly speaks of mining, which, much like agriculture, forestry and energy production, generates a large portion of the gross national product of many of these countries. It directs attention not only to low-commodity prices but, also, to the impacts of the Structural Adjustment Programmes that were being implemented in African countries over the 1980s and to the debt crisis of Latin America, noting that the Latin American 'continent's natural resources are now being used not for development but to meet financial obligations to creditors abroad'.[74] It then calls for international economic exchanges to meet two conditions in order to benefit all: to guarantee, on the one hand, 'the sustainability of ecosystems on which the global economy depends' and, on the other, the satisfaction of all economic partners on the basis of equitable exchange, assigning special responsibility to the World Bank and the International Development Association (as it was then known) as the main channels for multilateral finance for developing countries.[75] It also observes the role that transnational companies can play in sustainable development, a question particularly relevant as 'developing countries come to rely more on foreign equity capital', but warning that 'if these companies are to have a positive influence on development, the negotiating capacity of developing countries vis a vis transnationals must be strengthened so they can secure terms which respect their environmental concerns'.[76]

A second theme elaborates further on the interconnected nature of the environment and development. It notes that the extraction of minerals (as in the case of agriculture, the diversion of watercourses, emissions, commercial forests and genetic manipulation) illustrates 'human intervention in natural systems during the course of development' that, until not long ago, were 'small in scale and their impact limited' but were becoming 'more drastic in scale and impact, and more threatening to life-support systems both locally and globally'. For development to be sustainable, as a minimum, it 'must not endanger the natural systems that support life on Earth: the atmosphere, the waters, the soils, and the living beings'.[77]

---

[74] 2. The Interlocking Crises, paras 18–20. Para 20 states 'The production base of other developing world areas suffers similarly from both local failures and from the workings of international economic systems. As a consequence of the 'debt crisis' of Latin America, that continent's natural resources are now being used not for development but to meet financial obligations to creditors abroad. This approach to the debt problem is short-sighted from several standpoints: economic, political, and environmental. It requires relatively poor countries simultaneously to accept growing poverty while exporting growing amounts of scarce resources'.

[75] III. International Cooperation and Institutional Reform 1. The Role of the International Economy, 75.

[76] ibid 80.

[77] I. The Concept of Sustainable Development, 9.

68 *Mining and Minerals in International Law and Policy*

In connection to this, the Brundtland Report elaborates on standards for the use of non-renewable resources like fossil fuels and minerals, whose use implies a reduction of the stock available for future generations, recommending that 'the rate of depletion should take into account the criticality of that resource, the availability of technologies for minimizing depletion, and the likelihood of substitutes being available' and that this use be calibrated with recycling 'to ensure that the resource does not run out before acceptable substitutes are available'.[78]

On the question of resource scarcity, the Report distances itself from the position held under the Stockholm document. Observing constant patterns of metals consumption and the role of technology in achieving greater efficiency in use, recycling and substitution, it places emphasis on 'modifying the pattern of world trade in minerals' by allowing exporters 'a higher share in the value added from mineral use, and improving the access of developing countries to mineral supplies, as their demands increase' as a most immediate need, once again stressing the first theme identified.[79]

C. The 1992 Rio Declaration and Agenda 21

The Brundtland Report paved the way for convening the 1992 United Nations Conference on Environment and Development (UNCED) in Rio de Janeiro.[80] UNCED adopted the Rio Declaration and Agenda 21, the Convention on Biological Diversity, the Framework Convention on Climate Change and the Statement of Principles for a Global Consensus on the Management, Conservation and Sustainable Development of all Types of Forests.[81] The instruments developed at UNCED consolidated the trends initiated in the 1972 Stockholm Declaration and set the guiding principles for environmental law and sustainable development.

The Rio Declaration is 'the most significant universally endorsed statement of general rights and obligations of states affecting the environment' today.[82] First, it reaffirmed existing customary law on transboundary matters. In effect, under public international law, states exercise sovereignty over the natural resources within their territories and are bound not to cause environmental harm beyond

---

[78] ibid 12.

[79] See III. Strategic Imperatives. 5. Conserving and Enhancing the Resource Base, 63.

[80] Agenda 21: 1.2. 'This global partnership must build on the premises of [GA Resolution] 44/228 of 22 December 1989, which was adopted when the nations of the world called for the United Nations Conference on Environment and Development, and on the acceptance of the need to take a balanced and integrated approach to environment and development questions'.

[81] Rio Declaration on the Environment and Development, 13 June 1992, 31 ILM 874 (1992); Agenda 21, 13 June 1992, UN Doc A/CONF 151/26 (1992); Convention on Biological Diversity, 5 June 1992, 31 ILM 818 (1992); Framework Convention on Climate Change, 9 May 1992, 31 ILM 849 (1992); Statement of Principles for a Global Consensus on the Management, Conservation and Sustainable Development of all Types of Forests, 13 June 1992, 31 ILM 881 (1992).

[82] P Birnie, A Boyle and C Redgwell, *International Law and the Environment*, 3rd edn (Oxford, Oxford University Press, 2009) 112.

The Environment, Natural Resources and Sustainable Development   69

their national jurisdiction. The principle is set in the Charter of the United Nations and reiterated in numerous conventions and international declarations as well as in landmark cases.[83] Second, the Rio Declaration and the Rio instruments systematised new or emerging principles of law on the protection of the global environment.[84] The preambles of both conventions define biodiversity and climate change as 'common concern of mankind', what underlies their universal character and the need for global cooperation to prompt their protection.[85] Global environmental responsibilities to assist in achieving those goals may have *erga omnes* character; they are common but differentiated between developed and developing countries and commit to the application of a precautionary approach.[86] Third, the Rio Declaration articulated policies and 'ideals' that would be further developed in Agenda 21.[87]

The Rio Declaration lays out the thrust of sustainable development in 27 principles balancing the priorities of developing and developed countries.[88] It builds upon the Stockholm Declaration but refocuses on the central concept of sustainable development 'with the goal of establishing a new and equitable global partnership through the creation of new levels of cooperation among states, key sectors of societies and people'.[89] As endorsed by the Rio instruments, sustainable development does not only bring about a compromise between development and environmental protection, but proposes an integrative approach to development that considers the importance of equity within the economic system.[90]

The Rio Declaration constitutes the basic normative framework for subsequent conferences in 2002 and 2012.[91] Although it is a soft-law instrument, its drafting in mandatory terms, its negotiation by consensus as a 'package deal'

---

[83] Charter of the United Nations. See eg Protocol to the 1979 Convention on Long-Range Transboundary Air Pollution on Heavy Metals, Aarhus, 24 June 1998, UNTS vol 2237, 4; Convention on Biological Diversity, adopted on 5 June 1992 and entered into force on 29 December 1993, UNTS vol 1760, 79 (Art 3). See also 1972 Stockholm Declaration on Human Environment (Principle 21 and 22); 1992 Rio Declaration on Environment and Development. Landmark cases trace back to the Trail Smelter arbitration between Canada and the United States (*Trail Smelter* case (United States, Canada), 16 April 1938 and 11 March 1941, RIIA III 1905).

[84] Birnie, Boyle and Redgwell, *International Law and the Environment* (2009) 112.

[85] ibid.

[86] ibid 130ff.

[87] ibid 112.

[88] ibid.

[89] Rio Declaration on the Environment and Development, 13 June 1992, 31 ILM 874 (1992).

[90] P Birnie and A Boyle, *International Law and the Environment*, 2nd edition (Oxford, Oxford University Press, 2002) 45.

[91] In Resolution 47/190 of 22 December 1992 the General Assembly endorsed the Rio Declaration and urged that necessary action be taken to provide effective follow-up. Since then, the Declaration, whose application at national, regional and international levels has been the subject of a specific, detailed review at the General Assembly's special session on Rio+5 in 1997, has served as a basic normative framework at ensuing global environmental gatherings, namely the World Summit on Sustainable Development in Johannesburg in 2002 and Rio+20, the United Nations Conference on Sustainable Development in 2012.

70   *Mining and Minerals in International Law and Policy*

and the consensus effectively struck between developed and developing countries, which was not as palpable in the 1972 Stockholm Conference, all help to confer authority and influence in the systematisation and further development of international law.[92]

Between the Brundtland Report and the Rio Conference, the world had witnessed sweeping changes following the end of the Cold War, symbolised in the fall of the Berlin Wall in 1989, the 'Washington Consensus',[93] and the spread of globalisation.[94] The concerns of developing countries regarding the unfavourable terms of trade and depressed commodity prices are acknowledged in Agenda 21 but, attuned to the broader changes of the time, it calls for promoting an 'open, equitable, secure, non-discriminatory and predictable multilateral trading system that is consistent with the goals of sustainable development and leads to the optimal distribution of global production in accordance with comparative advantage'. It establishes a link between a combination of improved market access for the exports of developing countries and sound macroeconomic and environmental policies, along with a positive environmental impact, as a pathway to realising contributions towards sustainable development.[95]

Agenda 21 broadly refers to minerals as 'land resources'[96] or hosted in fragile mountains ecosystems[97] and includes 'environmentally sound mining' as an income-generating activity for promoting integrated watershed development and alternative livelihood opportunities in programmes for sustainable mountains development.[98] There are also references to mining as a 'human-made interference', such as forest poaching and unmitigated shifting cultivation, from which forests

[92] P Birnie, A Boyle and C Redgwell, *International Law and the Environment* (2009) 112–14.
[93] See ch 4.I.
[94] AE Bastida, 'Mining Law in the Context of Development' in P Andrews-Speed (ed), *International Competition for Resources: The Role of Law, State and Markets* (Dundee, Dundee University Press, 2008) 101–36.
[95] Agenda 21, ch 2. International Cooperation to accelerate sustainable development in developing countries and related domestic policies, establishing the promotion of sustainable development through trade as a programmatic area (A and B). See para 2.5; also para 2.19. On minerals and WTO Law, see ch 4.I.A.
[96] Agenda 21: ch 10. Integrated Approach to the Planning and Management of Land Resources. '10.1. Land is normally defined as a physical entity in terms of its topography and spatial nature; a broader integrative view also includes natural resources: the soils, minerals, water and biota that the land comprises. These components are organized in ecosystems which provide a variety of services essential to the maintenance of the integrity of life-support systems and the productive capacity of the environment. Land resources are used in ways that take advantage of all these characteristics. Land is a finite resource, while the natural resources it supports can vary over time and according to management conditions and uses'.
[97] Ch 13. Managing Fragile Ecosystems: Sustainable Mountain Development, 13.1. 'Mountains are an important source of water, energy and biological diversity. Furthermore, they are a source of such key resources as minerals, forest products and agricultural products and of recreation. As a major ecosystem representing the complex and interrelated ecology of our planet, mountain environments are essential to the survival of the global ecosystem'.
[98] Section II. Conservation and Management of Resources for Development. 13. Managing fragile ecosystems: sustainable mountain development B. Promoting integrated watershed development and alternative livelihood opportunities in programmes Objectives 13.15.

must be protected,[99] and to providing input to non-point source pollutants to marine pollution, which requires its control and a change in current practices.[100]

Agenda 21 underlines the need for guidelines for natural resources development, particularly for forests and different aspects of environmental management. In 1991, the Berlin Guidelines emerged as an outcome of the Round Table on Mining and the Environment organised by the United Nations Environment Programme (UNEP) and the German Foundation for International Development. They served as basis for the first edition of the 1994 Environmental Guidelines for Mining Operations prepared by the UN Department of Economic and Social Development and its Commission for Sustainable Development, and UNEP, at the request of a number of countries looking for environmental guidance, and were revised in 2002.[101] The Fundamental Principles for the Mining Sector developed in the Berlin Guidelines acknowledge the need of recognizing: (i) environmental management as high priority, notably during the licensing process and through the development and implementation of environmental management systems; (ii) socio-economic impact assessments and social planning in mining operations from the earliest stages of project development; and (iii) participation of and dialogue with affected parties on the environmental and social aspects of all phases of mining activities.

Agenda 21 does not refer to standards of use of minerals as previous documents do. This is consistent with the general shift in the Rio Declaration away from specific conservation provisions regarding natural resources, in contrast to the previous documents as the World Charter of Nature.[102] The idea that sustainable development entails limits in the use of land, water and other natural resources is spelt out in the Biodiversity and Climate Change Conventions, and the precautionary principle can also be understood as an element of sustainable resource utilisation[103] or management.

D. 2002 Johannesburg Declaration and Plan of Implementation

Whereas UNCED's main concern related to balancing environmental protection and economic development, the World Summit on Sustainable Development (WSSD) held in Johannesburg in 2002, which adopted the Johannesburg Declaration on Sustainable Development and its Plan of Implementation (PoI),

---

[99] B. Enhancing the protection, sustainable management and conservation of all forests, and the greening of degraded areas, through forest rehabilitation, afforestation, reforestation and other rehabilitative means, 11.13. g.

[100] A. Integrated management and sustainable development of coastal and marine areas, including exclusive economic zones. B. Marine environmental protection. 17.28.

[101] Berlin II Guidelines for Mining and Sustainable Development ('Berlin Guidelines') (UN, 2002).

[102] Birnie, Boyle and Redgwell (n 82) 199.

[103] ibid.

72 *Mining and Minerals in International Law and Policy*

emphasised efforts to integrate the interdependent and mutually reinforcing pillars of sustainable development, ie, economic development, social development and environmental protection (para 5, Declaration and para 2, PoI),[104] drawing attention to the social dimension.[105] The Declaration recognises poverty eradication, changing patterns of consumption and production and the protection and management of the natural resource base for economic and social development as 'overarching objectives of and essential requirements for sustainable development' (para 11, Johannesburg Declaration) and it also identifies the deep division between rich and poor and the developed and developing world as a 'a major threat to global prosperity, security and stability' (para 12), noting that the continuing challenges to the global environment with increasing loss of biodiversity, depletion of fish stocks, desertification and climate change (para 13) and the compounded dimension that globalisation has added to all such challenges, confronting us with an uneven distribution of benefits and costs.[106]

The PoI reaffirms the commitment to the Rio Principles, the implementation of Agenda 21 and the achievement of the internationally agreed development goals set in the United Nations Millennium Declaration, as well as the outcomes of the major UN Conferences and international agreements since 1992 (para 1, PoI). The Summit acknowledges the outcomes of the Monterrey Consensus on Financing for Development agreed at the International Conference on Financing for Development held in Monterrey, Mexico, on 18–22 March 2002 and at the WTO Ministerial Conference held in Doha in 2001.[107] As reflected in these documents, attitudes to foreign direct investment had changed in the intervening years. The emphasis was not only on establishing enabling conditions for investment, but also on doing this in such a manner so as to achieve national development priorities.[108]

Critical stances against the disruptive impacts of the mining sector on the environment, local communities and economies that had widely been expressed for some time in industrialised and democratic societies, started to take hold in an ever-larger number of countries as investment geographically materialised across the globe. The period is characterised by the very influential line of scholarship on the so-called 'resource curse', which saw an inverse correlation between resource endowment and development in many countries.[109] Over those years, and amidst

---

[104] A/CONF.199/20 Distr: General 4 September 2002, World Summit on Sustainable Development, Johannesburg Declaration on Sustainable Development and Plan of Implementation of the World Summit on Sustainable Development.

[105] N Schrijver, 'Development – The Neglected Dimension' (2001).

[106] Para 14; see further PoI – V. Sustainable Development in a Globalizing World 47.

[107] 'Monterrey Consensus of the International Conference on Financing for Development', International Conference on Financing for Development, Monterrey, Mexico, 18–22 March 2002; DOHA WTO Ministerial 2001: Ministerial Declaration, WT/MIN(01)/DEC/1, 20 November 2001 (adopted on 14 November 2001).

[108] Bastida, 'Mining Law in the Context of Development' (2008).

[109] See ch 2.VII.

The Environment, Natural Resources and Sustainable Development   73

strong opposition to the World Bank's participation and support of projects involving extractive industries, the Bank commissioned the Extractive Industries Review, an independent study to assess such interventions in the context of the affirmed mission of promoting poverty reduction and sustainable development. The report called for the Bank to reform its social and environmental standards and to finance projects only upon meeting the right conditions, advocating for 'pro-poor and corporate governance, including proactive planning and management to maximize poverty alleviation through sustainable development; much more effective social and environmental policies; and respect for human rights'. It placed emphasis on enhancing governance until the risks of developing these major projects might be borne.[110]

The quality of governance and institutions, which were put forward as explanations of the positive correlation between resource wealth and development in a few countries, took centre stage in policy prescriptions of international governmental organisations, with a focus on transparency, accountability, participation and partnerships, as pathways to promote rule of law environments and counter the 'resource curse'. Corporate social responsibility (CSR) gained traction and nine of the largest mining companies mobilised to convene the Global Mining Initiative, which, under the auspices of the World Business Council for Sustainable Development, commissioned the International Institute for Environment and Development to prepare a scoping study. This recommended the design and scope of the Mining and Metals Sustainable Development Project (MMSD), a two-year independent research and consultation process launched in 2000 to gain understanding of the steps required for the transition of the industry towards sustainable development.[111]

The role of mining and minerals in the material fabric of society, and the role of mining as an activity that can potentially contribute to sustainable development, are acknowledged for the first time in the text. Section 46 in IV of the PoI, On Protecting and managing the natural resource base of economic and social development, states:

> 46. Mining, minerals and metals are important to the economic and social development of many countries. Minerals are essential for modern living. Enhancing the contribution of mining, minerals and metals to sustainable development includes actions at all levels to:
>
> a.   Support efforts to address the environmental, economic, health and social impacts and benefits of mining, minerals and metals throughout their life cycle, including workers'. health and safety, and use a range of partnerships, furthering existing activities at the national and international levels among interested Governments, intergovernmental organizations, mining companies and workers and other

---

[110] Extractive Industries Review, 'Striking a Better Balance. The World Bank Group and Extractive Industries. The Final Report of the Extractive Industries Review' (December 2003).
[111] See further D Franks, *Mountain Movers: Mining, Sustainability and the Agents of Change* (London, Earthscan, 2015).

74   *Mining and Minerals in International Law and Policy*

> stakeholders to promote transparency and accountability for sustainable mining and minerals development;
>
> b.   Enhance the participation of stakeholders, including local and indigenous communities and women, to play an active role in minerals, metals and mining development throughout the life cycles of mining operations, including after closure for rehabilitation purposes, in accordance with national regulations and taking into account significant transboundary impacts;
>
> c.   Foster sustainable mining practices through the provision of financial, technical and capacity-building support to developing countries and countries with economies in transition for the mining and processing of minerals, including small-scale mining, and, where possible and appropriate, improve value-added processing, upgrade scientific and technological information and reclaim and rehabilitate degraded sites.'

More broadly, when calling for changing unsustainable patterns of consumption and production, the PoI appeals to the promotion of corporate environmental and social responsibility and accountability to improve performance through the use of voluntary initiatives, codes of conduct, certification and public reporting, encouraging dialogue with local communities as well as the incorporation of sustainable development into the decision-making processes of financial institutions.[112]

The PoI also acknowledged the role of small-scale mining as a source of livelihoods, in the framework of the strengthening of actions aimed at poverty eradication and sustainable natural resource management. Section II, Poverty Eradication, 10(d) and (f) of the Plan set out the need to include actions to:

> 10
>
> (d)   Provide financial and technological support, as appropriate, to rural communities of developing countries to enable them to benefit from safe and sustainable livelihood opportunities in small-scale mining ventures'
>
> ...
>
> (f)   Provide support for natural resource management for creating sustainable livelihoods for the poor.

These provisions mainstreamed mining in a sustainable development framework from planning to closure signalling an important normative reference for policy initiatives and standards in the industry. It has been criticised for falling short of the recommendations of the World Bank's commissioned Extractive Industries Review.[113] It has also been seen as spelling out a 'sustainable development consensus' within mainstream narratives rooted in the economic underpinnings

---

[112] III. Changing unsustainable patterns of consumption and production. Call to enhancing corporate environmental and social responsibility and accountability (para 18). See also V. Sustainable development in a globalizing world (paras 49 and 50).

[113] This point was raised by Dalupan in 'Mining and Sustainable Development' (2005).

The Environment, Natural Resources and Sustainable Development   75

of neoliberalism.[114] The recognition of the role of small-scale mining in rural livelihoods was significant as it had notoriously been neglected under the influential mining policies drafted and implemented over the 1990s.

In the late 1990s, the link between trade in minerals as diamonds in fostering and financing armed conflict in Angola and Sierra Leone became better understood. The UN Security Council adopted a series of resolutions imposing sanctions and conflict resources were object of subsequent prominent initiatives.[115] The following years would see the emergence of the transnational governance of mining and minerals through: (a) a wide set of voluntary initiatives such as the Extractive Industries Transparency Initiative (EITI) and the Kimberley Process Certification Scheme (KPCS), both launched in 2003;[116] (b) new institutions and sets of governance guidance, such as the Intergovernmental Forum on Mining, Minerals, Metals and Sustainable Development (IGF),[117] or new programmes within existing institutions, such as the Responsible Mineral Development Initiative within the 2010 World Economic Forum (WEF), as well as pursuits by global civil society in this field, from Global Witness to Oxfam America and new organisations, such as the Natural Resource Governance Institute (NRGI),[118] and industry bodies as the International Council on Mining and Metals (ICMM),[119] all populating the global governance landscape of mining and minerals; (c) the review of performance standards of international organisations; (d) the expansion of laws for extra-territorial application;[120] and (e) further development of supply chain, procurement and CSR requirements.[121]

The UN Guiding Principles on Business and Human Rights (UNGP), endorsed by the Human Rights Council in 2011, have crystallised the consensus on the issue of the growing role of transnational and national business in development and their impacts on human rights, the corresponding obligations of states in preventing and responding to them, as well as the responsibility of business in respecting

---

[114] TL Field, *State Governance of Mining, Development and Sustainability* (Cheltenham and Northampton, Edward Elgar Publishing, 2019) quoting Sara L Seck, 'Transnational corporations and extractive industries' in S Alam, S Atapattu, CG Gonzalez, J Razzaque (eds), *International Environmental Law and the Global South* (Cambridge, Cambridge University Press 2015) 380.

[115] See D Dam-de Jong, 'A Rough Trade'? Towards a More Sustainable Minerals Supply Chain' (2019) *Brill Open Law* 1–32.

[116] See ch 4.V.C.

[117] The IGF emerged from the 2002 World Summit of Sustainable Development. It supports countries to leverage mining for sustainable development to ensure 'negative impacts are limited, and financial benefits are shared'. IGF, '2018 IGF Annual Report'. Published by the International Institute for Sustainable Development (IISD). The Mining Policy Framework serves as policy guidance and as an assessment tool on six thematic areas: the legal and policy environment; financial benefit optimisation; socioeconomic benefit optimisation; environmental management; post-mining transition; and artisanal and small-scale mining, establishing a platform for developing national policies.

[118] The Natural Resource Charter, developed by a group of academics and practitioners, was launched in 2010 and formed the basis of implementation actions of the NRGI, established in 2013.

[119] Established in 2001 (following the then existing International Council on Metals and the Environment).

[120] See ch 4.V.C.

[121] See ch 4.V.D.

76   *Mining and Minerals in International Law and Policy*

human rights through due diligence measures.[122] The UNGP point at both transnational and national corporations, and at the obligations of states in running business, including the extraterritorial obligations of home states. Corporate responsibility to respect human rights had been recognised in other soft law instruments, such as the UN Global Compact, the ILO Tripartite Declaration of Principles Concerning Multinational Enterprises and Social Policy, and the OECD Guidelines for Multinational Enterprises.

E. 2012 Rio+20

The 2012 UN Conference on Sustainable Development (Rio+20), the last one to date, urged a focus on efforts to integrate and ensure enhanced coherence in sustainable development regarding its dimensions and supporting policies and institutions, and further stressed the need to eradicate poverty and radically shift consumption and production patterns.[123] It also called for the elaboration of the SDGs that would subsume the Millennium Development Goals, due in 2015, and would streamline the urgent need for climate action, consolidating a new development agenda post-2015. Agenda 2030, containing the SDGs, was approved in September 2015.[124] As such, 2015 set a milestone in international development cooperation.[125]

---

[122] See ch 4.V.A.

[123] GA Resolution 66/288 adopted on 27 July 2012, 'The Future We Want' (endorsing the Outcome Document of the United Nations Conference on Sustainable Development held in Rio de Janeiro on 20–22 June 2012 (A/RES/66/288)).

[124] GA Resolution 70/1. Transforming our world: the 2030 Agenda for Sustainable Development, 25 September 2015 (approving the Sustainable Development Goals). Agenda 2030 included the framework for financing sustainable development set at the Third International Conference on Finance for Development held in Addis Ababa from 13–16 July 2015 (GA Resolution 69/313. Addis Ababa Action Agenda of the Third International Conference on Financing for Development, 27 July 2015). This Resolution emphasises the role of public policies and domestic resource mobilisation to achieve the SDGs. It warns of the challenges faced by countries relying on natural resources exports, encouraging their processing, productive diversification, and investment in value addition as well as addressing 'excessive tax incentives' particularly concerning the extractive industries. It also underscores the role of corporate transparency and accountability and encourages countries to act on the implementation of measures to promote transparency and acknowledge voluntary initiatives as EITI. It refers to continuing sharing of best practice and the promotion of peer learning and capacity-building for the negotiation of contracts 'for fair and transparent concession, revenue and royalty agreements and for monitoring the implementation of contracts'.

[125] On 18 March 2015, the Third UN World Conference on Disaster Risk Reduction held in Sendai, Japan, approved the Sendai Framework for Disaster Risk Reduction 2015–2030 (UN General Assembly Resolution 69/283. Sendai Framework for Disaster Risk Reduction 2015–2030, 3 June 2015). This updated and succeeded the earlier Hyogo Framework for Action 2005–2015: Building the Resilience of Nations and Communities to Disasters. On 18 June 2015, Pope Francis released *Laudato Si*, the Encyclica calling for a radical shift of the individual and collective attitudes with regard to our planet – 'our common home' – and of the global economic system refashioning the relationship with the Earth as responsible stewardship, identified with a 'culture of care', and emphasising an interpretation of 'dominion' as stewardship. *Encyclical Letter Laudato Si of the Holy Father Francis on Care for Our Common Home*. See D Shelton, 'Dominion and Stewardship' (2015) 109 *American Journal of International Law Unbound* 132.

The Environment, Natural Resources and Sustainable Development   77

Mining has a place as one of the thematic areas and cross-sectoral issues in the framework for setting up courses of action and follow-ups. The drafting of paras 227 and 228 (V.A) reflects recent developments for countering the resource curse and upholding transparency and anti-corruption. They state that:

> 227. We acknowledge that minerals and metals make a major contribution to the world economy and modern societies. We note that mining industries are important to all countries with mineral resources, in particular developing countries. We also note that mining offers the opportunity to catalyse broad-based economic development, reduce poverty and assist countries in meeting internationally agreed development goals, including the Millennium Development Goals, when managed effectively and properly. We acknowledge that countries have the sovereign right to develop their mineral resources according to their national priorities and a responsibility regarding the exploitation of resources, as described in the Rio Principles. We further acknowledge that mining activities should maximize social and economic benefits, as well as effectively address negative environmental and social impacts. In this regard, we recognize that governments need strong capacities to develop, manage and regulate their mining industries, in the interest of sustainable development.

> 228. We recognize the importance of strong and effective legal and regulatory frameworks, policies and practices for the mining sector that deliver economic and social benefits and include effective safeguards that reduce social and environmental impacts, as well as conserve biodiversity and ecosystems, including during postmining closure. We call upon governments and businesses to promote the continuous improvement of accountability and transparency, as well as the effectiveness of the relevant existing mechanisms to prevent illicit financial flows from mining activities.

The intervening years between Johannesburg and Rio+20 witnessed the dramatic rise of mineral prices, driven at unprecedented levels by the demand of China and other countries undergoing industrialisation. China and Chinese enterprises have been playing a predominant role in the mining and minerals sector and have exercised an impact in the geographies and modalities of investment. The UN Economic Commission for Africa (UNECA) steered the International Study Group for the Review of African Mining Regimes (2007–2011), which led to the recommendation of the essential tenets of the Africa Mining Vision.[126] The Vision emphasised the role of minerals in building linkages between mining and other sectors of the economy (rather than as inputs in global value chains or tax earners) and inspired a new generation of legal and institutional reforms across the continent with provisions on local content, environment protection, transparency and accountability.[127] A range of approaches coalesced in Latin America at the time, from profound constitutional reforms which, as in the case of Bolivia, enshrined

---

[126] UNECA, 'Minerals and Africa's Development – The International Study Group Report on Africa's Mineral Regimes' (2011).

[127] NV Nwogu, 'Mining at the Crossroads of Law and Development: A Comparative Review of Labor-Related Local Content Provisions in Africa's Mining Laws through the Prism of Automation' (2019) 28 *Washington International Law Journal* 139.

78   Mining and Minerals in International Law and Policy

the preeminent role of mineral resources in the model for a plural economy in the very same constitutional chart,[128] to progressive incorporation of sustainability tools into regulatory frameworks. Some countries, such as Costa Rica and Ecuador, a few provinces in Argentina and municipalities, eg in Argentina and Colombia, implemented bans to mining, or processes or substances used in it.[129]

F. Agenda 2030 and the SDGs

Agenda 2030 set in place the SDGs, comprising 17 goals and 169 targets, in a process hailed as widely participative.[130] It is guided by the principles of the Charter of the United Nations, including full respect for international law, grounded in the Universal Declaration of Human Rights, international human rights treaties, the Millennium Declaration and the 2005 World Summit Outcome, and informed by other instruments, such as the Declaration on the Right to Development. Agenda 2030 reaffirms the outcomes of all major UN conferences and summits that have shaped the foundations for sustainable development. The SDGs strive to pursue focused and coherent action to guide the decisions to be adopted until 2030, which is measurable upon indicators.[131]

'Our common vision' (I.4), 'The Future We Want', recognises that 'protecting and managing the natural resource base of economic and social development' is one of 'the overarching objectives of and essential requirements for sustainable development', while the sustainable management and efficient use of natural resources is established as a specific target (12.2) in SDG 12 on sustainable consumption and production, with important implications for promoting recycling and circular economy models. Furthermore, while mining and minerals have not specifically been dealt with under the SDGs, the goals speak directly to them, notably by enhancing its contribution to those relating to work and economic growth (SDG 8), industry, innovation and infrastructure (SDG 9), and affordable energy

---

[128] The constitutional reforms in Bolivia and Ecuador aimed at aligning their structures and the state's functions with the concept of 'living well'/'good living' (*vivir bien/buen vivir*), which is rooted in the pluricultural identity of each of these countries, and draws a close connection between man and nature. See AE Bastida and L Bustos, 'Towards Regimes for Sustainable Mineral Resources Management. Constitutional Reform, Law and Judicial Precedents in Latin America' (2017) 9 *International Development Policy (Revue Internationale de Politique de Développement)* 235.

[129] See AE Bastida, 'Latin America's policy priorities on mining and sustainable development, and opportunities for EU cooperation', Strategic Dialogue on Sustainable Raw Materials for Europe (STRADE) EU Horizon 2020 Project; European Policy Brief No 5/2018, July 2018.

[130] T Etty, V Heyvaert, W Burns, C Carlarne, D Farber and J Lin, 'By All Available Means: New Takes on Established Principles, Actions and Institutions to Address Today's Environmental Challenges' (2015) 4 *Transnational Environmental Law* 235.

[131] The global indicator framework for the SDGs was prepared by the Inter-agency and Expert Group on SDG Indicators (IAEG–SDGs) established by the United Nations Statistical Commission on 6 March 2015, and adopted by Resolution adopted by the GA on Work of the Statistical Commission pertaining to the 2030 Agenda for Sustainable Development (A/RES/71/313) on 6 July 2017.

The Environment, Natural Resources and Sustainable Development 79

(SDG 7) or by requiring management actions in those related to the land-based environment (SDG 15), 'life below water' (SDG 14), and clean water and sanitation (SDG 6), with many more interlinked connections between different goals. SDG 16 promotes peaceful and inclusive societies, access to justice and building effective, accountable and inclusive institutions at all levels, with specific targets on supporting the rule of law (16.3), reducing corruption and bribery (16.5) and developing 'effective, accountable and transparent institutions at all levels'. ASM has particular connections with SDG 8, SDG1 (no poverty), SDG 2 (zero hunger) and SDG 5 (gender equality) due to its linkages with rural economies.[132]

SDG 17 is a cross-cutting goal concerning the means of implementation (finance, technology, capacity-building, trade) and the revitalisation of the 'global partnership for sustainable development' in which the private sector is envisaged to play an important role. It also points at systemic issues related to policy and institutional coherence for sustainable development, as enhancing policy coherence (17.14), respect for policy space and leadership (17.15), and encouraging effective partnerships (public, public–private and civil society) (17.17).

The UN Environment Assembly adopted Resolution 4/19 on Mineral Resource Governance in its fourth session that took place on 11–15 March 2019.[133] The Resolution recalls UNCHE, its Action Plan and Recommendation 56 on mining and minerals as well as the World Charter for Nature and the Berlin Guidelines, and reaffirms the Johannesburg Plan of Implementation of the WSSD adopted on 4 September 2002 and the Outcome Document of Rio+20 adopted on 27 July 2012 acknowledging the contribution of minerals and metals to society and the call to government and business to further upon accountability and transparency in the sector. It also recalls GA Resolution 70/1 adopting the SDGs and refers in particular to SDG 7 (access to affordable, reliable, sustainable and modern energy for all) and SDG 12 (sustainable consumption and production patterns) underlining the contribution of mining to their achievement. The Resolution notes that 'clean technologies, highly depending on metals and minerals, are important to combat climate change issues'.

The Resolution welcomes the Global Resource Outlook 2019: Natural Resources for the Future We Want report and takes note of the reports UN Environment and International Resource Panel, Mineral Resource Governance in the 21st Century. Gearing Extractive Industries towards Sustainable Development, 2019 (developing the comprehensive concept of 'Sustainable Development License to Operate'); Mine Tailings Storage: Safety is No Accident (UNEP – GRID ARENDAL, 2017) and Sand and Sustainability: Finding new solutions for environmental governance of global sand resources (UNEP–GRID 2019).

---

[132] G Hilson and R Maconachie, 'Artisanal and small-scale mining and the Sustainable Development Goals: Opportunities and new directions for sub-Saharan Africa' (2020) 111 *Geoforum* (May) 125.
[133] UN Environment Assembly Resolution 4/19 Mineral Resource Governance. Adopted on 15 March 2019 at Fourth session Nairobi, 11–15 March 2019 (UNEP/EA.4/Res.19).

80 *Mining and Minerals in International Law and Policy*

It recognises that 'sustainable management of metal and mineral resources contributes significantly to the achievement of the Sustainable Development Goals'; and that there is a need to advance knowledge on 'regulatory approaches, implementation practices, technologies and strategies for the sustainable management of metal and mineral resources' across the whole life-cycle and post-mining. It also anticipates the need to advance on gathering information on sustainable practices, identifying knowledge gaps and options for implementation strategies and reviewing assessments of governance initiatives and approaches on sustainable management of metal and mineral resources for reporting to the fifth UN Environment Assembly. Finally, it encourages governments, businesses, non-governmental organisations, academia and international institutions to promote awareness, due diligence best practice along the supply chain, capacity-building and public–private partnerships and continuous uptake of transparency.

The IRP report, 'Mineral Resource Governance in the 21st Century. Gearing Extractive Industries towards Sustainable Development', criticises existing approaches, such as the 'Social License to Operate' as insufficient to make significant progress towards sustainability. It puts forward the concept of 'Sustainable Development Licence to Operate' as a holistic integrative governance approach to decision-making calling on the 'shared responsibility' of 'host' and 'home' countries in the value chain to achieve the SDGs. It is a bold call to systemic governance and transformations to sustainability.

A series of documents are also pointing at the potential contribution of the sector across all scales to advancing the SDGs, and are developing guidance for management to steer public policy,[134] corporate strategies and operational practice.[135] Likewise, spearheaded by the SDGs, reports with novel concepts are emerging,[136] while guidance documents are maturing, consolidating and growing in sophistication, showing greater mainstreaming of human rights, as well as strengthened understanding of the existing fragmentation of legal and regulatory regimes in the sector and the need of steering actions towards integrating environmental sustainability and the social dimension into economic decisions.[137]

---

[134] See UNDP and Swedish Environmental Protection Agency, 'Extracting Good Practices. A Guide for Governments and Partners to Integrate Environment and Human Rights into the Governance of the Mining Sector' (2018); UNDP, 'Assessing the Rule of Law in Public Administration: the Mining Sector' (2019).

[135] UNDP, World Economic Forum and Columbia Centre on Sustainable Investment, Sustainable Development Solutions Network, 'Mapping Mining to the Sustainable Development Goals: An Atlas' (2016).

[136] See eg R Sánchez (ed), *La bonanza de los recursos naturales para el desarrollo: dilemas de gobernanza*, ECLAC Books, no 157 (LC/PUB.2019/13-P) (Santiago, Economic Commission for Latin America and the Caribbean (ECLAC), 2019) and World Economic Forum, 'Mining and Metals in a Sustainable World 2050' (September 2015).

[137] N Woodroffe and T Grice, 'Beyond Revenues: Measuring and Valuing Environmental and Social Impacts in Extractive Sector Governance' (NRGI, September 2019) (calling for more effective modelling and measurement of the environmental and social impacts of extraction to inform decision-making processes regarding public policy and regulations). See more generally IISD, 'Modelling for Sustainable Development. New Decisions for a New Age' (IISD, July 2019) (there is a growing realisation of the

The Environment, Natural Resources and Sustainable Development   81

Crucially, they are calling for more holistic approaches to planning development that go beyond the mere management of impacts through tools for modelling integrated decisions.[138] This growing refinement of standards is also being captured in responsible investment principles and certification schemes,[139] and helps to reflect on the role of business in moving beyond risk management to analyse the net positive contributions of projects to the well-being of humans and ecosystems in the long term.[140] A quite extended view in some documents is on the achievement of mining contributes with 'net positive gains'.

G. The Paris Agreement and Other Multilateral Environmental Agreements

The Paris Agreement builds upon the 1992 UN Framework Convention on Climate Change and charts global action towards limiting the rise of global temperature to well below 2°C and above pre-industrial levels, striving to set such a limit at 1.5°C on the basis of nationally determined contributions (NDCs).[141] SDG 7, on clean and affordable energy, and SDG 13 further steer actions in this direction. The Paris Agreement is the most prominent international treaty calling for dramatic economy-wide changes in the operating conditions of carbon-emitting processes, including mining.

As acknowledged by UN Environment Resolution 4/19, minerals are at the forefront of climate action as they provide the inputs for building the infrastructure required for the transition to meet the Paris Agreement in a carbon-constrained future. But unprecedented demand may either help or hinder achieving the SDGs by exercising unbearable pressure on local ecosystems, water systems and communities. At the same time, host countries and companies will have increased commitments to reducing their own emissions as well as the material footprint derived from their operations, amidst scenarios of declining ore grades and growing energy and water intensity.[142] It will be vital for host countries to shift their energy systems to renewables.[143]

---

need towards a more holistic approach to planning. Modelling for sustainable development can play an important role in improving decision-making and avoiding the emergence of future environmental, social and economic crises). See also IRP, 'Mineral Resource Governance in the 21st Century' (2020).

[138] ibid.

[139] Initiative of Responsible Mining Assurance (IRMA), Principles of Engagement.

[140] T Hodge, 'Towards Contribution Analysis' in T Addison and A Roe (eds), *Extractive Industries. The Management of Resources as a Driver of Sustainable Development* (Oxford, Oxford University Press, 2018) 369–94.

[141] Article 2.1 a; Art 3, Paris Agreement. See ch 4.

[142] Addison, 'Climate Change and the Extractive Sector' in T Addison and A Roe (eds), *Extractive Industries. The Management of Resources as a Driver of Sustainable Development* (Oxford, Oxford University Press, 2018) 471.

[143] ibid.

82   *Mining and Minerals in International Law and Policy*

At the heart of the Paris Agreement lie the NDCs which each Party commits to prepare, communicate and maintain (Article 4, para 2), and which identifies the domestic mitigation measures each country undertakes to reduce national emissions and adapt to the impacts of climate change. The Paris Agreement acknowledges the role of non-state actors, including the fundamental role of the private sector – their business impacts on climate, as well as the climate impacts on business and supply chains – in seeking to achieve the objectives of the Paris Agreement with civil society, consumers and investors increasingly requiring climate action.

International organisations are adapting their programmes for climate action, eg, the Climate-Smart Facility developed by the World Bank, seeking to minimise the environmental, social and climate footprint of extraction and providing further guidance on embedding policies within the SDGs.[144]

Beyond the Paris Agreement, which illustrates direct requirements impinging on *process* or operating conditions of mineral development, the body of multilateral environmental treaties has also implications in terms of *access* to land for mining – a number of international treaties ban or could potentially restrict mining from certain type of areas[145,146] – and *product* controls or bans on end products.[147] Soft law standards have also been particularly important in this field.[148]

---

[144] IRP, 'Mineral Resource Governance' (n 137).

[145] Convention on the Conservation of Migratory Species of Wild Animals (with appendices). Concluded in Bonn on 23 June 1979. UNTS vol 1651, 1-28395, 333; Convention on Wetlands of International Importance especially as Waterfowl Habitat. Concluded at Ramsar, Iran, on 2 February 1971. UNTS vol 996, I-I-I583, 245; Convention to Combat Desertification in Countries Experiencing Serious Drought and/or Desertification Particularly in Africa, 17 June 1994, 33 ILM 1328 (1994). See G Pring, 'International Law and Mineral Resources', *Mining, Environment and Development* series (UNCTAD, 2000).

[146] The Convention for the Protection of the World Cultural and Natural Heritage aims at the identification, protection, conservation and transmission to future generations of cultural and natural heritage property of Outstanding Universal Value worldwide, as they 'need to be preserved as part of the world heritage of mankind as a whole'. States party to the Convention commit to adopt policies, eg to promote their integration into planning programmes, as well as abstaining of undertaking measures that could deliberately result in their damage. The Operational Guidelines state that legislation and regulation at national and local level must ensure 'the protection of the property from social, economic and other pressures or changes that might negatively impact the Outstanding Universal Value', establishing buffer zones to provide an 'added layer of protection to the property' wherever necessary. Mining is cited as one of the activities that could severely deteriorate the natural beauty or scientific value of natural properties and in specific cases, place the enlisted property under 'Ascertained Danger' in which case the Committee can inscribe it in the List of World Heritage in Danger. Convention for the Protection of the World Cultural and Natural Heritage. Adopted by the General Conference of the United Nations Educational, Scientific and Cultural Organization at its 17th session, Paris, 16 November 1972. UNTS, vol 1037, 151; Operational Guidelines for the Implementation of the World Heritage Convention. United Nations Educational, Scientific and Cultural Organisation. Intergovernmental Committee for the Protection of the World Cultural and Natural Heritage.WHC.17/01 12 July 2017, and Decision 39 COM 11.

[147] Pring and Siegele, 'International Law and Mineral Resources' in AE Bastida, T Wälde and J Warden–Fernandez (eds), International and Comparative Mineral Law and Policy: Trends and Prospects (The Hague, Kluwer Law International, 2005) 127–47.

[148] Relevant UNEP/UN Environment Initiatives include 1978 Draft Principles on Shared Natural Resources; 1991 Environmental Management and Sustainable Development in Technical Assistance; 1982 Guidance Document on Transboundary Movements of Hazardous Waste Destined for Recovery Operations; 1984 Guidelines on Offshore Mining and Drilling, Banned and Severely Restricted

Law, Sustainable Resources Management and the Paradigm of Sustainability 83

Biodiversity mainstreaming efforts under the Convention on Biological Diversity have been strengthened under the Strategic Plan for Biodiversity 2011–2020 and the Aichi biodiversity targets in 2010,[149] and reiterated under the Cancun Declaration in 2016,[150] which called for their integration in policies in specific economic sectors.[151] Mining was later included among these sectors.[152]

The Minamata Convention on Mercury adopted in 2013, which entered into force in 2017, provides the foremost example of product ban and control. It is a remarkable instrument aimed at protecting human health and the environment from mercury emissions. It comprehensively deals with sources of mercury and trade. In connection with artisanal and small-scale gold mining and processing of gold with mercury amalgamation, states parties to the treaty commit to 'take steps to reduce, and where feasible eliminate, the use of mercury and mercury compounds in, and the emissions and releases to the environment of mercury from, such mining and processing' (Article 7, 2). If ASM activities are significant, they must develop national action plans and provide reviews of progress.

V. Law, Sustainable Resources Management and the Paradigm of Sustainability

While sustainable development has reached normative status under international law,[153] there is considerable uncertainty about the scope, exact meaning and legal implications of sustainable development. This section will review the status of sustainable development under international law and the constitutive substantive and procedural elements of sustainable development, pointing at some issues

---

Chemicals; 1987 Exchange of Information about Chemicals and International Trade. The Awareness and Preparedness for Emergencies at Local Level (APELL), a programme developed by UNEP in conjunction with governments and industry with the purpose of minimising the occurrence and harmful effects of technological accidents and environmental emergencies, developed the APELL Handbook which was revised in 2015 within the context of the Sendai Framework for Disaster Risk Reduction (2015–2013). A Handbook for mining was developed in 2001. UN Environment is calling for global action and a 'zero-failure' approach to tackle tailing dam failures. C Roche, K Thygesen, E Baker (eds), 'Mine Tailings Storage: Safety Is No Accident. A UNEP Rapid Response Assessment' (United Nations Environment Programme and GRID–Arendal, Nairobi and Arendal, 2017).

[149] Decision X/2. The Strategic Plan for Biodiversity 2011–2020 and the Aichi Biodiversity Targets. Adopted at the 10th COP meeting, Nagoya, 18–29 October 2010, Agenda item 4.4.

[150] Cancun Declaration on Mainstreaming the Conservation and Sustainable Use of Biodiversity for Well-Being. Adopted at the 13th COP meeting on 3 December 2016.

[151] See PR Whitehorna, LM Navarro, M Schröterd, M Fernandez, X Rotllan-Puigg and A Marque, 'Mainstreaming biodiversity: A review of national strategies' (2019) 235 *Biological Conservation* 157.

[152] Sharm El-Sheikh Declaration Investing in Biodiversity for People and Planet. Adopted at the 14th COP meeting on 16 November 2018. Mainstreaming of Biodiversity in the Energy and Mining, Infrastructure, Manufacturing and Processing Sectors. CBD/COP/DEC/14/3. 14th COP, Sharm El-Sheikh.

[153] See N Schrijver, 'Introductory Note' to the ILA New Delhi Declaration of Principles of International Law Relating to Sustainable Development (2002) 49 *Netherlands International Law Review* 299.

84   *Mining and Minerals in International Law and Policy*

relevant to sustainable mineral resources management. It will finally then on the principle of integration and its importance for law, policy and institutional coherence at all levels.

A. The Status of Sustainable Development under International Law

The International Court of Justice, in the *Gabčikovo-Nagymaros* case, recognised the existence of sustainable development as a *concept* when expressing that the

> need to reconcile economic development with protection of the environment is aptly expressed in the concept of sustainable development. For the purposes of the present case, this means that the Parties together should look afresh at the effects on the environment of the operation of the Gabčikovo power plant. In particular, they must find a satisfactory solution for the volume of water to be released ...[154]

In his separate opinion, Judge Weeramantry upheld that sustainable development is a *principle* with normative value, rather than a mere concept. It is a 'principle of reconciliation' that steers a course between development and environmental protection.[155] An interpretation of the duty to prevent or at least mitigate potential harm to the environment by development activities as a *principle* of general international law was later upheld by the arbitral tribunal of the Iron Rhine Arbitration (Belgium/Netherlands) in May 2005 (confirming the position of Judge Weeramantry in the *Gabčikovo-Nagymaros* case).[156] In turn, the ICJ in the *Pulp Mills* case recalled sustainable development as an *objective* to guide negotiations between the parties when interpreting the need 'to strike a balance between the use of the waters and the protection of the river consistent with the objective of sustainable development'.[157] In the *Shrimp/Turtle* case, the WTO Appellate Body stressed the general acceptance of the *concept* 'as integrating economic and social development and environmental protection' by construing the Preamble to the WTO Agreement, which commits parties to 'the optimal use of the world's resources in accordance with the objective of sustainable development'.[158]

Scholarship shows great variance on the scope and status of the concept but, nonetheless, all views contend that the principle of integration is essential for realising sustainable development. For Dupuy, sustainable development is a

---

[154] *Gabčíkovo-Nagymaros Project (Hungary/Slovakia)*, Judgment, ICJ Reports (1997) 78, [140].

[155] *Gabčíkovo-Nagymaros Project*, Separate Opinion of Judge Weeramantry, 85.

[156] Iron Rhine ('Ijzeren Rijn') Railway between the Kingdom of Belgium and the Kingdom of the Netherlands, Decision of 24 May 2005, RIAA XXVII, 35–125, [59].

[157] *Pulp Mills on the River Uruguay (Argentina v Uruguay)*, Judgment, ICJ Reports (2010) 14, 74–75, [177]).

[158] 38 ILM 121 (1999) [129] at no 107.

'conceptual matrix' for articulating and reconciling the often inconsistent provisions of international economic law and international environmental law.[159] For Lowe, it is an interstitial norm that fulfils a hermeneutical function in modifying primary rules in judicial decisions.[160] Birnie, Boyle and Redgwell observe the procedural role of law in sustainable development by stating that whereas 'international law may not require development to be sustainable, it does require development decisions be the outcome of a process which promotes sustainable development'.[161] They also observe that 'an interpretation which makes the process of decision-making the key legal test of sustainable development, rather than the nature of the development, is implicitly supported by the *Gabčikovo-Nagymaros* case'. This approach distinguishes between the components of sustainable development (eg, the obligation to carry out environmental impact assessments (EIA), the duty to cooperate, the integration of development and environmental considerations in decision-making, taking into account the needs of intra- and inter-generational equity), some of which have reached the status of customary international law and some others having normative significance.

Barral systematises these different strands of scholarship and findings arising from the decisions of international tribunals. She contends that by being widely endorsed as an objective in 'hundreds of treaties', sustainable development aims at regulating state conduct through obligations of means or of best efforts or 'due diligence' obligations – as opposed to obligations of result – and that these obligations can be tested against the core constitutive elements of the concept.[162]

As an objective, sustainable development must thus influence the decision-making process of legal subjects; they will have to strive to achieve a balanced decision, considering environmental, social and economic aspects. A number of tools will also help to measure the adequacy of the conduct states adopt in the light of their obligation to promote sustainable development. On the other hand, as a hermeneutical tool, a review of the decisions of international courts sheds light on its use in assisting in the redefinition of conventional obligations. Parties are called on to review or adapt provisions with a view that these are to be consistent with the objective of sustainable development.

---

[159] P Dupuy, 'Où en-est le droit international de l'environnement à la fin du siecle?' (1997) 101 Revue générale de droit international public 873. See also, P Dupuy and J Viñuales, *International Environmental Law*, 2nd edn (Cambridge, Cambridge University Press, 2018) 60.

[160] V Lowe, 'Sustainable Development and Unsustainable Arguments' in A Boyle and D Freestone (eds), *International Law and Sustainable Development: Past Achievements and Future Challenges* (Oxford, Oxford University Press, 1999).

[161] Birnie, Boyle and Redgwell (n 84) 126–27; A Boyle and D Freestone, 'Introduction', in Boyle and Freestone, *International Law and Sustainable Development* (1999).

[162] V Barral, 'Sustainable Development in International Law: Nature and Operation of an Evolutive Legal Norm' (2012) 23 *The European Journal of International Law* 2.

86   *Mining and Minerals in International Law and Policy*

B. The Core Constitutive Elements of Sustainable Development

The Rio Declaration lays down the *substantive* and *procedural* elements of sustainable development. The substantive elements comprise the integration of the environmental dimension into the development process, the right to development, the sustainable use of natural resources and intra- and intergenerational equity. The *procedural* elements include public participation, access to information and environmental impact assessments (EIA). Integrated decision-making processes constitute the bedrock of sustainable development. Integration is the principle that holds all other principles together;[163] it is a technique to be used for achieving the objective of sustainable development.[164]

The New Delhi Declaration of Principles of International Law Relating to Sustainable Development adopted by the 70th Conference of the International Law Association (ILA) on 6 April 2002 ('the New Delhi Declaration')[165] identified seven principles that seek to integrate international environmental law, human rights law and international law in the field of development, with a view towards contributing to the further development of international law in the field of sustainable development and ensuring that their consolidation will serve as guidance for law-making or interpretation at domestic level.[166,167] These principles are: (i) integration and interrelationship, in relation to human rights and social, economic and environmental objectives; (ii) the duty of states to ensure sustainable use of natural resources (sustainable development having evolved from its original conception as a principle of conservation of resources, to a focus on their sustainable use while protecting biodiversity and biological resources);[168] (iii) equity and poverty eradication; (iv) common but differentiated responsibilities of states and other relevant actors,[169] drawing on the principle whereby developed countries have a heightened responsibility to promote sustainable development considering their contribution to environmental degradation and climate change;[170] (v) a precautionary approach

---

[163] J Dernbach, 'Achieving Sustainable Development: The Centrality and Multiple Facets of Integrated Decisionmaking' (2003) 10 *Indiana Journal of Global Legal Studies* 1, Art 10.

[164] Barral, 'Sustainable Development in International Law' (2012).

[165] The New Delhi Declaration updates and builds on the ILA Seoul Declaration on the Progressive Development of Principles of Public International Law relating to a New International Economic Order.

[166] Principle 27, Rio Declaration on Environment and Development. Ch 39 of Agenda 21 called for 'the further development of international law on sustainable development, giving special attention to the delicate balance between environmental and developmental concerns'.

[167] Schrijver, 'Introductory Note' (2002) 305.

[168] See Pinto, 'The Legal Context' (1998).

[169] New Delhi Declaration, Principle 3, 303.

[170] Rio Declaration, Principle 7 and the 1992 Framework Convention on Climate Change (UNFCCC) fully endorses the principle of common but differentiated responsibilities. The principle has reflected in differentiated treatment and legal commitments, and a duty to realise technology and financial transfers.

Law, Sustainable Resources Management and the Paradigm of Sustainability   87

to human health, natural resources and ecosystems that provides guidance in the case of uncertainty of the environmental impacts of development;[171] committing states and other relevant actors to avoid activities that can be harmful to 'human health, natural resources or ecosystems, including in the light of scientific uncertainty'; (vi) public participation, access to information and justice;[172] and (vii) good governance, which in the wording of the ILA Principles, demands from states and international governmental organisations the adoption of democratic and transparent decision-making procedures and financial accountability and measures to combat corruption; respect for the principle of due process, the rule of law and human rights; and the implementation of public procurement according to the WTO Code on Public Procurement. Good governance demands full endorsement of the Rio Declaration principles and social inclusion in decision-making. Good governance also requires respect for internal democratic governance and effective accountability from non-state actors, as well as CSR (an approach that is evolving towards a standard of responsible business conduct).

The principle of sustainable use of natural resources has reached firm status under treaty law but, unlike the extensive regimes existing on fisheries and water bodies, or for forestry protection, there is no comprehensive convention elaborating on guiding principles on mining and minerals.[173] Many reasons have been hypothesised to explain the 'invisibility' of specific regulation, such as challenges to establishing general principles due to the diversity of minerals, their uses and methods of extraction and wide range of environments in which it takes place, as well as the fact that their impacts are usually confined within the boundaries and jurisdiction of particular states.[174]

For some, mining is the quintessentially unsustainable activity; for others, WSSD and Rio+20 aptly express the accommodation of mining in a sustainable development framework. For others yet, mining can be compatible with sustainable development if the broader context, as well as the pre-Rio documents in the evolution of international environmental law, which deal with standards of

---

[171] New Delhi Declaration, Principle 3, 303.

[172] Principle 10 of Rio expresses that 'Environmental issues are best handled with the participation of all concerned citizens, at the relevant level'. It calls for 'appropriate access to information concerning the environment'; 'the opportunity to participate in decision-making processes' and 'effective access to justice and administrative proceedings'.

[173] See a review of calls for global action in D Humphreys, AE Bastida and A Hermann, 'Platforms for Strategic Dialogues on Mining and Minerals: A possible way forward', STRADE Strategic Dialogue on Sustainable Raw Materials for Europe (STRADE) EU Horizon 2020 Project; European Policy Brief No 4/2017.

[174] Dalupan (n 63). It has been observed that overarching multilateral governance initiatives for metals and minerals markets 'are practically non-existent' due to stark differences 'in interests, objectives, and instruments of choice': HG Hilpert and SA Mildner (eds), 'Fragmentation or Cooperation in Global Resource Governance? A Comparative Analysis of the Raw Materials Strategies of the G20', Stiftung Wissenschaft und Politik (SWP) and the Federal Institute for Geosciences and Natural Resources (BGR) RP (Berlin, 1 March 2013).

88 *Mining and Minerals in International Law and Policy*

resources use, are considered.[175] The latter is a pathway that had been discontinued and the one that UNEA Resolution 4/19 on Mineral Resources Governance calls to re-engage with.[176] A few years ago, following the inclusion of mining and minerals in the Plan of Implementation of WSSD in 2002, Dalupan pointed out that the general references to 'sustainable mining practices' and 'contribution of mining to sustainable development' fell short of proposing general criteria or binding governance regimes which advance on their interpretation, scope and application on mining and minerals. There has been indeed scarce enquiry into the elaboration of the precautionary principle, common but differentiated responsibility and sustainable use in the context of mining and minerals.[177]

As reviewed earlier in this chapter, the 1972 Stockholm documents dealt with aspects of resource utilisation and of shared benefits pertinent to sustainable use. The reference to UNCHE and the World Charter for Nature in UNEA Resolution 4/19 provide some pointers into the analysis of sustainability as we consider an industry that extracts metals which are depleted at the site of extraction but could eventually be used indefinitely. The recent reports of the International Resource Panel assert that this requires transformations towards systemic governance at all levels, including mainstreaming natural resource accounting.

C. Integrated Decision-Making Processes for Sustainable Resource Management

Widely acknowledged in international treaties and declarations, and broadly endorsed in states' constitutional charts and domestic legislation, sustainable development provides the normative basis for designing and redesigning regimes of natural resources law. Principle 4 of Rio establishes the 'centrality' of integrated decision-making process. Integrated decision-making processes promote the identification of issues in legal, governance and policy regimes; the use of tools to progressively advance sustainability and the SDGs, and of criteria for their evaluation. Integrated decision-making is the answer to the fragmented, piecemeal processes that have resulted in unsustainable outcomes.[178] I will expand on some aspects related to the principle of integration here from the point of view of the task of governments at national and sub-national levels (I will return to these

---

[175] Dalupan (n 63) 164.

[176] See IV.A above.

[177] ibid 166.

[178] Dernbach, 'Achieving Sustainable Development' (2003) (stating that 'Integrated decision-making offers a useful set of analytical tools to move national governments and other decisionmakers in the direction of sustainable development. It does so by identifying a basic set of issues that need to be addressed in all law and policymaking, and by providing a set of criteria against which to evaluate laws and policies in which sustainable development is sought or claimed').

Law, Sustainable Resources Management and the Paradigm of Sustainability 89

points in chapter six, which deals with mining law regimes under the jurisdiction of nation-states).

Procedural integrated decision-making denotes the means to integrate environmental and social dimensions into economic decisions in a simultaneous and coherent manner. It is a method or manner to think about all these factors in the decision-making process.[179] In the case of decisions about large-scale industrial projects, this entails multiple decisions expressed in multi-faceted licencing processes (EIAs, water permits, discharges, land access and community agreements). *Substantive* integrated decision-making provides, in turn, an avenue for the realisation of specific goals, such as the SDGs.

Regarding the *scope* of integration, Dernbach distinguishes between resource-based, issue-based and place-based integration, emphasising that the latter provides a more specific, manageable and localised locus for integration, which is consistent with the principle of subsidiarity. Sustainable resource management requires a combination of these. At the level of projects, place-based integration provides the 'right geographic scale' for decisions as they involve multi-level decisions at national and sub-national level. For this to occur, each level should steer action through the formulation of a vision and strategy, as well as sustainability indicators to facilitate monitoring.

Sustainability expands the *temporal* scale of decisions, as these should involve future scenarios (which are uncertain) to achieve intergenerational equity. The temporal dimension of decisions reinforces the need for a continuing flow of information about the environmental, social, climate and economic impacts of the activity, ecosystems and communities such decisions will ultimately affect, to facilitate flexible and adaptive management as well as actions to problems that might emerge.[180]

Integrated decision-making processes involve multiple layers of decisions and decision-makers, which should work in a mutually supportive manner towards sustainable development.[181] Integration occurs *vertically* through coordination and cooperation between different levels of authority within nation-states (eg, at the various federal, provincial and local levels) where each level is working within the sphere of their competence towards the same objective (although higher levels in a hierarchy usually correspond to 'formal authority over lower levels'). Vertical integration can also occur through softer modes at an international level (eg, by cooperation among nations and through the relationship with

---

[179] Walsh, 'El ambiente y el paradigma de la sustentabilidad' (2000); Dernbach (n 163) quoting K Wheeler, 'Introduction' in K Wheeler and A Perraca Bijur (eds), *Education for a Sustainable Future: A Paradigm of Hope for the 21st Century* (New York, Kluwer Academic/Plenum Publishers, 2000).

[180] Dernbach (n 163): 'From a law and policy perspective, the transition to sustainability will require the design and implementation of policies with much longer time frames than are used in most other decision-making. Another approach to this issue, implicit in the Kyoto Protocol, is to develop laws and policies directed toward interim goals, and periodically to set new or more ambitious goals with corresponding implementing mechanisms'.

[181] See UNGP, Principle 8 (on ensuring policy coherence). On vertical integration see Dernbach (n 163).

90   *Mining and Minerals in International Law and Policy*

the governing body of international climate change and environmental agreements). Integration between many decision-makers at the same hierarchical level also occurs *horizontally*. Rather than by coercion or through higher governance structures, coordination occurs through collaboration. The need here is for coordinating mechanisms (eg, spatial planning agendas, land use mechanisms at local government levels), information-sharing and cooperation measures.[182]

Attention to the role of law in integrated decision-making has focused for a long time on the *procedural* dimension. But it has been observed that taking into account environmental and social dimensions in decision-making is not a sufficient condition for sustainable outcomes. The SDGs have come to provide *substantive* content and direction to decision-making processes.

In terms of the appropriate institutional setting for integrated decision-making processes, recent years have witnessed a shift from sectoral and silo agencies in public administration to 'whole-of-government' or 'joined-up government' approaches that work as formal and informal networks. The movement is driven by increased complexity of problems, which require collaborative solutions, and open government approaches that engage citizens in planning, implementing and evaluating public services, and the growing role of Internet in changing the interaction between government and citizens.[183]

This chapter has explored the evolution of the treatment of mining and minerals in international law and international policy, from early claims over natural resources to exercising political and economic self-determination and control by peoples, to their place within the global sustainable development agenda. Sustainable development has been set as an objective of the global community and its elements are guiding decision-making processes. Further implementation of the SDGs is also opening avenues for the elaboration of guidance for their operationalisation. The SDGs hold great potential for customising commitments and obligations in processes and agreements at the national and local levels.

To be sure, the greater visibility of mining and minerals in the global sustainable development agenda underscores heightened international awareness of their role in a sustainable and equitable future. But the uptake of sustainable development is still very much unfinished business.[184] The hardest challenges are still to be found in how to operationalise sustainable development and transition towards societies that fully consider ecological sustainability simultaneously with social and economic equity when taking decisions about economic projects at all levels, from communities to national governments to global businesses, while internalising those costs.

---

[182] A few countries in Latin America show experimentation in multi-stakeholder consultation and collaboration in policy design and territorial planning.

[183] UN, 'Chapter 3: Taking a whole-of-government approach', United Nations E-Government Survey (2012), available at https://publicadministration.un.org/egovkb/Portals/egovkb/Documents/un/2012-Survey/Chapter-3-Taking-a-whole-of-government-approach.pdf.

[184] J Otto and J Cordes, *The Regulation of Mineral Enterprises: A Global Perspective on Economics, Law and Policy* (Colorado, RM MLF, 2002).

Law, Sustainable Resources Management and the Paradigm of Sustainability   91

The next chapter will look briefly into developments in the fields of international economic law (particularly on investment law), human rights and anti-corruption, and into the question of the responsibility of non-state actors. It will also examine emerging transnational governance. At one level, this will advance understanding of the international and transnational levels of legal and normative ordering concerning mining and minerals; the tension between values and objectives enshrined in these variegated fields of international law, and the extent to which they might help or hinder sustainability. At another level, this will provide insights into the interpenetration of these fields of international law and domestic legal systems, and the interplay of transnational standards, laying the grounds for elaboration of the configuration of authority concerning the regulation of mining and minerals.

4

Mining and Minerals in Fields of International Law and Governance

Chapter three reviewed the emerging attention to mining and minerals under international law against the backdrop of the post-war world order, following the creation of the United Nations and the Bretton Woods system, and the transition of international law as a system of coexistence and coordination of international relations (mainly between European states) towards a universal system of cooperation and including subjects of international law other than states, notably intergovernmental organisations. The progressive development of the principle of Permanent Sovereignty over Natural Resources, the development of the legal regime applicable to mining and minerals in areas beyond national jurisdiction, notably over the seabed in international waters, and most recently through the inclusion of mining and minerals in global action plans to advance sustainable development, all constitute key aspects of the law and governance of mining and minerals from an international law and policy perspective.

Over recent decades, the fields of international economic law, international human rights law, international environmental law and anti-corruption law, among others, have undergone significant development, with large numbers of countries making commitments through ratification of treaties which have important implications for the law and governance of mining and minerals. Each of these fields includes its own principles and institutions and is embedded in different normative values that might result in framing minerals as commodities and raw materials, real property and commercial assets, fruits of nature or natural heritage, the land where they lie as having special cultural and spiritual significance, or the environment their extraction affects, as commons.[1] These fragmented regimes reflect the diverging objectives and values of different actors in a 'pluralistic (global) society' and have mostly developed in a self-contained manner, without looking for coherence with other related fields.[2]

---

[1] On these developments for a range of regimes of natural resources law see L Cotula, 'Land, Property and Sovereignty in International Law', (2017) 25 *Cardozo Journal of International and Comparative Law* 219; R Barnes, *Property Rights and Natural Resources* (Oxford, Hart Publishing, 2009) 12.

[2] 'Fragmentation of International Law: Difficulties Arising from the Diversification and Expansion of International Law'. Report of the Study Group of the International Law Commission, Finalised by Martti Koskenniemi, International Law Commission, UN General Assembly, 58th session, Geneva, 1 May–9 June and 3 July–11 August 2006. A/CN.4/L.682, 13 April 2006. Also, E Benvenisti and GW Downs, 'The Empire's New Clothes: Political Economy and the Fragmentation of International Law' (2007) 60 *Stanford Law Review* 595.

Mining and Minerals in International Economic Law   93

This chapter will briefly review how mining and minerals are being dealt with under these specialised fields of international law, which is vital to the understanding of the complexity of the legal landscape. The focus of this chapter will be on international economic law, including WTO law and international investment law. It will also point at another evolving aspect of international law and policy of natural resources: the responsibility of transnational corporations and other business enterprises, the debate on their accountability, and the evolving standard of responsible business conduct. Finally, this chapter will address key governance initiatives that relate to, or have been specifically designed for, mining and minerals.

I. Mining and Minerals in International Economic Law

Mining and minerals, as other natural resources, have been in the background of the evolution of international economic law in the post-war period and are core components of the process of economic globalisation.[3] International economic law is a key block of the global architecture for trade and investment designed in the aftermath of the Second World War, which rests upon the institutions created by the Bretton Woods Conference in 1944. The Atlantic Charter of 1941, the joint declaration issued by US President Roosevelt and UK Prime Minister Churchill set the foundations for establishing a liberal economic order to bolster international economic transactions on the basis of comparative advantage and equal conditions to market access, articulating the post-war concerns for security of supply and access to natural resources.[4] The Bretton Woods Conference resulted in the creation of the core international financial and economic institutions for the regulation of money and trade: the International Monetary Fund (IMF); the International Bank for Reconstruction and Development (IBRD); also known as the 'World Bank'; and subsequently the conclusion of the General Agreement on Tariffs and Trade (GATT).[5]

---

[3] '[G]overnance and management of natural resources have formed a pivotal backdrop to the evolution of international economic law in the post-war period and have been critical components of the process of economic globalisation'. J Faundez and C Tan, 'Introduction: International Economic Law, Natural Resources and Sustainable Development' (June 2015) 11 *International Journal of Law in Context* 109.

[4] It states that '[T]hey will endeavor, with due respect for their existing obligations, to further the enjoyment by all states, great or small, victor or vanquished, of access, on equal terms, to the trade and to the raw materials of the world which are needed for their economic prosperity'. The Atlantic Charter, Declaration of Principles Issued by the President of the United States and the Prime Minister of the United Kingdom, 14 August 1941.

[5] The Articles of Agreement of the IMF include as a purpose of such institution 'To facilitate the expansion and balanced growth of international trade, and to contribute thereby to ... the development of the productive resources of all members as primary objectives of economic policy' (Art I (ii)), while the Articles of Agreement of the IBRD state as a purpose 'To promote the long-range balanced growth of international trade and the maintenance of equilibrium in balances of payments by encouraging international investment for the development of the productive resources of members, thereby

94 *Mining and Minerals in Fields of International Law and Governance*

The Bretton Woods institutions provided the foundations for the process of globalisation and the expansion of the neoliberal programme unleashed in the late 1980s, entailing the unprecedented rise of the economic interdependence of the world in the Internet era. Following the severe debt crisis of the 1980s and the curtailment of external finance, these institutions urged developing countries to undertake extensive economic policy reforms as a condition to access funding. The 'Washington Consensus' epitomised this set of economic policy reforms, including fiscal discipline; the redirection of public expenditure priorities; tax reform; financial and trade liberalisation; a competitive exchange rate; elimination of barriers to FDI; privatisation of state enterprises; deregulation of market entry and competition, and ensuring secure property rights.[6] A great number of developing countries ratified international economic treaties, including multilateral and bilateral investment protection treaties, and undertook extensive processes of reform of their domestic legal systems to support the creation of stable and predictable environments for investment. International economic law transitioned from comprising a few scattered rules to becoming perhaps 'the most important field of international law', as defined by: (i) the *volume* of treaties and decisions of international organisations and international bodies setting voluntary standards in a large number of areas; (ii) the *scope* of rules, and the extent to which they deal with matters traditionally considered as falling within the realm of the exclusive domestic jurisdiction of states, and (iii) their *efficacy*, due to enhanced enforceability in light of the creation of international tribunals competent to adjudicate disputes regarding issues of international economic law.[7] International economic law crystallised the tenets of the Washington Consensus, signalling a substantial departure from the New International Economic Order (NIEO), in which developing countries had sought to steer the international economic system toward supporting their development objectives.[8]

The most radical prescriptions of the neoliberal programme have been partially delegitimised through financial and economic crises (and alternative models of development and societies), paving the way for both more regulation and state intervention in the economy and calls for increased policy space and the operationalisation of the Sustainable Development Goals (SDGs).[9]

---

assisting in raising productivity, the standard of living and conditions of labor in their territories' (Art I (iii)). The GATT preamble, in turn, includes among its objectives 'the full use of the resources of the world'.

[6] The 'Washington Consensus' was a blueprint originally designed for Latin America by international institutions such as the World Bank and the International Monetary Fund in the early 1990s. J Williamson, 'What Washington means by policy reform' in J Williamson (ed), *Latin American Adjustment: How Much Has Happened?* (Washington, Institute for International Economics, 1990).

[7] J Faundez, 'International Economic Law and Development Before and After Neo-Liberalism' in J Faundez and C Tan (eds), *International Law, Economic Globalization and Development* (Cheltenham and Northampton, Edward Elgar Publishing, 2010) 10–33.

[8] ibid.

[9] M Krajewski and RT Hoffman, 'Introduction' in *Research Handbook on Foreign Direct Investment* (Cheltenham and Northampton, Edward Elgar Publishing, 2019) 2. See ch 3 on the Monterrey Consensus.

International economic law encompasses a broad range of disciplines dealing with the bilateral or multilateral conduct of states in economic affairs, as well as with the conduct of private parties in cross-border economic and business transactions. These include international law related to trade, investment, economic integration, intellectual property rights, financing and monetary aspects. It also relates to the field of law and development.[10]

A. Mining and Minerals under WTO Law

Minerals play a key role in the organisation of the global economy and international trade law, setting the rules and customs governing trade linkages between countries and overseeing demands from Member States in the implementation of regulations that, among others, set restrictions to the import and export of minerals and other natural resources.[11] The GATT, which came into force in 1948, provided the foundations of the international trade regime, which has been constructed on a multilateral basis. The GATT was aimed at being applied provisionally but remained in place until the conclusion of the Uruguay Round in 1994, which set up the World Trade Organisation (WTO). The WTO's main objective is to promote trade liberalisation and to administer the international trade regime.[12] The original 23 parties to the GATT have expanded to 164 WTO Member States by 2016.

Trade agreements generally grant preferential access to markets and offer a transparent and predictable rules-based system. As a counterpart, they require actions to reduce barriers and promote trade, thereby setting restrictions on the policy space of contracting parties, including with regard to the scope of permissible counter-measures. The key principles of the international trade regime are the non-discrimination principles of Most-Favoured Nation (MFN) and National Treatment.[13] MFN prohibits discrimination between trading partners and requires that any advantage or privilege granted to one WTO member applies immediately and unconditionally to 'like products' originating from any other WTO Member State, except for provisions set by applicable bilateral and regional free trade agreements.[14] The national treatment principle, in turn, prohibits discrimination

---

[10] See Ch 2.VII.

[11] K Kulovesi, 'International Trade: Natural Resources and the World Trade Organization', in E Morgera and K Kulovesi (eds), *Research Handbook on International Law and Natural Resources* (Cheltenham and Northampton, Edward Elgar Publishing, 2016), 46–65, 52.

[12] International trade law had evolved through eight successive rounds of trade negotiations by then. The package adopted in the Uruguay Round expanded the original scope on reducing tariffs and related trade barriers, and included new trade agreements, notably the General Agreement on Trade in Services, the Agreement on Trade-related Aspects of Intellectual Property, the Agreement on Technical Barriers to Trade and the Agreement on Subsidies and Countervailing Measures.

[13] Kulovesi, 'International Trade' (2016) 52–53.

[14] ibid.

by the receiving state against goods imported from another WTO Member State with respect to taxation and regulations applied by the receiving state. This means that WTO Member States are required to treat imported and locally produced 'like' products as having equal standing. Apart from these two principles, the WTO regime also imposes quantitative trade restrictions upon its members. The MFN and national treatment principles, along with the prohibition on quantitative trade restrictions, place limitations on the policy space of governments for addressing environmental problems and protecting natural resources.[15]

Minerals are defined under the category of 'primary products', a term that is used as a synonym of 'primary commodity', which refers to products in their natural form or which have undergone processing in order to be marketed in substantial volumes in international trade (Ad Article XVI Section B, para 2, GATT).[16] A threshold issue under the WTO system is when natural resources qualify as 'goods' or 'products' within the meaning assigned by it. The majority view in the literature is that WTO rules apply to natural resources as they are extracted or harvested only. This implies that WTO members are free to decide whether, and to what extent, they will undertake mining or harvesting their natural resources. But if they decide to do so, they will generally have to make the extracted or harvested resources available to other WTO members.[17]

New trade agreements have started to include environmental and sustainable resource management provisions. Swift changes in the use of minerals and extraction of ore embedded in circular economy models need supportive multi-level trade policies. This nexus is starting to be explored.[18]

B. Mining under International Investment Law

i. The 'Treatification' of International Investment Law

Until the 1990s, the relationship between host states and foreign investors in respect of large resource projects situated in developing countries was typically

---

[15] ibid.

[16] See MG Desta, 'Commodities, International Regulation of Production and Trade', *Max Planck Encyclopedia of Public International Law*, Max Planck Foundation for International Peace and the Rule of Law under the direction of Rüdiger Wolfrum, available at https://opil.ouplaw.com/view/10.1093/law:epil/9780199231690/law-9780199231690-e1511.

[17] M Bronckers and K Maskus, 'China Raw Materials: A Controversial Step Towards Evenhanded Exploitation of Natural Resources' (2014) 13 *World Trade Review* 393. See further I Espa, *Export Restrictions on Critical Minerals and Metals: Testing the Adequacy of WTO Disciplines* (Cambridge, Cambridge University Press, 2015). See analysis on the *China – Raw Materials* and *China – Rare Earths* cases and potential lessons for sustainable management of mineral commodities in I Espa and M Oehl, 'Rules and Practices of International Law for the Sustainable Management of Mineral Commodities, including Nickel, Copper, Bauxite and Rare Earths', in report of ILA Sydney Conference (2018) 'Role of International Law in Sustainable Natural Resource Management for Development', ILA Committee on the Role of International Law in Sustainable Natural Resource Management for Development, section III.1, 9–11.

[18] OECD and RE-CIRCLE Resource Efficiency and Circular Economy Project, 'International Trade and the Transition to a Circular Economy' Policy Highlights (2018).

governed by investment or development contracts (ie, private law instruments) and domestic investment law taking the form of codes or statutes.[19] Today, even though domestic investment law and contracts usually include standards of treatment and due process provisions, the role of state contracts in protecting foreign investment has been replaced to a great extent by international investment agreements taking the form of treaties, ie, instruments of international law.[20] Indeed, since the late 1980s, there has been an ostensible movement towards what has been called the 'treatification' of international investment law, meaning that foreign investors in many parts of the world are largely protected by bilateral and/or multilateral investment treaties.[21]

The international investment regime has been built on a bilateral, rather than multilateral, basis.[22] The most common type of investment treaty consists of Bilateral Investment Treaties (BITs), which are forged between two countries to promote and protect investment made by investors of one country in the territory of the other, and which offer both countries substantive protections or guarantees and procedural protections to covered investors. Other investment treaties comprise bilateral and regional free trade agreements[23] incorporating investment chapters or provisions (such as the North American Free Trade Agreement (NAFTA), having been replaced by the United States–Mexico–Canada Agreement (USMCA) with effect from March 2020). By September 2019, it was reported that there were 2354 BITs and 313 treaties with investment provisions in force.[24] There is no global agreement on investment, but there are specific investment issues that relate to trade; these are dealt with under the WTO system. The General Agreement on Trade in Services (GATS) covers foreign investment in services as one of the four modes of trading services. The Agreement on Trade-Related Investment Measures (TRIMs), which applies to measures that affect trade in goods only, in turn prohibits investment measures related to trade that are inconsistent with core provisions of the 1994 GATT (Article III on national treatment, or Article XI on quantitative restrictions), such as local content restrictions. By ratifying international investment agreements, contracting states are bound to conform to their provisions under domestic law and they can no longer invoke domestic law to defend against breaches of international law.

International investment treaties often provide for the settlement of disputes by means of consultations and negotiations between the parties or between

---

[19] See ch 2.VII.

[20] J Viñuales, 'Foreign Direct Investment: International Investment Law and Natural Resource Governance' in Morgera and Kulowesi (eds), *Research Handbook* (2016) 27.

[21] J Salacuse, 'The Emerging Global Regime for Investment' (2010) 51 *Harvard International Law Journal* 427. See also J Salacuse, *The Three Laws of International Investment – National, Contractual, and International Frameworks for Foreign Capital* (Oxford, Oxford University Press, 2013).

[22] Salacuse, 'Emerging Global Regime' (2010).

[23] See ICSID, Other Investment Treaties, available at icsid.worldbank.org/en/Pages/resources/Other-Treaties.aspx.

[24] UNCTAD, Investment Policy Hub, International Investment Agreements Navigator.

the host state and a covered foreign investor, and for recourse to international arbitration by the parties or a foreign investor, which enforces the commitments made by states and makes breaches actionable through a direct right of redress on the part of private investors. By September 2019, 163 countries had signed, and 154 had deposited their instruments of ratification of, the International Convention on the Settlement of Investment Disputes between states and Nationals of Other States (ICSID) concluded in 1965 under the auspices of the World Bank.[25] Since the late 1990s, the number of cases of treaty-based investor–state disputes submitted to ICSID tribunals has grown exponentially. The cumulative number of known investor–state cases had risen to at least 1,023 as of 31 December 2019,[26] with 745 having been brought before ICSID.[27] Other investment arbitrations were initiated under the Arbitration Rules of the United Nations Commission on International Trade Law (UNCITRAL), the Stockholm Chamber of Commerce and the Cairo Regional Centre for International Commercial Arbitration, or were submitted to ad hoc arbitration. Twenty-four per cent of all cases registered under the ICSID Convention were related to mining and oil and gas activities.[28] Mining projects are prone to investor–state disputes because their investment features, such as large upfront capital expenditure and the implementation of unmovable assets with a long payback period,[29] increase the risk of interference by the host country authorities through expropriation or other regulatory measures, and national judiciaries may not be equipped to deal with the complexities presented by such projects.

ii. Investment Standards and International Mining Disputes

At the core of each investment treaty is the treatment promised to be provided by the host country to investors from the home country. By constraining the host country's behaviour (attaching safeguards to its freedom in taking administrative or legislative actions) and disciplining its actions that are held to violate treaty-based protective standards, the objective is to protect foreign investors against the risk that results from 'placing their assets under a host country's jurisdiction'.[30] Standards of treatment of foreign investment in a host country embedded in invest-ment protection treaties usually include guarantees against unlawful expropriation or lawful expropriation without compensation; fair and equitable treatment; full protection and security; national treatment (treatment of foreign investors like domestic investors in the host state in like circumstances); most-favoured-nation treatment (meaning that an investor from a home state covered by the treaty is

---

[25] See ICSID, Database of ICSID Member States.

[26] United Nations Conference on Trade and Development, Investment Dispute Settlement Navigator.

[27] ICSID, 'The ICSID caseload: Statistics' (2020) 1, 7.

[28] ibid 12.

[29] HG Burnett and LA Bret, *Arbitration of International Mining Disputes* (Oxford, Oxford University Press, 2017) 39.

[30] Salacuse, 'Emerging Global Regime' 440, 445.

given the best treatment available to any other foreign investor in the host state); and treatment in accordance with international law (also known as the minimum international standard of treatment that the host state is required to afford to foreign investors in their capacity as 'aliens', a wider group of protected subjects than 'investors').[31] This standard denotes those rules of general international law that a state must always observe in its relations towards aliens, ie, non-nationals.

As suggested by Resolution 1803 on PSONR, historically the main concern regarding investment disciplines related to expropriation without compensation and to potential denials of justice were frequently related.[32] The basic principles of customary international law on expropriation, which recognise a state's sovereign right to expropriate, provide that foreign-owned property may not be expropriated, or be subject to a measure tantamount to expropriation, unless four conditions are met: (i) the measure is for a public purpose; (ii) it is taken in accordance with applicable laws and due process; (iii) it is non-discriminatory; and (iv) it is accompanied by full compensation.[33]

A distinction has been drawn between *direct expropriation*, which entails the actual taking of property by direct means, including the loss of all, or almost all, useful control over property, and *indirect taking*, where the measure deprives the owner of substantially the whole of the anticipated economic benefit of the property, without formally expropriating him.[34] A number of well-known direct expropriations of mining and oil operations took place during the 1960s and 1970s,[35] but they are rarer today.[36] While *direct expropriation* affects the legal title itself, in *indirect expropriation* the investor maintains formal title over its investment but is substantially deprived of the economic use and enjoyment of rights to it.[37] Increased taxes, in-country beneficiation requirements, state or nationals' equity participation, denials, withdrawals or non-renewal of mining licences or permits as well as changes in environmental regulations, bans and moratoriums, are among the measures alleged to have resulted in partial or

---

[31] ibid 445; Burnett and Bret (n 29) 267.

[32] Viñuales, 'Foreign Direct Investment' (2016) 31.

[33] See Burnett and Bret (n 29) 268.

[34] See UNCTAD, 'Expropriation', UNCTAD Series on Issues in International Investment Agreements II (New York and Geneva, 2012). There is no generally accepted and clear definition of the concept of indirect taking and what distinguishes it from non-compensable regulation.

[35] See ch 3.III.

[36] A recent ICSID case was *Quiroborax SA, Non-Metallic Minerals SA and Allan Fosk Kaplún v Plurinational State of Bolivia* concerning the revocation in 2004 of mining concessions in Salar de Uyuni (upon a Decree issued by the President grounded in a law adopted in 2003 that had vested the Executive with the power to declare null the mineral rights liable to sanctions by laws and regulations). The Tribunal found that this constituted direct expropriation as it effectively transferred the title of mining concessions to the state. ICSID Case No ARB/06/2. In another ICSID case, *Carnegie Minerals Limited v Republic of The Gambia*, the Tribunal found that revocation of the mining licence and the confiscation of minerals' stockpiles amounted to unlawful expropriation. ICSID Case No ARB/09/19 (Award, 14 July 2015, not public, see Burnett and Bret (n 29) 270.

[37] Burnett and Bret (n 29) 269.

100 *Mining and Minerals in Fields of International Law and Governance*

total dispossession of mining companies' investors and referred by investors to arbitration tribunals.[38]

With regard to *indirect expropriation*, one important manifestation is the so-called *regulatory taking*, where deprivation of property takes place through regulatory interference by a host state in the use of an investor's property or with the enjoyment of the property's benefits. In this context, a main challenge lies in drawing a distinction between, on the one hand, the legitimate exercise of regulatory powers to tax and provide for the protection of the environment and other issues of public interest that, therefore, are not subject to compensation, and, on the other hand, measures amounting to expropriation that require compensation.[39] *Creeping expropriation*, in turn, results from the cumulative effect of a series of acts or measures that incrementally deprive the investor of the economic value or benefit of its investment or ownership rights, where no individual act or measure in itself would amount to an expropriation.[40]

The Fair and Equitable Treatment (FET) standard does not have a precise content, in that most investment protection treaties do not include a definition; its content and scope are determined by arbitral tribunals on a case-by-case basis. Arbitral jurisprudence, however, shows ample use of prior arbitral rulings and increasing convergence on the application of the FET standard to discipline the exercise of the sovereign powers of host states.[41] The FET standard often overlaps with, and is believed by many to include, the international minimum standard of treatment applicable to aliens, a category of subjects of which investors form a part.[42] The protection of investors' legitimate expectations; the requirement of stability, predictability and consistency of the legal framework; procedural due process and denial of justice; and substantive due process and protection against

---

[38] ibid 43–53. An example of an indirect expropriation claim is provided by the case brought by Glamis Gold, Ltd., a Canadian mining corporation, in which it argued that the United States, through federal and state actions, had expropriated the mining rights it owned in its Imperial Project (which had been acquired in accordance with the General Mining Law of 1872 that applies to public lands in the US). The project is located in the vicinity of an Indian Pass Area that had been categorised as a Critical Environmental Concern under the California Desert Conservation Area Plan, established in turn under the Federal Land Policy and Management Act. Glamis specifically alleged that regulations adopted by the State of California requiring backfilling and recontouring of open-pit mining operations where the project was located had rendered their project economically unfeasible. The Tribunal found that those measures were not of an economic impact amounting to rendering their investment valueless and so denied Glamis' claim for the expropriation of the granted mining rights. *Glamis Gold, Ltd v United States of America*, UNCITRAL. Award of 8 June 2009, § 14.

[39] See UNCTAD, 'Expropriation' (2012). Burnett and Bret (n 29) 273.

[40] Burnett and Bret (n 29) 273.

[41] S Schill, 'Fair and Equitable Treatment, the Rule of Law and Comparative Public Law', in S Schill (ed), *International Investment Law and Comparative Public Law* (Oxford, Oxford University Press, 2010) 159.

[42] ibid. See also UNCTAD, 'Fair and Equitable Treatment', UNCTAD Series on Issues in International Investment Agreements II (New York and Geneva, 2012) 8; A Newcombe and L Paradell, *Law and Practice of Investment Treaties: Standards of Treatment* (Kluwer Law International, Alphen aan den Rijn, 2009) 255.

Mining and Minerals in International Economic Law   101

discrimination and arbitrariness[43] have been identified as components of the FET standard in the literature and arbitral jurisprudence.[44]

An investor's legitimate expectations may be based on assurances, undertakings or representations arising from contractual or non-contractual commitments, legal provisions of written or verbal communications from high-level government officials – on which the investor reasonably and legitimately relies in making the investment. Host states may be liable for breaching the FET standard if they are found to fail honouring those assurances.[45] One of the constituent elements of the FET standard, which is also linked to the international minimum standard of treatment (of aliens *qua* aliens), is due process.[46] Due process can be described as a set of principles regarding 'minimum standards in the administration of justice of such elementary fairness and general application in the legal systems of the world that they have become international legal standards'.[47] For instance, some of these principles are: no unlimited detention without trial; no identity between prosecutor and judge; and the right to have a defence and to be heard before condemnation.[48] As regards the application of this principle in international investment case law, a denial of due process has been found in cases whenever there is a lack of participatory procedure or the local judicial system has not made any (timely) response to the investor's demands.[49] Arbitral tribunals have been reluctant to establish a FET standard violation based on mere deficiencies or irregularities in the procedure.[50]

The poor interface between mining titles and environmental and social regulation is increasing regulatory risk and leads to disputes being referred to arbitral tribunals. I have argued that such cases are often due to deficits of legal and

---

[43] Schill, 'Fair and Equitable Treatment' (2010) 159–60.

[44] J Stone, 'Arbitrariness, the Fair and Equitable Treatment Standard, and the International Law of Investment' (2012) 25 *Leiden Journal of International Law* 77; R Dolzer, 'Fair and Equitable Treatment: A Key Standard in Investment Treaties' (2005) 39 *International Lawyer* 87.

[45] In *Gold Reserve Inc v Bolivarian Republic of Venezuela*, the claimant had held the Brisas mining concession for more than 20 years and the Unicorn mining concession for more than 10 years without receiving objections from any government administration. The concessions were terminated on grounds of alleged failure to comply with a number of mining titles' obligations and failure to commence exploitation within seven years, citing the claimant's lack of solvency (§ 26 and 28, Award). The Tribunal found that the claimant had 'good reasons to rely on the continuing validity of its mining titles and rights and an expectation that it would obtain the required authorization to start the exploitation of the concessions' (§ 579, Award) and that the reasons for termination were due to 'the change of political priorities' of the administration (§ 580, Award). The same award interpreted the host state had breached the FET standard through a conduct displaying a 'lack of transparency, consistency and good faith in dealing with an investor' (§ 591, Award). ICSID Case No ARB(AF)/09/1.

[46] Newcombe and Paradell, *Law and Practice of Investment Treaties* (2009) 238, 244 and 279.

[47] W Friedmann, 'The Uses of General Principles in the Development of International Law' (1963) 57 *American Journal of International Law* 290.

[48] ibid 290.

[49] R Kläger, *Fair and Equitable Treatment in International Investment Law* (Cambridge, Cambridge University Press, 2011) 227.

[50] ibid.

102   *Mining and Minerals in Fields of International Law and Governance*

regulatory design.[51] Delays or denials of operating permits and claims for breaches of 'legitimate expectations' on the part of investors are often caused by: confusion and ambiguity regarding the rights of exploration holders and in the transition from exploration to exploitation; weaknesses in the sequencing of environmental and social permits and assessments, and of mining titles, paucity of environmental and social information available for decision-making prior the granting of titles; shortcomings in guidance for the preparation of environmental and social impact assessments, and in the participation of local communities, as well as deficiencies in the coordination between government authorities granting different types of titles and permits.[52]

iii. A 'Global Regime Governing Investment'

BITs and other investment treaties have undeniably transformed the relationship between host states and foreign investors. For some, the conclusion of such treaties and the interpretation of standards such as 'fair and equitable treatment' through arbitral awards is showing the emergence of a 'global regime governing foreign investment',[53] a kind of public *lex mercatoria* regulating host states' powers as exercised in relation to foreign investors, thus filling a 'quasi-constitutional' function linked to the rule of law.[54] It must, however, be kept in mind that the conclusion of investment treaties is still an *exercise* of sovereignty by the state parties to the treaty; the issue is usually how the particular treaty invoked before an arbitral tribunal treats the host country's regulatory measures that are alleged to violate the substantive guarantees set forth in the treaty.

In connection with arbitral awards issued in mining disputes, Burnett and Bret have noted that the publication of a considerable number of these awards is contributing to expanding knowledge of the sources on which customary law relating to the mining industry might develop.[55] Drawing on the literature on the

---

[51] AE Bastida and L Bustos, 'Towards Regimes for Sustainable Mineral Resources Management. Constitutional Reform, Law and Judicial Precedents in Latin America' in G Charbonnier; H Campodónico and S Tezanos Vásquez (eds), Special Issue on Alternative Pathways to Sustainable Development: Lessons from Latin America (2007, special issue) *International Development Policy, Revue internationale de politique de développement*; see also ch 6.VI below.

[52] IGF, 'Background Document: Legal Framework of Environmental and Social Impact Assessment in the Mining Sector' (January 2019). See also ch 6.

[53] See J Salacuse, 'Making transnational law work through regime-building: the case of international investment law' in P Bekker, R Dolzer and M Waibel (eds), *Making Transnational Law Work in the Global Economy – Essays in Honour of Detlev Vagts* (Cambridge, Cambridge University Press, 2010) 406.

[54] Cf Schill (n 41) 154, observing that 'fair and equitable treatment can be understood as embodying the rule of law as a standard that the legal systems of host states have to embrace in their treatment of foreign investors' (159). See also K Vandevelde, 'A Unified Theory of Fair and Equitable Treatment' (2010) 43 *International Law and Politics*, 52. The author explains that '[I]nternational arbitral awards interpreting the fair and equitable treatment standard have incorporated the substantive and procedural principles of the rule of law into that standard'.

[55] Burnett and Bret (n 29) 299–300.

development of '*lex petrolea*', they observe that a '*lex mineralia*' is emerging, ie, 'transnational rules that supplement or, in some rarer cases, supplant domestic rules governing certain categories of mining disputes.[56] As examples, they point to international disputes regarding: (i) expropriation or nationalisation of foreign-owned entities; and (ii) the validity and application of stabilisation provisions, from which awards one could draw emerging guiding principles for dealing with this kind of dispute. Furthermore, the authors underscore that arbitral awards are: (i) relying significantly on transnational environmental and social standards and principles as yardsticks for assessing culpability of a party's conduct; and (ii) contributing to the further development and dissemination of technical standards for valuation of mineral properties (eg, CIMVAL and JORC).[57]

The use of the analogous '*lex petrolea*' has not gone uncriticised. To be sure, treaties, international custom and general principles of law are the main sources of international investment law, with jurisprudence and doctrine being subsidiary means for the determination of rules of law. Most arbitrations of investment disputes are treaty-based; therefore, certain principles and procedural rules are enshrined under treaties but not under international custom. What has actually occurred is that, as a result of the large volume of BITs and multilateral treaties that have been concluded (the 'treatification' of international investment law phenomenon), there has been a standardisation of investment protection that to a certain extent competes with custom, but the former should not be confused with the latter.[58] It has further been argued that recognising common principles of petroleum or mining law and their application, including by a series of arbitral tribunals, does not justify the use of the terms '*lex petrolea*' or '*lex mineralia*', which could rather be expressed more clearly as 'transnational petroleum law' or 'transnational mining law'.[59]

iv. Investment Treaties and the Question of Policy Space

The design of investment treaties, the content of arbitral decisions dealing with investor–state disputes and the rise in such disputes all advance on aspects of a public policy nature, on the capacity of the state to regulate for the public interest. There is extensive debate as to what should be the proper counterweight to the rights of investors protected under international investment agreements. While the current system was merely an exception to the principle of PSONR, over time it has 'grown out of proportion' and come to be perceived as the rule rather than the

---

[56] ibid.

[57] ibid.

[58] See J Pérez-Vera, 'Las fuentes del Derecho Internacional de las inversiones y el riesgo jurídico estatal' (2007) *Revista Internacional de Arbitraje* 17.

[59] See T Daintith, 'Against "*Lex Petrolea*"' (2017) *Journal of World Energy Law and Business* 1. See further A Maniruzzaman, 'The *Lex Mercatoria* and International Contracts: A Challenge for International Commercial Arbitration?, (1999) 14 *American University International Law Review* 657; Bekker, Dolzer and Waibel (eds), *Making Transnational Law Work in the Global Economy* (2010).

exception, with expanding standards covering a wider range of disciplines,[60] often at the expense of the policy space that states require to implement commitments to advance the SDGs and climate action. This disparity is especially problematic for developing countries, which are in the process of building and strengthening their institutions, often with limited economic means.[61]

One great source of controversy has been the extensive use of umbrella clauses that, whenever in place, elevate breaches of contractual clauses to breaches of international (conventional) law, thereby providing direct recourse to arbitral tribunals. Another such critique has been the widening interpretation of state actions and omissions included under the FET standard, particularly on the range of government actions interpreted as creating 'legitimate expectations'.[62] Last but not least, the juxtaposition of a broadening protection afforded to foreign investors compared with the conspicuous absence of business obligations under international law, a matter that has attracted a great deal of attention in the context of the NIEO, has become ever more apparent and is a matter of renewed discussion and framing along the agenda to promote the SDGs and protect and respect human rights.[63]

As a reaction, a counter trend is seeking to rebalance the regime by placing greater emphasis on each state's policy space, which would include general exceptions in investment treaties to protect public health, safety or the environment.[64] More recent BITs are showing greater understanding of their public policy implications by referring to sustainable development, the environment, labour rights or health and safety, global standards such as the UN Global Compact and the OECD Guidelines for Multinational Enterprises and the UN 2030 Agenda for Sustainable Development; human rights obligations and standards; and the preservation of regulatory space more generally.[65] Meanwhile, human rights law is starting to feature in the reasoning of arbitral tribunals, and it is being argued that the SDGs should inform the assessment of international investment agreements.[66]

Greater emphasis on coherence between international legal subsystems is stressing that the conclusion of investment and trade treaties should be preceded by human rights impact assessments which take account of the overall positive and negative impacts of trade and investment treaties on human rights, including the

---

[60] See Viñuales (n 20) 30; G Van Harten, *Investment Treaty Arbitration and Public Law* (Oxford University Press, 2007) (arguing that an international judicial body should replace the current investment arbitration in line with criteria of public law adjudication).

[61] UN Human Rights Council, 'Protect, respect and remedy: a framework for business and human rights: report of the Special Representative of the Secretary-General on the Issue of Human Rights and Transnational Corporations and Other Business Enterprises, John Ruggie,' 7 April 2008, A/HRC/8/5,36.

[62] See Viñuales (n 20) 31ff.

[63] Krajewski and Hoffman, 'Introduction' (2019) 2.

[64] Viñuales (n 20). See UNGP, Principle 9.

[65] IIA Issues Note, 'Taking Stock of IIA Reform: Recent Developments', no 3, UNCTAD (June 2019).

[66] L Johnson, 'FDI, international investment agreements and the sustainable development goals' in Krajewski and Hoffman (n 9) 126–48.

realisation of the right to development, and which fully consider the human rights obligations of states consistently with the primacy clause of Article 103 of the UN Charter. It is also argued that future economic treaties should include provisions expressly dealing with human rights obligations.[67] Furthermore, in 2017, UNCITRAL mandated its Working Group III to work on the reform of the investor–state dispute settlement system.

II. Mining and Minerals in International Human Rights Law

A. The Human Rights System

The UN Charter is the starting point of a normative system that establishes obligations for states to protect human rights, and mechanisms of protection through monitoring international mechanisms imposed upon the parties in a treaty regarding those obligations. It also grounds international cooperation towards the universal respect, and realisation, of human rights and fundamental freedoms (Article 1.3, UN Charter).[68] Actions towards this objective are considered paramount to 'peaceful and friendly relations among nations based on respect for the principle of equal rights and self-determination of peoples' (Article 55, UN Charter).

The Universal Declaration of Human Rights[69] and the implementing International Covenants on Civil and Political Rights and on Economic, Social and Cultural Rights of 1966[70] form the crux of human rights (the International Bill of Human Rights). The Universal Declaration of Human Rights sets out the core principles of universality, interdependence and indivisibility, equality and non-discrimination,[71] and that human rights simultaneously entail both rights

---

[67] UN, Economic and Social Council, Committee on Economic, Social and Cultural Rights. General comment No 24 (2017) on state obligations under the International Covenant on Economic, Social and Cultural Rights in the context of business activities, E/C.12/GC/24, 10 August 2017, para 13.

[68] See M Pinto, *Temas de derechos humanos*, 4th edn (Buenos Aires, Editores del Puerto, 2006) 15–16.

[69] GA Resolution 217 (III). International Bill of Human Rights. Adopted at its 183th plenary meeting, 10 December 1948.

[70] International Covenant on Civil and Political Rights. Adopted by the General Assembly of the United Nations on 19 December 1966. UNTS, vol 999, 172. International Covenant on Economic, Social and Cultural Rights. Adopted by the General Assembly of the United Nations on 16 December 1966. UNTS, vol 993, 3.

[71] Reaffirmed by the Vienna Declaration adopted at the World Conference on Human Rights in Vienna on 25 June 1993. Endorsed by GA Resolution 48/121. World Conference on Human Rights. Adopted at its 85th plenary meeting, 20 December 1993. See Art 5. 'All human rights are universal, indivisible and interdependent and interrelated. The international community must treat human rights globally in a fair and equal manner, on the same footing, and with the same emphasis. While the significance of national and regional particularities and various historical, cultural and religious backgrounds must be borne in mind, it is the duty of states, regardless of their political, economic and cultural systems, to promote and protect all human rights and fundamental freedoms.'

106   *Mining and Minerals in Fields of International Law and Governance*

and obligations from duty bearers and rights' owners. These have been reiterated in numerous international and regional human rights conventions, declarations, and resolutions, as well as constitutions.[72] While in a first stage of the evolution of human rights law, these have been identified in resolutions of the UN General Assembly, in a second stage these have been crystallised into treaties.[73]

By ratifying treaties that consecrate human rights, states are bound to the *substantive* obligation of respecting, protecting and fulfilling those rights; abstaining from interfering with their enjoyment; guaranteeing the full enjoyment and exercise of the rights protected to every person within their jurisdiction, and adopting all necessary measures for their effectiveness.[74] The objective of 'progressively achieving full realisation of rights' is a fundamental concept steering the obligations of states that become parties to treaties that promote economic, social and cultural rights inasmuch as they entail a commitment to adopting the necessary measures at a domestic level, as well as through international assistance and cooperation, to the maximum extent of their available resources in accordance to the level of development.

States ratifying human rights treaties undertake *erga omnes partes* obligations. They are bound to other states parties and also to individuals or groups under their jurisdiction.[75] Governments must adopt domestic legislation and undertake actions consistent with their obligations and duties under those treaties. If they fail to put in place domestic legal proceedings that adequately deal with human rights abuses, they are subject to the individual complaints or communications available under regional or international levels.

B. Human Rights and Resource Development

Mining can provide the resources needed for furtherance of human rights and the SDGs. But operations can also potentially infringe on the whole spectrum of human rights, civil and political, and economic, social, cultural and environmental, in various ways. Operations can have deleterious effects and breach the rights to water and the environment. Mining projects might involve the acquisition of land from vulnerable local landowners, landholders or indigenous peoples. They may lack formal title and face dispossession and displacement that may breach their right to food when people depend on land for their livelihoods, the interdependent rights of health and shelter, with heightened gender impacts, and the right to

---

[72] European Convention for the Protection of Human Rights and Fundamental Freedoms. Signed at Rome, on 4 November 1950 (came into force on 3 September 1953), UNTS vol 213, 221. American Convention on Human Rights: Pact of San José, Costa Rica. Signed at San José, Costa Rica, on 22 November 1969, UNTS vol 1144, I-17955, 144: African Charter on Human and Peoples' Rights. Concluded at Nairobi on 27 June 1981, UNTS vol 1520, 1-26363, 217.

[73] Pinto, *Temas de derechos humanos* (2006) 45–46.

[74] ibid 47.

[75] ibid 58, 59.

property recognised under human rights instruments, including the Universal, the African and the American Declarations. There have been known cases of security forces in mining sites whose behaviour has posed threats to the lives of community groups, artisanal miners and opposition leaders, and mining has been linked to fostering conflict through the sale of its products to finance armed factions.

Human rights law places emphasis on the duty of states to protect and uphold fundamental human rights which are relevant to land rights and use, and which have often been disregarded in non-integrated regimes of mineral and land tenure. These include: the right 'to own property alone as well as in association with others' and to not being 'arbitrarily deprived of … property' enshrined in Article 17 of the Universal Declaration of Human Rights and regional conventions; the right of everyone to adequate standards of living, including housing, and the continuous improvement of living conditions established under Article 11 of the International Covenant on Economic, Social and Cultural Rights; the right of a people not to be 'deprived of its own means of subsistence' set forth under Article 1 of the same Covenant; and Article 1 of the International Covenant on Civil and Political Rights. Infringements might trigger the application of legal safeguards which, depending on applicable law, 'include due process, non-discrimination, public purpose and compensation', and the right of free, prior and informed consent held by indigenous peoples.[76]

There has been growing recognition under international law of the rights to land and participation of indigenous peoples. Convention No 169 Concerning Indigenous and Tribal Peoples in Independent Countries concluded under the umbrella of the International Labour Organization (ILO) in 1989, acknowledges the rights of ownership and possession over the lands that they traditionally occupy and the rights to participate in the use, management and conservation of natural resources pertaining to them.[77] In lands on which the state retains ownership of minerals or subsoil resources, the Convention establishes the duty of governments to put in place procedures for the consultation of peoples *prior* to undertaking or permitting exploration or exploitation in order to ascertain whether, and to what extent, their interests might be impaired. It also provides for the participation of peoples in the benefits of those activities, wherever possible, and for receiving fair compensation for any damages resulting from those activities (Article 15).

The Convention provides for the relocation of peoples as an exceptional measure and only with their 'free and informed consent', mandating 'appropriate procedures' for 'effective representation of the peoples concerned' under national law whenever consent has not been obtained. If return to their lands is not possible, they are entitled to 'lands of quality and legal status at least equal to that of

---

[76] See L Cotula, *Human Rights, Natural Resource and Investment Law in a Globalised World. Shades of Grey in the Shadow of the Law* (London, Routledge, 2012); J Ezirigwe, 'Human Rights and Property Rights in Natural Resources Development' (2017) 35 *Journal of Energy and Natural Resources Law* 201.

[77] Convention (No 169) Concerning Indigenous and Tribal Peoples in Independent Countries. Adopted by the General Conference of the International Labour Organisation at its 76th session, Geneva, 27 June 1989, UNTS vol 1650, 383, Art 14.

the lands previously occupied by them, suitable to provide for their present needs and future development', or to monetary compensation, if they so prefer, under relevant guarantees (Article 16). In all cases when applying these provisions, governments must respect the special cultural and spiritual relationship of indigenous peoples with the lands and territories they occupy and use, particularly the collective aspects of their relationship. 'Land' includes the concept of territories, covering 'the total environment of the areas which the peoples concerned occupy or otherwise use' (Article 13).

Regarding projects affecting indigenous peoples' lands, territories or other resources, particularly those related to the development, use or exploitation of mineral and water, or other resources, the UN Declaration on the Rights of Indigenous Peoples instead requires states to: (i) to consult and cooperate in good faith with indigenous peoples through their own representative institutions with a view to obtaining their free and informed consent prior to their approval; (ii) to provide effective mechanisms for just and fair compensation; and (iii) to adopt the actions required to mitigate adverse impacts of an environmental, economic, social, cultural or spiritual nature.[78] Following from that, no relocation can take place except with their free, prior and informed consent of the peoples and after agreement on just and fair compensation, as well as with the option to return, whenever possible (Article 10).

The Inter-American Court of Human Rights has upheld the collective rights of indigenous peoples to their lands and property and interpreted the responsibility of states to adopt domestic legislation to fulfil their obligations to grant collective titles, consult peoples and conduct appropriate assessments. In *Saramaka v Suriname*, the Saramaka people had initiated a complaint against Suriname before the Inter-American Commission of Human Rights to protect their land rights. The Saramaka asserted that Suriname had not conducted proper consultation when granting gold and logging concessions on territories they traditionally occupied, and alleged widespread environmental degradation, displacement, destruction of sacred sites and failure to provide economic benefits out of the development on their land. The Inter-American Court of Human Rights upheld the right to property of the Saramaka people, protected under Article 21 of the American Convention of Human Rights. The Court found that Suriname had failed to provide effective measures to recognise the right to the use and enjoyment of the territory traditionally held by the Saramaka people, when it granted concessions over those lands without proper consultation. The Court also held Suriname had violated Article 25 (right to judicial protection) as it had failed to provide effective domestic access to justice for the protection of the right to property in accordance with communal traditions, and Article 3 (right to judicial personality and domestic legal effect). The judgment found that the state had to: adopt appropriate domestic legislation in consultation with the Saramaka; grant collective title to

---

[78] GA Resolution 61/295. Declaration on the Rights of Indigenous Peoples. Adopted at 61st session, 107th plenary meeting on 13 September 2007, Art 32.

the Saramaka over their territory; obtain their free, prior and informed consent, and conduct environmental and social impact assessments prior to development activities on their lands; issue a public apology, and pay compensation for 'environmental degradation, destruction of territory by logging and market value of timber illegally harvested'.[79]

In *Sarayaku v Ecuador*, concerning the lack of consultation of the Kichwa Sarayaku People on the granting of an oil licence in their territories, the Inter-American Court of Human Rights found the state to be responsible for violating the right to communal property and to cultural identity, protected under Articles 21 and 1.1 and 2 of the American Convention of Human Rights.[80] The Court held that 'the obligation to consult, in addition to being a treaty-based provision, is also a general principle of international law' (§ 164) (this is one of the sources of international law in accordance with Article 38 of the Statute of the ICJ).[81] It concluded that by not consulting the Sarayaku on the execution of the project, Ecuador had breached its obligations 'under the principles of international law and its own domestic law' to adopt all necessary measures to guarantee their participation in the decision-making process, following their own institutions and mechanisms, on policies and affairs that could impact their territory, life, cultural and social identity, thereby affecting their rights to communal property and cultural identity (§232).[82]

International human rights law is evolving to acknowledge the broader spectrum of property rights, tenure and entitlements over natural resources as well as rights to participation, consent and benefit from resources development of local people, which include indigenous peoples, peasants and rural women.[83] On one hand, the contrasting values and fragmented nature of regimes of investment law and human rights law has placed host states under international authorities exercising a judiciary function which can result in their liability under both types of regimes. On the other, rights-based approaches to resources are challenging the traditional structures and modes of regulation enshrined in resources' regimes.

Another important facet of such challenges is that both host and home states, as duty-bearers towards the protection of human rights, can be held responsible

---

[79] *Saramaka People v Suriname*, Judgment (Preliminary Objections, Merits, Reparations and Costs), Inter-American Court of Human Rights, 28 November 2007, Series C No 172.

[80] *Kichwa Indigenous People of Sarayaku v Ecuador*, Judgment (Merits and Reparations). Inter-American Court of Human Rights, 27 June 2012.

[81] See ch 1.II.A.

[82] The Court also found the state to be responsible for placing the right to life and to personal integrity of the Sarayaku at risk (these being protected under Arts 4(1) and 5(1) of the American Convention), in connection to their obligation to guarantee the right to communal property pursuant to Arts 1(1) and 21 of the Convention, referring to the manner the operating company conducted oil exploration and dealt with explosives, which were placed at various locations in indigenous' territory; and for breaching the right to judicial guarantees and to judicial protection under Arts 8(1) and 25 of the American Convention.

[83] GA Resolution 73/165. Declaration of Rights of Peasants and Other People Working in Rural Areas. Adopted at 73rd session, 17 December 2018. See J Gilbert, *Human Rights and Natural Resources* (Oxford, Oxford University Press, 2018) 34–62.

for the acts of non-state actors, including business enterprises. This highlights the importance of states adopting and implementing coherent legal frameworks for investment which are fully embedded in human rights and meet their obligations towards their peoples.[84]

The report prepared by the Special Representative on Business and Human Rights distinguished between the state duty to *protect* human rights – the bedrock of human rights law – and corporate responsibility to *respect* human rights – which exists independently of states' duties. It emphasised that respecting human rights basically meant to do no harm; in other words, not infringing on the rights of others. This implies companies must exercise due diligence – to have systems in place that ensure compliance with national laws and manage 'the risk of human rights harm' in order to avoid it.[85] To implement due diligence processes, the report indicated that companies should adopt human rights policies to be integrated throughout their teams, conduct human rights assessments, track performance and monitor and audit developments. The International Bill of Human Rights and the core ILO conventions are indicated as the substantive benchmarks of those processes. The framework emerging from this report was implemented through the UN Guiding Principles on Business and Human Rights.[86]

Emerging guidance provides orientation for the implementation of governments' and companies' actions to fulfil their human rights duties.[87] The integration of human rights issues in the design of law, regulations and procedures, and right from the planning stage of projects, is crucial. Recommended tools to improve effectiveness include sanctions, incentives, due diligence and human rights impact assessments.

III. Mining and Anti-Corruption Instruments

The abuse of the fiduciary duties by those in the public and private sectors obtaining private and undue advantage is at the heart of definitions of corruption.[88]

---

[84] See the General Comment No 24 on State obligations under the International Covenant on Economic, Social and Cultural Rights in the context of business activities of the Committee on Economic, Social and Cultural Rights, UN Economic and Social Council, approved on 10 August 2017 (including extraterritorial obligations) (UN Doc E/C.12/GC/24, 10 August 2017).

[85] UN Human Rights Council, Protect, respect and remedy: a framework for business and human rights: report of the Special Representative of the Secretary-General on the Issue of Human Rights and Transnational Corporations and Other Business Enterprises, John Ruggie, 7 April 2008, A/HRC/8/5, 25.

[86] Human Rights Council Res 17/4, UN Doc. A/HRC/RES/17/4, 6 July 2011; see further V.A below.

[87] UN Guiding Principles on Business and Human Rights, 'Addendum on Principles for responsible contracts: integrating the management of human rights risks into State-investor contract negotiations: guidance for negotiations', Report of the Special Representative of the Secretary-General on the issue of human rights and transnational corporations and other business enterprises, United Nations General Assembly, A/HRC/17/31/Add.3, 25 May 2011, Human Rights Council, 17th Session.

[88] Transparency International defines corruption as 'abuse of power for private gain'. UNDP, 'Tackling Corruption, Transforming Lives: Accelerating Human Development in Asia and the Pacific' (2008). J Nye, 'Corruption and Political Development: A Cost–Benefit Analysis' (1967) 61 *American Political Science Review* 2.

The significant financial flows and direct opportunities for interactions between government officers at different levels and agencies and resource companies make the extractive industries particularly vulnerable to corruption risks. A wide range of instruments have emerged in relatively recent years to deal with both sides of bribery transactions.

The United Nations Convention against Corruption (entered into force in 2005) promotes measures for preventing and combatting corruption, strengthening international cooperation and technical assistance including on asset recovery, and encouraging 'integrity, accountability and proper management of public affairs and public property' (Article 1).[89] It applies to the 'prevention, investigation and prosecution of corruption and to the freezing, seizure, confiscation and return of the proceeds of offences established in accordance with this Convention' (Article 2).

A set of OECD instruments deal with the offering of bribes to foreign public officials. The Convention on Combating Bribery of Foreign Public Officials in International Business Transactions entered into force on 15 February 1999 criminalises bribery and corruption while the Recommendations for Further Combating Bribery of Foreign Public Officials in International Business Transactions, and on Tax Measures for Further Combating Bribery of Foreign Public Officials in International Business Transactions, both from 2009, and on Bribery and Officially Supported Export Credits from 2006, further strengthens commitments to prevent, identify and investigate foreign corruption.[90] The OECD Recommendation on Public Procurement of 2015 provides a comprehensive approach to updating procurement systems at all government levels and in state-owned enterprises.

Framed within actions to countering the resource curse, the promotion of transparency and accountability to combat corruption has run high in the global resource agenda from 2000s, through prominent initiatives as the Extractive Industries Transparency Initiative (EITI).[91] There has also been heightened research, awareness and recommendations on the role of resource contracts and laws in shaping transparent procedures and promoting accountability. Responsible business criteria, including human rights, can be embedded in contracts,[92] licensing, and in public procurement processes, which are increasingly required to be transparent and accountable to counter corruption risks.

---

[89] Resolution adopted by the UN General Assembly 58/4 of 31 October 2003. United Nations Convention against Corruption. Entered into force on 14 December 2005 in accordance with Art 68(1), UNTS vol 2349, 41.

[90] See also OECD, Responsible Business Conduct in Government Procurement Practices (June 2017).

[91] See ch 3.IV.D.

[92] See OECD Guiding Principles for Durable Extractive Contracts (2019); Annotated WAOML Miners' and Investors' Modern Model Mining Code Draft – Anti-Corruption Part, developed by WAOML; see Model Mining Development Agreement – Transparency Template prepared by Howard Mann et al, 2012 (a supplement to the Model Mining Development Agreement developed by the Mining Law Committee, IBA, 2010).

IV. The Responsibility of Transnational Corporations and Business Enterprises

The regulation of corporations' conduct within the territorial boundaries of a state belongs to the realm of municipal law. But effective regulation of global companies at national level for all sectors is challenged due to the

> extensive network of decision-making and operational structures formed by their headquarters, branches, subsidiaries and other forms of investment in independent company units throughout the world and their flexibility in transferring seats of production as well as profits within the framework of the organization as a whole.[93]

These characteristics are compounded when operating in the extractive sectors in low- and middle-income countries that are in the process of building or consolidating their institutions. Key concerns revolve around the dominant role of transnational corporations in their economies and their vulnerability to interference in domestic politics,[94] the asymmetries of power and information for striking fair deals, and the challenges to maximise revenue at host state and mostly local level. Faced with the changing role of non-state actors, a fundamental point of contention has been linked to the state-centric nature of traditional international law and the *lacunae* to hold corporations accountable. As said earlier, corporations do not have binding obligations under international law.[95] Transnational governance frameworks are setting standards on responsible business conduct concerning fundamental international legal norms.

The next section will look at the development of those standards and the range of initiatives that have emerged to engage non-state actors in the governance of the extractive industries.

V. Transnational Mining and Minerals Standards and Governance

A range of soft law instruments or non-binding rules emerging from United Nations bodies have shaped standards of responsible business conduct. Soft

---

[93] P Malanczuk, *Akehurst's Modern Introduction to International Law*, 7th edn (London and New York, Routledge, 1997) 102.

[94] ibid 102–03.

[95] The Open-ended Intergovernmental Working Group on Transnational Corporations and Other Business Enterprises with Respect to Human Rights (OEIGWG) established by Resolution 26/9 of the UN Human Rights Council (26th session, 26 June 2014) has the mandate to 'elaborate an internationally legally binding instrument to regulate, in international human rights law, the activities of transnational corporations and other business enterprises' with a view to strengthening corporate accountability. It released a revised draft instrument which served as basis for negotiations at the fifth session of the OEIGWG. See further J Nayak, *An International Framework for Advancing Business and Human Rights Beyond the UN Guiding Principles: Proposal for an Inclusive, Stepwise and Multistakeholder Approach*, PhD Thesis (CEPMLP University of Dundee, 2014).

law instruments are relevant in terms of standards-setting and as precedents to formal law. These coalesce with a growing and disparate range of other non-state norms emanating from the broad range of actors involved in the sector, or affected by mining operations. These include not only host states but also mining companies and their home states, international organisations and financial institutions, financial investors, downstream companies as refineries and firms that use minerals as inputs to their products and their home states, as well as civil society networks.

At least four groups of norms have been developed and are relevant to the mining and minerals sector.[96]

A. Standards Set by Intergovernmental Organisations

I have referred to the Draft UN Code of Conduct for Transnational Corporations that emerged in the context of work on the New International Economic Order and was finally shelved in 1992.[97] A working group formed in 1998 prepared the Draft UN Norms on the Responsibilities of Transnational Corporations and other Business Enterprises with Regard to Human Rights in 2003. This was an attempt to develop a set of norms establishing the obligation of transnational corporations to promote, secure and respect the fulfilment of human rights, and protect human rights recognised in international and national law.[98] The draft encountered wide criticism and was never endorsed.

In 2005, the UN Secretary General appointed Professor John Ruggie as Special Representative on Business and Human Rights with the mandate to identify and clarify standards of corporate responsibility and accountability for transnational corporations and other business enterprises with regard to human rights, the role of states, advance research and a compilation of best practices

---

[96] John Ruggie distinguishes between 'the traditional standard-setting role performed by inter-governmental organizations; the enhanced accountability mechanisms recently added by some intergovernmental initiatives; and an emerging multi-stakeholder form that involves corporations directly, along with states and civil society organizations, in redressing sources of corporate-related human rights abuses' (Human Rights Council, 'Business and Human Rights: Mapping International Standards of Responsibility and Accountability for Corporate Acts'. Report of the Special Representative of the Secretary-General (SRSG) on the issue of human rights and transnational corporations and other business enterprises (A/HRC/4/035) 9 February 2007, 46). He refers to these type of norms as 'soft law'.

[97] See ch 3.III.

[98] Norms on the Responsibilities of Transnational Corporations and Other Business Enterprises with regard to Human Rights. Approved by the United Nations Sub-Commission on the Promotion and Protection of Human Rights. UN Doc E/CN.4/Sub.2/2003/12/Rev 2 (55th session: Geneva, 2003). See D Weissbrodt and M Kruger, 'Norms on the Responsibilities of Transnational Corporations and Other Business Enterprises with Regard to Human Rights' (2003) 97 *American Journal of International Law* 901.

114 *Mining and Minerals in Fields of International Law and Governance*

on the subject.[99] The report submitted to the Human Rights Council on 3 June 2008 began:

> The root cause of the business and human rights predicament today lies in the governance gaps created by globalization – between the scope and impact of economic forces and actors, and the capacity of societies to manage their adverse consequences. These governance gaps provide the permissive environment for wrongful acts by companies of all kinds without adequate sanctioning or reparation.[100]

The report offered a common framework identifying 'differentiated but complementary responsibilities' of states and business: the state duty to protect against human rights abuses by third parties, including business entities; the corporate responsibility to respect human rights; and the need for more effective access to remedies.[101] The Special Representative was further mandated to develop guidance for the implementation of the Framework, which was submitted in this final report to the Human Rights Council.[102] The Human Rights Council endorsed the Guiding Principles on Business and Human Rights (UNGP) in Resolution 17/4 of 16 June 2011.[103] In the same Resolution, it established a working group on human rights and transnational corporations and other business enterprises.

I pointed out in chapter three that the UNGP has crystallised the consensus on the issue of the growing role of transnational and national business in development and their impact on human rights, the corresponding obligations of states in preventing and responding to them, as well as the responsibility of business in respecting human rights through due diligence measures. The UNGP points at both transnational and national corporations, and at the obligations of states in running business, including the extraterritorial obligations of home states. It has a global approach, calling on all relevant states and business actors to act in accordance with their corresponding duties and responsibilities.

Corporate responsibility to respect human rights had been recognised in other soft law instruments, such as the UN Global Compact, the ILO Tripartite Declaration of Principles Concerning Multinational Enterprises and Social Policy, and the OECD Guidelines for Multinational Enterprises. These have all been reviewed and strengthened in their approaches to business and human rights.

The UN Global Compact, launched on 26 July 2000, provides a 'framework for businesses' seeking to shape operations and strategies along the lines of 10 universally recognised principles in the areas of human rights, labour, environment

---

[99] Office of the High Commissioner on Human Rights, Human Rights and Transnational Corporations and other Business Enterprises, Human Rights Resolution 2005/69, E/CN.4/RES/2005/69, 20 April 2005.

[100] ibid para 3.

[101] UN Human Rights Council, 'Protect, respect and remedy: a framework for business and human rights: report of the Special Representative of the Secretary-General on the Issue of Human Rights and Transnational Corporations and Other Business Enterprises', John Ruggie, 7 April 2008, A/HRC/8/5.

[102] A/HRC/17/31.

[103] UN Human Rights Council. 17/4 Human Rights and transnational corporations and other business enterprises. A/HRC/RES/17/4, 6 July 2011 (endorsing Guiding Principles on Business and Human Rights: Implementing the United Nations 'Protect, Respect and Remedy' Framework).

and anti-corruption.[104] Through its local networks, it promotes alignment with those principles and with the UNGP Guiding Principles. The above-mentioned ILO Tripartite Declaration of Principles Concerning Multinational Enterprises and Social Policy (adopted in 1977, and as amended in 2000, 2006 and 2017)[105] sets forth principles in the fields of employment, training, working conditions and industrial relations, recommended to governments, employers and workers. It intends to further realise the ILO Declaration on Fundamental Principles and Rights at Work.

B. Intergovernmental Initiatives with Accountability Mechanisms

A few initiatives have moved beyond standard-setting to establish mechanisms to improve accountability. The Declaration on International Investment and Multinational Enterprises recommending the observance of the Guidelines for Multinational Enterprises ('the Guidelines'), were first adopted by OECD governments in 1976 and initially aimed at facilitating direct investment among OECD members. They have gone through various revisions, the last one dated 5 May 2011 to align with the UNGP.

The Guidelines constitute the most comprehensive framework backed by governments to support businesses to promote responsible conduct. They establish non-binding principles on human rights, environment and climate change, information disclosure, employment and industrial relations, combating bribery and extortion, consumer interests, science and technology, competition and taxation. Business must fulfil the requirements of the applicable national law as well as internationally recognised norms. They recommend companies follow due diligence processes to identify, prevent and mitigate the potential or actual adverse impacts they cause, contribute to, or are directly related to.[106] Importantly, the Guidelines provide for an enhanced mechanism for accountability: National Contact Points (NCP), organised in adhering countries. These establish a non-judicial review procedure whose main function is to raise awareness about the Guidelines and contribute to resolving issues that relate to their implementation in specific circumstances. Complaints can be put forward for the NCP to investigate multinationals that do not follow the guidelines. A series of sectoral tools have

---

[104] www.unglobalcompact.org.

[105] See ILO, 'Tripartite Declaration of Principles Concerning Multinational Enterprises and Social Policy' (Geneva, International Labour Office, 2017).

[106] Responsible Business Conduct comprises two aspects concerning business and society: the positive contributions that business can make to sustainable development and inclusive growth (through added value); and the avoidance of adverse impacts. The latter requires conducting processes of effective due diligence for identifying, preventing, mitigating and accounting for how they deal with actual and potential adverse impacts 'in their own operations, their supply chain and other business relationships'. OECD, 'Due Diligence Guidance for Responsible Business Conduct' (2018).

116 *Mining and Minerals in Fields of International Law and Governance*

been developed to implement the guidelines in different sectors and contexts.[107] In 2018, the OECD adopted the Due Diligence Guidance for Responsible Business Conduct[108] to support enterprises on the implementation of the Guidelines, taking into consideration a broad range of risks.

The IFC's Sustainability Framework,[109] which includes the Environmental and Social Performance Standards, sets up the requirements that clients must meet throughout the life of investment in projects funded by IFC. The Standards relate to social and environmental assessment and management systems, labour and working conditions, pollution prevention and abatement, community health, safety and security, land acquisition and involuntary resettlement, biodiversity conservation and sustainable natural resource management, indigenous peoples and cultural heritage. Enhanced mechanisms for accountability for compliance include review by an Ombudsman, who can handle complaints from persons affected by social and environmental impacts of projects funded by IFC or MIGA. The Performance Standards are used as reference for due diligence processes conducted as required by the Equator Principles' Financial Institutions.

The World Bank's Environmental and Social Standards (ESS) establishes a set of 10 Environmental and Social Standards to support borrower's projects to identify and assess environmental and social risks.[110] These Standards seek to:

(a) support Borrowers in achieving good international practice relating to environmental and social sustainability;

(b) assist Borrowers in fulfilling their national and international environmental and social obligations;

(c) enhance non-discrimination, transparency, participation, accountability and governance; and

(d) enhance the sustainable development outcomes of projects through ongoing stakeholder engagement.[111]

C. Multi-Stakeholder Governance

The Voluntary Principles on Security and Human Rights is a set of principles, developed in 2000 by the governments of the United States, the United Kingdom, Norway and the Netherlands, companies in the extractive and energy sectors,

---

[107] For example, OECD, 'Due Diligence Guidance for Responsible Supply Chains of Minerals from Conflict-Affected and High-Risk Areas', 3rd edn (2016); 'Risk Awareness Tool for Multinational Enterprises in Weak Governance Zones' (2006), and 'Due Diligence Guidance for Meaningful Stakeholder Engagement in the Extractive Sector' (2017).

[108] OECD, Due Diligence Guidance for Responsible Business Conduct' (2018).

[109] IFC Sustainability Framework includes the Environmental and Social Performance Standards (updated 1 January 2012).

[110] The World Bank, 'World Bank Environmental and Social Framework (World Bank, Washington DC, 2016).

[111] World Bank Environmental and Social Framework, ix.

Transnational Mining and Minerals Standards and Governance   117

and NGOs (including Amnesty International, The Fund for Peace, Human Rights Watch and Oxfam). They provide guidance for companies to balance the needs for safety and security of their operations within a framework of respect for human rights and fundamental freedoms.

The Kimberley Process Certification Scheme (KPCS) is a joint initiative of governments, industry and civil society organisations to stop trade of conflict diamonds. It tracks sales and exports of rough diamonds through the certification of shipments. Certificates are issued with the authority of participating governments. Schemes should be implemented through binding legislation by participating governments and supported by appropriate penalties for infringements by individuals or companies. The scheme was established between 2000 and 2002, and followed a series of resolutions of the UN Security Council.[112]

The EITI was announced in 2002 by the then British Prime Minister Tony Blair in a publication prepared for the World Summit for Sustainable Development in Johannesburg, and later launched at the Lancaster Conference.[113] The EITI is a joint initiative of governments, companies and civil society organisations that developed its principles and format, which evolved in subsequent iterations, from a Statement of Principles towards a set of Rules to consolidate into a global governance standard.[114] It initially focused on the publication by companies of what they pay to governments, and the disclosure by governments on what they receive. The Standard now adopts a comprehensive approach including the whole upstream value chain of the extractive industries, starting from the granting of exploration and exploitation licences, followed by the monitoring of production and tax collection, and finally income distribution and expense management.[115] It is implemented through a process that brings together representatives of governments, companies and civil societies in a 'multi-stakeholder forum' which constitutes the main decision-making body for the implementation of EITI; and requires independent validation of the information submitted by an independent auditor perceived as trustworthy and technically competent. EITI aims to enhance transparency and accountability – the governance of the extractive industries – as well as their development outcomes,[116] seeking to contribute to better managing the resources administered by governments, which are of public interest.

The last version of the Standard adopted in 2019 incorporated section 8 with a recommendation for its implementation taking into consideration the initiatives

---

[112] See D Dam-de Jong, 'A Rough Trade'? Towards a More Sustainable Minerals Supply Chain' (2019) *Brill Open Law* 1.

[113] EITI International Secretariat, 'The EITI Standard 2019' (Oslo, 17 June 2019) and Guidance Notes.

[114] See EITI, 'The EITI Standard 2019' (2019) ch II.

[115] Collier developed the steps of the Extractive Industries value chain in the book *The Bottom Billion*. This concept has been taken as a reference, with different variations, for the elaboration of the *Natural Resource Charter* (Natural Resource Governance Institute); 'Extractive Industries Value Chain' (World Bank), as well as the EITI.

[116] A Mejía Acosta, 'The Impact and Effectiveness of Accountability and Transparency Initiatives: The Governance of Natural Resources' (2013) 31 *Development Policy Review* 89.

and experience of open data. Implementing countries are encouraged to orient their government systems towards the practice of open data and systematic disclosure, and incorporate its principles, including data opening without any restriction, enabling users to obtain and reuse data easily and freely. In this manner, the Standard has established a nexus with open government initiatives at international and regional levels, as well as with the trend towards open government systems. The SDGs have incorporated as a target the development of effective and transparent institutions, which promote accountability at all levels (SDG 16.6).

The Open Government Partnership was established in 2011 as an international platform for governments strengthening links with citizens.[117] It promotes the cross-cutting principles of transparency, participation and accountability in government agendas and requires four types of commitment to be endorsed by countries in Open Government Declarations. These refer to access to information about government activities; support to citizen participation in decision-making processes and public policy formulation; implementation of high standards of professional integrity in public administration; and expansion of access to technology with the objective of opening information and promoting accountability. Governments commit to develop National Action Plans that identify their commitments and are subject to independent review, in collaboration with civil society organisations.

The International Open Data Charter[118] and the Global Partnership for Sustainable Development Data[119] were launched on occasion of the adoption of the SDGs in 2015. The Charter is based on six principles that guide the access, opening and use of data, and according to which the data should be published in open formats as a common practice, updated and complete, accessible and usable, comparable and interoperable, aimed at improving governance and citizen participation, and for innovation and inclusive development.

D. Corporate Self-Regulation

The practice of disciplining the behaviour of individual firms or through regulation of a collective group of firms through private codes of conduct started in highly industrialised countries, prompted by consumer and supplier demand, reputation, increased efficiency and community pressure,[120] and was part and parcel of a range of broader factors including a turn from regulation to governance.[121] Beginning with *voluntary* forms of self-regulation, *mandated* forms started to

---

[117] The Open Government Partnership.
[118] International Open Data Charter. See opendatacharter.net.
[119] Global Partnership for Sustainable Development Data. See www.data4sdgs.org.
[120] K Webb, 'Voluntary initiatives and the law' in R Gibson, *Voluntary Initiatives. The New Politics of Corporate Greening* (Peterborough, Broadview, 1999) 42.
[121] O Lobel, 'The Renew Deal: The Fall of Regulation and the Rise of Governance in Contemporary Legal Thought' (2004) 89 *Minnesotta Law Review* 342.

emerge over time, as governments required groups or sectors to enforce broadly defined norms.[122]

The global expansion of mining in the 1990s entailed the spread of (then mostly Western) companies, comprising a few that had started to embrace the practice of corporate social responsibility through environmental standards. There was a stark contrast between increasing opposition to, and regulation of, mining in industrialised and democratic societies and what was then called 'the race to the bottom' to attract investors in the developing world. By the late 1990s, the widespread view of mining as a 'dirty industry' prompted the need for collective action, initially by nine of the major companies, which was steered towards changing the public perceptions about the harmful, disruptive effects of mining, and gaining understanding on the way forward. They called to convene the Global Mining Initiative, under the auspices of the World Business Council for Sustainable Development, which resulted in the commissioning of a scoping study to the International Institute for Environment and Development. This recommended the design and scope of the Mining and Metals Sustainable Development Project (MMSD), a two-year independent process of research and consultation launched in 2000, which produced the report 'Breaking New Ground',[123] aimed at producing research and analysis assessed the minerals sector and how it could best contribute in the transition to sustainable patterns of economic development.[124]

The MMSD report found that most organisations involved in mining did not have sustainable development policies. It recommended the development of such policies, along with integrated management systems, to generate change internally and to mainstream sustainable development to add value.[125] Research commissioned by the MMSD project had pointed at the numerous corporate codes of conduct, standards and best practices rules. While initially focused on environmental management aspects, attention expanded on social aspects and ranged from minimising the social impacts of new investments to demonstrating commitment to social advancement, communicating and cooperating with local stakeholders, and contributing to local development. These actions started then to be seen as necessary to obtain access to land and a 'social licence to operate', and as part and parcel of a strategy for long-term corporate survival and managing environmental and social risks.

Since the MMSD, there has been a continuing trend towards mainstreaming and consolidating standards, which are crystallising in the concept of 'responsible mining'. A prominent industry-led initiative is Towards Sustainable Mining (TSM),

---

[122] On a categorisation of self-regulation forms, see J Blake, 'Constitutionalising Self-Regulation' (1996) 59 *The Modern Law Review Limited* 27. At the national level, countries such as Canada, the US, Denmark, Germany, Britain and France have undertaken initiatives to promote CSR, including corporate governance. In the US, the Sarbanes-Oxley Act of 2002 aims at improving the accuracy and reliability of corporate disclosure.

[123] See MMSD, *Breaking New Ground* (London, Earthscan, 2002).

[124] ibid xiv.

[125] ibid 393–94.

120　*Mining and Minerals in Fields of International Law and Governance*

launched in 2004 by the Mining Association of Canada (MAC). Members agreed to commit to the TSM Guiding Principles and report their performance against 23 indicators through TSM Progress Reports. It was adopted by other five business councils on four continents: Finland, Argentina, Botswana, the Philippines and Spain.

The International Council on Mining and Metals (ICMM) also followed the MMSD process. Created in 2003, the ICMM brought together 26 mining and metal companies and 35 regional and commodities associations. Its objective is to strengthen environmental and social performance. ICMM requires mining companies to commit to the ICMM 10 Principles. The Principles are supposed to respond to key challenges identified by the MMSD's agenda for change.[126] Several companies are aligning their corporate policies towards a sustainable development business.[127] Companies have also steadily been following voluntary initiatives as created by the Task Force on Climate-related Financial Disclosures (TCFD) for use by companies in providing climate-related financial risk information to investors, lenders and other stakeholders.[128]

In parallel, civil society and independent organisations have been engaged in promoting sustainability in the mining sector, mainly in relation to responsible sourcing. In 2004, the Alliance for Responsible Mining (ARM) was established to contribute to sustainable development within artisanal and small-scale mining (ASM). ARM works to support small and medium miners in their journey to certification. An independent party audits mining operations, after which compliant mining operators are granted a Fairmined Certification. Once certified, miners can sell their Fairmined-certified gold to markets. The Mining Certification Evaluation Project (MCEP) launched by the WWF-Australia looked to assess whether an independent third-party certification of environmental, social and economic performance could be applied to the large-scale mining sector.[129] The MCEP acted as a test for understanding the feasibility of a global certification initiative which 'confirmed the deep challenges associated with implementing a single certification system within the context of the geographical and product diversity of the minerals sector'.[130]

Responsible sourcing has been a current concern among civil society organisations. In 2004, Earthworks launched the No Dirty Gold international campaign with the aim of ensuring that gold mining operations (mainly the jewellery market)

---

[126] ICMM, 'Mining Principles', available at www.icmm.com/mining-principles. In 2014, the China Chamber of Commerce of Metals, Minerals and Chemicals launched the first edition of the 'Guidelines for Social Responsibility in Outbound Mining Investment'.

[127] De Beers, for example, together with the Diamond Development Initiative is piloting a programme called GemFair, which seeks to 'create a secure and transparent route to market for ethically sourced ASM diamonds'.

[128] Rio Tinto and Glencore, for example, have reported TCFD in their 2018 Annual Sustainability Reports (Rio Tinto Annual Report, 2018, 13; Glencore Annual Report, 2018, 35).

[129] MCEP: www.resolve.ngo/docs/mining-certification-evaluation-project.pdf.

[130] J Potts, M Wenban-Smith, L Turley and M Lynch, 'State of Sustainability Initiatives Review'. Standards and the Extractive Economy, Intergovernmental Forum on Mining, Minerals, Metals and Sustainable Development (2018).

Transnational Mining and Minerals Standards and Governance 121

respect human rights and the environment. In 2005, the Council for Responsible Jewellery Practices was established, congregating a group of 14 diamond and gold jewellery businesses. Its main objective has been to become a standard and a certification organisation for the jewellery supply chain, from mine to retail.[131] The Council for Responsible Jewellery Practices became the Responsible Jewellery Council (RJC) in 2008. The RJC Standards Committee agreed the final revisions to the Code of Practices Standard and Guidance on 25 January 2019, as the culmination of an 18-month multi-stakeholder consensus-building process.[132]

In 2006, the Initiative for Responsible Mining Assurance (IRMA) was launched with the aim to develop a standard in consultation with a broad group of stakeholders, for the certification of an environmental performance at mine sites globally. It addresses both aspects of due diligence – gauging actions to reduce potential harm – and steps towards continuous improvement.[133] Different to No Dirty Gold campaign and the RJC, IRMA has self-proclaimed as a 'multi-commodity initiative focused on developing an FSC-style standard and corresponding governance model for large scale mining'.[134]

Incorporated in 2015, the Aluminum Stewardship Initiative (ASI) was created to administer an independent third-party certification programme for the aluminum value chain. The first certification under the ASI Standard began in 2018. On the steel industry side, ResponsibleSteel was created as a multi-stakeholder standard and certification initiative to operate along the steel supply chain. The ResponsibleSteel Standard Version 1-0 was launched in November 2019.

Progressive corporate strategies have been moving away from the more limited concept of corporate social responsibility towards 'shared value', embracing more innovative forms around system change and seeking to mainstreaming the SDGs. The 'Principles for Responsible Investment' and the spread of strategies to deal with 'Environmental, Social and Governance' (ESG) risks are permeating corporate strategies and shaping the conceptualisation of 'responsible mining' as the business operational standard.

This spectrum of impacts and risks for governments, communities and ecosystems requires from operating companies high-level engineering excellence and risk management. The practice of responsible investment is gaining traction in the mining sector and in minerals sourcing. It seeks to embed investment analysis and decision-making processes in environmental, social and governance (ESG) considerations for risk management and for generating sustainable outcomes.

Apart from soft norms, and as part and parcel of the global resource governance movement, a few Western jurisdictions, home countries to important investors in mining, have adopted laws of extra-territorial application. These

---

[131] Responsible Jewellery Council: www.responsiblejewellery.com/about-rjc.
[132] Code of Practices Standard 2019, available at www.responsiblejewellery.com/files/RJC-COP-April-2019.pdf.
[133] IRMA: responsiblemining.net/what-we-do/approach/.
[134] Potts, Wenban-Smith, Turley and Lynch, *State of Sustainability Initiatives Review* (2018) 15.

122 *Mining and Minerals in Fields of International Law and Governance*

have been designed to complement EITI by imposing mandatory reporting requirements to extractive companies on payments to public administrations. Article 1504 of the Dodd-Frank Act (the 'Wall Street Reform and Consumer Protection Act') adopted in July 2010 and applicable to companies which are subject to the supervision of the Securities and Exchange Commission (SEC) in the US, requires companies operating in oil and gas, and mining abroad, to report payments made to foreign governments. In the EU, the European Parliament and EU Council approved requirements demanding from companies operating in the extractive industries, including in the wood sector, to disclose annually their payments to public administrations, to be disaggregated both at country and at project level. The norms refer to the EITI.[135] In Canada, the Extractive Sector Transparency Measures Act (ESTMA), in force from 1 June 2015, also requires the disclosure of payments to public administrations both in Canada and abroad, while Switzerland has also adopted a resolution along the same lines.

This chapter has provided a glimpse into the remarkable developments in the fields of human rights, the environment and anti-corruption, as well as of international economic law, as they relate to mining and minerals. Each of these fields of international law are establishing obligations (eg, banning mining products or areas from mining; setting emissions' reductions requirements) and sets of standards and safeguards (eg, for treatment of investment as standards of expropriation and due process; standards for consultation of indigenous peoples). Overall, they can be seen as efforts to limit the exercise of public powers in global and national governance.

The implications for transnational and domestic legal systems are wide-ranging. They might place core aspects of the law and governance of mining and minerals, which typically belong to the realm of municipal systems, under the jurisdiction of international courts. They might also connect with, mandate or influence the development of national law and regulations, expanding on the criteria and actors involved in decision-making processes about mining projects at domestic level. The growth of certain areas of law or procedural aspects have often occurred inorganically, without a prior assessment of the legal baseline with a view to gauging impacts and regulatory risks from the perspective of the nation-state and result in internal contradictions of the whole constellation of the state's rights and duties.

The next chapter will look at regimes for mining and minerals in the global commons.

---

[135] EU Directive 2013/34/EU of the European Parliament and the Council of 26 June 2013 and EU Directive 2013/50/EU of 22 October. On conflict minerals, see Article 1502 of the 'Dodd-Frank Act' in the US, and Regulation (EU) 2017/821 of the European Parliament and of the Council of 17 May 2017 laying down supply chain due diligence obligations for Union importers of tin, tantalum and tungsten, their ores, and gold originating from conflict-affected and high-risk areas (to become operative on 1 January 2021).

5

Mining and Minerals Regimes in the Global Commons

From an international law perspective, and in spatial terms, there are three fundamental categories of resource regimes: those that apply to resources subject to territorial sovereignty; those that apply to the global commons (resources beyond the territorial sovereignty of any particular state); and regimes applicable to transboundary or 'shared' resources.[1]

Even though the bulk of mining activity occurs onshore, marine mining has long taken place on shallow near shores in many countries (less than a 50m water depth), concentrating mainly on aggregates (eg, in many European countries, China, and Pacific Island states) and also on diamonds (Namibia and South Africa), tin (Indonesia), magnesium, salt, sulphur, gold and heavy minerals.[2] The global community is starting to pay attention to the formidable scale of sand and aggregate extraction, which is understood to be an example of the activities triggering the Anthropocene age: a new geological epoch triggered by human intervention rather than nature.[3] Likewise, although until recently the prospects of mining seawards and into the deep seabed seemed remote, science and technology are moving fast and, coupled with increasing mineral demand and pressure on land-based resources, an expansion of marine mining, particularly in the deep seabed, is getting closer. Concerns about the impact of deep seabed mining on ocean ecosystems are growing and being framed within calls for coherent governance of these global commons consistent with SDG 14. Mineral exploration efforts are also starting to take place in outer space.

Chapter three defined 'territorial sovereignty' and reviewed the development of the principle of PSONR and the inclusion of mining and minerals in global action plans to advance sustainable development. It noted that the development of the legal regime applicable to mining and minerals in areas beyond national

---

[1] O Schachter, *Sharing the World's Resources* (New York, Columbia University Press, 1977). J Barberis, *Los Recursos Naturales Compartidos entre Estados y el Derecho Internacional* (Madrid, Tecnos, 1978).

[2] E Baker, F Gaill, A Karageorgis, G Lamarche, B Narayanaswamy, J Parr, C Raharimananirina, R Santos and R Sharma, 'Offshore Mining Industries' in United Nations, Division for Ocean Affairs and the Law of the Sea, Office of Legal Affairs (ed) *The First Global Integrated Marine Assessment: World Ocean Assessment I* (Cambridge, Cambridge University Press, 2014) 363–78.

[3] UNEP, Sand and sustainability: Finding new solutions for environmental governance of global sand resources. GRID–Geneva, United Nations Environment Programme (Geneva, Switzerland, 2019).

124 *Mining and Minerals Regimes in the Global Commons*

jurisdiction, notably over the international seabed, and the concept of 'common heritage of mankind' were core aspects of attention. This chapter begins by reviewing the provisions of the 1982 United Nations Convention on the Law of the Sea (UNCLOS), which came into force in 1994,[4] regarding the extent of territorial sovereignty over maritime areas. It then analyses the status and concepts underlying regimes in the global commons.

I. Extent of Territorial Sovereignty Over Maritime Zones

While considerable controversy has long existed as to the extent of territorial sovereignty beyond land territory, UNCLOS clarifies the status and extent of the rights of states over maritime zones. In effect, it draws a distinction between different categories of maritime zones over which the coastal state exercises 'graduated degrees of sovereign rights and obligations',[5] with national jurisdiction of coastal states diminishing 'as one moves seawards from the coastlines'.[6]

The *territorial sea* is the belt of sea adjacent to the land territory of coastal states (Article 2, UNCLOS), which can have a breadth of up to 12 nautical miles as established by the coastal state and in accordance with UNCLOS. Coastal states exercise *full sovereignty* over the territorial sea, except for the right of innocent passage recognised to foreign flagged vessels (Article 17, UNCLOS).[7] Sovereignty of coastal states over the territorial sea extends to the air space, bed and subsoil (and all resources in it) to an unlimited depth.[8]

The *Exclusive Economic Zone* (EEZ) is the area beyond and adjacent to the territorial sea, which extends up to 200 nautical miles 'from the baselines from which the breadth of the territorial sea is measured' (Articles 55 and 57, UNCLOS). Coastal states have '*sovereign rights* for the purpose of exploring and exploiting, conserving and managing the natural resources, whether living or non-living, of the waters superjacent to the seabed and of the seabed and its subsoil' (Article 56(1)(a), emphasis added).[9] The rights of coastal states concerning the seabed and

---

[4] UNCLOS, 10 December 1982, 21 ILM 1261 (1982).

[5] R Pincus and S Ali, *Diplomacy on Ice: Energy and the Environment in the Arctic and Antarctic* (New Haven and London: Yale University Press, 2015) 46.

[6] C Joyner, *Antarctica and the Law of the Sea* (Dordrecht, Martinus Nijhoff, 1992) 76. See also Pincus and Ali, Diplomacy on Ice (2015) 46, and R Murray and A Dey Nuttall, *International Relations and the Arctic: Understanding Policy and Governance* (Amherst, Cambria Press, 2014).

[7] Ships of all States – whether coastal or land-locked – enjoy the right of innocent passage through the territorial sea (Art 17, UNCLOS). Passage – navigation – is innocent so long as it is not prejudicial to the peace, good order or security of the coastal State (Art 19, UNCLOS).

[8] R Lagoni, 'Oil and gas deposits across national frontiers' (1979) 73 *American Journal of International Law* 216 (citing H Lauterpacht, *International Law (Oppenheim)*, 8th edn (London: Longmans, Green & Co, 1955) 462; H Bonfils, *Traité de Droit International Public (Fauchille)*, 8th edn (Librairie Arthur Rousseau, Paris, 1925) 99.

[9] See also Pincus and Ali (n 5) 46.

Extent of Territorial Sovereignty Over Maritime Zones 125

its subsoil will be exercised in accordance with the continental shelf regime established in Part VI of UNCLOS (Article 56(3)).

The *Continental Shelf* (CS) comprises 'the seabed and subsoil of the submarine areas that extend beyond its territorial sea throughout the natural prolongation of its land territory to the outer edge of the continental margin, or to a distance of 200 nautical miles from which the breadth of the territorial sea is measured where the outer edge of the continental margin does not extend up to that distance' (Article 76). The outer limits of the CS cannot extend beyond 350 nautical miles 'from the baselines from which the breadth of the territorial sea is measured' or 100 nautical miles from the 2500 metre isobath (Article 76(5)).

For purposes of establishing the outer limits of continental shelves exceeding 200 nautical miles, coastal states must submit the particulars and supporting scientific and technical data to the Commission on the Limits of the Continental Shelf (Article 76(8) and Annex II of UNCLOS). Unlike the EEZ, that must always be claimed by coastal states, the CS does not need to be claimed.[10] It 'exists *ipso facto* and *ab initio*', not depending on occupation or express proclamation.[11]

The coastal state holds 'sovereign rights for the purpose of exploring [the CS] and exploiting its natural resources' (Article 77).[12] It holds exclusive rights to authorise and regulate drilling for any purpose (Article 81). These sovereign rights include mineral and other non-living resources of the seabed and subsoil, together with living organisms belonging to sedentary species, within the 200 nautical miles' zone.[13] The coastal state defines the conditions under which exploration and exploitation of such resources is conducted through laws and regulations.[14]

Within the 200-mile zone, the regimes of the EEZ and CS coexist.[15] Beyond the 200-mile zone, only the CS regime applies. As the adjacent waters of the CS area beyond 200 miles are high seas, the coastal states' rights over that area are slightly different than those over the EEZ. Although there are generally the same rights regarding exploration and exploitation, there are differences in relation to living organisms belonging to sedentary species and on payment for the exploitation of non-living resources in the outer CS (to be distributed to state parties under UNCLOS, Article 82).[16]

The Arctic Ocean coastal states (Russia, Canada, the US, Denmark and Norway) have advanced territorial claims over the seabed areas in the Arctic, in the context of the delimitation of the outer continental shelves. The region is faced with growing challenges brought about by climate change and increased interest

---

[10] This means there could be a CS without an EEZ, but there could not be an EEZ without a CS. R Churchill and A Lowe, *The Law of the Sea*, 3rd edn (Manchester, Manchester University Press, 1999) 145.

[11] Churchill and Lowe, *The Law of the Sea* (1999) 145. Cf Art 77 UNCLOS.

[12] ibid. See also Pincus and Ali (n 5) 46.

[13] Churchill and Lowe (n 10) 151.

[14] ibid.

[15] ibid 151.

[16] ibid 121.

in its resources.[17] There are currently no prospects for a framework convention on the Arctic, but increased focus is being cast on the applicable regime under UNCLOS.[18]

Article 82(2) of UNCLOS establishes that coastal states must make annual payments or contributions in kind (at a rate of up to seven per cent) in relation to the exploitation of mineral resources of the continental shelf beyond 200 nautical miles from the baselines from which the breadth of the territorial sea is measured (Article 82(1) UNCLOS), except for developing states that are net importers of the resources produced from its CS (para 3). Payments must be made through the International Seabed Authority (ISA, or 'the Authority') for distribution among state parties based on an equitable sharing criterion as set up under paragraph 4. This Article has not yet been triggered in practice.[19]

Followed ratification of UNCLOS, many countries established constitutional provisions and mining codes at domestic level setting out definitions of state ownership and jurisdiction of minerals over offshore areas, whenever applicable. Individual countries have also enacted specific laws and regulations to govern mineral development in the seabed in areas under their jurisdictions, in line with UNCLOS.[20]

II. Mining Regimes in the Global Commons

International law provides for specific regimes related to mineral resources in relation to the global commons, the sea and space, as well as the legal framework for Antarctica. The 'global commons' refer to areas and natural resources beyond the realm of the national jurisdiction of any individual state, and which belong to the international community as a whole.[21]

A basic principle in resource regime design addresses the question of ownership and property over these resources. For a long time, these resources were subject to 'open access' and were part of the freedom of the high seas.[22] The status

---

[17] See K Schönfeldt (ed), *The Arctic in International Law and Policy* (Oxford, Hart Publishing, 2017).

[18] T Stephens and D VanderZwaag, 'Polar oceans governance: shifting seascapes, hazy horizons' in T Stephens and D VanderZwaag (eds), *Polar Oceans Governance in an Era of Environmental Change* (Cheltenham and Northampton, Edward Elgar Publishing, 2014) 10–11.

[19] Recent oil discoveries off the east coast of Canada could potentially trigger this Article. See RJ Harrison, 'Article 82 of UNCLOS: The day of reckoning approaches' (2017) 10 *The Journal of World Energy Law and Business* 488. A key question is whether the coastal state or the industry bears this cost.

[20] UK Deep Sea Mining Act 2014; Singapore Deep Seabed Mining Act 2015; Tonga Seabed Mining Act 2014; Tuvalu Seabed Minerals Act 2014; Cook Islands Seabed Minerals Act 2009 Act to amend the Seabed Minerals Act 2009 (2015); Fiji International Seabed Mineral Management Decree 2013; New Zealand Exclusive Economic Zone and Continental Shelf (Environmental Effects) Act 2012.

[21] N Schrijver, 'Managing the global commons: common good or common sink?' (2016) 37 *Third World Quarterly* 1252. The global commons typically comprise the high seas, the deep seabed, the atmosphere, Antarctica and the Outer Space. See also S Buck, *The global commons: An introduction* (Washington DC, Island Press, 1998).

[22] Schrijver, 'Managing the global commons' (2016) 1256.

of resources in international areas as a 'heritage of mankind' emerged in connection with the progressive development of international law and has been reflected in the reform of the law of the sea as well as in space law. In space law (much earlier than in the context of the law of the sea negotiations), the principle was incorporated in the 1967 Outer Space Treaty, using its own terminology, and later in the Moon Agreement.[23]

The legal status of the common heritage of mankind doctrine under international law has been hotly debated among scholars. Whereas some are of the view that it is a rule of *jus cogens*, 'a new peremptory norm of general international law from which no derogation is permitted',[24] others see it as a 'philosophical notion with the potential to emerge and crystallise as a legal norm'.[25] An eclectic interpretation endorses legal significance to the concept and, at most, *jus cogens* status to some of its main elements, as the non-appropriation rule.[26]

A. The Seabed Mining Regime

The prospect of incalculable mineral wealth lying on the bottom of the sea was the subject of great controversy and dominated negotiations for an ocean governance regime during the third United Nations Conference on the Law of the Sea from 1973 to 1982. The deep seabed mining regime was called a 'laboratory' for testing the ideas emerging from the NIEO agenda.[27] It found expression in the doctrine of common heritage of mankind famously articulated by Maltese ambassador Arvid Pardo in a speech delivered at the UN General Assembly in November 1967.[28] UNCLOS only came into force in 1994 upon the introduction of significant changes to Part XI of the regime regulated under the 1982 UNCLOS through the Agreement relating to its implementation.[29] These changes addressed the claims

---

[23] The Declaration of Legal Principles Governing the Activities of States in the Exploration and Use of Outer Space (GA Resolution 1962 (XVIII), 13 December 1963) stated that 'The exploration and use of outer space shall be carried on for the benefit and in the interests of all mankind' (Art 1).

[24] N Schrijver, Sovereignty over Natural Resources. Balancing Rights and Duties (Cambridge, Cambridge University Press, 1997) 221 (in reviewing various positions on the status of the doctrine).

[25] C Joyner, 'Legal Implications of the Concept of the Common Heritage of Mankind' (1986) 35 ICQL 190, 199.

[26] Schrijver, Sovereignty over Natural Resources' (1997) 221–22.

[27] F Paolillo, 'The Future Legal Regime of Seabed Resources and the NIEO: Some Issues' in K Hossain, *Legal Aspects of the New International Economic Order* (Frances Pinter Publishers Ltd., London, 1980) 165–66. See also Schrijver (n 21) 1252. See ch 3.III.

[28] GA, Agenda Item 92. Examination of the question of the reservation exclusively for peaceful purposes of the sea-bed and the ocean floor, and the subsoil thereof, underlying the high seas beyond the limits of present national jurisdiction, and the use of their resources in the interests of mankind (A/6695; A/C.1/952). First Committee, 1515th meeting, 1 November 1967. See ED Brown, *Sea-bed Energy and Minerals: The International Legal Regime; Vol 2 Sea-Bed Mining* (The Hague, The Netherlands, Martinus Nijhoff, 2001) 3.

[29] UNCLOS, 10 December 1982, in force from 16 November 1994, 21 ILM 1261 (1982). Agreement relating to the Implementation of Part XI of the UNCLOS of 10 December 1982, New York, 28 July 1994, UNTS vol 1836, 3.

128 *Mining and Minerals Regimes in the Global Commons*

of industrialised nations on aspects such as subsidies to the Enterprise – a supra-national mining company envisaged in this Part – and compulsory transfer of technology.[30] The revisions reflected a move towards a private investment-friendly regime providing for 'a stable environment for investors', guaranteed 'access to the resources of the seabed to all qualified investors', and a taxation regime seen as attractive to the miner while benefitting the international community.[31]

Schrijver has summarised the diverging positions on the administration of a resource regime for seabed resources, which in essence enshrines the long-held distinction between 'first come, first served' v competitive bidding as the basis of criteria to allocate resources:[32]

> At the risk of over-generalization, it could be said that most industrialized nations have preferred to establish an agency which would simply register claims of potential miners, allocate mining sites to them, and collect royalties and taxes. In their view such a liberal sea-bed mining regime would best serve their interests and, according to some, those of humankind. The developing countries, on the other hand, have insisted on a strong International Seabed Authority invested with the exclusive right to manage the resources, acting for humankind as a whole.

Article 150 of UNCLOS states that '[A]ctivities in the Area' must be carried out with a view to 'foster[ing] healthy development of the world economy and balanced growth of international trade, and to promote international coopera-tion for the over-all development of all countries, especially developing States' to ensure a range of objectives that include the 'orderly, safe and rational manage-ment of the resources of the Area'.

i. Common Heritage of Mankind

For centuries the traditional principle of *freedom of the high seas* ruled the use of maritime areas, comprising the freedom to navigate, conduct commerce and fishing. UNCLOS came to limit dramatically this principle, by extending rights of coastal states and by adopting the new principle defining the deep seabed and its resources in areas beyond national jurisdiction as the *common heritage of mankind*.

Under typical categories of ownership regimes, *res communis* denotes property that is not owned by anyone but can be used by everyone (and hence not amena-ble to appropriation), unlike *res nullius* property, which refers to property that does not belong to anyone but is subject to appropriation. There has been consen-sus in understanding the seabed and resources as *res communis*, but divergences on its implications. Industrialised nations have argued that, by application of the

---

[30] M Lodge, 'International Seabed Authority Regulations on Prospecting and Exploration for Polymetallic Nodules in the Area' in AE Bastida, T Wälde, and J Warden–Fernandez (eds), *International and Comparative Mineral Law and Policy: Trends and Prospects* (The Hague, Kluwer Law International, 2005).

[31] ibid 173.

[32] Schrijver (n 24) 219.

principle of freedom of the high seas, they are open to use on a 'first come, first served' basis in practice by nations having the technological resources to access such resources. By contrast, developing nations have argued for the adoption of the concept of the *common heritage of mankind* as concerned with the international administration, management and use of resources, including an appropriate oversight, with the aim of benefitting the common interest of people.[33]

The key UNCLOS Articles are Article 136, stating that 'The Area [defined as 'the sea-bed and ocean floor and the subsoil thereof, beyond the limits of national jurisdiction' under Article 1] and its resources ['all solid, liquid or gaseous mineral resources in situ in the Area at or beneath the seabed, including polymetallic nodules' as per Article 133(a)] are the common heritage of mankind'; and paragraph 2 of Article 137, which sets forth 'All rights in the resources of the Area are vested in mankind as a whole, on whose behalf the Authority shall act'.

The doctrine of the *common heritage of mankind* as implemented under UNCLOS has been characterised by the following features:[34]

- Non-appropriation. The Area and its resources cannot be subject to claims, the exercise of sovereignty nor appropriation by anyone (para. 1 of article 137); 'the resources are not subject to alienation' (para. 2 of article 137);

- Administration by the international community. The 'Authority' established under Section 4, Part XI (article 156 and ss.) is set to fulfil a double function as a 'global regulatory agency' with the mandate of organising and controlling activities in the Area (through an Assembly, a Council and a Secretariat) and as a 'deep seabed miner' through the 'Enterprise', which is empowered to carry out activities including exploration and exploitation, as well as the transportation, processing and marketing of minerals. It is worth noting that the Enterprise has not been established yet;

- Benefit sharing: Activities in the Area must be conducted for the benefit of mankind as a whole, irrespective of the geographical location of States, whether coastal or landlocked, taking into consideration the needs of developing countries (article 140), and equitable revenue-sharing (article 140 and provisions on the transfer of technology, article 144);

---

[33] See CR Buxton, 'Property in Outer Space: The Common Heritage of Mankind Principle vs. the First in Time, First in Right, Rule of Property' (2004) 69 *Journal of Air Law and Commerce* 4, 689; Schrijver (n 24) 219. See further bibliography: K Baslar, *The Concept of the Common Heritage of Mankind in International Law* (Dordrecht, Martinus Nijhoff, 1998), AA Cançado Trindade, 'International Law for Humankind towards a New Jus Gentium' (2005) 316 *Recueil Des Cours* 316, 365, ED Brown, 'Freedom of the high seas versus the common heritage of mankind: fundamental principles in conflict' (1982–1983) 10 *San Diego Law Review* 521; I Brownlie, 'Legal status of natural resources in international law (some aspects)' (1979) 162 *Recueil Des Cours* I; RJ Dupuy, 'La notion de patrimoine commun de l'humanité appliquée aux fonds marins' in C-A Colliard, *Droit et libertés à la fin du XXe siècle: Influence des données économiques et technologiques. Etudes offertes à Claude-Albert Colliard* (Paris, Editions Pedone, 1984) 197–205; M Lodge, 'The deep seabed' in D Rothwell, A Oude Elferink, K Scott, T Stephens (eds), *The Oxford Handbook of the Law of the Sea* (Oxford, Oxford University Press, 2015) 226–53.

[34] See Joyner, 'Legal Implications' (1986) 191–92 and Schrijver (n 24) 219–20.

130   *Mining and Minerals Regimes in the Global Commons*

- Use of the Area for peaceful purposes (article 141);

- Respect for the interests of future generations, relevant to decision-making on the use and distribution of resources, implied in the very same notion of 'heritage'.[35]

The Authority has noted the acute challenges entailed in integrating and implementing these principles into the legal framework, in a context of evolving technological and scientific knowledge, and of commercial uncertainty. On the one hand, this should be 'adaptive, practical and technically feasible', striving to apply the precautionary principle.[36] On the other, this should be embedded in an understanding of the financial and economic model for deep seabed mining, and factors influencing supply, demand and prices, taking into account the interests of importing and exporting countries, particularly those of developing countries, for developing equitable sharing criteria.[37]

ii. The Mining Code

The Mining Code refers to all the rules, regulations and procedures adopted by ISA to govern prospecting, exploration and exploitation of marine minerals in the Area. The legislative regime for the Area established under Part XI and Annex III of UNCLOS on 'Basic Conditions of Prospecting, Exploration and Exploitation', the 1994 Agreement relating to the Implementation of Part XI of UNCLOS and the Mining Code all conform a single integrated system, and together with supplementary regulations and recommendations, they are, overall, the most developed international governance regime for mineral resource activities.

The specific sets of regulations, which constitute part of the Mining Code, include: (i) the Regulations on Prospecting and Exploration for Polymetallic Nodules in the Area, adopted on 13 July 2000, and which have been updated in 2013;[38] (ii) the Regulations on Prospecting and Exploration for Polymetallic Sulphides in the Area, adopted on 7 May 2010;[39] and (iii) the Regulations on

---

[35] See Joyner (n 25) 195, and Schrijver (n 24) 220.

[36] ISA, 'Consideration, with a view to adoption, of the draft strategic plan of the International Seabed Authority for the period 2019–2023,' ISBA/24/A/4, 6, available at www.isa.org.jm/sites/default/files/files/documents/isba24_a4-en.pdf.

[37] ibid 7.

[38] Regulations on Prospecting and Exploration for Polymetallic Nodules in the Area, ISBA/6/A/18. Approved at 76th meeting, 13 July 2000; Decision of the Council of the International Seabed Authority relating to amendments to the Regulations on Prospecting and Exploration for Polymetallic Nodules in the Area and related matters, ISBA/19/C/17. Approved at 190th meeting, 22 July 2013; Decision of the Assembly of the International Seabed Authority regarding the amendments to the Regulations on Prospecting and Exploration for Polymetallic Nodules in the Area, ISBA/19/A/9. Approved at 142nd meeting, 25 July 2013.

[39] Decision of the Assembly of the International Seabed Authority relating to the regulations on prospecting and exploration for polymetallic sulphides in the Area, ISBA/16/A/12/Rev.1. Adopted at 130th session, 7 May 2010.

Prospecting and Exploration for Cobalt-Rich Ferromanganese Crusts in the Area, adopted on 27 July 2012.[40] These regulations include provisions for applying for exploration rights and the standard terms of exploration contracts, as well as for the protection and preservation of the marine environment. There are also other general procedural provisions[41] and recommendations issued by the Legal and Technical Commission of the Authority for guiding contractors on the submission of reports, assessment of environmental impacts and training.[42]

iii. *The Enterprise and the 'Parallel System'*

Either the Enterprise or state parties or qualified state-sponsored entities, in association with the Authority, are entitled to carry out the exploration and exploitation of the Area (Article 153), which can occur simultaneously due to the 'parallel system'. The Enterprise may apply on an equal footing with other applicants and must provide the same contractual undertakings.

The Enterprise is a supra-national mining company authorised to carry out activities in the Area as well as the transportation, processing and marketing of minerals recovered from the Area (Article 170). The mining regime under 1982 UNCLOS envisaged substantial competitive advantages for the Enterprise, which were at the heart of long-held disagreements between negotiating parties. The modified text of 1994, on the contrary, guaranteed exclusive rights to miners, security of tenure, stability of expectations and title to any mineral extracted and due process through extensive judicial and arbitral remedies to protect such rights. The Enterprise has not been established yet and it is thought that in the future it might operate in association with others through joint ventures. There are ongoing deliberations at the Authority on the development of rules and regulations for governing future joint ventures.[43]

---

[40] Decision of the Assembly of the International Seabed Authority relating to the Regulations on Prospecting and Exploration for Cobalt-rich Ferromanganese Crusts in the Area, ISBA/18/A/11. Approved at 138th meeting, 27 July 2012.

[41] Decision of the Assembly of the International Seabed Authority concerning overhead charges for the administration and supervision of exploration contracts, ISBA/19/A/12. Adopted at 142nd meeting, 25 July 2013; Decision of the Council of the International Seabed Authority relating to the procedures and criteria for the extension of an approved plan of work for exploration pursuant to section 1, para 9, of the annex to the Agreement relating to the Implementation of Part XI of the United Nations Convention on the Law of the Sea of 10 December 1982, ISBA/21/C/19. Adopted at 212th meeting, 23 July 2015.

[42] Recommendations for the guidance of contractors on the content, format and structure of annual reports ISBA/21/LTC/15; Recommendations for the guidance of contractors for the reporting of actual and direct exploration expenditure ISBA/21/LTC/11; Recommendations for the guidance of contractors for the assessment of the possible environmental impacts arising from exploration for marine minerals in the Area ISBA/19/LTC/8; Recommendations for the guidance of contractors and sponsoring States relating to training programmes under plans of work for exploration ISBA/19/LTC/14.

[43] IISD Reporting Services, 1st Part of the 25th Annual Session of the International Seabed Authority (ISA) 25 February – 1 March 2019 | Headquarters of the International Seabed Authority, Kingston, Jamaica. Available at http://enb.iisd.org/oceans/isa/2019-1.

132 Mining and Minerals Regimes in the Global Commons

A central feature of the system consists of the reservation of areas as developed states apply for exploration rights to the ISA; this has been called the 'parallel system'.[44] These areas are held in a 'site bank' for activities to be conducted by developing states or by the Authority through the Enterprise.[45] In the case of applications for polymetallic nodules, the area and value of the application (which should not necessarily cover a single continuous area) should be of such an extent as to allow two mining operations of 'equal estimated commercial value'.[46] The Authority's Secretariat is entrusted with the responsibility of conducting resource assessments in these areas. The first group of reserved areas date back to the late 1980s and early 1990s and were contributed under the interim regime so-called 'pioneer investor regime' adopted by the third UN Conference on the Law of the Sea, adopted prior to the entry into force of UNCLOS. These were mostly situated in the Clarion-Clipperton Zone (in the Central Pacific Ocean south and southeast of Hawaii).[47] A second group of reserved areas was designated after the establishment of ISA in 1994.[48] In the case of polymetallic sulphides and cobalt-rich crusts, as applicants have found it hard to collect enough survey data to identify two sites in accordance with the requirements of the regulations, they have been authorised to offer a future equity interest in a joint venture with the Enterprise as an option to contributing a reserved area.[49]

iv. The Regime for Prospecting, Exploring and Mining in the Area

Prospecting is unrestricted and non-exclusive; it does not require a permit, but rather a written undertaking from the prospector to comply with the relevant applicable rules and submission of an annual report. The scope of the regime of prospecting as a general survey may overlap with marine scientific research, which is open to all states.

Exploration rights are granted upon a contract. They are exclusive and cover an area of up to 150,000 km^2 for a period not exceeding 15 years and subject to relinquishment obligations for half of the area over the first eight years of the contract.[50] The maximum size of the areas allocated depends on each type of mineral pursuant to the relevant regulations.[51] Contractors are required to propose

---

[44] UNCLOS, Annex III, Art 8.

[45] ISA, 'Current Status of the Reserved Areas with the International Seabed Authority', Policy Brief 01/2019.

[46] Regulation 15, ISBA/6/A/18.

[47] ISA, 'Current Status of the Reserved Areas with the International Seabed Authority'.

[48] ibid.

[49] ibid.

[50] Regulation 24(1) – UNCLOS Arts 153–56 and Annex III, Arts 3–4 and 16. Agreement Annex Section 1–9. Lodge, 3.5.

[51] For polymetallic nodules, the total area allocated to the contractor under the contract must not exceed 150,000 km^2 subject to relinquishment obligations (except for the case the area does not exceed 75,000 km^2) – Reg 25, ISBA/19/C/17. For cobalt-rich ferromanganese crusts, the total area covered by the application, a 'cobalt crust block' is one or more cells of a grid as provided by the Authority,

Mining Regimes in the Global Commons 133

a training programme for nationals of developing states, which will be incorporated as a schedule into the contract. They must submit a contingency plan prior to commencing activities and annual reports on their activities thereafter. The procedure starts with an application to the Authority for approval of an exploration plan of work, submission of a declaration of responsibility and evidence of qualification standards, compliance with environmental regulation and payment of an application fee (USD 250,000). The Authority's Legal and Technical Commission has issued guidelines for contractors to follow on environmental impact assessments for the exploration of polymetallic nodules.[52] Although non-binding, they may eventually contribute to form part of a code of best practices for contractors. Since 2001, 30 15-year contracts for exploration for polymetallic nodules, polymetallic sulphides and cobalt-rich ferromanganese crusts in the deep seabed have been signed between the ISA and a range of contractors.[53]

UNCLOS provides for the Member States' obligation to protect and preserve the marine environment. The Authority is entrusted with the responsibility to set rules, regulations and procedures for preventing, reducing and controlling pollution of the marine environment from activities carried out in the Area, as well as for protecting and preserving the biodiversity of the marine environment. The Authority has approved an environmental management plan for the Clarion-Clipperton Zone that designates a network of areas of particular environmental interest, indicating that it 'gives effect to the precautionary approach as called for by the Regulations' and that it will be applied in a flexible manner to allow improvements as further 'scientific, technical and environmental baseline and resource assessment data are supplied by contractors and other interested bodies'.[54]

Regarding exploitation regulations, in 2017 the Authority released the Draft Regulations on Exploitation of Mineral Resources in the Area (ISBA/23/LTC/CRP.3). This has gone through further revisions and been open to stakeholders'

---

which may be square or rectangular in shape and no greater than 20 km^2 in size. The area covered by each application for approval of a plan of work for exploration for cobalt crusts shall be comprised of not more than 150 cobalt crust blocks, which shall be arranged by the applicant in clusters (Reg 12, ISBA/18/A/11). The contractor shall relinquish portions of the area allocated to it to revert to the Area. A contractor shall not be required to relinquish any additional part of such area when the remaining area allocated to it after relinquishment does not exceed 1,000 km^2 (Reg 27, ISBA/18/A/11). For polymetallic sulphides, the total area allocated to the contractor under the contract shall not exceed 10,000 km^2. The contractor shall relinquish portions of the area allocated to it to revert to the Area. A contractor shall not be required to relinquish any additional part of such area when the remaining area allocated to it after relinquishment does not exceed 2,500 km^2 (Reg 27). A 'polymetallic sulphide block' means a cell of a grid as provided by the Authority, which shall be approximately 10 km by 10 km and no greater than 100 km^2. The area covered by each application for approval of a plan of work for exploration for polymetallic sulphides shall be comprised of not more than 100 polymetallic sulphide blocks which shall be arranged by the applicant in at least five clusters (Reg 12, ISBA/16/A/12/Rev.1).

[52] Recommendations for the guidance of contractors for the assessment of the possible environmental impacts arising from exploration for marine minerals in the Area, ISBA/19/LTC/8.

[53] See ISA website, Deep seabed minerals contractors, available at www.isa.org.jm/deep-seabed-minerals-contractors.

[54] Decision of the Council relating to an environmental management plan for the Clarion-Clipperton Zone, ISBA/18/C/22. Approved at 180th meeting, 26 July 2012.

134　*Mining and Minerals Regimes in the Global Commons*

submissions.[55] The Draft intends to crystallise the doctrine of common heritage of mankind while striking a balance with investors' concerns. To promote adaptation to evolving knowledge, the Draft envisages the regulations will be reviewed every five years.[56] It raises key points of contention regarding the operationalisation of the polluter-pays principle, the precautionary principle and an ecosystem approach as well as enforcement provisions.[57] Some aspects have been further researched through studies and background notes, as the use of the contract as security by the contractor, the scope of insurance policy coverage, closure plans, settlement of disputes and payable fees. A few key provisions are the subject of further research, such as the economic benefit-sharing system and regional environmental management plans.

B. The Question of Banning Mining in Antarctica

Under the 1959 Antarctic Treaty System (ATS), the 1988 Convention on the Regulation of Antarctic Mineral Resource Activities (CRAMRA) was negotiated between 1982 and 1988.[58] It was designed to regulate mineral resource development for managing environmental degradation in a rational and orderly manner, with a view to ensuring the ATS's primary purpose of using Antarctica for peaceful purposes only.[59] CRAMRA acknowledged in its Preamble:

> [T]he unique ecological, scientific and wilderness value of Antarctica and the importance of Antarctica to the global environment; … that Antarctic mineral resource activities could adversely affect the Antarctic environment or dependent or associated ecosystems; and that the protection of the Antarctic environment and dependent and associated ecosystems must be a basic consideration in decisions taken on possible Antarctic mineral resource activities.

It followed that no mining was allowed except in accordance with CRAMRA (Article 3). CRAMRA foresaw the embedding of 'intrinsic, wilderness and, aesthetic values, concepts now found in the Madrid Protocol'.[60]

---

[55] Draft Regulations on Exploitation of Mineral Resources in the Area, ISBA/24/LTC/WP.1/Rev.1, 24th session, LTC session, part II, 2–13 July 2018; see also ISBA/25/C/WP.1 and ISBA/25/C/18 considered by the Council of ISA in the second part of 25th session, July 2010. See 26th session, Council session, part I, 17–21 February 2020. Comments on the draft regulations on the exploitation of mineral resources in the Area.

[56] ISA, 'Consideration, with a view to adoption, of the draft strategic plan of the International Seabed Authority for the period 2019–2023,' 5, available at www.isa.org.jm/sites/default/files/files/documents/isba24_a4-en.pdf.

[57] See 26th session, Council session, part I, 17–21 February 2020. Comments on the draft regulations on the exploitation of mineral resources in the Area.

[58] Antarctic Treaty, 1 December 1959, UNTS Vol 402, 71 (adopted by the seven states with territorial claims to parts of Antarctica: Argentina, Australia, Chile, France, New Zealand, Norway and the UK, plus Belgium, Japan, South Africa, the then Soviet Union and the US – the original '12 Consultative Parties'). See L Goldsworthy and A Hemmings, 'The Antarctic Protected Area Approach' (2008) 106.

[59] See F Orrego Vicuña, *Antarctic Mineral Exploration: The Emerging Legal Framework* (Cambridge, Cambridge University Press, 1988).

[60] Goldsworthy and Hemmings, 'Antarctic Protected Area Approach' (2008) 111.

In June 1988 all the Consultative Parties agreed on the CRAMRA text and this was open for signature in Wellington, New Zealand in November 1988 (requiring the ratification of all signatory states). Christopher Joyner explains that 'despite its attributes as a preclusive management regime', the Convention was 'stillborn'. The environmental community argued that making mining lawful in Antarctica would lift the policy of 'voluntary restraint' acting as an incentive to prospecting (which could lead to discoveries and mining) resources in Antarctica, leading to environmental degradation.[61] In June 1989, Australia and France (both states signatory to the Antarctic Treaty) decided not to sign the agreement. This meant CRAMRA never entered into force as it was not ratified. Joyner suggests that environmental considerations might well have shifted Australia's position on mining in Antarctica. In January–February 1989, oil spills occurred in Antarctic waters followed by the major oil spill disaster in Alaska when the tanker *Exxon Valdez* hit a reef.[62] CRAMRA's shelving meant shifting attention from a *resource regime* regulating mining against environmental degradation to a system of *comprehensive environmental protection* from degradation *before* it occurs.[63]

This was the thrust of the Protocol on Environmental Protection to the Antarctic Treaty (Madrid Protocol), adopted in 1991 and in force since 1998.[64] The Protocol designated Antarctica as a 'natural reserve' (Article 2) and prohibited 'any activity relating to mineral resources, other than scientific research' (Article 7). Interpreted with other provisions of the Protocol, such a restriction means a moratorium on mining for a 50-year period (until 2048), subject to review.[65] The ban may only be lifted in a two-step procedure: first, upon the unanimous vote of the Consultative Parties involved in the negotiation and the adoption of a binding legal regime governing mining; and second, upon two-thirds of votes of those Parties.[66]

C. Exploring the Moon and Other Celestial Bodies

The Treaty on Principles Governing the Activities of States in the Exploration and Use of Outer Space, including the Moon and other Celestial Bodies (the 'Outer

---

[61] C Joyner, *Governing the Frozen Commons. The Antarctic Regime and Environmental Protection* (Columbia, South Carolina: University of South Carolina Press, 1998) 149.

[62] Joyner, *Governing the Frozen Commons* (1998) 150.

[63] Joyner (n 61); M Weber, 'Power Politics in the Antarctic Treaty System' in T Stephens and DL VanderZwaag (eds), *Polar Oceans Governance in an Era of Environmental Change* (Cheltenham, Edward Elgar, 2014) 92.

[64] Protocol on Environmental Protection to the *Antarctic Treaty*. Adopted 4 October 1991, entered into force 14 January 1998, 30 *ILM* 1455.

[65] See Art 25 of Protocol. See Joyner (n 61) 166–69. See D Leary, 'From Hydrocarbons to Psychrophiles: The "Scramble" for Antarctic and Arctic Resources' in Stephens and VanderZwaag (eds), *Polar Oceans Governance* (2014) 142.

[66] Goldsworthy (n 60) 111.

Space Treaty') is the fundamental framework governing space exploration.[67] It has been ratified by more than 100 countries. Signed during the Cold War, its purpose was to ensure international cooperation and agreement on the use of outer space for peaceful purposes. Article I of the 1967 treaty states that 'The exploration and use of outer space, including the moon and other celestial bodies, shall be carried out for the benefit and in the interests of all countries, irrespective of their degree of economic or scientific development and shall be the province of all mankind'.[68] It highlights that outer space shall be free for exploration by all countries without any discrimination, on the basis of equality and in accordance to international law. Article II affirms that 'Outer space, including the moon and other celestial bodies, is not subject to national appropriation by claim of sovereignty, by means of use or occupation, or by any other means'. Article III of the treaty sets forth that exploration and use of outer space is to be conducted in accordance to international law 'in the interest of maintaining international peace and security and promoting international cooperation and understanding'.

The Moon Agreement defines the moon and its natural resources as 'the common heritage of mankind' (Article 11(1)), which finds expression particularly on the establishment of an 'international regime, including appropriate procedures, to govern the exploitation of the natural resources of the moon as such exploitation is about to become feasible' (Article 11(5)).[69] The purpose of such a regime would be promoting 'the orderly and safe development of the natural resources of the moon' as well as their 'rational management', the 'expansion of opportunities in the use of those resources' and 'equitable sharing by all states parties in the benefits derived from those resources, whereby the interests and needs of the developing countries, as well as the efforts of those countries which have contributed either directly or indirectly to the exploration of the moon, shall be given special consideration' (Article 11(7)). In practice, only 15 countries have ratified, and two have signed, the Moon Agreement and, with the exception of France, none of them are space-faring nations. Those countries 'unbound' by the Moon Agreement and with the ability to develop the required technology would argue for the historical principle of 'first come, first served' to access resources.[70] Even such a reduced number of ratifications is, for some authors, significant, as it 'delegitimises any unilateral action by interested states'.[71]

---

[67] Treaty on Principles Governing the Activities of States in the Exploration and Use of Outer Space, including the Moon and Other Celestial Bodies. UNTS No 8843. Opened for signature on 27 January 1967, 205.

[68] Article 1 of the 1967 Outer Space Treaty.

[69] Agreement Governing the Activities of States on the Moon and other Celestial Bodies. UNTS, Volume No 1363, 3. Opened for signature on 18 December 1979. Entry into force on 11 July 1984, in accordance with Art 19(3).

[70] Buxton, 'Property in Outer Space' (2004) in connection to the US.

[71] Schrijver (n 21).

The US has recently adopted a national act recognising entitlements to asteroid or space resources.[72] The move responds to growing private sector's interest in mining and using extra-terrestrial resources, and their concerns for certainty and a clear legal framework.[73] Luxembourg, in turn, sought to compete with the US by putting in place a legal framework aiming at guaranteeing companies based in Luxembourg (whether national or not) property rights for space resources. The legality of these national acts is questionable and contrary to the non-appropriation principle.[74]

This chapter has reviewed the mining and minerals regimes in the global commons. The ancient dispute between free access and common management as competing approaches underlies the debates on the design of resource regimes for every each of the global commons. The international community has managed to cooperate in the design of the deep seabed mining regime, which is based on the principle of common heritage of mankind. It calls for the operationalisation of broad principles (the precautionary principle, sustainable resource use, intergenerational equity, common but differentiated responsibilities and integration), all subject to intense debate.

---

[72] US Commercial Space Launch Competitiveness Act, H.R.2262 – 114th Congress (2015–2016) encompassing the Space Resource Exploration and Utilization Act, H.R.1508 – 114th Congress (2015–2016), which establishes that 'A U.S. citizen or company engaged in commercial recovery of an asteroid resource or a space resource shall be entitled to any asteroid resource or space resource obtained, including to possess, own, transport, use, and sell it according to applicable law, including U.S. international obligations'.

[73] It has been said that it could take 20 to 30 years to develop the technology required for those purposes.

[74] F Tronchetti, 'The Space Resource Exploration and Utilization Act: A move forward or a step back?' (2015) 34 *Space Policy* 6.

6

Mining Law Regimes at the Level of Nation-States (and their Interface with Local Levels)

While sovereignty constitutes the cornerstone doctrine of international law, the determination of the constitutional, legal and regulatory rules applicable to resources within the territories of nation-states belongs to the realm of municipal law.[1] States as sovereigns hold authority to govern and regulate access and management of minerals within their territories. They have traditionally done so through mining law regimes or 'systems' which, at their core, usually establish a nexus between three forms of ownership and rights or entitlements: (i) primary ownership on minerals over the subsoil; (ii) rights to explore and extract minerals (through licences or contractual forms); and (iii) the interface with the surface rights owners and holders to the land, as well as entitlements to water and other natural resources. The latter might connect mining law regimes with local levels of normative ordering. The principle of 'public purpose' or 'public utility' has characteristically grounded specific principles (eg separation of surface from mineral resources' ownership; precedence of mining over other land uses), rules and regimes to provide miners with 'access' to land and resources. The very same existence and justification of a specific law to govern mining, its scope and approach, depends of course on the extent to which a state assigns importance, and values, minerals, land and resources. Some countries might rely on a patchwork of contracts only, with little overall consistency to constitute a generalised framework for mining activities.[2]

Broad systems of mining law can be distinguished along legal traditions and historical patterns of dissemination, with the caveat put forward by Anthony Scott when noting that 'systems of mining law are not easily classified into distinct national or theoretical types'; most systems are very old and they have survived because they have been adapted to changing circumstances.[3]

---

[1] C Redgwell, 'Property Law Sources and Analogies in International Law' in A McHarg, B Barton, A Bradbrook and L Godden (eds), *Property and the Law in Energy and Natural Resources* (Oxford, Oxford University Press, 2010) 101–12.

[2] P Cameron and M Stanley, *Oil, Gas, and Mining. A Sourcebook for Understanding the Extractive Industries* (Washington, The World Bank Group, 2017) 4.

[3] A Scott, *The Evolution of Resource Property Rights* (Oxford, Oxford University Press, 2008). See A McHarg, B Barton, A Bradbrook and L Godden, 'Property and the Law in Energy and Natural Resources' in McHarg, Barton, Bradbrook and Godden, *Property and the Law* (2010) 7.

Mining Law Regimes at the Level of Nation-States 139

In Western tradition, the origins of these systems date back to Roman law, and concepts and practices found in medieval Europe which were later diffused with territorial expansions, colonialism and globalisation. Unlike the oil and gas regimes (having generally outgrown mineral regimes) that do show some standardisation in the use of common contracts, there is greater variation in mining laws across jurisdictions and regarding different minerals; and property/tenure systems are still preponderant in a few countries with regards to metallic minerals. These have been called one of the basic infrastructure linking global trade and investment with mining territories,[4] the other being transnational mining contracts.

This chapter will describe in a general manner broad systems of primary minerals ownership; typologies of regimes of acquisition or granting of mineral rights, and their interface with surface rights, as structural features of comparative mining law regimes as often categorised by (Western) scholarship, delving, to do so, into their historical origins. It will also examine the principle of 'public purpose' or 'public utility', which has characteristically underpinned specific rules and regimes to deal with mining. Last, it will enquire into their interface with evolving constitutional norms and administrative law, as well as fields of international law aimed at strengthening the rule of law and, further, to achieving the goals of sustainability.

The chapter deals with these core features, which can be understood as mining law *sensu stricto*,[5] comprising the definitions of minerals ownership as well as the rules and procedures to access rights for exploring and exploiting minerals, which (until the establishment of the deep seabed mining regime under UNCLOS, the United Nations Convention on the Law of the Sea) has always eminently been a matter of *domestic law*. The overall legal framework of mining and minerals at national levels (mining law *sensu lato*), usually encompasses the multi-layered framework governing mineral resources' development and the relationships between the state, the miners and surface rights holders, local communities as well as other actors involved in the activity,[6] and the regulatory procedures to get permission from different administrative agencies to operate, often at lower government levels. It also comprises, more broadly, the whole range of contracts and with those areas of law which have implications in the various aspects of mineral investment and development, financing, infrastructure, taxation, competition, planning and management. This framework covers regulations setting up limits to meet a range of public interest objectives, such as ensuring fair competition between economic

---

[4] D Szablowski and B Campbell, 'Struggles over extractive governance: Power, discourse, violence, and legality' (2019) 6 *The Extractive Industries and Society* 636.

[5] Tenure has been defined, in general terms, as a right, term, or mode of holding or occupying. See a general definition in *Blacks Dictionary of Law*, 2nd edn (Union, New Jersey, The Lawbook Exchange Ltd, 1995) 1145. Land tenure means the rights and terms under which land is held, including the rights and obligations of the holder. See J Bruce, 'Review of tenure terminology' (1998) 1 *Tenure Brief* 1–2, Land Tenure Center, University of Wisconsin, and E Liedholm-Johnson, 'Mineral Rights: Legal Systems Governing Exploration and Exploitation' (2010) 4 Institutionen för infrastruktur, Fastighetsteknik 38.

[6] See AD Cançado Trindade, 'Princípios de Direito Minerário Brasileiro' in MM Gomes de Souza (ed), *Direito Minerário em Evoluçao* (Belo Horizonte, CEAMIN and Mandamentos Editora, 2009) 48.

140 *Mining Law Regimes at the Level of Nation-States*

actors, protecting labour rights and the health and safety of workers or consumers, protecting the environment, planning land uses and ensuring the sustainable management and development of natural resources.

I. Ownership and Jurisdiction Over Minerals in Situ

A fundamental question in traditional resource regimes is who owns, is *primarily* entitled to and has the legal capacity to use, enjoy and dispose of minerals in situ? It is very hard to generalise or build typologies on this subject, not least because similar terminology is used to signify different situations across different jurisdictions and different lines of scholarship (eg, what the *regalian* doctrine entails), but also because there is a great divergence along legal, political and economic divides that also influences the status of ownership over surface land, legal traditions in which mining law regimes are embedded and scholarship positions are laid down. Definitions of ownership might have been drafted in recent constitutional or peace agreements in some countries. In many others, they may have evolved over time and be subject to legislative change, judicial interpretation and scholarship contention. Broadly speaking, the legal status of primary mineral ownership sets the basis for the regimes of acquisition or granting (or 'disposal') of mineral rights, and their legal status, and might provide the grounds for setting royalties and specific fiscal terms.

A related crucial question in resource regimes is who holds jurisdiction, the power to control, regulate and manage natural resources (which does not necessarily square with ownership) or matters relevant to their management.[7] Depending on their constitutional structures, subnational levels of government might hold powers to make laws and regulate and/or enforce minerals access and management (including powers of taxation), while municipalities may hold powers to decide on land use planning that might conflict with minerals development.

Comparative regimes generally distinguish between two main legal doctrines of mineral ownership in situ, whereby minerals are attributed to whoever owns the land (the doctrine of landownership, often called the 'accession system'), or they are attributed to, or controlled by the state (the *regalian* and domanial doctrines). In Western tradition, these doctrines developed under Roman law over different periods, and ideas and practices found in medieval Europe, themselves the object of wide dissemination. Furthermore, civil law scholars usually incorporate *res nullius* as another legal doctrine to define ownership in situ.

Civil law concepts of ownership are based on the concept of *dominium*, the ultimate right to use and dispose of a thing subject to public interest reasons.[8]

---

[7] N Haysom and S Kane, *Negotiating natural resources for peace: Ownership, control and wealth-sharing*, Briefing Paper, Centre for Humanitarian Dialogue, October 2009.

[8] L Aladeitan, 'Ownership and Control of Oil, Gas and Mineral Resources in Nigeria: Between Legality and Legitimacy' (2012) 38 *Thurgood Marshall Law Review* 159, 160.

Ownership and Jurisdiction Over Minerals in Situ   141

In Anglo-American legal systems, ownership is more closely assimilated to a bundle of rights. The collation of rights comprising ownership include as 'standard incidents of ownership' the right to dispose of the property (*ius disponendi*), the right to use the property (*ius utendi*), the right to draw the fruits of the property (*ius fruendi*), and the right to neglect, or to fail to develop, the property (*ius abutendi*).[9] In general terms, assets with public or state ownership are subject to the specific rules of administrative law although there are important variations in civil law and in common law countries.

A. The Landownership Doctrine

The basic principle of the land ownership doctrine is that minerals belong to the owner of the land where deposits are found. This regime has traditionally been the case in English common law countries. It is based on early Roman law, which considered that minerals were an integral part of the soil, whether they were located on the surface (such as quarries) or in the subsurface.[10]

This regime has commonly been defined by the maxim *cuius est solum, ejus est usque ad coelum et ad inferos*. The maxim is said to have been coined by Accursius, the thirteenth-century glossator of the *Iustinian's Digest*, and was later used in early English common law (in *Bury v Pope* of 1586), and famously stated by Lord Edward Coke around 1628,[11] and later by Blackstone in 1766, and then widely diffused in English and American courts.[12] In the famous debate before the French National Assembly on the enactment of the 1791 French Law of Mines, the arena for two antagonistic positions on the question of mineral ownership in situ and systems to allocate mineral rights,[13] the physiocrat Merlin argued for this, which he called the 'accession theory', drawing on the legal fiction of the subsurface as appurtenant to the surface land.[14]

This system applies to onshore minerals and oil and gas in situ in private lands in the US.[15] In the UK today, there is a presumption that the surface owner owns the underlying strata and all subjacent minerals in the absence of any evidence to

---

[9] H Mostert, *Mineral Law: Principles and Policies in Perspective* (Cape Town, Juta, 2012) 9. See also TL Field, *State Governance of Mining, Development and Sustainability* (Cheltenham and Northampton, Edward Elgar Publishing, 2019).

[10] See Scott, *Evolution of Resource Property Rights* (2008) 194.

[11] See a critical analysis in HD Klein, '*Cujus Est Solum Ejus Est … Quousque Tandem*' (1959) 26 *Journal of Air Law and Commerce* 3, 237.

[12] JG Sprankling, 'Owning the Centre of the Earth' (2008) 55 *UCLA Law Review* 979.

[13] This section partially draws on AE Bastida, 'The Perennial Questions of Ownership, Mineral Rights, and Land Rights: From Principles to Practice', Rocky Mountain Mineral Law Foundation, Proceedings of the International Mining and Oil & Gas – Law, Development, and Investment Conference, panel on Ownership of Minerals, Cartagena, 23 April 2013.

[14] See NJ Campbell, 'Principles of Ownership in the Civil Law and Common Law Systems' (1956–1957) 31 *Tulane Law Review* 303.

[15] R Basset and A Irvine, 'United States' in *Getting the Deal Through – Mining in 31 jurisdictions worldwide* (London, Law Business Research Ltd, 2013) 211. The landownership system was also in

142 *Mining Law Regimes at the Level of Nation-States*

the contrary, but the rights to a range of minerals are owned or vested in the Crown either by common law or statute. Evidence may consist of a document (most commonly a deed) of severance, by which the original owner had disposed of the surface and retained the minerals (or some of the minerals), or vice versa. In effect, case law has established that different strata may be in separate ownership.[16] In some land areas in some provinces in Canada, minerals or mineral rights are also held privately due to either historical land grants or earlier mining legislation.[17] Even under the landownership system, the state might be willing to exercise a regulatory function regarding what is otherwise a private law situation.[18] The former 1991 South African Minerals Act is one example in which minerals were vested in the landowner – and thus their acquisition was ruled by property law – but then a licence was required from the state to enable the holder of rights to exercise them.[19] While the first component might be a private law matter, the second one has a public law licensing component necessary to exercise the rights so acquired.[20]

Two countervailing trends can broadly be observed on the application of the landownership system over an extended period. The first is that, as this system implies placing mineral resources in situ under the sphere of private property and private law, it has generally been withdrawn as the importance or strategic nature of some minerals is acknowledged, or political-economic changes occur. The adoption of this system in feudal Britain meant that the minor nobility benefitted at the expense of the monarchy.[21] But this principle did not apply to gold and silver (metals used for coinage), on which the Crown established its royal prerogative in 1568. The royal prerogative also applied to land owned by the Crown, in Britain and its colonies.[22] Over time, coal also came to be deemed

---

place in the Russian Empire, from the adoption of a manifesto in June 1782, to 1917. See A Kursky and A Konoplyanik, 'State Regulation and Mining Law Development in Russia from 16th to 21st Century' in AE Bastida, T Wälde, J Warden-Fernandez (eds), *International and Comparative Mineral Law and Policy: Trends and Prospects* (The Hague, Kluwer Law International, 2005) 969–1008. In Brazil, the landownership system was adopted with the advent of the First Republic in 1891 and was in place until the Constitution of 1934 which separated surface property from mineral resources' ownership, which was attributed to the Nation. PH de Castro Júnior and T de Mattos Silva, *Compensaçao Financeira pela Exploração de Recursos Minerais* (Belo Horizonte, Editora D'Placido, 2018) 22.

[16] P Morgan, 'An Overview of the Legal Regime for Mineral Development in the United Kingdom' in AE Bastida, T Wälde and J Warden – Fernandez (eds), *International and Comparative Mineral Law and Policy: Trends and Prospects* (The Hague, Kluwer Law International, 2005) 1086 (referring to *Cox v Glue* (1848) 5 CB 533 as per H Halvey and C Masson (eds) *Halsburys Laws of England*, 4th edn (London, Butterworths, 1998) vol 31 'Mines Minerals and Quarries'). *Mineral Law and Policy: Trends and Prospects* (The Hague, Kluwer Law International, 2005) 1086.

[17] M Bourassa and A Lacy, 'Canada' in 'GTDT: Market Intelligence' (2019).

[18] M Dale, 'South African Mineral Law. Present and Future' in 'Global Issues in Corporate Mining Strategy and Government Policy,' CEPMLP Dundee Annual Mining Seminar, 4–8 June 2001. See also M Dale, 'Security of Tenure as a Key Issue Facing the International Mining Company: A South African Perspective' (1996) 14 *Journal of Energy & Natural Resources Law* 305.

[19] ibid. This operated in a similar manner to a driving licence.

[20] ibid.

[21] Scott (n 3).

[22] ibid.

Ownership and Jurisdiction Over Minerals in Situ 143

royal prerogative and excluded from surface land ownership. This all occurred either by common law or statute.[23]

A second, more recent, trend, has found application of the land ownership doctrine with increasing recognition of indigenous peoples' land and resource ownership. In Canada, some comprehensive land claim agreements acknowledge indigenous ownership rights over the surface, which in some areas also includes the subsurface. This is the case of the Nunavut Land Claim Agreement between the Inuit of the Territory of Nunavut and the Government of Canada settling in 1993 all land claims by the Inuit, granting title to 19 per cent of the land in Nunavut, including mineral rights to two per cent of Nunavut.[24] In Papua New Guinea, where more than 98 per cent of land is held by customary landholders, the Mining Act of 1992 and mineral policy framework has gone to an unusual effort to identify and accommodate the rights of landholders without conceding minerals ownership, which is vested in the state,[25] while the Mining Act of the Autonomous Government of Bougainville of 2015 proclaims that 'All minerals existing on, in or below the surface of customary land in Bougainville are the property of the owners of the customary land' (Article 8).[26] Only minerals in or below land that is not owned by customary landowners is proclaimed as property of the Autonomous Government of Bougainville (Article 9.1).

In Latin American countries, as in many others, the landownership system has more frequently and widely applied to construction materials such as stone, sand and gravel, and quarry materials. Unlike other minerals, these deposits do not pose major geological difficulties and are relatively abundant. These materials do not need processing and are most commonly traded and consumed in domestic markets; their production and prices are subject to the fluctuations of economic activity, particularly the construction industry, but they are not exposed to the extraordinary ups and downs of international metal prices.[27]

Whenever minerals belong to the surface owner, these are subject to common property law and rights can be obtained by purchase, lease or private contracts as established under the applicable regime, or by entering into royalty agreements.[28] As explained, in the UK and US, rights on minerals can be 'severed' from surface rights and transferred through separate transactions.

---

[23] See Morgan, 'Mineral Development in the United Kingdom' (2005) 1083–85.

[24] See comment in J Donihee and A Lucas, 'Canadian Impact and Benefit Agreements with Local and Indigenous People' in Bastida, Wälde, and Warden-Fernandez, J (eds), *International and Comparative Mineral Law* (2005) 718. The Inuvialuit Final Agreement, which back in 1984 required entering into negotiations of so-called Impact and Benefit Agreements. In practice, Impact and Benefit Agreements are being sought for by project developers even when Aboriginal rights are limited to surface rights in order to secure land access. See ibid 718.

[25] C Filer, 'The Role of Land-Owning Communities in Papua New Guinea's Mineral Policy Framework' in Bastida, Wälde and Warden-Fernández (n 15) 903–31.

[26] Autonomous Region of Bougainville (No 3 of 2015). Bougainville Mining Act 2015.

[27] See ch 2.

[28] See R Bassett and R Ihnen Becker, 'Myth or Reality: Has Environmental Regulation Destroyed the US Mining Industry?' in Bastida, Wälde and Warden-Fernández (n 15) 697–711.

144　*Mining Law Regimes at the Level of Nation-States*

B. The *Regalian* and Domanial Doctrines

i. *The* Regalian *Doctrine*

A group of scholars has defined the *regalian* doctrine as wherever minerals are *unowned* resources on which the state controls access, holding the power to administer mineral wealth through the granting of rights and concession, or otherwise as unowned, but in which ownership is attributed to the collective body in the nature of a faculty or power over mines to regulate their use through concessions and grants, and the exercise of public order, providing for the conservation of soil and mine safety and 'receiving, as the sovereign, a portion of the product obtained from the exploitation'.[29] In other words, they are 'res nullius but subject to imperium', ie, the jurisdiction of state law. Campbell explains that, as other categories of things considered *res nullius*, such as treasure troves, the state 'participates in a specified percentage of the property upon the occasion of its discovery or reduction to possession'.[30] Yet another group of authors calls the *regalian* doctrine what others refer to as the *domanial* doctrine.

While there are some antecedents of the *regalian* system in post-classic Roman Law – more precisely in the *Theodosian Code*[31] – the sources of the *regalian* system date back to the Middle Ages. Mines were regarded as *iura regalia* or royal rights, a right enjoyed by the sovereigns by virtue of their prerogatives.[32] The concept of *iura regalia* is certainly influenced and linked to the concept and structure of territorial ownership in a stratified and fragmented feudal society.[33] *Usufruct, emphyteusis* and *superficie* provided the legal basis for the concept of double ownership whereby the feudal lords gained legitimacy to claim and receive the tithe.[34] The concept of mines as *iura regalia* was regarded as a principle of political and economic law, instrumental in substantiating the participation of the Crown in mining.[35]

---

[29] NJ Campbell, 'Principles of Ownership in the Civil Law and Common Law Systems'. See E Catalano, *Código de Minería Comentado* (Buenos Aires, Zavalía Editor, 1999) 63 (who speaks of '*régimen de patronato minero*').

[30] Campbell, 'Principles of Ownership' (1999).

[31] C Pharr (transl), *The Theodosian Code and Novels and the Sirmondian Constitutions* (Princeton, Princeton University Press, 1952) Title 19: Minerals, Mines, and Miners (*De Metallis et Metallaris*) 10.19.3, 283–85. See also J Vildósola Fuenzalida, *El dominio minero y el sistema concesional en América Latina y el Caribe* (Caracas, OLAMI/ECLAC, 1999) 13–14. Vergara Blanco observes that at this time mines had clearly become considered linked to a public interest or function, but this falls short of a comprehensive prior declaration of 'state' ownership over mines. A Vergara Blanco, 'El problema de la naturaleza jurídica de la riqueza mineral' (2006) 33 *Revista Chilena de Derecho* 215–44.

[32] See the thorough study of A Vergara Blanco, *Principios y sistema de derecho minero. Estudio histórico y dogmático* (Santiago de Chile, Editorial Jurídica de Chile, 1992) 54–55. Vergara transcribes the 'Capitulaciones' as per F Morales Padrón, *Teoría y leyes de la Conquista* (Madrid, Ediciones Cultura Hispánica, Centro Iberoamericano de Cooperación, 1979).

[33] Vildósola Fuenzalida, *El dominio minero* (1999) 100–01.

[34] ibid; and 55–58.

[35] This is also contained in the *Bergregal* of the Roman–German Sacred Empire, the *Dixième* and *Royal Demesne* in France, *Fondinae Regales* in England and *Regalía* in Spain. See Vildósola Fuenzalida (n 31) 100.

This was extended and applied throughout medieval Europe.[36] It is then in medieval Europe where the juridical idea of mineral wealth as royal patrimony of the political body finds its roots.[37]

The *regalian* system provided the basis for the mining law regimes in place in different vice-royalties across Spanish America.[38] Due to the strategic importance of mineral resources, mines from the outset were regarded as *iura regalia*.[39] The hallmark of the *regalian* principle is the distinction between the *original* (also called 'radical') *dominium* that was placed under the Crown, and the *dominium utile*, which was granted by the Crown to whoever discovered the mine. This provided the legal basis for collecting a royalty, ie, a share in mineral production.

The original patrimonial ownership of mines evolved into acquiring the status of a sovereign power with the emergence of the nation-state and the development of the concept of sovereignty as an abstraction.[40] Vergara Blanco notes that the original 'patrimonial' character has remained strong and continued to inform interpretations of mining ownership as closer to property concepts.[41] The author, as is true of other scholars informed in public and administrative law, has tended to interpret the *regalian* system as an antecedent in the evolution to the *domanial* system.[42]

ii. The Domanial Doctrine

According to the *domanial* doctrine, the state holds ownership over minerals in situ.[43] Definitions and terminology vary enormously but, in general terms and beyond categorisations, the state holds ownership as a juridical entity or as a representative of the collective body.[44] Definitions generally suppose the state can undertake mining either through state-owned companies or decentralised entities, or by granting rights to private entities (some laws requiring state equity).

---

[36] ibid.

[37] Vergara Blanco, 'El problema' (2006).

[38] The 1783 *New Spain–México Ordinances* were applicable throughout the Spanish–American territory during the last phase of the Vice-Royalties and are recognised as the premier source of most of the first Mining Codes enacted by independent states in Spanish America *Reales Ordenanzas para la Dirección, Rejimen y Gobierno del Importante Cuerpo de la Minería de Nueva-España y de su Real Tribunal Jeneral de orden de Su Majestad,* (printed in Madrid, 1783, and reprinted in Santiago de Chile, Imprenta de la Opinión, 1833). These have been said to be influential far beyond their territorial application and become a source of the US 1872 Mining Act. J Lacy, 'Going with the Current: the Genesis of the Mineral Laws of the United States', Proceedings of 41st Annual Rocky Mountain Mineral Law Institute (1995) 10–33.

[39] Vergara Blanco, *Principios y sistema de derecho minero* (1992) and Vildósola Fuenzalida (n 31).

[40] Vildósola Fuenzalida (n 31).

[41] Vergara Blanco (n 31).

[42] Vergara Blanco (n 32); H Zaballa and S Arbeleche, 'Evolución de la intervención estatal en la legislación minera argentina' (2014) 1 *Revista Argentina de Derecho de la Energía, Hidrocarburos y Minería* 101.

[43] See Vergara Blanco, *Sistema de derecho minero* (Santiago de Chile, Legal Publishing, 2013) 197–98.

[44] Campbell (n 29).

146 *Mining Law Regimes at the Level of Nation-States*

In centrally planned economies and often in mixed economies, states own both the minerals in situ and land.[45]

In civil law tradition, the legal regime of public ownership presupposes the protection and performance of a general interest function; this justifies the existence of exceptional privileges and limitations. A core principle of public ownership is that assets cannot be alienated because they are affected to public utility (principle of *inaliénabilité* or *inalienabilidad*). Hence, they are not capable of prescription.[46] In effect, public ownership is defined by two conditions: that property belongs to a public legal entity (as the state); and that it is attributed public utility (*utilité publique*).[47] Nevertheless, the nature of public ownership has been the subject of fierce doctrinal controversy. Mainstream French and Spanish legal scholarship construe public ownership as having a proprietary nature. In contrast, the 'functional' doctrine of public ownership argues that public ownership is a legal technique with a purely functional aim: to create a title for plain administrative intervention that legally empowers the administration to regulate the use of those things classified as public, in accordance with the general interest; ie, rather than a bundle of assets, public ownership provides the legal underpinnings for powers ('*potestades*'). It identifies the *regalian* doctrine as an antecedent to the *domanial* doctrine, with this functional aim in mind, public ownership being a technical concept.[48]

In recent decades, to facilitate financing and encourage capital intensive investment, it has become more widely accepted that the state may be empowered to grant administrative real property rights (*droits réeles administratifs*) on public ownership regarding activities that can best be performed by the private sector.[49] Grants are subject to the regulatory powers of the state to ensure that they are granted and operated in accordance with the general interest.

In essence, the public nature of mineral resources entails that they belong to the *populus*, to the people, to everyone; and that they are administered by the competent organs of the state for the benefit of the people and regulated under administrative law.[50] To date, there has been a varied and intense debate on the precise meaning of each particular definition of ownership in civil law countries.[51]

---

[45] Olawuyi observes that African jurisdictions vest ownership rights over natural resources in the sovereign, and also interprets that the origins of this dominial system are found in the regalian doctrine. D Olawuyi, *Extractive Industries Law in Africa* (Cham, Switzerland AG, Springer Nature, 2018).

[46] ibid.

[47] See R Chapus, *Droit administratif général*, 15th edn (Paris, Montchrestien, 2001) vol 2, 376ff.

[48] Vergara Blanco (n 32) 197–98.

[49] eg 2011 Guinean Mining Code: 'A Concession is an immoveable, divisible, right which can be subleased; this right may be mortgaged in order to secure loans to finance mining operations' (Art 35).

[50] Vergara Blanco (n 31).

[51] Under the 2011 Guinean Mining Code, 'Mineral Substances or fossil substances contained in the subsoil or existing on the surface, as well as ground waters and geothermal deposits are, on the territory of the Republic of Guinea and in the exclusive economic Zone, the property of the state and cannot be the object of any form of private appropriation, save as otherwise provided in this Code, and in the Code on Private and State-Owned Land (*Code Foncier et Domanial*)' (Art 3). In Mexico, the 1917

Ownership and Jurisdiction Over Minerals in Situ 147

In many jurisdictions, constitutional provisions and the relevant mining laws provide that mineral resources are owned by the people and the state acts as *trustee* (rather usual in 'common law' jurisdictions) or as a 'guardian', 'custodian', 'agent' or 'administrator' (whatever the definition under the law of particular jurisdictions) to manage resources and allocate exploration and exploitation rights. The South African Mineral and Petroleum Resources Development Act states in Article 3(1) that 'Mineral resources are the common heritage of all the peoples of South Africa and the State is the custodian thereof for the benefit of all South Africans'. The Preamble to this law acknowledges that South Africa's mineral and petroleum resources belong to the nation and that the state is the custodian thereof. There are contested views on the nature of the rights vested in the state by the Act.[52] In *De Beers Consolidated Mines Ltd v Ataqua Mining (Pty) Ltd* the Court held that 'the objects of the Act ... do not vest ownership in the state ... "State's Custodianship" ... do not mean that minerals are *res publicae* ... [The Act] controls the use of the "resource"'.[53] In Kenya, 'Every mineral (a) in its natural state in, under or upon land in Kenya; (b) in or under a lake, river, stream, or water courses in Kenya; (c) in the exclusive economic zone and an area covered by the territorial sea or continental shelf, is the property of the Republic and is vested in the national government in trust for the people of Kenya'.[54]

The constitution of Bolivia establishes that all-natural resources are property of the Bolivian people and is to be managed by the State (Article 311, II 2).[55] Some countries vest ownership in the President or political authority on behalf of the people. Under the Mines Act in Zambia, ownership is vested as witnessed in Article 3(1): 'All rights of ownership in, searching for, and mining and

---

Political Constitution qualified the *direct* domain of all-natural resources as inalienable and imprescriptible and belonging to the Nation. In the Philippines, the 1995 Mining Act stated that 'All mineral resources in public and private lands within the territory and exclusive economic zone of the Republic of the Philippines are owned by the State'. Philippines, Mining Act of 1995 (Act No 7942, Section 2). The 1973 Spanish Law of Mines provides a good example of a traditional definition of mineral resources (it refers to orebodies and other geological resources) as assets of public ownership. Ley de Minas 22/1973, 21 July 1973, BOE-A-1973-1018, Art 2.1.

[52] Badenhorst and Mostert interpret the provisions of the Act in the sense that mineral and petroleum resources are *res publicae*, according to the ordinary private law of property. They also refer to another opinion (by J Glazewski, *Environmental Law in South Africa* (Durban, Butterworths 2001) 464–68) arguing that there is no definition of state ownership (and that custodianship does not equal ownership), 'the landowner still remains owner of unsevered mineral and petroleum resources, subject to the public trust doctrine'. PJ Badenhorst and H Mostert, *Mineral and Petroleum Law of South Africa*, 4th edn (Cape Town, Juta Law, 2008) 13–14 and 15. Michael Dale has suggested that either ownership of unmined minerals still vests in the landowner as the South African state has not reserved explicitly to itself ownership of mineral resources under the Act; or the state has impliedly reserved to itself the right to prospect and miner, or the grant of rights may be construed as purely a regulatory power. See M Dale, 'Comparative International and African Mineral Law as Applied in the Formation of the New South African Mineral Development Legislation' in Bastida, Wälde and Warden-Fernández (n 15) 827.

[53] *De Beers Consolidated Mines Ltd v Ataqua Mining (Pty) Ltd* and Others (3215/06) ZAFSHC 74 (13 December 2007).

[54] Mining Act, 2016, Part II, 6.

[55] 'Los recursos naturales son de propiedad del pueblo boliviano y serán administrados por el Estado'.

148 *Mining Law Regimes at the Level of Nation-States*

disposing of, minerals are hereby vested in the President on behalf of the Republic'.[56] In Malawi, 'The entire property in minerals in, under or upon any land or waters ... are vested in the Republic on behalf of the people of Malawi ...'.[57] In Tanzania, the Mining Act provides that:

> The entire property in and control of all minerals in, and under or upon any land, rivers, streams, water courses throughout Tanzania, area covered by territorial sea, continental shelf or the exclusive economic zone is the property of the United Republic and shall be vested in the President in trust for the People of Tanzania.[58]

C. The *Res Nullius* Doctrine

The *res nullius* doctrine contends that minerals belong to no one until they have either been discovered or reduced to possession.[59] This means that surface ownership does not entail a proprietary interest neither on the subsoil nor on the minerals it might lie in.[60] Scholarship in countries with a civil law tradition has typically distinguished between two subsidiary theories that elaborate on ownership acquisition when minerals are not primarily owned by anybody. The first postulates that mines are acquired by the first occupier, namely, the one who excavates the mine first and reduces it into possession.[61] This theory was postulated by the French economist Turgot under the term 'occupation theory' (following the application of the Roman doctrine of acquisition by *occupatio*), in a brief published in 1764. As a physiocrat, Turgot believed in not interfering with the natural laws of society and industry and regarded land (and agricultural labour) as a main source of wealth.[62] Turgot advocated legal and economic reasons for the adoption of the occupation theory, such as the fact that the right of occupation fostered competition and suggested that payment of royalties on minerals to the state should be abolished. His brief is considered to be an early economic analysis of the efficiency of a form of mineral tenure.[63] The second theory attributes ownership of mines to the first discoverer.

Drawing on the debate in the French Assembly that would result in the adoption of the 1791 Law of Mines, Mirabeau inspired the adoption of the definition stating that mines were 'at the Nation's disposal' ('*à la disposition de la Nation*'), which was also incorporated into the subsequent 1810 Law of Mines. It has been

---

[56] *Mines and Minerals Development* No 11 of 2015. Date of Assent: 14 August 2015.

[57] Mines and Minerals Act 2018, section 4(1).

[58] Mining Act, 2010, section 5(1) (Rev ed 31 October 2018).

[59] Campbell (n 29).

[60] ibid.

[61] P Crabbe, 'Turgot's Brief on Mines and Quarries: An Early Economic Analysis of Mineral Land Tenure (1985) 2 *Natural Resources Journal* 267. Some authors draw a distinction between the *res nullius* and the 'occupatio' doctrine.

[62] ibid.

[63] ibid.

construed that the state intervenes as a tutor of those resources (not as owner) and as a representative of the general interest, to grant minerals concessions.[64] A fundamental argument put forward by Mirabeau was that property of mines should fall on whoever discovers the vein first, upon a concession granted by the nation.[65]

D. Interpreting States' Duties to Manage Resources

In recent years, debates on the scope and nature of state ownership over mineral resources have resurfaced in some countries, particularly in the reasoning of judicial decisions under certain constitutional structures, along lines of interpretation on the state's duty to manage resources and derive revenue in ways that contribute to sustainable development, taking account of all the dimensions of the concept and within a framework of the rule of law and good governance: transparency and accountability; inclusiveness; responsive public management; and efficient and equitable management of resource revenue.[66]

The notion of resource ownership as a duty, rather than as a power, vested on the Government to use resources as established in the Constitution, emerges, as an example, from the judgment of Sudershan Reddy J in *Reliance Industries Limited v Reliance Natural Resources Limited* of the Supreme Court of Justice of India, which grounded the principles applicable to the development of 'scarce natural resources' in constitutional provisions, stating that:[67]

> 21. ... Natural Gas belongs to the people of India, and vests in the Union of India, to be held for the purposes of the Union. The Constitution of India commands the Government to frame policy to prevent the distribution of such resources in a manner that may be inimical to national development.
>
> ...
>
> 88. While the word 'vest'; could normally partake of at least a portion of the full bundle of rights associated with ownership, the phrase 'shall vest'; as used in Article 297 of the

---

[64] L Latty, '*La loi du 21 avril 1810 et le Conseil général des mines avant 1866. Les procès-verbaux des séances*', *Documents pour l'histoire des techniques* (2008) 16, available at journals.openedition.org/dht/803 (quoting sources that characterise the system as 'regalian').

[65] H-G Riqueti Mirabeau (comte de), 'Discours sur la Propriété de Mines', 21 March 1791, 356 and 'Second Discours sur la Propriété de Mines', 27 March 1791, 377 in *Œuvres Oratoires de Mirabeau, ou recueil de ses discours, rapports, adresses, opinions, discussions, réparties, etc., à l'Assemblée Nationale, ou recueil de ses discours, rapports, adresses, opinions, discussions, réparties, etc., à l'Assemblée Nationale* (Paris, Librairie de Pierre Blanchard, 1819) vol 1, 356–84 (see particularly 367–75).

[66] R Ako and N Uddin, 'Good Governance and Resource Management in Africa' in F Botchway (ed), *Natural Resource Investment and Africa's Development* (Cheltenham, Edward Elgar, 2011) 23.

[67] Commentators have noticed that in Reddy's judgment 'ownership' is not a power vested on the Government; it is rather an obligation or duty placed on the Government to 'make use' of resources as established under the Constitution. See Z Hossain and AP Kumar, 'The New Jurisprudence of Scarce Natural Resources: An Analysis of the Supreme Court's Judgment in Reliance Industries Limited v Reliance Natural Resources Limited' (2010) 7 SCC 1, (2010) 4 *Indian Journal of Constitutional Law* 105.

150 *Mining Law Regimes at the Level of Nation-States*

Constitution implies a deliberate, and not an incidental, act by a body at the various constitutional moments that have informed our Constitution. That body is the people as a nation. It is now a well-established principle of jurisprudence that the true owners of 'natural wealth and resources'; are the people as a nation.[68]

To be sure, either by interpreting *dominium* ('resource ownership') as entailing a duty of states to exercise corresponding functions of resource management and derived revenue to benefit the people, the ultimate and true owners, or by exercising *imperium*, the jurisdictional power to control over resources, what emerges is that, upon developments in particular contexts, those powers might be qualified *internally* by constitutional and legal reforms guiding the manner in which the state can undertake or authorise mining and by the redistribution of those powers through rather extended processes of decentralisation; and *externally* through obligations derived from international law.

II. Typologies and Functions of Mining Law Regimes

While broad types exist along different legal traditions and as a function of economic interest and the place of mining in domestic economies, at their most elementary, mining law regimes are usually comprised of a 'nucleus' consistent of:[69]

(a) a definition of primary mineral ownership (both in the subsoil and once extracted);

(b) the system establishing the modalities, criteria, rules and procedures for governing access to these resources (how mineral rights are acquired, held, transferred and terminated),[70] which includes, inter alia,[71] a categorisation of mineral rights, providing for uniform rights and obligations for each category of mineral right, the size, shape, or area, including survey and demarcation procedures, if applicable, and title registration;

(c) the rules and procedures to access land as well as to use other resources (eg, water, timber) for operational purposes (with a growing interface with land and other regimes that balance competitive uses), as well as rules and procedures to establish and use subsidiary facilities;

---

[68] ibid.

[69] A Vergara Blanco, *Sistema de Derecho Minero* (2013). On an analysis of the autonomy and foundational principles of mining law, see W Freire, 'Direito Minerário: Fundamentos e Hermenêutica' in W Freire and T de Mattos (eds), *Aspectos controvertidos do Direito Minerário e Ambiental. Enfoque Multidisciplinar* (Belo Horizonte, Jurídica Editora, 2013) 105.

[70] I use 'mineral rights' as a generic term, to encapsulate the different types of specific entitlements to prospecting, exploration and extraction, a mining act can set forth. 'Mining' right is a type of mineral right entitling minerals extraction.

[71] T Wälde, 'Mineral Development Legislation: Result and Instrument of Mineral Development Planning' (1988) 12 *Natural Resources Forum* 177.

Typologies and Functions of Mining Law Regimes   151

(d) the rights and obligations of the parties involved, including those of the mineral rights holders in relation to the minerals, land and adjacent mineral rights;

(e) the method and procedures for settlement of disputes; and

(f) the administrative rules and intervention powers of government authorities derived from public interest (monitoring and compliance, inspection, rational and efficient use of resources, health and safety, environmental regulation – often in conjunction with regulatory regimes applicable to operations).

This nucleus of principles and rules constitute a legal 'micro-system'[72] or 'subsystem' which establish the scenario for an industry: (i) usually recognised as of national interest or public purpose and associated to wealth creation (and/or where mines or mineral resources are considered as assets linked to public utility); (ii) consisting at its core of the extraction of depletable natural resources; and (iii) which is subject of arduous relationships with surface and local rights holders at the mine site,[73] and surrounding areas and communities.

As described in chapter two, industrial mining consists of a series of sequential stages that begin with reconnaissance, prospecting, exploration and discovery of mineral deposits and continue through ore extraction and processing to the closure and remediation of sites.[74] A feasibility study is the basis for the decision to mine, which also comprises environmental and social impact assessments and the evaluation of the commercial viability of the project (eg, whether water supply is sufficient, infrastructure and transportation costs, environmental and social factors). Each successive stage, from exploration to exploitation, typically involves increasing time and expenditure and less land than the previous stage. Moreover, discovery risk declines as activity moves from one of these phases on to the next.

Mining law regimes *stricto sensu* basically establish the rules and procedures governing how mineral rights are acquired, held, transferred and terminated. There are obvious limitations to any attempt to produce a categorisation distinguishing between different types. The type of mineral, public interest on ensuring security of supply or its importance for the economy, and scale of mining, among others, are all concerns that might inform the regulatory design of mining regimes and produce categories of mineral rights. In addition, the legal context in each country confers a specific meaning to the extent of the rights and obligations enshrined under mining laws, eg, the extent of protection against government regulation and/or intervention.[75]

---

[72] AD Cançado Trindade, 'Princípios de Direito Minerário Brasileiro' in MM Gomes de Souza (ed), *Direito Minerário em Evoluçao* (Belo Horizonte, CEAMIN and Mandamentos Editora, 2009) 52.

[73] Catalano, *Curso de Derecho Minero*, 5th edn (Buenos Aires, Zavalía Editor, 1999) 15–17.

[74] UNEP, 'Mining: Facts, Figures and Environment' (2000) 23 *Industry and Environment* 23.

[75] See J Southalan, *Mining Law and Policy. International Perspectives* (Sydney, The Federation Press, 2012) 45.

152 Mining Law Regimes at the Level of Nation-States

I here suggest two ways of drawing a typology of mining law regimes *stricto sensu*. The first one is defined around the *legal form* established for the allocation of mineral rights (possessory forms as free entry or claim-staking; licensing and contracts). The second one revolves around the *process* of allocation of mineral rights (*open access, bidding or discretionary*).

A. Possessory, Licensing and Contractual Systems

The sequence of activities through which minerals are converted from unknown geologic resources to marketable commodities has been legally captured in sequential exclusive entitlements of exploration and exploitation rights, with the discovery of minerals determining the transition between one phase (and legal category of rights) and the other. Some countries provide for *reconnaisance* licences (that usually grant non-exclusive rights to enter upon and carry out tasks on the surface in the search for minerals) and phases beyond exploitation, while others make provisions for retention licences that allow holders to keep their rights while temporarily suspending the concomitant obligations to title maintenance. As a counterpart to title over mineral rights, holders are subject to a varying range of obligations and powers of the state supervisory authorities, such as fixed or gradual fees, minimum working or expenditure commitments, reporting requirements and exploration programmes. These, together with time and space constraints in the allocation of mineral rights and obligatory relinquishments, are designed to protect the public interest in the exploitation of the state's mineral wealth.

From the point of view of the legal instrument used as a method for allocation of mineral rights, in which the root of *title* lies, one may distinguish between 'possessory', 'licensing' and 'contractual' approaches, in addition to hybrid approaches whenever we consider not only the method of title acquisition but also the instrument for setting rights and obligations. Within these categories, distinct forms are discernible.

i. Background – 'The Free Mining' Tradition – Possessory Systems

As in other fields of the law of energy and natural resources, systems of private property law in Western tradition have greatly influenced the development of the fundamental principles of mining law,[76] but medieval concepts and the practices of communities of miners emerging by then still resonate in legal texts and mindsets today. In many cases, these have coexisted over time, or have preceded systems crystallising a greater role of the state set within administrative law.[77]

---

[76] See See A McHarg, B Barton, A Bradbrook and L Godden, 'Property and the Law in Energy and Natural Resources' in McHarg, Barton, Bradbrook and Godden (n 1) 1–16.

[77] ibid. See also L Godden, 'Governing Common Resources: Environmental Markets and Property in Water' in McHarg, Barton, Bradbrook and Godden (n 1) 413.

Typologies and Functions of Mining Law Regimes   153

As mining is among the most ancient economic activities, mining law regimes are deeply embedded in millennial laws and customs. Their function has typically been to set rules to provide access or permission to miners to extract minerals, favouring mining over other land uses, and they have existed ever since there have been 'structures of public government, economic interest in minerals and technical ability to extract them'.[78] Even in the absence of structures of public government, customary rules of allocation of mineral rights among communities of miners have been frequent in history and are not uncommon among miners operating at small or artisanal scale in some sites.

In Western tradition,[79] it is often said that a first antecedent of legal rules governing mining has been found in relation to the exploitation of the silver mines of Laurion in Attica, apparently inherited from ancient civilisations,[80] although the evidence is disputed.[81] Under those rules, the authority would grant rights for exploitation to individuals for terms of three to ten years, under the condition to continuously operate the mine and the payment of a large stipend to the public authority. A ruler's authority to recognise rights to individuals to undertake the activity constituted an early expression of core concepts that would be further developed under Roman Law over different periods, itself the object of wide dissemination.

The origins of possessory systems of allocation of mineral rights (and other self-initiated systems) are found in the 'free mining' tradition. It denotes the customs of communities of miners in mining districts in medieval Germany, which practices have famously been illustrated in the imprints of Agricola's *De Re Metallica*[82] and became widespread in medieval Europe.[83] The system encourages mining by

---

[78] Wälde, 'Mineral Development Legislation' (1988).

[79] On historical antecedents in China, Golas observes that evidence of a role of the state in mining only emerges late in the Warring States period with regard to iron (around −300), while interest of emperors or governments to exercising more control directly over production emerges later by the Han court (−117). Over the two millenia of the imperial period, official attitudes to mining were ambivalent and fluctuated around the extent of involvement by government. Policies also fluctuated and generally provided guidance for dealing with individual situations, but there was no body of formal mining law. Contractual practices would follow the pattern used in the agricultural sector. Some specific characteristics of mining leases would include their validity until the mine depletion under condition of being maintained in continuous production. PJ Golas, *Science and Civilisation in China* (New York, Cambridge University Press, 1999) Vol 5, part 13: Mining, 416–19.

[80] John Lacy suggests that these rules represent a first example of a merger of the concepts of 'royal patrimony and the right of capture' that would be crystallised in modern mineral laws. These mines formed the economic backbone of Athens during the time of controlling power of the state: the revenues derived from them supported the supremacy of Athens and its position as a seapower. While the active operation of these mines extended over some 500 years, from 700 to 200 BC, the period of most literary reference was from 400 to 300 BC. See Hoover and Hoover, 'Note from the Translators' in G Agricola, *De Re Metallica* (New York, Dover Publications Inc, 1950) 27.

[81] Scott (n 3) 192–93.

[82] Agricola, *De Re Metallica* (1950) xxvi.

[83] J Graulau, 'Ownership of mines and taxation in Castilian laws, from the middle ages to the early modern period: the decisive influence of the sovereign in the history of mining' (2011) 26 *Continuity and Change* 13. R Richardson, 'Governing Western Mineral Resources: The Emergence of Collaboration' (003) 43 *Natural Resources Journal* 566.

154 *Mining Law Regimes at the Level of Nation-States*

establishing a self-initiated process to access land; not only a right to explore but also title to the surface land (as it is based in the assumption that mining is the best use of land).[84] The role of the authority under this system is limited to the administration of a system of registry or mineral rights.[85] Campbell puts forward an important caveat when stressing that this system should not be confused with systems that attribute mineral ownership to the state, in which 'discovery and subsequent denouncements are merely procedural steps in the acquisition of [mineral rights] from the state'.[86]

The processes of wide dissemination of mining law and 'free mining' in particular, compounded by colonialism and patterns of investment and trade are remarkably illustrated with the Gold Rushes of the late nineteenth century, a truly global phenomenon, extending to the Western US, Canada, Australia, New Zealand and South Africa.[87] The expansion to the West in the US was favoured by these self-constituted, customary rules based on the allocation of mineral rights by application of the 'rule of discovery' and the act of possession (in which the root of title lies).[88] This system formed the basis for mineral tenure regimes still in place in public lands in the US and in most provinces in Canada (within the so-called 'claim staking' or 'free entry' system)[89] and even in Sweden, and used to be the norm in Europe. Mineral tenure regimes designed around 'the rule of discovery' were imported to the Spanish vice-royalties in America and across the Portuguese colonies. These influenced the mining codes adopted by the countries across the region in the late nineteenth century, and some elements of it underlie the regimes of mining codes from the 1990s, starting with Chile in 1983 and extending to Peru, Mexico and Argentina.

ii. Licensing

Licensing regimes denote legally protected entitlements obtained by a sequence of mineral rights (permits, licences, leases, claims and/or concession, whatever the nomenclature, which collectively are here called 'mineral rights') obtained upon specific conditions to authorise, primarily, exploration and extraction.[90] If there is

---

[84] B Barton, 'The History of Mining Law in the US, Canada, New Zealand and Australia, and the Right of Free Entry' in Bastida, Wälde and Warden-Fernández (n 15) 646.

[85] P McDade, *Materials on Mineral Law – A Survey of United Kingdom, Comparative and International Legal Issues Relating to Hard Minerals* (Dundee, Centre for Petroleum and Mineral Law Studies, University of Dundee, *undated*) J1–07; Campbell (n 29).

[86] Campbell (n 29).

[87] Barton, 'The History of Mining Law' (n 84) 643.

[88] Scott (n 3) 218. Barton (ibid) 646.

[89] Alberta, Nova Scotia and Prince Edward Island have replaced this system.

[90] T Wälde, 'Third World Mineral Development: Recent Issues and Literature' (1984) 2 *Journal of Energy and Natural Resources Law* 282.

no government participation required,[91] the Government may grant titles under the mining code through licensing and regulate investment through administration and supervision.[92]

Licensing regimes vary greatly and most of them are 'composite structures' in between private and public law.[93] These include (i) *law-based regimes* in which the root of the title lies in the law, like the concession system in some countries in Latin America; and (ii) *adjudicative regimes*, in which the root of the title lies in a judicial decision (eg, Chile and some provinces in Argentina). There are also *custom-based regimes*, in which the root of the entitlement lies in commonly accepted customs within a group (eg, of miners or local communities).

Within licensing regimes, one can also distinguish modalities which might be more influenced by public law, such as (i) *administrative-based regimes* in which the root of title lies in an administrative act of granting, and (ii) *contract-based regimes* in which the root of the title lies in a contract (eg mining licences are considered contracts under the mining laws of Ghana and Kenya).[94] It is worth noting that the term 'concession' under comparative resources law does not have a single and univocal definition. While in some legal systems the term has no clear legal connotation, in others, as in the French legal system, concession is classified as a species of administrative contracts,[95] or as unilateral administrative acts (as in German, Swiss and Italian legal doctrine).[96] In common law systems, a concession may take the form of a grant, a licence or a lease, or that of a state contract.[97]

As in the oil and gas sector, the sequence of mineral titles granting exploration and exploitation rights is today indeed predominantly governed by administrative law. In the US, the 'claim staking' system still applies to hard rock minerals in public federal lands, but has been subject to steady limitations in their scope as specific administrative regimes, eg to rule coal, have been set in place. In Canada, the provinces of Alberta, Nova Scotia and Prince Edward have moved to administrative regimes.[98] In Australia, administrative titles have gradually superseded the

---

[91] Tanzania, for example, requires from any mining operation under a mining licence or a special mining licence, not less than 16% non-dilutable free carried interest Government shares in the capital of a mining company 'depending on the type of mineral and the level of investment'. The Government is also entitled to acquire up to 50% of the shares of the mining company (section 10.-(1)).

[92] T Wälde, 'Methods of Mineral Investment Promotion', UN Regional Seminar on Mining Exploration and Investment Potential in West Africa, 11–15 December 1989, Yamoussoukro, Côte D'Ivoire, 339.

[93] McDade (n 85).

[94] MK Ayisi, 'The legal character of mineral rights under the new mining law of Kenya' (2017) 35 *Journal of Energy & Natural Resources Law* 25.

[95] Chapus, *Droit Administratif Général* (2001).

[96] P Fischer, 'Concessions' in R Bernhardt and Max-Planck-Institut Fur Auslandisches Offentliches Recht Und Volkerrec, *Encyclopedia of Public International Law* (London-Amsterdam, North Holland, 1981–1990) 715–21.

[97] S Toriguian, *Legal Aspects of Oil Concessions in the Middle East* (Beirut, Hamaskaine Press, 1972) 17. See also Fischer, 'Concessions' (1981–1990).

[98] B Barton, 'Reforming the Mining Law of the Northwest Territories. Prepared for the Canadian Arctic Resources Committee', Northern Minerals Programme working papers, 3 (1998) 652.

156 *Mining Law Regimes at the Level of Nation-States*

claim 'as of right by entry' since the 1890s.[99] By that time, free entry was also disappearing in New Zealand. Under the 1991 Crown Minerals Act, permits would be allocated by the Minister on a discretionary basis, to be exercised pursuant to the corresponding minerals programme, and mining operations were required to comply with the environmental provisions of the Resource Management Act, adopted that same year.[100]

In the EU, the influential 1810 French Law of Mines combined a system of administrative concessions with a definition of mineral rights as property rights (epitomising the liberal ideas of the time of its enactment). It subsequently evolved through many amendments to provide for more regulatory powers of the state limited by the increasing powers of the EU and its Directives, which shaped the competitive procedure established by the selection of a candidate.[101] The 1982 German Mining Act also adopted an administrative concession system; mining permissions originate in a grant, which requires first of all, and among other requirements, evidence of the applicant's reliability and financial capacity, and of an economically reasonable extraction.[102] In the administrative concession system adopted by the 1973 Spanish Law of Mines the first applicant has a right of priority, provided that the proposed studies and exploration work are deemed convenient.[103] In Latin America, the model of 'legal concessions' that was predominant in the 1990s is still in place in a few countries while in others it coexists or has been replaced by administrative concessions. Under the 2002 Colombian Mining Code, the mining concession is regarded as an adhesion contract since its terms, conditions and methods cannot be pre-negotiated. In Bolivia, the system of 'legal concessions' under the 1997 Mining Code has been substituted by administrative contracts. Russia and most of the Central Asian Republics have adopted administrative concession or licensing systems with discretionary powers in all significant aspects of tenure rules and procedures.

iii. Contractual Regimes

Contractual regimes include, again, a great variety of arrangements. Most usually, countries using mining agreements rely on a hybrid of mining laws granting title to conduct exploration, exploitation and ancillary activities, and agreements fixing terms and conditions for large-scale, industrial mining. The choice for the use of contractual over licensing regimes might be influenced by knowledge of the geological prospectivity of some areas, or the strategic nature of some minerals. Small projects might be governed by the general licensing system, while large-scale

---

[99] ibid 653–54.
[100] ibid 657.
[101] T Lauriol, 'Reform of the French Mining Code' (1994) 9 Oil & Gas Law and Taxation Review 289.
[102] JC Pielow, 'Mining Law in Germany' in Bastida, Wälde and Warden-Fernández (n 15) 1037–65.
[103] See P Legoux, 'Legislations Minières des États Membres de la Communauté Européenne', *Revista de Administración Pública* 113 (Madrid, Centro de Estudios Constitucionales, 1987) 365–98, and translated into Spanish in *Revista de Derecho de Minas y Aguas*, vol III (1992) 35–57.

projects rely on model or ad-hoc mining agreements.[104] Agreements can be used to allocate financial risks and rewards between the government and the miner; to grant mining titles; to provide the miner with assurance on core investment issues or specify further conditions convenient to attract investors (eg strengthening security of title; including stabilisation clauses; providing recourse to international arbitration if not BIT is in place to do so); to control large infrastructure projects; to coordinate the functions of different government agencies regarding permits' assessment, approval and control; or to structure actions around impacts and development locally and nationally (eg local content; shared used infrastructure; articulation with communities' agreements);[105] some agreements recognise the Government or other parties equity in the project.

It is most helpful to draw distinctions between types of mining agreements by examining the manner they deal with the main functions – control, risk, revenue-sharing – in project development, and their specific terms, rather than their label.[106] But classifications are usually drawn around the following main forms:[107] (i) the *concession* (sometimes called 'mining development') agreement, which involves wholly owned foreign equity ownership and entitlement to mineral rights; (ii) *investment promotion agreements*, which might apply to all large investment projects and seek to provide further assurances as stabilisation provisions;[108] (iii) *service contract* forms, where no ownership/equity linkage exists between the project and the foreign contractor (turnkey, management, technical assistance and related contracts belong to this non-equity form of long-term industrial cooperation);[109] (iv) *joint ventures*, where several partners partake in equity and ownership;[110] (v) *production-sharing agreements*, which are used more extensively in the oil and gas sector;[111] and (vi) agreements used to coordinate the functions of the various government agencies involved in permitting and infrastructure approval and monitoring of works.[112]

---

[104] This is the case in Papua New Guinea, for example, according to the Mining Act 1992. The Mineral Resources Authority negotiates so-called 'mining development contracts' as agent for the state (according to Mineral Resources Authority Act 2018, certified 5 July 2018).

[105] See generally Southalan, *Mining Law and Policy* (2012) 173ff.

[106] T Wälde, 'Investment policies in the international petroleum industry – responses to the current crisis' in N Beredjick and T Wälde (eds), *Petroleum Investment Policies in Developing Countries* (London, Graham & Trotman, 1988) 13.

[107] See M Likosky, 'Contracting and Regulatory Issues in the Oil and Gas and Metallic Minerals Industries (2009) 18 *Transnational Corporations* 1.

[108] D Barberis, *Negotiating Mining Agreements: Past, Present and Future Trends* (London, Kluwer Law International, 1998).

[109] Y Omorogbe and P Oniemola, 'Property Rights in Oil and Gas under Domanial Regimens' in A McHarg, B Barton, A Bradbrook and L Godden, *Property and the Law in Energy and Natural Resources* (Oxford, Oxford University Press, 2010) 126.

[110] Omorogbe and Oniemola, 'Property Rights' (2010) 127. Southalan (n 78) 174–75.

[111] Omorogbe and Oniemola (n 109) 125. CCSI, 'Natural Resource Contracts as a Tool for Managing the Mining Sector' (June 2015).

[112] A Fitzgerald, *Mining agreements: negotiated frameworks in the Australian minerals sector* (Sydney, Prospect Media, 2002).

158 *Mining Law Regimes at the Level of Nation-States*

Mining agreements can interact with the general legal framework to implement and/or complement the law; in some jurisdictions, these have also been used to substitute it.[113] As explained in chapter two, agreements have often been used in jurisdictions lacking fully developed legal frameworks for mining. In a few jurisdictions, mining agreements become statutes by parliamentary approval.[114] Whenever the function of agreements is filling in regulatory gaps, these will naturally be superseded over time as laws and regulations evolve, and there is indeed an observed trend to more 'legislated terms', and the provisional use of model mining agreements.[115] This approach has been recommended as case-by-case negotiations to fill in gaps can prove very costly and time-consuming.[116] Either by exercising a function as 'gap-fillers' or by carving out a specific regime for the project, they have been under scrutiny for their potential role in crafting legal enclaves, insulated from the broader regulatory context, often raising key questions about their legality and constitutional standing.[117]

Agreements provide a framework to govern the relationship between the Government and the miner,[118] which will necessarily change over time as the conditions of the initial bargain change, markets fluctuate and societies expectations' evolve. During the 2000s, and at times of high commodity prices, the most extensive changes occurred when the initial bargain was negotiated at times of low prices (mid-1980s to 1999) and there was no internal adaptation system in the agreement; or changing host government administrations embraced development models which entailed a backlash against foreign and/or private investment or with reversals to policies of privatisation.[119] Host governments would argue for the application of the *clausula rebus sic stantibus* as basis for renegotiation and adjustments; that governments have a unilateral rights to change or revoke the contract on the basis of their sovereign powers, or for the jurisdiction on national courts.[120] In contrast, foreign investors would counter exposure to host government powers by arguing for the application of the principle *pacta sunt servanda*, stabilisation

---

[113] Southalan (n 75) 177; Barberis (1998).

[114] Southalan (n 75) 177.

[115] CCSI, 'Natural Resource Contracts' (2015).

[116] E Dietsche, 'Balancing mining contracts and mining legislation: experiences and challenges' (2019) 32 *Mineral Economics* 153.

[117] See K Tienhaara, *The Expropriation of Environmental Governance: Protecting Foreign Investors at the Expense of Public Policy* (Cambridge, Cambridge University Press, 2009); L Cotula, 'Reconsidering Sovereignty, Ownership and Consent in Natural Resource Contracts: From Concepts to Practice' in M Bungenberg, M Krajewski, C Tams, J Terhechte and A Ziegler (eds), *European Yearbook of International Economic Law* (Springer, 2018) 143–74.

[118] M Frilet and K Haddow, 'Guiding Principles for Durable Mining Agreements in Large Mining Projects' (2013) 31 *Journal for Energy and Natural Resources Law* 467.

[119] TW Wälde, 'Renegotiating acquired rights in the oil and gas industries: Industry and political cycles meet the rule of law' (2008) 1 *Journal of World Energy Law & Business* 55.

[120] ibid.

clauses, internationalisation of applicable law and recourse to international arbitration particularly direct investor–state arbitration under investment.[121]

Jurisdictions relying on mining agreements generally show a gradual shift from broad provisions and land extensions, as well as reduced government control and oversight, to better understanding of balancing of benefits, local content and community development, eg through a 'planning and reporting structure'.[122] International organisations have paid a great deal of attention in recent years to supporting efforts to publish contracts, assist in negotiation and develop guidance for negotiation and drafting.[123] Emphasis is placed on adaptive clauses and mechanisms for self-adjustment to prevent continuous renegotiation.

It has been said that that 'direct investment agreements between the mining companies and the Host States … include flat royalty rates and fixed tax rates [which] are generally ill-suited to accommodate significant operational or economic changes'.[124] Likewise, it has been observed that stabilisation provisions, whenever in place, should distinguish between the pay-back period of the initial investment (in which the terms might be more comprehensive), and the remainder period, that should provide for flexibility and dynamic adaptation.[125] The debate is moving into this direction, calling for a radical departure from traditional agreements to partnership approaches around agreed objectives. Furthermore, innovative forms as so-called 'environmental agreements' concluded between different levels and agencies of government administrations and companies, and complemented through protocols with indigenous communities, have emerged to fill in and supplement regulatory gaps, improve the governance of the many environmental and socio-economic aspects of large projects and their impacts and communities' participation, and strengthen management, monitoring and enforcement mechanisms.[126]

---

[121] ibid.

[122] J Southalan, 'Mining State Agreements: Understanding the Framework' in Legalwise Mining Agreements Intensive, 28 March 2018.

[123] OECD Guiding Principles for Durable Extractive Contracts developed by the OECD Policy Dialogue on Natural Resource-based Development's Work Stream 3 on 'Getting Better Deals' and endorsed at the Twelfth Plenary Meeting of the Policy Dialogue on Natural Resource-based Development on 20–21 June 2019 (now submitted for consideration and 'possible endorsement' of the Governing Board of the OECD Development Centre). See also G7 CONNEX Initiative. Sites: resource-contracts.org; oecd.org/dev/natural-resources.htm; connex-unit.org.

[124] H Burnett and LA Bret, *Arbitration of International Mining Disputes: Law and Practice* (Oxford International Arbitration Series) (Oxford, Oxford University Press, 2017) 30.

[125] See also J Otto, 'Resource Nationalism and Regulatory Reform'(RMMLF, 2013).

[126] NA Affolder, 'Rethinking Environmental Contracting' (2010) 21 *Journal of Environmental Law and Practice* 155.

160 *Mining Law Regimes at the Level of Nation-States*

B. Open Access, Bidding and Discretionary Processes of Allocation

From the point of view of the process of allocation or acquisition of mineral rights, a distinction can be drawn between the following:

(i) Open access or direct application processes whereby mineral rights are acquired by application of the prior appropriation rule, '*prior in tempore potiore in iure*', under a first-come, first-served basis. Again, there are variations ranging from: (a) *self-initiated regimes* in which the process consists of (i) the registration of discovery, as the free-entry or claim-staking system in US and Canada; or (ii) an administrative act; or (iii) by adjudication, whereby mineral rights are granted by a judicial act following objective, non-discretionary criteria; and (b) *administrative regimes* in which an application is assessed following an administrative process vis-à-vis subjective criteria, such as whether the applicant meets certain economic or financial conditions. A variation on the first-come, first-served criteria is the 'first-come, first considered' method, under which the first application is considered first and accepted provided the applicant meets certain subjective criteria, such as technical and economic qualifications. The 1973 Spanish Law of Mines, the Tanzanian Mining Act and the system that applies in New Zealand all exemplify this approach.[127]

(ii) Bid or tender processes distinguish between (a) *competitive bidding*, calling for selecting candidate (according to the bid terms);[128] and (b) *direct negotiation*, with a candidate selected on discretionary basis (which for obvious reasons, are highly discouraged).[129]

Open access licensing regimes are commonly used to incentivise mineral exploration while competitive bidding processes are used whenever prospective

---

[127] B Barton, 'An Overview of Mining Law in New Zealand' (1998) 7 *Mineral Resources Engineering* 336. See J Otto and J Cordes, *The Regulation of Mineral Enterprises: A Global Perspective on Economics, Law and Policy* (Colorado, RMMLF, 2002), 3–23.

[128] See CCSI, 'Competitive Bidding in Mining. Country Index' (May 2019).

[129] France and Germany provide examples of legal forms whereby the granting authority chooses the applicant by means of a competitive bidding procedure. The Tanzanian Mining Act adopted an alternative tendering system (where the Minister considers the invitation of applications by tender) for prospecting and mining certain types of minerals, in certain locations, for public interest reasons. A successful bid is selected on the proposed operations programme and expenditure commitments, financial and technical resources and previous experience of the applicant in the conduct of prospecting and mining operations. The subsurface laws of the Russian Federation and Central Asian Republics (Kazakhstan, Kyrgyzstan, Tajikistan, Turkmenistan and Uzbekistan) establish that mineral rights should be granted mostly through tenders and auctions. See M Valdez and S Baimagambetov, 'Comparative Mineral Law of Russian Federation and Central Asian Republics' in Bastida, Wälde and Warden-Fernández (n 15) 1009–36. Southalan (n 75) 48. See further A Gourley, 'Key elements of a model mining code: a Middle East case study' (2019) 32 *Mineral Economics*, 187–204.

areas have already been identified. Open access regimes are far more common in mining than in oil and gas. Ken Haddow explains that this is because offering a proven mineral reserve in a bid is preceded by a costly and lengthy programme that requires advancing from regional geological surveying through prospecting, exploration and evaluation.[130] As described in chapter two, it is commonly held that most deposits that are located close to the surface and can easily be targeted have already been found. The odds of discovering a mine are calculated at a ratio of '1 in 10,000 mineral occurrences (no drilling and no calculated mineral resources or reserves) ... and 1 in 1,000 deposits (meaning a discovery with drill indicated resource and/or reserve estimates)'.[131] The 10,000:1 odds determine that regional surveys are generally carried out by national geological surveys, often supported by international cooperation projects.[132] New discoveries require advancing and testing geo-scientific ideas creatively, which entails significant skills, technology, costs, time and 'tolerance of risk'.[133]

Haddow assimilates prospecting and exploration rights to 'a right to test a geological idea – and to develop it through data collection, interpretation and re-thinking – and, subject to conditions, to enjoy the benefit of that effort if it proves successful.'[134] This task differs from oil and gas exploration where costs are extremely high but the odds of finding mineralisation of potential economic value following successful indication from remote sensing (and the odds that those findings then progress to confirmation of actual economic value) are also high. Investment recovery is also much faster in the oil and gas industry than in the hard rock minerals industry, which affects value and the length of exposure to political and economic changes.

The allocation of mineral rights constitutes, together with the transition from exploration to exploitation rights the two crucial 'moments' of the mining law regime process. I will elaborate on this point in section VI below.

III. The Interface with Land Rights

Mining law regimes usually set forth rules and processes to govern the relationship between mineral rights, and surface holders and owners. The basic principle of traditional mineral tenure regimes has been towards precedence of mineral tenure, on the assumption that mining is a more valuable land use, and so these

---

[130] K Haddow, 'Should Mineral Rights for Hard-Rock Minerals be Awarded by Tender?' (2014) 32 *Journal of Energy & Natural Resources Law* 337.

[131] ibid 338.

[132] ibid 339.

[133] There is a considerable amount of initiatives to conduct geological surveys. The objective is not only identifying key mining deposits but also positioning government teams in mining conventions.

[134] ibid 339.

162　*Mining Law Regimes at the Level of Nation-States*

rules facilitate access to land for mining use independently of surface rights holders' will, or otherwise attempting to reconcile the underlying interests over the land.[135] This principle is often spelled out in the relevant mining code or even in the Constitution, while the applicable rules and procedures might be established under the mining law or either the land law.

Such higher value has historically consisted of the value of minerals extracted. In his famous treatise on mining and metallurgy, Giorgio Agricola observes the importance of mining, first due to the key role of minerals for other economic activities ('[I]n all the works of agriculture, as in other "arts", implements are used which are made of metals … for this reason the metals are of the greatest necessity to man'), and second, because a piece of land derives much richer yields when it is mined than when it is tilled:

> [O]f all ways whereby great wealth is acquired by good and honest means, none is more advantageous than mining; for although from fields which are well tilled … we derive rich yields, yet we obtain richer products from mines; in fact, one mine is often much more beneficial to us than many fields.[136]

The interface of state ownership over minerals in the subsoil, mineral tenure and land ownership is a subject of great variation under comparative law as the legal status of land differs along political and institutional configurations, historical developments and different notions of land law. In most countries, the state holds ownership over minerals in situ. Some countries, like China and many countries in Africa, the state also holds ownership of the land while recognising surface land users' rights. In most countries, land tenure status varies widely, ranging from public to private lands, to communal, undocumented, or customary forms of tenure. In all cases, mining has typically been considered a public purpose/public interest activity, assigning precedence of mining land use, grounding the exercise of powers of eminent domain for land expropriation or compulsory acquisition.

Mining law regimes often establish rules and procedures for: (i) accessing and occupying land, favouring agreement with surface owners and holders; (ii) authorising the expropriation or compulsory acquisition or cession of surface lands, or the establishment of compulsory easements if no agreement is reached;[137] (iii) setting forth the compensation for the use or acquisition of surface lands and

---

[135] AA Debrah, H Mtegha and F Cawood, 'Social licence to operate and the granting of mineral rights in sub-Saharan Africa: Exploring tensions between communities, governments and multinational mining companies' (2018) 56 *Resources Policy* 95; B Barton, 'Reforming the Mining Law of the Northwest Territories: Prepared for the Canadian Arctic Resources Committee', Northern Minerals Programme working papers, 3 (1998).

[136] Agricola (n 80) xxvi.

[137] eg through compulsory sale; in case of unreasonable opposition from the surface owner only (eg, South Africa); through 'cession of land' in the 1982 German Mining Act; this is regarded as an expropriation (by the state) in favour of an individual or legal entity of private law (§§ 77ff BbergG). See JC Pielow, 'Mining Law in Germany' in Bastida, Wälde and Warden-Fernández (n 15) 1037–65. See V Nalule, *Mining and the Law in Africa. Exploring the social and environmental impacts* (Cham, Palgrave MacMillan, 2020) 89.

for damages, and eventually rules for conciliation and dispute resolution;[138] and (iv) using other resources (such as wood, grass and water) that might be useful to mining camps or operations. I will elaborate on the interface of these rules with the recognition of evolving environmental rights and human rights and standards, encompassing a changing and plural content of 'public interest' in section VI.C and D below.

IV. The Principle of 'National Interest' or 'Public Purpose' in Mining and Minerals

The separation of ownership on surface land from the subsurface, and the attribution of ownership or control rights over the state or a collective body to administer or grant mineral rights for exploration and exploitation, has typically been supported by reason of national interest in securing mineral supply and/or the assumption that it is an activity that contributes to development. Domestic mining law regimes often set rules establishing precedence of mining over other land uses through a declaration of mining as 'national interest' or 'public purpose' as grounds for the exercise of wide powers of eminent domain, ie to authorise expropriation, compulsory acquisition or the use of land for mining.

Economic efficiency arguments have most often been put forward to ground the design of special regimes facilitating and prioritising mining over other land uses and (under those old laws) over the will of landowners.[139] The point argued by Mirabeau in the famous debate in the French Assembly that led to the adoption of the 1791 Law of Mines, is the separation of mineral rights from surface rights – essential to the very existence of typical mining law systems in Western jurisdictions.[140] Mirabeau vehemently contended with economic efficiency arguments for establishing a system based on the economic and physical differentiation of the mine (then vein deposits in the subsurface) and the surface land, to best facilitate exploitation. He observed that the artificial division of land ownership does not always fit the full extent of mines. Land is divisible, but a mine is not.[141] Where mines occupy various land properties, mine operation would be subject to agreement with various landowners, adding costs and uncertainty to the success of the project. Furthermore, surface owners do not necessarily have the capital and expertise required to discover and operate a mine.[142]

---

[138] Some laws recognise a 'royalty' or participation to the landowner.

[139] There is abundant literature on the problems of dealing with numerous landowners in mineral deposits located in private lands in the United States of America. See, eg, WG Sumners, 'United States' in Cowles, R (ed), *World Coal Mining Law, a Comparative Survey* (London, International Bar Association, 1984).

[140] See section I.C above.

[141] ibid.

[142] ibid.

164 *Mining Law Regimes at the Level of Nation-States*

Nef provides an illustration of this point with reference to the private owner-ship of minerals and its impact on British coal mining:

> The private ownership of minerals which became a principle of English law ... was hardly an advantage to the subsequent development of mining ... innumerable disputes arose out of the artificial boundaries between colliery concessions, made to correspond with the boundaries between surface holdings. Even in the seventeenth century, when the area required by a single mining enterprise was much smaller than today, the necessity of leaving barriers of coal, which was one of the principal consequences of the private ownership of minerals, added to the expense of litigation, at the same time involved the loss of great quantities of coal, which could have been worked if the granting of mining leases had been taken out of private hands.[143]

From this perspective, national interest requires a balancing act between internal demand for minerals on the one hand, and the interests of surface landowners on the other. As an example, in England, the concept of national interest, defined by the courts as 'the greatest good of the greatest number' to make a differentiation from the private interest of the individual,[144] would require a balancing test by the courts to weigh it against the detrimental effect to landowners in the mining area.[145]

A few trends are worthy of note. First, securing 'critical minerals' as a matter of national interest for the energy transition has become core in specific legislation in many industrialised countries. Second, recognising special interest in minerals whose importance for local economies has typically been overlooked as 'development minerals', and, more generally, drawing finer categorisations of minerals and their linkages with development (eg the potential of major v minor metals for development) are emerging in policy and academic debate.

V. From *Thin* Tenure Regimes to *Thick* Regulation

I started this chapter by examining the question of ownership of minerals in situ. Whatever the definition and status of ultimate *ownership* or radical title over mineral resources, it does not always square with the *jurisdictional* power to regulate (including environmental and health and safety issues) and allocate and manage revenues, which can be assigned to subnational levels of governments (or to national governments) as per the constitutional and legal structure of a country.

Mining codes have historically provided rules for identifying ownership and allocating mineral rights, acknowledging the rights of surface landowners and including rules of rational use and exploitation. The review of traditional doctrines

---

[143] JU Nef, *The Rise of the British Coal Industry* (London, Studies in Economic and Social History, London School of Economics and Political Science, 1932) vol 1, 341.
[144] *Consett Iron Co Ltd v Clavering Trustees* (1935) 2 KB 42 in McDade (n 85).
[145] ibid.

From Thin Tenure Regimes to Thick Regulation   165

on primary mineral ownership traced Roman law concepts and practices in medieval Europe and identified the legal fiction of separation of ownership of minerals in situ (sometimes defined as ownership of the subsoil) from surface ownership for economic efficiency purposes. The objective has typically been to facilitate and encourage mining, the underlying assumption being that minerals were required either for local economies or as source of wealth or as essential inputs for industries elsewhere.

But public interest and the role of mining in society evolves over time. Public interest in other societal values (eg, ecosystems' integrity, indigenous peoples' and peasant communities' rights, cultural heritage, community lifestyles, and other land uses), recognised under an increasing web of laws and regulations, often diverges from the national interest in promoting mining, imposing restrictions on, or qualifying the decision-making processes relevant to the activity, or outright banning mining from territories. Likewise, the expectations about the benefits to be obtained from mining locally and nationally also change and societies expect that projects that go ahead contribute substantially to transform their economic prospects with minimum impact throughout and beyond closure.

In highly industrialised economies, mining became increasingly regulated from the 1960s, hand in hand with increased awareness on the value of the environment, water and other natural resources. In the US, the 'public trust' doctrine, which finds its roots in the Roman law category of *res communis* (things that are common to all such as air, water, the sea and its shores), emerged in judicial precedents and scholarship in the late 1960s and early 1970s, as a device to manage change and acknowledge community values in diffuse resources. In the background, governance theories were changing in the light of findings of 'capture' of public agencies and legislatures by focused minority interests at the expense of diffuse majorities.[146] For some, it amounted in effect to a rule of inalienability of 'trust resources' that was judicially enforced and would place those resources into public ownership.[147] '[T]he collection of adequate information, public participation in decisions, informed and accountable choices, and close scrutiny of private give-aways of environmental resources' were required regarding 'trust resources' such as water.[148]

The ensuing decade would witness formidable statutory developments on environmental, land and resource planning,[149] which would result in locating or relocating mineral tenure regimes within the procedures of planning law (as in the UK) or environmental law (as in Michigan, US) or of administrative law more generally (as in many EU countries, which replaced their liberal mineral tenure

---

[146] CM Rose, 'Joseph Sax and the Idea of the Public Trust' (1998) 25 *Ecology Law Quarterly* 354.

[147] JD Kearney and TW Merrill, 'The Origins of the American Public Trust Doctrine: What Really Happened in Illinois Central' (2004) 71 *University of Chicago Law Review* 799.

[148] CM Rose, 'Joseph Sax and the Idea of the Public Trust' (1998) 25 *Ecology Law Quarterly* 354.

[149] RJ Lazarus, 'Changing Conceptions of Property and Sovereignty in Natural Resources Law: Questioning the Public Trust Doctrine' (1986) 71 *Iowa Law Review* 631–716.

166   *Mining Law Regimes at the Level of Nation-States*

regimes with administrative concessions) in all cases interfacing with a web of regulations. This progression is in line with observed trends in the evolution of law (at least in Western legal systems) from a *thin* system that facilitates private ordering and administers private entitlements, to a *thicker* model of state regulation.[150] While the very same notion of public trust is rooted in *property* (or Crown or states' ownership of minerals in situ), broader regulatory developments find grounding on the exercise of the jurisdictional powers by virtue of *sovereignty*.[151] Yet, a third turn in the evolution of law in these economies points at the emergence of a *governance* paradigm consisting of participatory and collaborative processes in which both public and private actors along with civil society share responsibility for achieving common goals.[152]

Over those years, countries in the developing world would also transition eventually from general reliance on mineral tenure regimes towards the use of contractual forms such as joint ventures and service contracts that would ultimately allow the exercise of further powers of control under issues of ownership. Constitutional and legal reforms of the time would generally be informed by the lexicon of Permanent Sovereignty over Natural Resources and definitions of state ownership would usually qualify its character of non-alienability and non-prescriptibility. In many countries these definitions have been inimical to the sweeping reforms of the 1990s, which brought liberal mining law regimes back to centre stage accompanied by opening up to foreign direct investment with the ratification of international investment treaties that would globally discipline the regulatory powers of states. The constitutional and legal reforms of the time did not only focus on setting the conditions for market economies. They also strengthened bills of rights, recognised the right to a healthy environment and generally redistributed government powers and functions to subnational units.

In countries that inherited their legislation from colonial traditions, or middle- and low-income countries with exporting profiles and where legal frameworks have notably been influenced by international actors, there has been, at least over the last 15 years or so, an upward trend towards challenging mining and its precedence. In Latin America, this has found expression through the opposition from communities; legislation and regulations; municipal ordinances issued by local governments banning open pit mining using chemicals in their processes; and judicial decisions that have reinterpreted the traditional principle of public interest of mining precedence, as well as rights and obligations of states and investors in

---

[150] O Lobel, 'The Renew Deal: The Fall of Regulation and the Rise of Governance in Contemporary Legal Thought'(2004) 89 *Minnesotta Law Review*: see definition quote at 344 and 364 on evolution of law.

[151] Lazarus, 'Changing Conceptions of Property and Sovereignty' (1986).

[152] Lobel, 'The Renew Deal' (2004). See examples on collaborative governance processes emerging in Chile and Colombia in AE Bastida, 'Latin America's Policy Priorities on Mining and Sustainable Development, and Opportunities for EU Cooperation', European Policy Brief, Strategic Dialogue on Sustainable Raw Materials for Europe (STRADE) No 05 / 2018.

the light of constitutional charters of environmental and human rights.[153] In many African countries, inspired by the tenets of the Africa Mining Vision, great focus is being placed on local content and linkages between mining, other sectors of the economy, infrastructure development and value addition,[154] and emerging attention on the role of 'development minerals' and ASM to contribute to the SDGs. In all cases, the typical mining laws lie at the many interfaces with a growing range of fields of law and regulation at all levels.

VI. Mineral Law 'As Interfaces'

In previous sections I have looked very schematically into key aspects underlying the design of mining law and regulations which are inherent to the dynamics of exploration and mining and explored how these have typically been captured in different types of comparative mining law regimes. In democratic societies, mining laws and contracts operate within a framework of evolving constitutional provisions and administrative norms that protect and guarantee fundamental individual and collective rights by placing limits to the powers of government administrations to respect the rule of law, which might be further reinforced by international agreements. All in all, these qualify the various administrative processes relevant to mineral rights.

Mining laws interact with land regimes, other regulatory 'subsystems' and international law within evolving constitutional and administrative law structures. In thinking about the role of these regimes and interactions, it is useful to consider that, by establishing the rules and processes for the granting of mineral rights, mining laws essentially set a decision-making process that is significantly influenced by the extent and quality of information on geological prospects.

Key factors in the mineral supply process are as follows: (i) the information on mineral occurrences; (ii) the risks and resources involved in obtaining it; and (iii) who bears the risks, costs and the benefits from the rewards. Mining laws have typically been designed with an economic criteria, taking a varying range of approaches to deal with these issues along broader economic models that determine the role of the state in the economy, the importance of mining or certain minerals in the economy, attitudes to foreign investment and policy priorities. Along these lines, the spectrum ranges from property or tenure, to administrative systems and contractual regimes. These all entail important decisions on who

---

[153] AE Bastida and L Bustos, 'Towards Regimes for Sustainable Mineral Resources Management. Constitutional Reform, Law and Judicial Precedents in Latin America' (2017) 9 *International Development Policy, Revue internationale de politique de développement* 235. H Mostert, *Mineral Law: Principles and Policies in Perspective* (Cape Town, Juta, 2012).

[154] See AKK Camara, *Linking Mining and Infrastructure Development in Sub-Saharan Africa: Towards a Collaborative Framework for Sustainable Shared-Use of Rails and Ports Facilities for Minerals and Non-Minerals Activities*, PhD Thesis (CEPMLP University of Dundee, 2017).

168   *Mining Law Regimes at the Level of Nation-States*

is entitled to mine and to what extent and under what capacity these decisions will lay out different approaches on how to regulate for broader issues of public interest.

The extent of ratification of international treaties in the fields of investment and trade, and also the environment and human rights, and anti-corruption efforts undertaken by an impressive number of countries are all gradually reshaping the internal space for the exercise of sovereign powers to regulate the activity.[155] This internal reconfiguration has been reflected in, and compounded, by extensive domestic processes of constitutional and legal reform strengthening the rule of law, recognising the right to a healthy environment and expanding the charters of rights and guarantees. At the same time, most reforms have embraced decentralisation and have gradually implemented the transfer of powers and functions of central governments to subnational units. This is further recontouring the internal space of nation-states to govern and regulate mining.[156]

In many countries, each of these normative claims are being 'domesticated' as a matter of commitments undertaken under international treaties ratified, or as a matter of the evolution of domestic law, through constitutional and legal reform and judicial interpretation. For mining law specifically, this all entails, at a minimum, that the process to obtain and maintain legal entitlement to explore and mine will interface, on the one hand, with processes related to obtaining approval of environmental reports and assessments along with a wide range of operating permits, and, on the other, with processes to negotiate land access and the consent of all affected communities.[157] The great fragmentation of international law regimes translates domestically into a disparate constellation of regimes and duties, all of which are parallel and inconsistent systems that are being challenged in courts. This entails inherent contradictions and is posing great challenges for the regulatory design of coherent systems that will be able to work for supporting sustainable outcomes.

Government administrations are challenged to exercise their sovereign powers in ways they meet the goals of national interest in mining and the whole set of rights and interests of their citizens emerging from the interplay of national and international law. In many jurisdictions, each stage of regulatory processes is beginning to be examined from a broader range of criteria that also relate to types, holders and quality of information vital to advance sustainable development outcomes. Mining laws can thus have a fundamental role in defining the

---

[155] See N Schrijver, *Sovereignty over Natural Resources. Balancing Rights and Duties* (Cambridge, Cambridge University Press, 1997); R Barnes, *Property Rights and Natural Resources* (Oxford, Hart Publishing, 2009) 12. See ch 4.

[156] H Santaella Quintero, '*Un territorio y tres modelos de gestión: análisis de la necesidad de armonizar y constitucionalizar las competencias urbanísticas, ambientales y mineras sobre el territorio*' in JC Henao and S Díaz Ángel (eds), *Minería y desarrollo. Tomo V: Historia y gobierno del territorio minero* (Bogotá, Universidad Externado de Colombia, 2016) 175–226; Bastida and Bustos, 'Towards Regimes for Sustainable Mineral Resources Management' (2017).

[157] Southalan (n 75).

rules and procedures for decision-making based on information about the financial and technical aspects, and the environmental and human rights impacts of investment projects, environmental and socio-economic baselines, water basins, territorial agendas and institutional structures to make projects work for broader-based development while safeguarding environmental sustainability.

Such a potential role is far from being realised. The inherent contradictions involved in meeting a range of regulatory functions are starting to be addressed in a few jurisdictions through integrated regulation, environmental contracting, 'whole-of-government' innovations and through the use of regulatory risks impacts analysis which are beginning to pave the way to innovative platforms, tools and arrangements seeking to provide more coherent approaches to law and regulation.[158]

I will use here again the concept of 'interfaces' – used above to advance understanding of the connection between mining law regimes and the global economy[159] – to illuminate the intersections with variegated fields of law and regulation at national and subnational levels. 'Interfaces' has been defined by Kanetake as 'the points where the actors, norms and procedures belonging to respective [international and national] legal orders connect and interact with one another'. Interactions are furthered by overlapping 'subject matters' (of different fields of law at domestic level; between national and international law).[160] This section will explore some of these interactions, which pose questions for regulatory design and tools for sustainability. It will begin with some observations regarding the critical transition from exploration to mining, as this is often a crucial moment for the interface of various regulations along the mineral tenure process.

A. The Transition from Exploration to Exploitation Rights

Comparative law shows a wide spectrum of regulatory responses to the critical transition from exploration and discovery to mining. Regimes that place great emphasis on the needs and dynamics of private investment tend to provide assurances to those who commit resources to exploration, that they will be able to develop a successful discovery or, in other words, that they will be granted a right

---

[158] See New South Wales, Integrated Mining Policy; Alberta Energy Regulator, 'The Alberta Model for Regulatory Excellence April 2016' in Open Contracting Partnership and NRGI, 'Open Contracting for Oil, Gas and Mineral Rights: Shining a Light on Good Practice' (June 2018).

[159] See ch 1.I, referring to the use by Schill of the term 'interfaces' elaborated by Kanetake in the context of global energy relations.

[160] M Kanetake, 'The Interfaces between the National and International Rule of Law: A Framework Paper' in M Kanetake and A Nollkaemper (eds), *The Rule of Law at the National and International Levels. Contestations and Deference* (Oxford, Hart Publishing, 2018). S Schill, 'The Rule of Law and the Division of Labour Between National and International Law: The Case of International Energy Relations' in M Kanetake and A Nollkaemper (eds), *The Rule of Law at the National and International Levels. Contestations and Deference* (Oxford, Hart Publishing, 2018).

170 *Mining Law Regimes at the Level of Nation-States*

to proceed from exploration to the exploitation or mining stage (ie, 'the right to mine'). Typically, security or the guarantee of mineral tenure has been defined as a reasonable legal entitlement for extraction rights after successful completion of the exploration phase.[161] At the other end of the spectrum, a few regimes provide for the allocation of exploitation rights to the discoverer or to any other applicant at the government's discretion.[162]

A crucial issue relates to the conditions imposed upon the investor in return for such an entitlement. Here again, responses vary from single unified grants that entitle the holder to explore and extract, to an automatic transition from exploration to exploitation rights, to priority on the rights to mine,[163] all subject to specific procedures and meeting obligations, such as the approval of feasibility studies, mining plans, and environmental impact assessments and/or entering into community development agreements.[164] Another relevant and related question is the ability to transfer title to other companies that can undertake exploitation, a practice that is inherent to the dynamics of many junior companies.

To fully grasp the challenges involved in the critical transition from exploration to mining rights, one needs to understand another core aspect of regulatory design: the interface between mineral tenure or title, on the one hand, and regulatory conditions for the operation of those rights, on the other.

B. The Multi-Faceted Nature of the Title and Permitting Process

A core question in regulatory design is whether regulatory conditions for the exercise of rights (such as environmental and health and safety regulations, or requirements for entering into agreements with surface landowners or landholders) have been incorporated within the process to obtain mineral rights, or whether these are completely independent from the mineral licensing process.

To be sure, the overall process of acquiring mineral rights and the separate or inherent permits to operate (including the so-called 'social licence to operate') have become a complex and multifaceted affair. In the case of contracts, they often intertwine operational requirements within the process for granting mineral

---

[161] T Wälde, 'Investment Policies and Investment Promotion in the Mineral Industries' (1991) 6 *ICSID/Foreign Investment Law Journal* 102.

[162] See G Akpan, 'Towards a Regime of Secured Tenure in the International Mining Industry' (1998) 1 *OGLTR* 31.

[163] This is the criterion adopted by the legislation in force in the Russian Federation and Central Asian Republics. Upon making a commercial discovery, and obtaining the right to start mining operations, companies must obtain governmental approval of various technical reports. These include a feasibility study, EIA, and mining plans with a view to ensuring that the project minimises its impact on the environment and the population and guarantees the rational development of mineral resources. See Valdez and S Baimagambetov, 'Comparative Mineral Law of Russian Federation and Central Asian Republics' in Bastida, Wälde and Warden-Fernández (n 15).

[164] Southalan (n 75) 51.

Mineral Law 'As Interfaces' 171

rights.[165] To start with, and without going into questions of spatial land use planning, any project must go through processes of assessment and management of environmental and social impacts. This has widely been done through EIAs (aimed at identifying and mitigating environmental risks in projects) and environmental licensing processes. There is increased understanding that EIAs have been used to manage negative impacts rather than to strengthening the decision-making process, with insufficient efforts to promote public participation and inter-institutional coordination before the key decisions about projects have been taken, and they lack of an assessment of alternatives to reach a solution that integrates environmental and social outcomes.[166] EIAs might also be an insufficient tool for the full and unbiased assessment of impacts[167] and fall short of designing the required structures for supporting net positive outcomes.[168] Moreover, environmental baselines and knowledge about water basins are usually insufficient while they are crucial to inform the decisions of public administrations and business enterprises, and to render accountability to the public.

Regulatory innovation is starting to emerge in the form of environmental agreements and virtual platforms developed by governments in consultation with business and communities for accessing and generating information about projects, environmental assessments and land uses, as well as clarifying the role of the different stakeholders along the decision-making processes.[169]

The UN Guiding Principles have emphasised the importance of human rights impact assessments and meaningful consultation to potentially affected groups, which might be mainstreamed within risk assessments or environmental and social impact assessments, and inform the due diligence process, as well the importance of tracking through integration in internal business functions, decision-making and internal reporting processes.[170] Impacts must be assessed early on, at the

---

[165] Open Contracting Partnership and NRGI, 'Open Contracting for Oil, Gas and Mineral Rights: Shining a Light on Good Practice' (June 2018).

[166] A Williams and K Dupuy, 'Deciding over Nature: Corruption and Environmental Impact Assessments' (2017) 65 *Environmental Impact Assessment Review* 120; N Woodroffe and T Grice, *Beyond Revenues: Measuring and Valuing Environmental and Social Impacts in Extractive Sector Governance* (NRGI, September 2019).

[167] M Aguilar-Støen and C Hirsch, 'Bottom-Up Responses to Environmental and Social Impact Assessments: A Case Study from Guatemala' (2017) 62 *Environmental Impact Assessment Review* 225; M Dougherty, 'By the Gun or by the Bribe: Firm Size, Environmental Governance and Corruption Among Mining Companies in Guatemala' (2015) U4 Issue Paper 17; Williams and Dupuy, 'Deciding over Nature' (2017) 120; P De Sa, 'Mining and sustainable development: territorializing the mining industry' (2019) 32 *Mineral Economics* 131.

[168] Williams and Dupuy (n 166).

[169] Common Ground, the site developed by the New South Wales Government in Australia to provide 'clear explanations of mining and production titles' and 'describe the roles of community and governments in the decision making process for any proposed activity'. Government of New South Wales, Planning and Environment, Resources and Geoscience, at http://commonground.nsw.gov.au/#!. On environmental agreements, see Affolder, 'Rethinking Environmental Contracting' (2010).

[170] UN Guiding Principles, Principles 18 and 19. See further D Kemp and F Vanclay, 'Human Rights and Impact Assessment: Clarifying the Connections in Practice' (2013) 31 *Impact Assessment and Project Appraisal* 86.

172 *Mining Law Regimes at the Level of Nation-States*

stage of project design or contract negotiations. In the latter case, this would be the appropriate time to set the expectations and responsibilities of the parties and coherently respond, if needed, in the contractual undertakings. Considering human rights at this stage would also demonstrate that the state has policy space to negotiate and takes consideration of all its commitments and duties, thereby preventing potential international arbitration cases in the future.[171] It is also being advised that contractual stabilisation clauses, whenever used, should not impinge on 'the state's bona fine efforts to implement laws, regulations or policies, in a non-discriminatory manner, in order to meet its human rights obligations.'[172]

C. The Mineral Rights–Land Nexus: Spatial Planning

Old mining laws usually identify sites and types of lands (such as urban areas and military buildings). The conventional spatial scope of mining laws increasingly interfaces with a wide range of international, national and local laws and regulations protecting the environment and ecosystems; establishing consultation or consent with indigenous communities; or articulating the power of municipalities to decide on land uses.

The question of access to land and the *mineral rights–land rights interface* is strongly related to dramatic changes within societal attitudes to mining and resources use; to the value of land and ecosystems, and to the recognition and integration of rights of those affected by projects (and the development of environmental and human rights law). These all imply gradual changes in tenure regimes and regulation, to accommodate diverging interests, and result in challenging precedence of mining land use and regulating access and use. The question of the equitable accommodation of different interests has become crucial as a matter of the very same social legitimacy of projects.

A few jurisdictions are integrating mining as a use of land within systemic spatial planning and strategic impact assessments, differentiating between areas open to mining from those that are protected, or where access is qualified to obtaining some permits. In business terms, accommodation has been phrased as managing risks of uncertainty derived from a range of claims, interests and tenure situations that require different levels and types of contracting; a range of regulatory permits to comply with, and allocation of benefits at lower levels of government, and closer to communities affected by projects. This is not a passing and cyclical trend, but one that will see increased sophistication on forms of

---

[171] See Commentary in 'Principles for Responsible Contracts: Integrating the Management of Human Rights Risks into State–Investor Contract Negotiations: Guidance for Negotiators' (A/HRC/17/31/Add 3). It states: 'While human rights risks should always be considered in the context of business ventures … human rights risk management is essential in the negotiation of the contract or agreement that establishes and governs the project. This will contribute to ensuring the project's sustainability and success'.
[172] ibid, Principle 4.

Mineral Law 'As Interfaces'   173

collaboration and an *integrated* view of mining, minerals, land, water and ecosystems. It ultimately has important implications in terms of *where* to mine and on processes on *how* to mine, to negotiate access.[173]

D. The Processes of Consultation and Consent

The typical function of mining laws has been promoting mining, often through incentives to miners in the form of tenure rights which provided access to territories and lands. Decision-making in the process of acquisition, maintenance, transfer and cancellation of mineral rights in traditional mining law has historically been unidimensional. When referring to land holders and other land uses, these have often been based on the assumption of mining as an activity of public purpose or vital to the national interest.

Mining laws often provide procedures to notify the landowner, conduct a negotiation process, and criteria for determining the relevant compensation (often in conjunction with rules determining expropriation, easements, or similar). These typical, usually minimum and standardised provisions have been at the root of much conflict related to the engagement between miners, surface owners and holders, local communities and broader societies. A compounding factor has been the transformation of industrial mining – and the boundaries between what is technically possible, and environmentally and socially feasible – and, in some jurisdictions, the granting of mineral rights independently from geology and local context. Mining laws were historically designed for small operations. Mining operations are not confined to the site of extraction but use land for processing, waste storage, transportation, and power generation.

The underlying factor behind change of this *status quo* is the growing understanding of land as holding a multiplicity of values and indefinitely advancing benefits of an economic, social, environmental and cultural nature[174] – with more value assigned to other land uses such as conservation, wilderness, landscape, forestry, recreation, farming, urban settlement – and increased consideration for accounting for natural capital and ecosystem services into decision-making, as well as an expansion of the understanding of *risk* – away from confined business risks. Multiple claims are advanced by different actors under growing and disparate areas of law (at international, national and local levels as well as under customary norms) that can view land as a commodity; as storing biodiversity, heritage, cultural and environmental values, and providing ecosystem services; as the fundamental means to provide livelihoods and food security, or as

---

[173] See ECOWAS Model Mining and Minerals Development Act, June 2019. See the community provisions in the Model Mining Development Agreement, developed by the Mining Law Committee, International Bar Association, 2010, and in the Annotated WAOML Miners' and Investors' Modern Model Mining Code, developed by WAOML.

[174] MMSD, *Breaking New Ground* (London, Earthscan, 2002) 142.

174 *Mining Law Regimes at the Level of Nation-States*

inextricably linked to the very same identity of peoples.[175] This is all redefining not only the *extent of lands* available to mining, but also the *scope* and *contours* of the rules of engagement of mineral rights holders with other users and holders of land rights, challenging mining precedence as an overriding principle.

The timing of consultation and processes oriented to seeking consent poses great challenges in regulatory design. Except for projects in which a proven reserve has been shown – and where rights to which could be obtained through a bidding process similar to oil and gas regimes – the timing for 'prior and informed' consultation along the tenure and licensing processes during the exploration and evaluation of mineral occurrences challenges the redesign of inclusive and partici-patory regulations seeking to balance the interests of all parties involved.

In 1992, Papua New Guinea introduced innovations through a consultation process convened by the Minister within a 'development forum' *prior to* the grant of a 'special mining lease' with a view to considering the views of those who could be affected by the grant including landholders, national and provincial govern-ment, apart from the applicant (with the lease granted upon prior consultation with the provincial government, if any). The Act also established that applica-tions for mineral rights on land reserved for exclusive use under the Land Act or any other Act could only be granted upon consent of the Minister responsible for that reserved land.[176] In New South Wales, Australia, the title holder must develop a community consultation strategy at the stage of the exploration licence and exploration can only go ahead upon an access arrangement between the company and the landholder. Community engagement is only compulsory for granted mining or production leases. Conducting community consultation and engagement in the process of State agreements negotiations itself is also under debate.[177]

E. Administrative Processes and the Rule of Law

A key aspect of the processes of granting and maintaining mineral rights deals with the *substantive and procedural limits* for the exercise of state powers under the rule of law (which are increasingly determined and qualified by constitutional and legal duties to protect the environment and resource management, human rights and generally to regulate in the public interest). These substantive and procedural guarantees are usually recognised at constitutional level and under administrative

---

[175] See L Cotula, 'Land, Property and Sovereignty in International Law' (2017) 25 *Cardozo Journal of International and Comparative Law* 219.

[176] 1992 Mining Act of Papua New Guinea, Preliminary section and Art 3. C Filer, 'Development Forum in Papua New Guinea: Upsides and Downsides' (2008) 26 *Journal of Energy and Natural Resources Law* 120.

[177] Fitzgerald, Mining agreements (2002). Southalan (n 75). See further analysis of approaches in a range of jurisdictions in J Warden-Fernandez, 'Indigenous Communities' Rights and Mineral Development' (2005) 23 *Journal of Energy & Natural Resources Law* 395.

law, and consecrate the principles of proportionality, legality, due process and judicial review, among others.[178]

This domestic body of national law interacts with the international investment agreements ratified by states, which subject matter ultimately disciplines the exercise of public authority in accordance with the rule of law, expressed through standards of treatment of investment. These include respect for standards of due process (eg, the identification of who makes decisions along the award procedure, the criteria on which decisions are made, participatory procedures and appeal processes) and respect for legitimate investors' expectations (certainty, stability and consistency of the legal framework and of assurances made by government officers). Likewise, such domestic body of national law interacts with human rights treaties which also uphold substantive and procedural rights – as due process and judicial protection. The fragmented nature of processes and institutions, lack of transparency and accountability are all situations that often conspire against the overall quality of the decision-making processes and the standards of treatment.

F. Administrative Processes and Transparency Standards

The increasingly multi-layered and complex decision-making process has often been vulnerable to corruption risks[179] and to high politicisation through the undue exercise of discretionary powers by high and lower-ranking officials. In effect, mining, and extractive industries and natural resource projects more generally, are particularly prone to corruption due to the large profits the sector can generate and the opportunities for hiding transfers.[180] The potential for acts of corruption at all levels can take place during mineral rights awarding, the negotiation (and renegotiation) of contracts and bidding processes, the critical transition from exploration to exploitation, and of issuance of permitting processes (eg, the approval of environmental impact assessments),[181] as well as in the face of subsequent renewals[182] and the monitoring and enforcement of contractual, licensing and permitting obligations.[183]

Corruption might occur through bribery, embezzlement and/or the misappropriation of funds at the local level, and it may be favoured through 'a culture of clientelism and patronage, informal networks of local public officials, community leaders and local business elite', and also be an outcome of rushed processes of

---

[178] See G Corrêa da Fonseca Lima, 'Direitos e Garantias Fundamentais no Processo de Outorga de Direitos Minerários' in M Mendo, Gomes de Souza, *Direito Minerário em Evoluçao* (Belo Horizonte, Mandamentos Editora, 2009) 161–176.

[179] I Kolstad and T Søreide, 'Corruption in Natural Resource Management: Implications for Policy Makers' (2009) 34 *Resources Policy* 218.

[180] ibid 219.

[181] Williams and Dupuy (n 166) 120.

[182] ibid.

[183] See Kolstad and Søreide, 'Corruption' (2009) 222.

176 *Mining Law Regimes at the Level of Nation-States*

decentralisation – which have often occurred without appropriate assessment of the capacity of local economies and the capabilities of local authorities to manage large inflows of revenue and undertake new responsibilities.[184] Information asymmetries on geological factors and the value of the resource and projects' costs can also favour corruption, particularly at the planning stages (with impacts particularly on the revenue sharing arrangements in contracts).[185] Loopholes in the decision-making process, as a lack of coordination between government authorities, can also foster an environment for corrupt practices.[186] Advice consistently points out the need for transparent decision-making processes, with a standard of systematic disclosure emerging, and disclosure of contracts.[187]

VII. Redefining the Disciplinary Matrix of Mineral Law for Sustainability

In Western jurisdictions, mining codes have historically provided rules for identifying ownership and allocating mineral rights, acknowledging the rights of surface landowners and including rules of rational use and exploitation. They have also typically set the administrative rules and intervention powers of government authorities derived from public interest (monitoring and compliance, inspection, rational and efficient use of resources, health and safety, environmental regulation – often in conjunction with regulatory regimes applicable to operations). But they have not been conceived as frameworks for coordinating regulatory authority for their management and for providing the basis for transforming mineral resources into local (and national) wealth.

---

[184] OECD, 'Corruption in the Extractive Value Chain: Typology of Risks, Mitigation Measures and Incentives' (2016). This report states that 'The OECD Foreign Bribery Report shows the magnitude of the problem, finding that one in five cases of transnational bribery occur in the extractive sector'. 'The offenses include: bribery of foreign officials, embezzlement, misappropriation and diversion of public funds, abuse of office, trading in influence, favouritism and extortion, bribery of domestic officials and facilitation payments.'

[185] Kolstad and Søreide (n 178) 221. See also OECD Typology, 'On the Government's Side Insufficient Resources and Information to Assess the Country's Reserves' (2016).

[186] OECD Typology, 'Political Discretion and Poor Governance' (2016).

[187] Addendum on Principles for responsible contracts: integrating the management of human rights risks into State-investor contract negotiations: guidance for negotiations. Report of the Special Representative of the Secretary-General on the issue of human rights and transnational corporations and other business enterprises, United Nations General Assembly, A/HRC/17/31/Add.3, 25 May 2011, Human Rights Council, Seventeenth Session; see also L Caripis, 'Combatting corruption in mining approvals: assessing the risks in 18 resource-rich countries', Mining for Sustainable Development Programme (Transparency International Australia, 2018); Model Mining Development Agreement, developed by the Mining Law Committee (International Bar Association, 2010), and its supplement, the Transparency Template prepared by Howard Mann et al (2012); Annotated WAOML Miners' and Investors' Modern Model Mining Code Draft – Anti-Corruption Part, developed by WAOML.

Nowadays, changing societal awareness on the value of protecting ecosystems, environmental and land stewardship, human rights, the value of minerals in the economy from a developmental perspective and the rule of law and transparency are all bringing in a diverse range of broader interests of a public nature and, along with them, sets of criteria, information and expectations to consider in regulatory design. The vulnerability of the sector to corruption has been brought under scrutiny in recent years and with it the spotlight on the processes for awarding mineral rights. All these sets of contradictory challenges and emerging trends are redefining both mineral law (as a multi-level and multi-layered framework of law and regulation *and* as a field of study) and the governance of mining and minerals.

In a disciplinary matrix for sustainability, mineral law entails such multi-faceted legal, normative and institutional framework and their many 'interfaces' with coinciding (and at times conflicting) subject matter – the exercise of authority by institutions for sustainable resource management.

7

The Law and Governance of Mining and Minerals from a Global Perspective: 'An Overarching Vision'

The study of the law and governance of mining and minerals has not yet consolidated as an academic discipline in international scholarship. A first challenge in any attempt at systematisation is the many ways of *naming* the very same phenomenon – 'minerals and metals', or 'subsoil resources' or 'strategic resources' from the point of view of the sites of extraction or 'sustainable production and consumption'; or 'raw materials', 'commodities' or 'critical substances from the point of view of global markets, 'value chains' or 'responsible sourcing' initiatives. They are also seen as 'commercial assets' from the perspective of investors; or 'commons', 'fruits of nature' or 'natural heritage' from perspectives that place emphasis on the value of nature. Furthermore, the land where they lie can be considered as an accessory to mineral rights and interests in traditional patterns of mining law and tenure, or as endowed of special cultural, spiritual and economic significance if viewed from the standpoint of indigenous peoples, peasant communities or rural women. Additionally, they can also turn into 'recycled materials' or 'recovered inputs' as the circular economy is already underway. The different nominations reveal the many diverging values underlying related fields of law: international investment, trade, economics and finance, environment and human rights, and anti-corruption, as well as laws and regulations and national, and local levels, and transnational governance initiatives, which interconnect in many ways.

A second challenge is found in the *scope* and *breadth* of the subject matter. The study of 'mining' or 'mineral' or 'subsoil' law has usually been undertaken in resource-rich countries at domestic levels and scholarship has usually focused on the analysis of statutory Acts and precedents, and their relationship with other statutory and regulatory instruments, notably those concerning investment and the environment. From a global perspective, that is a crucial, but not the only, level of relations and legal ordering in this field. A global perspective as the analytical lens to examine the legal and normative phenomena concerning mining and minerals assists in capturing the existence of multiple layers of ordering at international, regional, transnational, national and local levels, and the complex interactions between them.

That expanded understanding is particularly relevant to this industry and type of natural resource. The mining industry is inherently global. Minerals and metals are unevenly spread throughout the Earth's crust and no country is fully self-sufficient. Mining constitutes a first stage in global production networks and is defined by the presence of transnational corporations. The traditional Western mining companies are being joined by a more diverse set of vertically integrated companies that trade minerals and/or use them as vital inputs for their products, as well as investors and lenders who determine the business, technologies and cost structures of operations. They are part of a growing constellation of actors active in resource governance at multiple levels. The prominent role of global and transnational of actors contrasts with the dramatic environmental, human rights, economic and governance impacts of operations at local level. The biggest paradox occurs whenever projects take place in jurisdictions and localities with poor governance. And there are many of them. The double – global and local – governance gap often works to the detriment of local communities, environments and economies if institutions are not in place to manage those impacts and plan for development.

In the Introduction of this monograph I referred to Twining, who observed that lawyers are challenged to shape 'overarching visions' of cosmopolitan disciplines of law in ways that grasp both complex and diverse legal phenomena and engage with the core challenges of our age (poverty, climate change, sustainability) and their implications for these disciplines. A third challenge in systematising the law and governance of mining and minerals from a global perspective then arises not only on the definition, scope and breadth of the subject matter, but also on its *normative guidance* and its implications.

A fourth challenge is that of much needed *diversity* in the structure and knowledge-making processes of the academic discipline. It is only through a dynamic and diverse 'community of practice' that more textured understandings of governance from global to local levels can be achieved. A diverse community can have an important role in shifting academic framings, practice and mindsets from a focus on extractives towards their role in transformative outcomes and in building sustainable futures. New framings are required for reusing and recycling minerals and for assessing the full value of primary resources for local peoples.

I. Conclusions

What transpires from this exploration of levels of normative ordering of mining and minerals is increasing, albeit fragmented, law and regulation of the field. This has historically been a chronically under-theorised and under-systematised area of enquiry in international scholarship. A disciplinary matrix of the law and governance of mining and minerals from a global perspective is embedded in the understanding of the geographical levels of relations and legal ordering concerning

180　*The Law and Governance of Mining and Minerals*

minerals access and management (and the diversity of sources); and of the various fields of law and regulation concerning sustainable resource management, which often conflict, overlap, and interpenetrate each other.

The key constituents of the international law and governance of mining and minerals have evolved against the backdrop of the post-war period. Firstly, the international law of natural resources has evolved from PSONR and the principles enshrined in UN General Assembly Resolution 1803 to multiple treaties and soft law that qualify states' exercise of their powers to fulfil duties towards investors, peoples, ecosystems and economies when managing land and natural resources. This is increasingly shaped by the grammar of human rights, finding expression in the distinctive legal recognition of the rights of indigenous peoples and growing treatment of the land rights of peasant communities under soft law, as well as in international court decisions. Secondly, there has been growing normative recognition of the role of transnational and national business in development and their impact on human rights, the corresponding obligation of states (both host states and home states) in preventing and responding to them, as well as the responsibility of business to respect human rights through due diligence measures, while the debate is advancing on establishing their accountability. Thirdly, such recognition of responsibilities is extending to a broader set of actors active in global minerals resource governance, notably international organisations, financial institutions, traders and consumers.

Mining and minerals have been included in the global development agenda of the international community with the aim of guiding decisions towards sustainability. Sustainable development calls upon all actors to make renewed efforts for cooperation at multiple levels to push sustainability into the mainstream decision-making process of economic activities. The purpose is to achieve sustainable resources management, and all the interconnected SDGs more broadly. This holds profound significance for normatively guiding governance and international cooperation at bilateral and multilateral levels, although their enforcement is very weak. At the same time, this illuminates the inherent contradictions underlying current fragmented systems of decision-making at all levels. There is currently neither a global convention regulating minerals governance nor comprehensive governance guidelines (considering both terrestrial and deep seabed mining). But there is an emerging line of work calling for systemic governance and emerging calls for global action and for cooperating around global value chains, which is bringing a minerals and mining governance dimension into the environmental law agenda.

On a more granular basis, countries entering into bilateral and multilateral treaties do often place core aspects of mining law, which typically belong to the realm of municipal systems, under the jurisdiction of international tribunals. Decisions emerging from arbitral investment tribunals are interpreting traditional concepts of mining law (such as 'security of tenure' and 'right to mine', crafted within the structure and internal logic of mineral tenure regimes) and

Conclusions 181

expanding their scope. Drawing on the scholarly work of Schill on energy law, it is apparent that domestic mining law and contracts work then as interfaces between national law and the international legal architecture governing international mineral markets and investment, and their common underpinnings in the concept of the rule of law as guiding 'the exercise of public authority'. In turn, decisions emerging from international human rights courts are establishing obligations to guarantee the rights to property and consultation of indigenous communities, which also relate to the rules and processes of mining laws. They thus redefine the contours of the internal space for the exercise of sovereign powers to regulate mineral rights. This internal space is often an arena of great tension reconfigured by a more textured identification of states' duties, as well as conflicting claims and values over projects.

At the level of nation-states, mineral law encompasses a constellation of norms that place tenure and contracts within a web of laws, regulations and contractual commitments. Mineral law, with its typical ownership–tenure–land nexus is becoming redefined – by either law and judicial interpretation, or both – with evolving notions of public interest, constitutional provisions and growing areas of law that shape and broaden the scope of decision-making over projects. Mineral law can work internally as interfaces between those disparate regimes. But at present, those decision-making processes are characterised by their many loopholes and incoherent nature and, broadly speaking, by a lack of systematic approaches to public administration instruments and structures both conceptually and in practice. A new impetus results from calls to 'constitutionalise', 'democratise', 'decolonise', 'diversify' and 'territorialise' mining law, and to adopt 'rights-based' and 'gender-sensitive' approaches. They place attention on the fact that the *local* level – land and land-holders, artisanal miners, ecosystems, local economies, local linkages and development – have been structurally neglected from decision-making processes. They coincide with more general calls to mainstream transparency, accountability and rule of law standards also for the mining sector.

Emerging policy approaches are implicitly addressing those deficits of design and calling for a wider understanding of the law as well as the governance of mining and minerals as establishing the rule of law framework for responsible investment and for steering the decision-making processes towards achieving common goals for sustainable resource management through deliberation and collaboration.

The complexification of problems and the widening circle of actors are demanding new forms of legal and normative ordering of social relationships in mining and minerals at all levels and across value chains that place dialogue, collaboration and coordination at their core if intended to work towards sustainable futures. Some initiatives are beginning to reflect such turns to multi-level, holistic, integrated and multi-stakeholder governance institutions and mechanisms with a view to achieving the interlinked SDGs.

II. A Research Agenda

Mineral law is developing from scattered international provisions, domestic tenure regimes and domestic and transnational contracts, to a multi-level and multi-layered subfield of natural resources law, practice and scholarship encompassing a broad range of issues. A global perspective enhances our understanding of mineral law as an under-theorised and long neglected field of study lying at the intersection of the global economy, environmental sustainability and climate action, and human rights and social equity, and at the crossroads of law and development.

This calls for a rich research agenda to advance scholarly understanding and debate, and eventually improve practice.

At international level, there is a need to further study the emerging development of rules, principles and policy on mining and minerals as an embryonic subfield of the international law of natural resources, further interpreting international resources regimes in the light of evolving sustainability concepts and principles, and examining the suitability of working on consensus on guiding principles for mining and minerals stewardship (as is in place for other natural resources), building on the UNGP and other instruments, with a view that they might evolve into binding instruments. In a sustainable future, minerals might only be extracted whenever demand cannot be met by recycling, which is already happening. But even that scenario raises crucial questions for global ethics, justice and the development of international law as there are growing concerns about the substantial amounts of minerals that will be extracted over the next few years to meet the demands of the energy transition and what it means for mineral-rich countries. Further work on the interaction between circular economy models and actions for a just resource transition are needed.

Likewise, the early documents in the evolution of sustainable development showed a concern for global equitable distribution, pointing at the issues raised by recycling and pricing. These are resurfacing in the literature, and in a few documents elaborated by international organisations, and deserve further research and reflection. This relates to a point raised by many voices: consolidating a global platform to address the serious problems within this sector (eg legacies of abandoned mines, tailings, boosting new technologies) and embracing new practices in development cooperation. This should have space within calls for placing efforts on reforming existing international organisations, enhancing multilateral processes and strengthening accountability of actors, to reflect plural agreements, amidst current challenges brought by a multipolar global order, technology and climate change.

There is also a need to diversify, and consolidate the theoretical framings for studying mineral law, including on renewed visions on the nature of resource ownership in situ in the light of stewardship, justice and accountability theories, and plural perspectives to the understanding of the local interface between projects and landholders, artisanal miners and communities.

There is great need to further understand the form and extent of interaction and interdependence of traditional concepts of mining law and the decisions of arbitral tribunals and human rights courts.

At domestic level, mineral law is evolving from its traditional focus on facilitating 'access' to mines and lands and calling for its redefinition and transformation under the matrix of sustainability and, more specifically, of integrated decision-making processes – with a heightened role for public law, public administration structures and private–public arrangements. The principles of cooperation and subsidiarity place coordination and collaboration at the heart of deliberative structures that bring inter-ministerial agencies, levels of government and groups of actors together around those processes. At the same time, there is much potential for emerging forms of transnational and global structures that seek collaboration and just distribution of benefits across a global value chain. It is time for regulatory innovations to provide the legal infrastructures for local sustainable development (mainstreaming FPIC, human rights, biodiversity and climate action, exploring the analysis of regulatory risks ex ante the adoption of new laws, design for sustainability based on the data revolution); for addressing the embedded inconsistencies in mining law regimes and their interface with a great range of laws and regulations, and for recalibrating a far more textured understanding of risks and rewards in decision-making processes about mining and minerals. There is also need for exploring framings for 'secondary' mines, for the use and recycling of minerals and for the overall uptake of the circular economy concept.

Shaping a cosmopolitan discipline of the law and governance of mining and minerals places the moral duty to each another at their core. It is a tall order that calls, as no other, for extensive dialogue, collaborative efforts and supportive global governance. This becomes crucial in the face of challenges to multilateral governance and a divisive international scenario.

SELECTED BIBLIOGRAPHY

Abraham, D, *The Elements of Power. Gadgets, Guns, and the Struggle for a Sustainable Future in the Rare Metal Age* (New Haven and London, Yale University Press, 2015).

Addison, T, 'Climate Change and the Extractives Sector' in T Addison and A Roe (eds), *Extractive Industries. The Management of Resources as a Driver of Sustainable Development* (Oxford, Oxford University Press, 2018).

Affolder, NA, 'Rethinking Environmental Contracting (2010) 21 *Journal of Environmental Law and Practice* 155.

Agricola, G, *De Re Metallica*, translated from the first Latin edition of 1556 into English from its first Latin version by Hoover, H and Hoover, L (New York, Dover Publications Inc, 1950).

Ako, R and Uddin, N, 'Good Governance and Resource Management in Africa' in F Botchway (ed) *Natural Resource Investment and Africa's Development* (Cheltenham, Edward Elgar, 2011), 21.

Aladeitan, L, 'Ownership and Control of Oil, Gas and Mineral Resources in Nigeria: Between Legality and Legitimacy' (2012) 38 *Thurgood Marshall Law Review* 159, 160.

Alam, S; Bhuiyan, JH and Razzaque, J (eds), *International Natural Resources Law, Investment and Sustainability* (London, Routledge, 2017).

Ali, SH, Giurco, D, Arndt, N, Nickless, E, Brown, G, Demetriades, A, Durrheim, R, Enriquez, MA, Kinnaird, J, Littleboy, A, Meinert, LD, Oberhänsli, R, Salem, J, Schodde, R, Schneider, G, Vidal O, and Yakovleva, N, 'Mineral Supply for Sustainable Development Requires Resource Governance' (2017) 543 *Nature* 367.

Al-Saman, Y, 'Evolution of the Contractual Relationship between Saudi Arabia and Aramco' (1994) 12 *Journal of Energy & Natural Resources Law* 257.

Arias M, Atienza M, Cademartori J, 'Large mining enterprises and regional development in Chile: between the enclave and cluster' (2014) 14 *Journal of Economic Geography* 73.

Arndt, N, Kesler, S and Ganino, C, *Metals and Society. An Introduction to Economic Geology* (Verlag Berlin Heidelberg, Springer Mineralogy, Springer International Publishing, 2015).

Anyaoku, Chief Emeka, 'The End of Multilateralism: Whither Global Governance?' (2004) 93 *The Round Table*193.

Asante, S and Stockmayer, A, 'Evolution of Development Contracts: The Issue of Effective Control' in *Legal and Institutional Arrangements in Minerals Development* (London, Mining Journal Books 1982) 57.

Auty R, 'Mining enclave to economic catalyst: large mineral projects in developing countries' (2006) 13 *Brown Journal of World Affairs* 135.

Auty, R and Mikesell, R, *Sustainable Development in Mineral Economies* (Oxford, Clarendon Press, 1998).

Ayuk, ET, Pedro, AM, Ekins, P, Gatune, J, Milligan, B, Oberle B, Christmann, P, Ali, S, Kumar, SV, Bringezu, S, Acquatella, J, Bernaudat, L, Bodouroglou, C, Brooks, S, Buergi Bonanomi, E, Clement, J, Collins, N, Davis, K, Davy, A, Dawkins, K, Dom, A, Eslamishoar, F, Franks, D, Hamor, T, Jensen, D, Lahiri–Dutt, K, Mancini, L, Nuss, P, Petersen, I and Sanders, ARD, 'Mineral Resource Governance in the 21st Century: Gearing extractive industries towards sustainable development. A Report by the International Resource Panel' (United Nations Environment Programme, Nairobi, 2020).

Baker, E, Gaill, F, Karageorgis, A, Lamarche, G, Narayanaswamy, B, Parr, J, Raharimananirina, C, Santos, R and Sharma, R, 'Offshore Mining Industries' in United Nations, Division for Ocean Affairs and the Law of the Sea, Office of Legal Affairs (ed), *The First Global Integrated Marine Assessment: World Ocean Assessment* I (Cambridge, Cambridge University Press, 2014) 363–78.

Selected Bibliography 185

Badenhorst, PJ and Mostert, H, *Mineral and Petroleum Law of South Africa*, 4th edn (Cape Town, Juta Law, 2008).

Baker, E, Gaill, F, Karageorgis, A, Lamarche, G, Narayanaswamy, B, Parr, J, Raharimananirina, C, Santos, R and Sharma, R, 'Offshore Mining Industries' in United Nations, Division for Ocean Affairs and the Law of the Sea, Office of Legal Affairs (ed) *The First Global Integrated Marine Assessment: World Ocean Assessment* I (Cambridge, Cambridge University Press, 2014) 363–78.

Barberis, D, *Negotiating Mining Agreements: Past, Present and Future Trends* (London, Kluwer Law International, 1998).

Barberis, J, *Los recursos naturales compartidos entre estados y el derecho internacional* (Madrid, Tecnos, 1978).

Barnes, R, *Property Rights and Natural Resources* (Oxford, Hart Publishing, 2009).

Barral, V, 'National Sovereignty over Natural Resources: Environmental Challenges and Sustainable Development' in Morgera, E and Kulovesi, K (eds), *Research Handbook on International Law and Natural Resources* (Cheltenham and Northampton, Edward Elgar Publishing, 2016) 3–25.

—— 'Sustainable Development in International Law: Nature and Operation of an Evolutive Legal Norm' (2012) 23 *The European Journal of International Law* 2.

Barrera-Hernández, L, Barton, B, Godden, L, Lucas, AR and Rønne, A, 'Introduction' in Barrera-Hernández, L, Barton, B, Godden, L, Lucas, AR and Rønne, A (eds), *Sharing the Costs and Benefits of Energy and Resource Activity. Legal Change and Impact on Communities* (Oxford, Oxford University Press, 2016) 1.

Barton, B, 'Reforming the Mining Law of the Northwest Territories: Prepared for the Canadian Arctic Resources Committee', Northern Minerals Programme working papers, 3 (1998).

—— 'The History of Mining Law in the US, Canada, New Zealand and Australia, and the Right of Free Entry' in Bastida, AE, Wälde, T, Warden–Fernandez, J (eds), *International and Comparative Mineral Law and Policy: Trends and Prospects* (The Hague, Kluwer Law International, 2005) 643.

Baslar, K, *The Concept of the Common Heritage of Mankind in International Law* (Dordrecht, The Netherlands, Martinus Nijhoff, 1998).

Bassett, R and Ihnen Becker, R, 'Myth or Reality – Has Environmental Regulation Destroyed the US Mining Industry?' in Bastida, AE, Wälde, T, Warden–Fernandez, J (eds), *International and Comparative Mineral Law and Policy: Trends and Prospects* (The Hague, Kluwer Law International, 2005) 697–709.

Bastida, AE, 'From *Extractive* to *Transformative* Industries: Paths for Linkages and Diversification for Resource-Driven Development' (2014) 27 *Mineral Economics* 73.

—— 'Mining Law in the Context of Development' in Andrews-Speed, P (ed), *International Competition for Resources: The Role of Law, State and Markets* (Dundee, Dundee University Press, 2008) 101–36.

—— 'The Perennial Questions of Ownership, Mineral Rights, and Land Rights: From Principles to Practice, a paper published in Rocky Mountain Mineral Law Foundation, Proceedings of the International Mining and Oil & Gas – Law, Development, and Investment Conference, panel on 'Ownership of Minerals' (Cartagena, 23 April 2013).

Bastida, AE and Bustos, L, 'Towards Regimes for Sustainable Mineral Resources Management. Constitutional Reform, Law and Judicial Precedents in Latin America' (2017) 9 *International Development Policy, Revue internationale de politique de développement* 235 (published both in English and Spanish).

Bastida, AE, Ifesi, A, Mahmud, S, Ross, J and Wälde, T, 'Cross-Border Unitization and Joint Development Agreements: An International Law Perspective' (2007) 29 *Houston Journal of International Law* 355.

Bastida, AE, Wälde, T, Warden-Fernandez, J (eds), *International and Comparative Mineral Law and Policy: Trends and Prospects* (The Hague, Kluwer Law International, 2005).

Bekker, P, *The Legal Position of Intergovernmental Organizations* (Dordrecht, Martinus Nijhoff Publishers, 1994).

Bekker, P, Dolzer, R and Waibel, M (eds), *Making Transnational Law Work in the Global Economy – Essays in Honour of Detlev Vagts* (Cambridge, Cambridge University Press, 2010).

Benvenisti, E and Downs, GW, 'The Empire's New Clothes: Political Economy and the Fragmentation of International Law' (2007) 60 *Stanford Law Review* 595.

186   Selected Bibliography

Birnie, P and Boyle, A, *International Law and the Environment*, 2nd edn (Oxford, Oxford University Press, 2002).

Birnie, P, Boyle, A and Redgwell, C, *International Law and the Environment*, 3rd edn (Oxford, Oxford University Press, 2009).

Blake, J, 'Constitutionalising Self–Regulation' (1996) 59 *The Modern Law Review Limited* 27.

Bosson, R and Varon, B, *The Mining Industry and the Developing Countries* (Washington DC, The World Bank, Oxford University Press, 1977).

Boulin, I, Gomez, L and de Casas, I, 'Human Rights Standards Applicable to Extractive Industries. Requirements in Relation to Indigenous Peoples Arising from the Jurisprudence of the Inter-American Human Rights System', a paper presented at the RMMLF (2013).

Bouvet, JP, *L'Unité de Gisement. Hydrocarbures et autres matiêres minérales* (Paris, L'Harmattan, 2004).

Boyle, A and Freestone, D, 'Introduction' in Boyle, A and Freestone, D (eds), *International Law and Sustainable Development: Past Achievements and Future Challenges* (Oxford, Oxford University Press, 1999).

Brilha, J, Gray, M, Pereira, DI and Pereira, P, 'Geodiversity: An integrative review as a contribution to the sustainable management of the whole of nature' (2018) 86 Environmental Science & Policy 19.

Bronckers, M and Maskus, K, 'China Raw Materials: A Controversial Step Towards Evenhanded Exploitation of Natural Resources' (2014) 13 *World Trade Review* 393.

Brown, ED, *Sea-Bed Energy and Minerals: The International Legal Regime*, Vol 2: 'Sea-Bed Mining' (The Hague, The Netherlands, Martinus Nijhoff, 2001).

—— 'Freedom of the High Seas versus the Common Heritage of Mankind: Fundamental Principles in Conflict' (1982–3) 20 *San Diego Law Review* 521.

Brown, R, 'New Mining Codes: Salient Features' (1986) *Commonwealth Secretariat*.

Brownlie, I, 'Legal Status of Natural Resources in International Law (Some Aspects)' (1979) 162 *Recueil Des Cours* 245.

Bruckner, KD, 'Community Development Agreements in Mining Projects' (2016) 44 *Denver Journal of International Law and Policy* 413.

Burnett, H and Bret, L, *Arbitration of International Mining Disputes: Law and Practice* (Oxford International Arbitration Series) (Oxford, Oxford University Press, 2017).

Busia, K and Akong, C, 'The African Mining Vision: Perspectives on Mineral Resource Development in Africa' (2017) 8 *Journal of Sustainable Development Law & Policy* 146.

Busse, M and Groning, S, 'The Resource Curse Revisited: Governance and Natural Resources' (2013) 154 *Public Choice* 1.

Buxton, The Concept of the Common Heritage of Mankind in International Law (1999) 13 *Emory International Law Review* 615.

Camara, AKK, *Linking Mining and Infrastructure Development in Sub-Saharan Africa: Towards a Collaborative Framework for Sustainable Shared-Use of Rails and Ports Facilities for Minerals and Non-Minerals Activities*, PhD thesis (CEPMLP University of Dundee, 2017).

Cameron, P, *Property Rights and Sovereign Rights: the Case of North Sea Oil* (London, Academic Press, 1983) 11.

Campbell, B (ed), *Mining in Africa. Regulation and Development* (London/New York, Pluto Press, 2009).

—— 'New Rules of the Game: The World Bank's Role in the Construction of New Normative Frameworks for States, Markets and Social Exclusion' (2000) 21 *Canadian Journal of Development Studies* 7.

—— (ed), *Regulating Mining in Africa: For Whose Benefit?*, Discussion Paper 26, (Uppsala, Nordiska Afrikainstitutet, 2004).

Campbell, B and Prémont, MC, 'What Is Behind the Search for Social Acceptability of Mining Projects? Political Economy and Legal Perspectives on Canadian Mineral Extraction' (2017) *Mineral Economics* 171.

Campbell, NJ, 'Principles of Ownership in the Civil Law and Common Law Systems' (1956–7) 31 *Tulane Law Review* 303.

Selected Bibliography   187

Cancado Trindade, AA, 'International Law for Humankind towards a New *Jus Gentium*' (2005) 316 *Recueil Des Cours* 365.

Catalano, E, 'El Derecho Europeo y Latinoamericano de Minas' in Proceedings of the III National Forum of Mining Law and the IV Latin American and The Caribbean Forum of Mining Legislation (October 1999).

Chapus, R, *Droit Administratif Général*, 15th edn (Paris, Montchrestien, 2001) vol 2.

Churchill, R and Lowe, A, *The Law of the Sea*, 3rd edn (Manchester, Manchester University Press, 1999).

Colangelo, AJ, 'What Is Extraterritorial Jurisdiction' (2014) 99 *Cornell Law Review* 1303.

Cotterrell, R, 'What is Transnational Law?' (2012) 37 *Law & Social Inquiry* 2.

Cotula, L, 'Land, Property and Sovereignty in International Law' (2017) 25 *Cardozo Journal of International and Comparative Law* 219.

—— *Human Rights, Natural Resource and Investment Law in a Globalised World. Shades of Grey in the Shadow of the Law* (London, Routledge, 2012).

——'Reconciling Regulatory Stability and Evolution of Environmental Standards in Investment Contracts: Towards a Rethink of Stabilization Clauses' (2008) 1 *The Journal of World Energy Law & Business* 158.

—— 'The New Enclosures? Polanyi, international investment law and the global land rush' (2013) 34 *Third World Quarterly* 1605.

Crawford, J, *Brownlie's Principles of Public International Law*, 9th edn (Oxford, Oxford University Press, 2019).

Crowson, P, *Inside Mining. The Economics of the Supply and Demand of Minerals and Metals* (London, Mining Journal Books Limited, 1998).

—— *Mining Unearthed. The Definitive Book on how Economic and Political Influences Shape the Global Mining Industry* (London, Aspermont, 2008).

—— 'The Resource Curse: A Modern Myth?' in Richards, J (ed), *Mining, Society and a Sustainable World* (Berlin/Heidelberg, Springer-Verlag, 2009) 3–36.

Cussianovich, E, 'La gobernanza de los recursos naturales desde la mirada de los ciudadanos' in Sánchez, R (ed), *La bonanza de los recursos naturales para el desarrollo: dilemas de gobernanza*, ECLAC Books, no 157 (LC/PUB.2019/13–P) (Santiago, Economic Commission for Latin America and the Caribbean (ECLAC) 2019) 257–276.

Daintith, T, 'Against "Lex Petrolea"' (2017) 10 *Journal of World Energy Law and Business* 1.

Dale, M, 'South African Mineral Law. Present and Future' in *Global Issues in Corporate Mining Strategy and Government Policy*, CEPMLP Dundee Annual Mining Seminar, 4–8 June 2001.

—— 'Security of Tenure as a Key Issue Facing the International Mining Company: A South African Perspective' (1996) 14 *Journal of Energy & Natural Resources Law* 305.

Dam-de Jong, D, *International Law and Governance of Natural Resources in Conflict and Post-Conflict Situations* (Cambridge, Cambridge University Press, 2015).

Dam-de Jong, 'A Rough Trade'? Towards a More Sustainable Minerals Supply Chain' (2019) *Brill Open Law* 1.

—— 'The Role of Informal Normative Processes in Improving Governance Over Natural Resources in Conflict–torn States' (2015) 7 *The Hague Journal on the Rule of Law* 219.

Dashwood, H, *The Rise of Global Corporate Social Responsibility: Mining and the Spread of Global Norms* (Cambridge, Cambridge University Press, 2012).

Debrah, AA, Mtegha, H and Cawood, F, 'Social licence to operate and the granting of mineral rights in sub–Saharan Africa: Exploring tensions between communities, governments and multinational mining companies' (2018) 56 *Resources Policy* 95.

Dernbach, J, 'Achieving Sustainable Development: The Centrality and Multiple Facets of Integrated Decisionmaking' (2003) 10 *Indiana Journal of Global Legal Studies*, 1, article 10.

de Sousa Santos, B, 'Law: A Map of Misreading. Toward a Postmodern Conception of Law' (Autumn, 1987) 14 *Journal of Law and Society* 279.

188 Selected Bibliography

Desta, MG, 'Commodities, International Regulation of Production and Trade', *Max Planck Encyclopedia of Public International Law*, Max Planck Foundation for International Peace and the Rule of Law under the direction of Rüdiger Wolfrum. Last updated in March 2010.

di Boscio, N and Humphreys, D, 'Mining and Regional Economic Development' in Bastida, AE, Wälde, T, Warden–Fernandez, J (eds), *International and Comparative Mineral Law and Policy: Trends and Prospects* (The Hague, Kluwer Law International, 2005) 589–604.

Dicken, P, *Global Shift. Mapping the Changing Contours of the World Economy*, 7th edn (London, Sage, 2015).

Dietsche, E, 'Diversifying Mineral Economies: Conceptualising the Debate on Building Linkages' (2014) 27 *Mineral Economics* 89.

Dolzer, R, 'Fair and Equitable Treatment: A Key Standard in Investment Treaties' (2005) 39 *International Lawyer* 87.

Donihee, J and Lucas, A, 'Canadian Impact and Benefit Agreements with Local and Indigenous People' in Bastida, AE, Wälde, T, Warden–Fernandez, J (eds), *International and Comparative Mineral Law and Policy: Trends and Prospects* (The Hague, Kluwer Law International, 2005) 718.

Dupuy, KE, 'Community Development Requirements in Mining Laws' (2014) 1 *Extractive Industries and Society* 200.

Dupuy, P, '*Où en-est le droit international de l'environnement à la fin du siecle?*' (1997) 101 Revue générale de droit international public 873.

Dupuy, P and Viñuales, J, *International Environmental Law*, 2nd edn (Cambridge, Cambridge University Press, 2018).

Dupuy, RJ, '*La notion de patrimoine commun de l'humanité appliquée aux fonds marins*' in *Droit et libertés à la fin du XXe siècle: Influence des données économiques et technologiques. Études offertes à Claude–Albert Colliard* (Paris, Pedone, 1984) 197–205.

Eggert, R, *Metallic Mineral Exploration: An Economic Analysis* (Washington DC, Resources for the Future, 1987).

El-Malik, W, 'State Ownership of Minerals under Islamic Law' (1996) 14 *Journal of Energy & Natural Resources Law* 315.

Ericsson, M and Löf, O, 'Mining's Contribution to Low- and Middle-Income Economies' in Addison, T and Roe, A (eds), *Extractive Industries. The Management of Resources as a Driver of Sustainable Development* (Oxford, Oxford University Press, 2018) 51–70.

—— 'Mining's contribution to national economies between 1996 and 2016' (2019) 32 *Mineral Economics* 223.

Eslava, N, 'Successful implementation of conflict mineral certification and due diligence schemes and the European Union's role: lessons learned for responsible mineral supply, STRADE Project (May 2018).

Etty, T, Heyvaert, V, Burns, W, Carlarne, C, Farber, D and Lin, J, 'By All Available Means: New Takes on Established Principles, Actions and Institutions to Address Today's Environmental Challenges' (2015) 4 *Transnational Environmental Law* 235.

Ezirigwe, J, 'Human Rights and Property Rights in Natural Resources Development' (2017) 35 *Journal of Energy and Natural Resources Law* 201.

Faundez, J, 'International Economic Law and Development Before and After Neo-Liberalism' in Faundez, J and Tan, C (eds), *International Law, Economic Globalization and Development* (Cheltenham and Northampton, Edward Elgar Publishing, 2010) 10–33.

Faundez, J and Tan, C, 'Introduction: International Economic Law, Natural Resources and Sustainable Development' (2015) 11 *International Journal of Law in Context* 109.

—— *Natural Resources and Sustainable Development* (Cheltenham and Northampton, Edward Elgar Publishing, 2017).

Fenwick, M, Siems, M and Wrbka, S, *The Shifting Meaning of Legal Certainty in Comparative and Transnational Law* (Oxford and Portland, Oregon, Hart Publishing, 2017).

Field, TL, *State Governance of Mining, Development and Sustainability* (Cheltenham and Northampton, Edward Elgar Publishing, 2019.

Fornillo, B, '¿*Commodities, bienes naturales o Recursos Naturales Estratégicos? La importancia de un nombre*' (2014) *Revista Nueva Sociedad* 252.

Selected Bibliography 189

Franks, D, *Mountain Movers: Mining, Sustainability and the Agents of Change* (London, Earthscan, 2015).

Freire, W, '*Direito Minerário: Fundamentos e Hermenêutica*' in W Freire and T de Mattos (eds), *Aspectos controvertidos do Direito Minerário e Ambiental. Enfoque Multidisciplinar* (Belo Horizonte, Jurídica Editora, 2013) 105.

Friedmann, W, 'The Uses of General Principles in the Development of International Law' (1963) 57 *American Journal of International Law* 290.

Frilet, M and Haddow, K, 'Guiding Principles for Durable Mining Agreements in Large Mining Projects' (2013) 31 *Journal of Energy & Natural Resources Law* 467.

Gathii, J and Odumosu-Ayanu, IT, 'The Turn to Contractual Responsibility in the Global Extractive Industry' (2015) 1 *Business and Human Rights Journal* 69.

Gilbert J, *Human Rights and Natural Resources* (Oxford, Oxford University Press, 2018).

Glenn, HP, 'Cosmopolitan Legal Orders' in Halpin, A and Roeben, V (eds), *Theorising the Global Legal Order* (Oxford, Hart Publishing, 2009) 25–37.

Godden, L, 'Governing Common Resources: Environmental Markets and Property in Water' in McHarg, A, Barton, B, Bradbrook, A and Godden, L (eds), *Property and the Law in Energy and Natural Resources* (Oxford, Oxford University Press, 2010) 413–36.

Goldsworthy, L and Hemmings, A, 'The Antarctic Protected Area Approach' in Hart, S (ed), *Shared Resources: Issues of Governance* (Gland, IUCN, 2008) 105–28.

Graulau, J, 'Ownership of Mines and Taxation in Castilian Laws, from the Middle Ages to the Early Modern Period: The Decisive Influence of the Sovereign in the History of Mining' (2011) 26 *Continuity and Change* 13.

Gudynas, E, '*Desarrollo sostenible: una guía básica de conceptos y tendencias hacia otra economía*', VI *Otra Economía –Revista Latinoamericana de economía social y solidaria–* 6 (1st Sem 2010) 43–66.

Gulley, AL, Nassar, NT and Xun, S, 'China, the United States, and competition for resources that enable emerging technologies' (2018) 115 *Proceedings of the National Academy of Sciences of the United States of America* 4111.

Haddow, K, 'Should Mineral Rights for Hard-Rock Minerals Be Awarded by Tender?' (2014) 32 *Journal of Energy & Natural Resources Law* 337.

Halpin, A and Roeben, V, 'Introduction' in Halpin, A and Roeben, V (eds), *Theorising the Global Legal Order* (Oxford, Hart Publishing, 2009) 1–23.

Halliday, T and Shaffer, G, 'Transnational Legal Orders' in T Halliday and G Shaffer, *Transnational Legal Orders* (Cambridge, Cambridge University Press, 2015).

Harris, J, Wise, T, Gallagher, K and Goodwin, N, *A Survey of Sustainable Development Social and Economic Dimensions* (Washington, Island Press, 2001).

Harrison, RJ, 'Article 82 of UNCLOS: The Day of Reckoning Approaches' (2017) 10 *The Journal of World Energy Law and Business* 488.

Harvey, B and Bice, S, 'Social Impact Assessment, Social Development Programmes and Social Licence to Operate: Tensions and Contradictions in Intent and Practice in the Extractive Sector' (2014) 32 *Impact Assessment and Project Appraisal* 327.

Hayes, S and McCullough, E, 'Critical minerals: A review of elemental trends in comprehensive criticality studies' (2018) 59 *Resources Policy* 192.

Haysom, N and Kane, S, *Negotiating Natural Resources for Peace: Ownership, Control and Wealth-Sharing*, Briefing Paper, Centre for Humanitarian Dialogue (October 2009).

Held, D, *Cosmopolitanism: Ideals and Realities* (Cambridge, Polity Press, 2010).

Held, D, McGew, A, Goldblatt, D and Perraton, J, *Global Transformations. Politics, Economics and Culture* (Cambridge, Polity Press, 1999).

Hilpert, HG and Mildner, SA (eds), *Fragmentation or Cooperation in Global Resource Governance? A Comparative Analysis of the Raw Materials Strategies of the G20*. A collaboration between the Stiftung Wissenschaft und Politik (SWP) and the Federal Institute for Geosciences and Natural Resources (BGR) RP (Berlin, 1 March 2013).

Hilson, G, 'Small-scale mining, poverty and economic development in sub-Saharan Africa: An overview' (2009) 34 *Resources Policy* 1.

190 Selected Bibliography

Hilson, G, Hilson, A, Maconachie, R, McQuilken, J and Goumandakoye, H, *Artisanal and small-scale mining (ASM) in sub-Saharan Africa: Re-conceptualizing formalization and 'illegal' activity* (2017) 83 *Geoforum* 80.

Hobe, S, 'Evolution of the Principle on Permanent Sovereignty Over Natural Resources: From Soft Law to a Customary Law Principle?' in Bungenberg, M and Hobe, S (eds), *Permanent Sovereignty Over Natural Resources* (Cham, Springer, 2015).

Hodge, A, 'Towards Contribution Analysis' in Addison, T and Roe, A (eds), *Extractive Industries. The Management of Resources as a Driver of Sustainable Development* (Oxford, Oxford University Press, 2018) 369–394.

Hossain, K, 'Introduction' in Hossain, K (ed), *Legal Aspects of the New International Economic Order* (London, Frances Pinter Publishers Ltd, 1980).

—— 'Introduction' in Hossain, K and Chowdhury, SR, *Permanent Sovereignty Over Natural Resources in International Law. Principle and Practice* (London, Frances Pinter Publishers, 1984).

Hossain, Z and Kumar, AP, 'The New Jurisprudence of Scarce Natural Resources: An Analysis of the Supreme Court's Judgment in Reliance Industries Limited v Reliance Natural Resources Limited (2010) 7 SCC 1' (2010) 4 *Indian Journal of Constitutional Law* 105.

Hufty, M, 'Governance: Exploring Four Approaches and Their Relevance to Research' in U Wiesmann and H Hurni (eds), *Research for Sustainable Development: Foundations, Experiences, and Perspectives.* Perspectives of the Swiss National Centre of Competence in Research (NCCR) North–South, University of Bern, vol 6 (Bern, Switzerland: Geographica Bernensia, 2011).

Humphreys, D, *The Remaking of the Mining Industry* (New York, Palgrave Macmillan, 2015).

Jessup, PC, *Transnational Law* (New Haven, Yale University Press 1956).

Johnson, L, 'FDI, international investment agreements and the sustainable development goals' in Krajewski, M and Hoffman, RT, *Research Handbook on Foreign Direct Investment*, (Cheltenham and Northampton, Edward Elgar Publishing Ltd, 2019) 126–48.

Joyner, CC, *Antarctica and the Law of the Sea* (The Hague, Martinus Nijhoff Publishers, 1992).

—— 'Legal Implications of the Concept of the Common Heritage of Mankind' (1986) 35 *International & Comparative Law Quarterly* 190.

—— *Governing the Frozen Commons. The Antarctic Regime and Environmental Protection* (Columbia, South Carolina, University of South Carolina Press, 1998).

Kanetake, M, 'The Interfaces between the National and International Rule of Law: A Framework Paper' in M Kanetake and A Nollkaemper (eds), *The Rule of Law at the National and International Levels. Contestations and Deference* (Oxford, Hart Publishing, 2018).

Kearney, JD. and Merrill, TW, 'The Origins of the American Public Trust Doctrine: What Really Happened in Illinois Central' (2004) 71 *University of Chicago Law Review* 799.

Kemp, D and Owen, JR, 'Community Relations and Mining: Core to Business But Not "Core Business"' (2013) 38 *Resources Policy* 523.

Kläger, R, *Fair and Equitable Treatment in International Investment Law* (Cambridge, Cambridge University Press, 2011) 227.

Krajewski, M and Hoffman, RT, 'Introduction' in Krajewski, M and Hoffman, RT, *Research Handbook on Foreign Direct Investment* (Cheltenham and Northampton, Edward Elgar Publishing Ltd, 2019).

Kriebaum, U and Reinisch, A, 'Property, Right to, International Protection' in *Max Planck Encyclopedia of Public International Law* (July 2009).

Kulovesi K, 'International Trade: Natural Resources and the World Trade Organization' in Morgera, E and Kulovesi, K (eds), *Research Handbook on International Law and Natural Resources* (Cheltenham and Northampton, Edward Elgar Publishing, 2016) 46–65.

Kumra, S, '*La gobernanza de los recursos naturales y su vínculo con los objetivos de desarrollo sostenible*' in R Sánchez (ed), *La bonanza de los recursos naturales para el desarrollo: dilemas de gobernanza*, ECLAC Books, no 157 (LC/PUB.2019/13–P) (Santiago, Economic Commission for Latin America and the Caribbean (ECLAC), 2019).

Kursky, A and Konoplyanik, A, 'State Regulation and Mining Law Development in Russia from 16th to 21st Century' in Bastida, AE, Wälde, T, Warden–Fernandez, J (eds), *International and Comparative Mineral Law and Policy: Trends and Prospects* (The Hague, Kluwer Law International, 2005) 969–1008.

Lagoni, R, 'Oil and Gas Deposits across National Frontiers' (1979) 73 *American Journal of International Law* 215.

Lazarus, RJ, 'Changing Conceptions of Property and Sovereignty in Natural Resources Law: Questioning the Public Trust Doctrine' (1986) 71 *Iowa Law Review* 631.

Liedholm-Johnson, E, *Mineral Rights: Legal Systems Governing Exploration and Exploitation*, vol 4, issue 112 of Meddelande (Institutionen för Infrastruktur, Fastighetsteknik, kungl Tekniska Högskolan), Royal Institute of Technology.

Lobel, O, 'The Renew Deal: The Fall of Regulation and the Rise of Governance in Contemporary Legal Thought' (2004) 89 *Minnesotta Law Review* 342.

Lodge M, 'The Deep Seabed' in Rothwell D, Oude Elferink A, Scott K and Stephens T (eds), *The Oxford Handbook of the Law of the Sea* (Oxford, Oxford University Press, 2015) 226–53.

Lowe, V, 'Sustainable Development and Unsustainable Arguments' in Boyle, A and Freestone, D (eds), *International Law and Sustainable Development: Past Achievements and Future Challenges* (Oxford, Oxford University Press, 1999).

Malanczuk, P, *Akehurst's Modern Introduction to International Law*, 7th edn (London and New York, Routledge, 1997).

Maniruzzaman, A, 'The *Lex Mercatoria* and International Contracts: A Challenge for International Commercial Arbitration? (1999) 14 *American University International Law Review* 657.

—— 'The New Generation of Energy and Natural Resource Development Agreements: Some Reflections' (1993) 11 *Journal of Energy & Natural Resources Law* 207.

Martin, P, Boer, B and Slobodian, L (eds), 'Framework for Assessing and Improving Law for Sustainability A Legal Component of a Natural Resource Governance Framework' (IUCN, 2016).

McHarg, A, Barton, B, Bradbrook, A and Godden, L, 'Property and the Law in Energy and Natural Resources' in McHarg, A, Barton, B, Bradbrook, A and Godden, L (eds), *Property and the Law in Energy and Natural Resources* (Oxford, Oxford University Press, 2010) 1–16.

Mejía Acosta, A, 'The Impact and Effectiveness of Accountability and Transparency Initiatives: The Governance of Natural Resources' (2013) 31 *Development Policy Review* 89.

Merino Blanco, E and Razzaque, J, *Globalisation and Natural Resources Law: Challenges, Key Issues and Perspectives* (Cheltenham and Northampton, Edward Elgar Publishing, 2011).

Meyersfeld, B, 'Empty Promises and the Myth of Mining: Does Mining Lead to Pro-Poor Development?' (2017) 2 *Business and Human Rights Journal* 31.

Mirabeau, H., 'Discours sur la Propriété de Mines' (21 March 1791) and 'Second Discours sur la Propriété de Mines' (27 March 1791) in Mirabeau, H and Cerutti, J, *Œuvres Oratoires de Mirabeau ou Recueil de ses Discours ... à l'Assemblée Nationale* (Paris, Librairie de Pierre Blanchard, 1819) vol 1, 356–84.

Mirovitskaya, N and Ascher, W (eds), *Guide to Sustainable Development and Environmental Policy* (Durham, Duke University Press, 2001).

Model Mining Development Agreement, developed by the Mining Law Committee (International Bar Association, 2010).

Morgera, E and Kulovesi, K, *Research Handbook on International Law and Natural Resources* (Cheltenham and Northampton, Edward Elgar Publishing, 2016).

Morgan, P, 'An Overview of the Legal Regime for Mineral Development in the United Kingdom in Bastida, AE, Wälde, T and Warden–Fernandez, J (eds), *International and Comparative Mineral Law and Policy: Trends and Prospects* (The Hague, Kluwer Law International, 2005).

Mostert, H, *Mineral Law: Principles and Policies in Perspective* (Cape Town, Juta, 2012).

Mudd, G, 'The Environmental Sustainability of Mining in Australia: Key Mega-Trends and Looming Constraints' (2010) 35 *Resources Policy* 98.

Murray, RW and Dey Nuttall, A, *International Relations and the Arctic: Understanding Policy and Governance* (Amherst, Cambria Press, 2015).

Nayak, J, *An International Framework for Advancing Business and Human Rights Beyond the UN Guiding Principles: Proposal for an Inclusive, Stepwise and Multistakeholder Approach*, PhD Thesis (CEPMLP, University of Dundee, 2014).

Nef, JU, *The Rise of the British Coal Industry* (London, Studies in Economic and Social History, London School of Economics and Political Science, 1932).

192   Selected Bibliography

Newcombe, A and Paradell L, *Law and Practice of Investment Treaties: Standards of Treatment* (Alphen aan den Rijn, Kluwer Law International, 2009).

Nwapi, C, 'Legal and Institutional Frameworks for Community Development Agreements in the Mining Sector in Africa' (2017) 4 *Extractive Industries and Society* 202.

Nwogu, NV, 'Mining at the Crossroads of Law and Development: A Comparative Review of Labor-Related Local Content Provisions in Africa's Mining Laws through the Prism of Automation' (2019) 28 *Washington International Law Journal* 137.

Nye, J, 'Corruption and Political Development: A Cost–Benefit Analysis' (1967) 61 *American Political Science Review* 2.

Oberle, B, Bringezu, S, Hatfield-Dodds, S, Hellweg, S, Schandl, H, Clement, J, and Cabernard, L, Che, N, Chen, D, Droz-Georget, H, Ekins, P, Fischer-Kowalski, M, Flörke, M, Frank, S, Froemelt, A, Geschke, A, Haupt, M, Havlik, P, Hüfner, R, Lenzen, M, Lieber, M, Liu, B, Lu, Y, Lutter, S, Mehr, J, Miatto, A, Newth, D, Oberschelp, C, Obersteiner, M, Pfister, S, Piccoli, E, Schaldach, R, Schüngel, J, Sonderegger, T, Sudheshwar, A, Tanikawa, H, van der Voet, E, Walker, C, West, J, Wang, Z and Zhu, B, 'Global Resources Outlook 2019: Natural Resources for the Future We Want, A Report of the International Resource Panel' (United Nations Environment Programme, Nairobi, 2019).

O'Faircheallaigh, C, 'Community Development Agreements in the Mining Industry: An Emerging Global Phenomenon' (2013) 44 *Community Development* 222.

Open Contracting Partnership and NRGI, 'Open Contracting for Oil, Gas and Mineral Rights: Shining a Light on Good Practice' (June 2018).

Olawuyi, D, *Extractive Industries Law in Africa*, (Cham, Springer Nature Switzerland AG, 2018).

Omorogbe, Y and Oniemola, P, 'Property Rights in Oil and Gas under Domanial Regimes' in A McHarg, A, Barton, B, Bradbrook, A and Godden, L (eds), *Property and the Law in Energy and Natural Resources* (Oxford, Oxford University Press, 2010) 125.

Orrego Vicuña, *Antarctic Mineral Exploration: The Emerging Legal Framework* (Cambridge, Cambridge University Press, 1988).

Otto, J, 'How Do We Legislate for Improved Community Development?' in T Addison and A Roe (eds), *Extractive Industries. The Management of Resources as a Driver of Sustainable Development* (Oxford, Oxford University Press, 2018) 673–694.

—— 'Resource Nationalism and Regulatory Reform' (RMMLF, 2013).

Owen, JR and Kemp, D, 'Social Licence and Mining: A Critical Perspective' (2012) 38 *Resources Policy* 29–35.

Paolillo, F, 'The Future Legal Regime of Seabed Resources and the NIEO: Some Issues' in Hossain, K and Chowdhury, SR (eds), *Permanent Sovereignty Over Natural Resources in International Law. Principle and Practice* (London, Frances Pinter Publishers, 1984).

Pritchard, R, 'Safeguards for Foreign Investment in Mining' in Bastida, AE, Wälde, T, Warden-Fernandez, J (eds), *International and Comparative Mineral Law and Policy: Trends and Prospects*, (The Hague, Kluwer Law International, 2005).

Orakhelashvili, A, *Akehurst's Modern Introduction to International Law*, 8th edn (London and New York, Routledge, 2019).

Otto, J and Cordes, J, The Regulation of Mineral Enterprises: A Global Perspective on Economics, Law and Policy (Colorado, RMMLF, 2002).

Pincus, RH and Ali, SH, *Diplomacy on Ice: Energy and the Environment in the Arctic and Antarctic,* (New Haven, Yale University Press, 2015).

Pinto, M, *Temas de derechos humanos*, 4th edn (Buenos Aires, Editores del Puerto, 2006).

Pinto, MCW, 'The Legal Context: Concepts, Principles, Standards and Institutions' in Weiss, F, Denters, E and de Waart, P (eds), *International Economic Law with a Human Face* (The Hague, Kluwer Law International, 1998).

Pring, G and Siegele, L, International Law and Mineral Resources in Bastida, AE, Wälde, T, Warden-Fernandez, J (eds), *International and Comparative Mineral Law and Policy: Trends and Prospects*, (The Hague, Kluwer Law International, 2005) 127–45.

Radetzki M, *State Mineral Enterprises: An Investigation into their Impact on International Mineral Markets* (Washington, Resources for the Future, 1985).

Selected Bibliography   193

Redgwell, C, 'Property Law Sources and Analogies in International Law' in McHarg, A, Barton, B, Bradbrook, A and Godden, L (eds), *Property and the Law in Energy and Natural Resources* (Oxford, Oxford University Press, 2010) 101–12.

Roe, A and Dodd, S, 'Dependence on extractive industries in lower income countries. The Statistical Tendencies' in Addison, T and Roe, A (eds), *Extractive Industries. The Management of Resources as a Driver of Sustainable Development* (Oxford, Oxford University Press, 2018).

Rose, CM, 'Joseph Sax and the Idea of the Public Trust' (1998) 25 *Ecology Law Quarterly* 351.

Rovere, MB, '*Efectos ambientales transfronterizos del Proyecto Minero Binacional Pascua Lama: el conflicto analizado desde la perspectiva internacional*' in Hart, S (ed), *Shared Resources: Issues of Governance* (Gland, IUCN, 2008) 129–47.

Roy, V, 'Stabilize, rebuild, prevent?: An overview of post–conflict resource management tools' (2017) 4 *The Extractive Industries and Society* 227–34.

Salacuse, J, 'From Developing Countries to Emerging Markets: A Changing Role for Law in the Third World' (1999) 33 *The International Lawyer* 880.

—— 'Making transnational law work through regime-building: the case of international investment law' in Bekker, P, Dolzer, R and Waibel, M (eds), *Making Transnational Law Work in the Global Economy – Essays in Honour of Detlev Vagts* (Cambridge, Cambridge University Press, 2010).

—— 'The Emerging Global Regime for Investment' (2010) 51 *Harvard International Law Journal* 427.

—— *The Three Laws of International Investment – National, Contractual, and International Frameworks for Foreign Capital* (Oxford, Oxford University Press 2013).

Sánchez, R (ed), *La bonanza de los recursos naturales para el desarrollo: dilemas de gobernanza*, ECLAC Books, no 157 (LC/PUB.2019/13–P) (Santiago, Economic Commission for Latin America and the Caribbean (ECLAC), 2019).

Santaella Quintero, H, '*Un territorio y tres modelos de gestión: análisis de la necesidad de armonizar y constitucionalizar las competencias urbanísticas, ambientales y mineras sobre el territorio*' in Henao, JC and Díaz Ángel, S (eds), *Minería y desarrollo. Tomo V: Historia y gobierno del territorio minero* (Bogotá, Universidad Externado de Colombia) 175–226.

Sauvant, K, 'The Negotiations of the United Nations Code of Conduct on Transnational Corporations Experience and Lessons Learned' (2015) 16 *The Journal of World Investment & Trade* 11–87.

Sbert, C, 'Re-Imagining Mining: The *Earth Charter* as a Guide for Ecological Mining Reform' (2015) 6 *IUCNAEL EJournal* 66.

Schachter, O, *Sharing the World's Resources* (New York, Columbia University Press, 1977).

Schill, S, 'Fair and Equitable Treatment, the Rule of Law and Comparative Public Law' in Schill, S (ed), *International Investment Law and Comparative Public Law* (Oxford, Oxford University Press, 2010).

—— 'The Rule of Law and the Division of Labour Between National and International Law: The Case of International Energy Relations' in M Kanetake and A Nollkaemper (eds), *The Rule of Law at the National and International Levels. Contestations and Deference* (Oxford, Hart Publishing, 2018).

Schönfeldt, K (ed), *The Arctic in International Law and Policy* (Oxford, Hart Publishing, 2017).

Siegel, S and Veiga, MM, 'Artisanal and small-scale mining as an extralegal economy: De Soto and the redefinition of "formalization"' (2009) 34 *Resources Policy* 52.

Scott, A, *The Evolution of Resource Property Rights* (Oxford, Oxford University Press, 2008).

Schachter, O, *Sharing the World's Resources* (New York, Columbia University Press, 1977).

Schill, S, 'Fair and Equitable Treatment, the Rule of Law and Comparative Public Law' in Schill, S (ed), *International Investment Law and Comparative Public Law* (Oxford, Oxford University Press, 2010) 159.

Schrijver, N, *Sovereignty over Natural Resources. Balancing Rights and Duties* (Cambridge, Cambridge University Press, 1997).

—— 'Managing the global commons: common good or common sink?' (2016) 37 *Third World Quarterly* 1252.

—— 'Fifty Years Permanent Sovereignty over Natural Resources. The 1962 UN Declaration as the *Opinio Iuris Communis*' in Bungenberg, M and Hobe, S (eds), *Permanent Sovereignty Over Natural Resources* (Cham, Springer, 2015) 15–28.

194 Selected Bibliography

—— 'Natural Resources, Permanent Sovereignty over', *Max Planck Encyclopedia of Public International Law*, Max Planck Foundation for International Peace and the Rule of Law under the direction of Rüdiger Wolfrum, last updated June 2008.

—— 'Development – The Neglected Dimension in the Evolution of the International Law of Sustainable Development' paper presented at International Law and Sustainable Development: Principle and Practice seminar (Amsterdam, 29 November–1 December 2001) 6.

—— 'Introductory Note' to the ILA New Delhi Declaration of Principles of International Law Relating to Sustainable Development (2002) 49 *Netherlands International Law Review* 299, 305.

—— 'Self-determination of peoples and sovereignty over natural wealth and resources' in United Nations Human Rights Office of the High Commissioner, *Realizing the Right to Development. Essays in Commemoration of 25 Years of the United Nations Declaration on the Right to Development*, United Nations Publication HR/PUB/12/4 (New York and Geneva, 2013) 95–102.

Shelton, D, 'Dominion and Stewardship' (2015) 109 *American Journal of International Law Unbound* 132.

Sierra Camargo, X, '*Derecho, minería y (neo)colonialismo. Una aproximación crítica a la regulación de la minería de oro a gran escala en Colombia*' (2014) 14 *Opera* 161.

Smith, D, 'Social Licence to Operate in the Unconventional Oil and Gas Development Sector. The Colorado Experience' Barrera-Hernández, L, Barton, B, Godden, L, Lucas, AR and Rønne, A (eds), *Sharing the Costs and Benefits of Energy and Resource Activity. Legal Change and Impact on Communities* (Oxford, Oxford University Press, 2016) 113–31.

Sovacool, B, Ali, S, Bazilian, M, Radley, B, Nemery, B, Okatz, J and Mulvaney, D, 'Sustainable minerals and metals for a low-carbon future' (2020) 367 *Science* 30.

Sprankling, JG, 'Owning the Centre of the Earth' (2008) 55 *UCLA Law Review* 979.

Stephens, T and VanderZwaag, D, 'Polar Oceans Governance: Shifting Seascapes, Hazy Horizons' in T Stephens and D VanderZwaag (eds), *Polar Oceans Governance in an Era of Environmental Change* (Cheltenham and Northampton, Edward Elgar Publishing, 2014) 1–17.

Stevens, P and Dietsche. E, 'Resource curse: An analysis of causes, experiences and possible ways forward' (2008) 36 *Energy Policy* 56.

Stone, J, 'Arbitrariness, the Fair and Equitable Treatment Standard, and the International Law of Investment' (2012) 25 *Leiden Journal of International Law* 77.

Sumners, WG, 'United States' in Cowles, R (ed), *World Coal Mining Law, a Comparative Survey* (London, International Bar Association, 1984).

Svampa, M, 'Commodities Consensus: Neoextractivism and Enclosure of the Commons in Latin America' (2015) *The South Atlantic Quarterly* 65.

Szablowski, D, *Transnational Law and Local Struggles. Mining, Communities and the World Bank* (Oxford, Hart Publishing, 2007).

Szablowski, D and Campbell, B, 'Struggles over extractive governance: Power, discourse, violence, and legality' (2019) 6 *The Extractive Industries and Society* 635.

Tienhaara, K, *The Expropriation of Environmental Governance: Protecting Foreign Investors at the Expense of Public Policy* (Cambridge, Cambridge University Press, 2009).

Tiess, G, *General and International Mineral Policy* (Verlag/Wien, Springer, 2011) ch 4.

Trubek, D and Santos, A, 'Introduction: The Third Moment in Law and Development and the Emergence of a New Critical Practice' in D Trubek and A Santos (eds), *The New Law and Development: A Critical Appraisal* (Cambridge, Cambridge University Press, 2006).

Twining, W, 'The Implications of "Globalisation" for Law as a Discipline' in Halpin, A and Roeben, V (eds), *Theorising the Global Legal Order* (Oxford, Hart Publishing, 2009) 39–59.

—— 'Diffusion of Law: A Global Perspective' (2004) 36 *The Journal of Legal Pluralism and Unofficial Law* 1.

—— *Legal Jurisprudence: Understanding Law from a Global Perspective* (Cambridge, Cambridge University Press, 2009).

UNEP, Mining – Facts, Figures and Environment (2000) 23 *Industry and Environment* 4.

Selected Bibliography 195

Vandevelde, K, 'A Unified Theory of Fair and Equitable Treatment' (2010) 43 *International Law and Politics* 43.

Van Harten, G, *Investment Treaty Arbitration and Public Law* (Oxford, Oxford University Press, 2007).

Vergara Blanco, A, *Principios y sistema de derecho minero. Estudio histórico y dogmático* (Santiago de Chile, Editorial Jurídica de Chile, 1992).

—— *Sistema de derecho minero* (Santiago de Chile, Editorial Jurídica de Chile, 2013).

Vidal, O, Goffé, B and Arndt, N, 'Metals for a Low-Carbon Society' (2013) 6 *Nature Geoscience* 894.

Vildósola Fuenzalida, J, *El dominio minero y el sistema concesional en América Latina y el Caribe* (Caracas, OLAMI/ECLAC, 1999).

Viñuales, J, 'The Resource Curse: A Legal Perspective' (2011) 17 *Global Governance: A Review of Multilateralism and International Organizations* 197.

—— 'Foreign Direct Investment: International Investment Law and Natural Resource Governance' in Morgera, E and Kulowesi, K (eds), *Research Handbook on International Law and Natural Resources* (Cheltenham and Northampton, Edward Elgar Publishing, 2016) 26–45.

Wälde, T, 'A Requiem for the "New International Economic Order". The Rise and Fall of Paradigms in International Economic Law' in Al–Nauimi, N and Meese, R (eds), *International Legal Issues Arising under the United Nations Decade of International Law* (The Hague, Martinus Nijhoff Publishers, 1995) 1209–48.

—— 'Investment policies in the international petroleum industry – responses to the current crisis' in N Beredjick and T Wälde (eds), *Petroleum Investment Policies in Developing Countries* (London, Graham & Trotman, 1988) 7.

—— 'Lifting the Veil from Transnational Mineral Contracts. A Review of Recent Literature' (1977) 1 *Natural Resources Forum* 166.

—— 'Mineral Development Legislation: Result and Instrument of Mineral Development Planning' (1988) 12 *Natural Resources Forum* 175.

—— 'Permanent Sovereignty over Natural Resources: Recent Developments in the Minerals Sector' (1983) 7 *Natural Resources Forum* 239.

—— 'Third World Mineral Development: Recent Issues and Literature' (1984) 2 *Journal of Energy and Natural Resources Law* 282.

—— 'Third World Mineral Investment Policies in the Late 1980s: From Restriction Back to Business' (1988) 3 *Mineral Processing and Extractive Metallurgy Review* 121.

Walsh, JR, '*El ambiente y el paradigma de la sustentabilidad*' in JR Walsh and ME Di Paola (eds), *Ambiente, Derecho y Sustentabilidad* (Buenos Aires, La Ley, 2000) 1–66.

Warden-Fernandez, J, 'Indigenous Communities' Rights and Mineral Development' (2005) 23 *Journal of Energy & Natural Resources Law* 395.

Webb, K, 'Voluntary initiatives and the law' in R Gibson, *Voluntary Initiatives. The New Politics of Corporate Greening* (Peterborough, Broadview, 1999) 42–50.

Weber, M, 'Power Politics in the Antarctic Treaty System' in Stephens, T and VanderZwaag, DL (eds), *Polar Oceans Governance in an Era of Environmental Change* (Cheltenham and Northampton, Edward Elgar Publishing, 2014).

Weissbrodt, D and Kruger, M, 'Norms on the Responsibilities of Transnational Corporations and Other Business Enterprises with Regard to Human Rights' (2003) 97 *American Journal of International Law* 901.

Wilson, E and van Alstine, J, 'Localising Transparency: Exploring EITI's Contribution to Sustainable Development' (International Institute for Environment and Development, 2014).

Woods, N, Betts, A, Prantl, J and Sridhar, D, 'Transforming Global Governance for the 21st Century', UNDP Human Development Report Office Occasional Paper (2013/09).

Zumbansen, P, 'Transnational Law, Evolving', King's College London Dickson Poon School of Law, Legal Studies Research Paper Series: Paper No 2014–29.

INDEX

A
access to land 82, 138, 150, 172–174
  open access processes 160–161
access to minerals
  international treaties 82
  national laws 150
  open access processes 160–161
  resource diplomacy 17
accession system 140, 141–143
accountability
  anti-corruption measures 110–111,
    175–176
  EITI 22, 23, 75, 111
  generally 7, 73–77, 87, 182
  Open Government Partnership 118
  responsible business conduct 93
  transnational governance 93, 112, 115–116
Accursius 141
Action Plan for the Human
    Environment 64–65
Africa
  Africa Mining Vision 15, 49, 77, 167
  African Charter on Human and Peoples'
    Rights 16, 107
  African Commission on Human and Peoples'
    Rights 16
  ASM sector 50–51
  Chinese investment 77
  CMV Guidebook 15
  environmental protection 77
  International Study Group for the Review
    of African Mining Regimes 77
  post-colonial mining laws 59, 166, 167
  regional governance 15–16
  state land ownership 162
  Structural Adjustment Programmes 67
  transnational enterprises 77
  UN Economic Commission for Africa
    (UNECA) 49, 77
  WAEMU Mining Code 15
  World Bank Strategy for African
    Mining 15, 47
Agenda 21 68–71, 72
Agenda 2030 10, 12, 50, 76, 78–81, 104

aggregates
  marine mining 31, 123
Agreement on Trade-Related Investment
    Measures (TRIMs) 97
Agricola, G 153, 162
Alcoa 42
Alliance for Responsible Mining (ARM) 120
aluminium 28, 30, 42
  recycled 32
Aluminium Stewardship Initiative (ASI) 121
American Declaration of the Rights and
    Duties of Man 107
Angola 75
Antarctica
  Antarctic Treaty System 134
  CRAMRA 12, 134–135
  environmental protection 135
  Exxon Valdez oil spill 135
  global commons 126, 126n
  Madrid Protocol 134, 135
  mining, generally 22
  mining moratorium 12, 134–135
arbitration
  international economic law 94
  transnational 13, 40, 47, 48, 58, 98–102,
    180–181
  UNCITRAL 98
ArcelorMittal Steel 42
Arctic Ocean
  territorial claims 125–126
Argentina 78, 154
  Mining Integration Treaty with Chile 13
Argentina 120
armed conflict
  demand fostering 14, 54, 62, 75
  trade financing 75
artisanal and small-scale mining (ASM)
  alluvial mining 34
  definition 42–43
  development potential 50–51
  extra-legal activities 20, 43
  generally 2, 34, 167
  illegal 43
  Johannesburg Declaration and PoI 74–75

198 *Index*

Minamata Convention on Mercury 83
social and environmental impacts 36
ASEAN 31
Atlantic Charter 93
Australia
community consultation 174
junior mining companies 41
licensing system 155–156
mineral production 31
transnational mining companies 41
Auty, R 49

B
banking sector
influence 44
policy documents 12
Barral, V 85
battery technology
boom 42
European Battery Alliance 17
metals required 28–29
bauxite 28
bentonite 30
Berlin Guidelines 71, 79
bidding processes 18, 160–161
Bilateral Investment Treaties (BITs) 97,
102, 105
biodiversity
Aichi targets 83
common concern of mankind 69
Convention on Biological Diversity 68, 83
New Delhi Declaration 86
planning law 173–174
Strategic Plan for 83
Birnie, P et al 85
Blackstone, Sir William 141
Blair, T 117
Blanco, V 145
Bolivia 16, 77–78, 156
Botswana 42, 120
Botswanan Act 59
Brazil 31
Bretton Woods Agreement 54, 93–94
bribery *see* **corruption, prevention**
Brown, R 59
Brundtland Report 65–68
Burnett, HG and Bret, LA 102–103
Bury v Pope 141
business conduct
accountability 93
responsible, evolving standard 93
transnational enterprises, responsibility 93,
110, 111, 112–115, 119, 180

C
Campbell, NJ 144, 154
Canada 120
claim-staking system 154, 160
indigenous ownership rights 143
junior mining companies 41
licensing system 155
mineral production 31
ownership rights 142, 143
transnational mining companies 41
transparency 122
carbon emissions
Paris Agreement 81
Caribbean
ECLAC 15–16
Mining Strategy for Latin America
and 47
Charter of Economic Rights and Duties
of States (CERDS) 56, 57
Chile 31, 154
Codelco 42
Mining Integration Treaty with
Argentina 13
China
investment in Africa 77
mineral demand and production 31, 77
recycled metals 32
state land ownership 162
transnational mining companies 41, 42, 77
Churchill, Sir W 93
CIMVAL 103
circular economy
see also sustainability
calls for, generally 3
EU Action Plan 17
generally 178
international trade law 96
national minerals policies 18–19
new business models 50
claim-staking system 154, 155, 160
climate change
see also environmental protection
Arctic Ocean 125–126
challenges, generally 2, 54, 182
common concern of mankind 69
Framework Convention on 68, 81
nationally determined contributions
(NDCs) 81, 82
New Delhi Declaration 86
Paris Agreement 10, 50, 81–83
Task Force on Climate-related Financial
Disclosures 120
World Bank Climate-Smart Facility 82

Index   199

closing operation   151
    duration and costs involved   38–39
coal   142–143, 164
cobalt   28
Coke LCJ   141
Colombia   78, 156
colonialism
    claims by former colonial powers   58
    independence from   53, 56
    investment by colonial powers   45
    post-colonial mining laws   15, 59, 139, 154,
       166
commodity prices
    environmental protection and   65, 67, 70
    rise   77
common heritage of mankind
    benefit sharing rule   129
    global commons   124, 127
    marine mining   124, 127, 128–130, 134
    minerals conceptualised as   3, 54, 58, 60, 124
    non-appropriation rule   127, 129
community agreements
    generally   9
community consultation *see* public
       consultation
community impacts *see* social impacts
       of mining operations
competition
    laws governing, generally   4
    Washington Consensus   94
concession agreements   45–46, 157
construction materials   30
consultation *see* public consultation
continental shelves   125–126
contracts
    allocation or acquisition of mineral
       rights   152, 156–159, 175–176
    anti-corruption measures   175–176
    breach, elevation to international law   104
    clausula rebus sic stantibus   158
    concession agreements   157
    exploration and extraction rights   138,
       169–170, 175
    investment promotion agreements   157
    investor protection   40
    joint ventures   157
    licensing under   155
    pacta sunt servanda   158
    production-sharing agreements   157
    service contracts   157
    stabilisation clauses   40, 47, 48, 158–159
    transnational   13–14, 47, 48, 49
    transparency   49

Convention on Biological Diversity   68, 83
Convention on the Settlement of Investment
       Disputes (ICSID)   98
copper   28, 29, 30
    recycled   32
corporate social responsibility   73, 87, 119,
       180
corruption, prevention
    Convention on Combating Bribery   111
    EITI   111
    international law   3, 13, 92, 110–111
    meaning of corruption   110–111
    national laws   175–176
    New Delhi Declaration   87
    OECD measures   111
    Sustainable Development Goals   79
    transparency and accountability   110–111,
       175–176
    UN Convention against Corruption   111
    UN Global Compact   115
cosmopolitan legal thought   11, 179
Costa Rica   78
coupled elements   30
critical minerals   18, 32–33, 164
cross-value chains   50
Crowson, P   29
customary law
    free mining customs   4–5, 152–154
    generally   9
    international   11

D
Dalupan, C   65, 88
De Beers Group   42
Debswana Diamond Company   42
Declaration on the Right to Development   78
demand
    cyclical nature   18
    derived-driven   29
    emerging technologies   28–29
deregulation
    Washington Consensus   94
Dernbach, J   89
developed economies
    mineral demands   30–31
developing countries
    see also development
    Africa Mining Vision   15, 49, 77
    Agenda 21   70–71, 72
    assisting to prevent environmental
       impacts   64
    Brundtland Report   66–67
    colonial legal heritage   15, 139, 154, 166

200   *Index*

development minerals   20, 43, 51, 56, 164, 167
financing development   67
foreign investment   94, 96–102
international development agencies   45
international economic law   94, 96–102
marine mining   126, 128, 129, 133
mineral demands   30–31
national laws   166
negotiating capacity   67
New International Economic Order   94
PSONR principle   55–61, 64, 166
'resource curse'   22, 48, 49, 72–73, 77, 111
transnational governance   14
Washington Consensus   94
development
see also developing countries
African Mining Vision   77
Agenda 21   70–71, 72
Agenda 2030   78–81, 104
Brundtland Report   65–68
commodity price rise   77
distributional justice   24, 53, 55, 70, 72, 85, 182–183
duty to cooperate for   58
environmental protection and   62–68
industrialisation   77, 78–81, 94
international law   95
Johannesburg Declaration and PoI   71–76, 79
laws governing, generally   4
Millennium Development Goals   76–77
mining's link to   2–3
MMSD   73, 87, 119
Monterrey Consensus on Financing for   72
PSONR principle   54–61, 64, 92, 123, 166
right to   58, 78, 86, 105
Rio Declaration   86, 87, 88
social ends, for   66
Stockholm Declaration   63–65, 66, 69, 70
Structural Adjustment Programmes   67
sustainable *see* sustainability
UN Millennium Declaration   72, 78
UN principles   57
WSSD   71–76, 79, 87
diamonds   30
ASM sector   34
EITI   75
financing armed conflict   75
Kimberley Process Certification Scheme   75, 117
marine mining   31, 123

discrimination
human rights law   107
international investment law   98–99, 101
Most-Favoured Nation principle   95–96, 98–99
national treatment principle   95–96, 98–99
distributional justice   24, 53, 55, 70, 72, 85, 182–183
Doha Conference   72
domanial **doctrine**   140, 145–148
Dupuy, P   84
Dutch disease   49

E
Economic Commission for Africa (UNECA)   49, 77
Economic Commission for Latin America and the Caribbean (ECLAC)   15–16
economic decision-making *see* **international economic law; investment**
economic law *see* **international economic law; international investment law**
Ecuador   16, 78
Eggert, R   36–37
energy
affordable, SDGs   78, 79
energy minerals   30
mining's energy usage   30
Paris Agreement   81
renewable   81
transition   1, 50, 164
Environment and International Resource Panel   79
environmental protection
see also climate change; pollution; sustainability
Action Plan for the Human Environment   64–65
African Mining Vision   77
Agenda 21   70–71, 72
Aichi biodiversity targets   83
Antarctica   135
ASM operations   36
Berlin Guidelines   71, 79
Brundtland Report   65–68
commodity prices and   65, 67, 70
common concern of mankind   69
Convention on Biological Diversity   68, 83
corporate social responsibility   73, 87, 119
development and   62–68
economic factors   65

Index 201

Environmental, Social and Governance risks 121
Environmental Guidelines for Mining Operations 71
evolution of environmental law 54, 58, 61
Forests, Statement of Principles 68
impact assessments 19, 37, 71, 85, 86, 151, 171, 175
impact of mining, generally 34–35, 41, 71
integrated decision-making 88–91
international cooperation, requirement for 8
international economic law 96
international investment law 100
international law, development 3, 54, 58, 61, 92
IRMA 121
IUCN 62, 65
Johannesburg Declaration and PoI 71–76, 79
Latin American regional governance 16
legal *see* international environmental law
marine mining 32, 123, 133–134
MCEP 120
mega-trends in environmental issues 9n
mining and, generally 3
New Delhi Declaration 86–87
No Dirty Gold campaign 120–121
Paris Agreement 10, 50, 81–83
planning law 173–174
product controls or bans 82–83
public consultation 16, 18, 173–174, 183
radioactive waste 64
Rio Declaration 68–71, 72, 86, 87, 88
social license to operate 41, 70–72
soft law instruments 11, 69–70, 82–83
Stockholm Declaration 62–65, 69, 70
Strategic Plan for Biodiversity 83
sustainable development principle 6, 9, 84
transboundary environmental harm 68–69
treaties 11, 18
UN Global Compact 114–115
UNCHE 62–65, 79
waste management 34–35
WCED 66
World Bank ESS 116
World Charter for Nature 64–65, 79, 88
World Conservation Strategy 65–68
Equator Principles 116
Escazú Agreement 16
ethical considerations
generally 8
soft law instruments 11

European Battery Alliance 17
European Union
allocation of property rights 156
Circular Economy Action Plan 17
European Green Deal 17
Innovation Partnership on Raw Materials 17
mining law, generally 22
payment disclosures 122
Raw Materials Initiative 16–17
recycling and substitution 17, 32
resource diplomacy 17
responsible sourcing 17
sustainable sourcing 17
exclusive economic zone (EEZ) 124–125
exploration
see also licensing/permitting
business fragmentation 30
duration and cost 38
evaluation 37
generally 33, 69–70
geographical expansion 7–8
geological surveying 37
junior exploration companies 30, 38, 41–42
marine mining 132–133
national laws 138, 151, 169–170
odds of discovering 37, 161
prospecting 36–37, 151, 161
PSONR principle 57, 64, 123, 166
rights 138, 161
territorial sovereignty 53, 61
transition to exploitation 169–170, 175
uncertainty surrounding results 40
expropriation
creeping 100
customary international law 99, 103
direct and indirect 99–100
international investment law 99–102
national laws 62, 63
extraction
see also licensing/permitting
calls to phase out 3
corporate duty to local population 19
cost assessment 37, 38–39
geographical expansion 7–8
illegal, UN Protocol Against 60
national laws 138, 151, 169–170
ownership of extracted minerals 4
pollution *see* pollution
rights 4, 53, 138, 169–170, 175–176
Extractive Industries Review 73, 74

202 *Index*

Extractive Industries Transparency
 Initiative (EITI) 22, 23, 75, 111,
 117–118, 122
Exxon Valdez oil spill 135

F
Fair and Equitable Treatment (FET)
 100–102, 104
Fairmined Certification 120
feasibility studies 151
 duration and cost 37, 38
financing *see* international investment law;
 investment
Finland 120
forests
 Agenda 21 70–71
 Statement of Principles 68
Fourth Revolution 1–2, 28
France 156
free mining customs 4–5, 152–154

G
Gabčikovo-Nagymaros case 84, 85
General Agreement on Tariffs and Trade
 (GATT) 93–94, 95
General Agreement on Trade in Services
 (GATS) 97
geological surveying 36–37, 132, 150, 161
Germany 156
Glencore 42
Glenn, P 10
global commons
 Antarctica *see* Antarctica
 Arctic 125–126
 benefit sharing rule 129
 common heritage of mankind 3, 54, 58, 60,
  124, 127, 128–130, 134
 definition 126, 126n
 Earth's atmosphere 67, 126n, 165
 high seas 125, 126–127, 128
 international law 123, 126–137
 legal status of doctrine 127
 non-appropriation rule 127, 129
 outer space *see* space resources
 peaceful purposes rule 130
 res communis doctrine 128, 165
 seabed *see* marine mining
 UNCLOS 12, 124–134, 139
Global Mining Initiative 73, 119
global perspective
 mining law, generally 6, 7–20, 178–183
 sustainability 6, 9

Global Resource Outlook 2019 79
globalisation
 Agenda 21 70–71, 72
 Bretton Woods Agreement 93–94
 challenges to multilateralism 54
 cosmopolitan legal thought 10–11, 26, 179
 diffusion of governance 26
 economic 93
 economic liberalisation 8, 46–47, 74–75,
  93, 94, 95
 generally 45
 international economic law 93–94
 international law and 53–54
 internationalisation of production 45
 Internet era 94
 mining industry 179
 mining law and 139
 production networks 30–32
 spread 70
 supply chains 14
 transnational companies *see* transnational
  enterprises
 value chain 8, 77, 117
gold 29, 32
 ASM sector 34
 Fairmined Certification 120
 Gold Rushes 154
 marine mining 32, 123
 No Dirty Gold campaign 120–121
 Responsible Jewellery Council 121
governance
 see also international law; national laws
 accountability 7, 73–74, 77, 87, 93, 111
 concept, generally 25–26, 166
 corporate social responsibility 73, 87, 119
 global perspective 26, 28
 good governance concept 25–26, 87
 impact of mining, generally 36
 International Resource Panel reports 88
 licensing generally 44
 mining industry stakeholders 43–44
 self-constituted charters 45–46
 transnational *see* transnational enterprises;
  transnational governance
 transparency 49, 73–74, 77, 79, 80, 87, 111
 UN Mineral Resource Governance
  Resolution 79, 80, 81, 88
 voluntary initiatives 75
gravel 30
Great Lakes Region
 Pact on Security, Stability and Development
  for 60, 60–61n

Index 203

H
Haddow, K 161
Huber, M 52
Hufty, M 25–26
human rights/human rights law
African Charter 16, 107
African Commission on Human and Peoples'
Rights 16
Agenda 2030 78–81
American Convention of Human
Rights 107, 108–109
consultation of indigenous peoples 18,
107–109, 172–174, 183
corporate responsibility 110, 112–115, 182
development of law, generally 3, 7, 13
due process principle 107
evolution 92, 105–106
home state 109–110, 180
host state 109–110, 180
ILO Convention 107–108
impact assessments 110, 171–172
indigenous peoples 3, 6, 44, 106–110,
172–174, 178, 180
Inter-American Court of Human
Rights 108
International Bill of Human Rights 105, 110
International Covenant on Civil and Political
Rights 55, 107
International Covenant on Economic, Social
and Cultural Rights 55, 107
international investment treaties 104–105
mining and minerals, generally 105–110,
111
national laws and 106
New Delhi Declaration 86–87
No Dirty Gold campaign 120–121
non-discrimination 107
potential impacts of mining operations 35,
41
progressively achieving rights 106
protection, state's duty 110
PSONR principle 61, 180
right to own property 107
social license to operate 41, 70–72
Stockholm Declaration 62–65
Sustainable Development Goals 80
transnational enterprises 110, 114–115,
180, 182
UN Charter 105
UN Global Compact 76, 104, 114–115
UN Guiding Principles 75–76, 110,
113–115, 171, 182

UN principles, generally 53, 105
Universal Declaration of Human Rights 78,
105, 107
Voluntary Principles 116–117
women 106, 109, 178
World Bank Extractive Industries
Review 73
hydrocarbons
transition from 1, 50, 164

I
illegal exploitation of natural resources
UN Protocol Against 60
impact assessments
Berlin Guidelines 71
environmental 19, 37, 71, 85, 86, 151, 171,
175
human rights 110, 171–172
social 19, 37, 71, 85, 86, 151, 171–172
India 31
indigenous peoples
consultation 18, 107–109, 172–174
culturally or spiritually significant land 3, 6,
92, 108, 173, 178
ILO Convention 107–108
international human rights law 44, 106–110,
178, 180
ownership rights 143
relocation 107–108
traditional mining rights 6, 74
UN Declaration on Rights of 108
Indonesia 31, 123
industrial mining 39–41, 173
industrialisation *see* **development**
infrastructure
cost assessment 37, 151
development, generally 167
laws governing, generally 4
remote sites 39–40
**Initiative for Responsible Mining Assurance
(IRMA)** 121
intellectual property rights
international law 95
**Intergovernmental Forum on Mining,
Minerals, Metals and Sustainable
Development (IGF)** 50, 75
internal rate of return (IRR) 39
International Bill of Human Rights 105, 110
**International Council on Mining and Metals
(ICMM)** 75, 120
**International Covenant on Civil and Political
Rights** 55, 107

204 Index

International Covenant on Economic, Social and Cultural Rights 55, 107
International Development Association 67
international economic law
  see also international investment law
  circular economy 96
  developing countries 94
  dispute resolution 94
  environmental provisions 96
  evolution 92, 93–94
  Fair and Equitable Treatment standard 100–102, 104
  foreign direct investment (FDI) 94
  GATT 93–94, 95
  intellectual property rights 95
  mining and minerals 93–105
  Most-Favoured Nation principle 95–96, 98–99
  national treatment principle 95–96, 98–99
  resource management provisions 96
  trade agreements 95–96
  Washington Consensus 94
  World Trade Organisation 93–94
International Finance Corporation (IFC)
  Sustainability Framework 116
international investment law
  see also international economic law
  arbitrariness, protection against 101
  Bilateral Investment Treaties (BITs) 97, 102, 105
  discrimination, protection against 98–99, 101
  dispute resolution 97–102
  due process principle 100, 101
  environmental protection measures 100
  expropriation 99–102, 103
  Fair and Equitable Treatment standard 100–102, 104
  foreign investors 97–102
  free trade agreements 97
  GATS 97
  generally 4, 7, 40, 92
  human rights 104–105
  ICSID 98
  investment protection 97–105
  legitimate expectations 100–102, 104, 175
  licence non-renewal 99
  Most-Favoured Nation (MFN) principle 98–99
  national treatment principle 98–99
  nationalisation and 103
  public policy implications 103–105

  regulatory taking 100
  SDG and climate change standards 104–105
  stability, predictability and consistency principle 48, 100, 131, 175
  standards 104–105
  tax measures 100
  transnational governance 13–14
  treaties 96–105
  TRIMs 97
International labour Organisation (ILO)
  Convention on Indigenous and Tribal Peoples 107–108, 110
  Declaration on Fundamental Principles and Rights at Work 115
  Tripartite Declaration 76, 114–115
international law
  access to land for mining 82
  Antarctica *see* Antarctica
  clausula rebus sic stantibus 58
  common heritage of mankind 3, 54, 58, 60, 124, 127
  contractual clauses, breach 104
  corruption, prevention 3, 13, 92, 110–111
  cosmopolitan legal thought 10–11, 26, 179
  customary 11, 61, 68–69, 99, 102–103
  development law 95
  due process principle 87, 97, 99, 100, 101, 107, 122, 131, 175
  economic criteria 167–168
  economic globalisation and 93
  economic law *see* international economic law; international investment law
  EITI standard 22, 23, 75, 111, 117–118, 122
  environmental *see* environmental protection
  evolution 44–51, 54, 92, 180
  expropriation 99, 103
  Fair and Equitable Treatment standard 100–102, 104
  freedom of the high seas 126, 128, 129
  global commons *see* global commons
  globalisation and 26, 53–54
  human rights *see* human rights/human rights law
  integrated decision-making 86, 87, 88–91
  intellectual property rights 95
  investment law *see* international investment law
  lex mineralia 103
  lex petrolea 103
  marine mining *see* marine mining
  Minamata Convention on Mercury 83

Index 205

mining and minerals 3, 8, 54, 87–88
nation-states bound by 13
national law interfaces 13, 168–176,
 180–183
national and subnational law and 8, 13
nationalisation and 103
New Delhi Declaration 86–87
pacta sunt servanda 58
product controls or bans 82
PSONR principle 55–61, 64, 68–69, 92, 99,
 123, 180
rule of law, generally 7, 40, 48, 73, 79, 87,
 139, 149, 167, 168, 174–175, 181
soft law instruments 11, 69–70, 75–76,
 82–83, 180
sources 11
sovereignty, doctrine generally 138
stability, predictability and consistency
 principle 48, 100, 131, 175
state-centric nature 112
sustainable development, normative
 status 83–91
sustainable development principle 84–85
territorial sovereignty 52–53, 61, 123–126,
 138
transboundary matters 68–69
transboundary resources 123
transnational governance *see* transnational
 enterprises; transnational governance
treaties 11, 12–13, 18, 47, 85, 94, 96–102
tribunals 94
UNCLOS 12, 124–134, 139
International Monetary Fund (IMF) 54, 93
International Open Data Charter 118
international policy
Agenda 21 68–71, 72
Agenda 2030 10, 12, 50, 76, 78–81, 104
banking sector 12
Brundtland Report 65–68
Cancun Declaration 83
Convention on Biological Diversity 68, 83
development 44–46
Framework Convention on Climate
 Change 68, 81
generally 3, 8
Johannesburg Declaration and PoI 71–76, 79
Minamata Convention on Mercury 83
New International Economic Order 12, 54,
 56–57, 60, 67, 94
Paris Agreement 10, 50, 81–83
PSONR principle 55–61, 64, 68–69, 92, 99,
 123, 180

Rio Declaration 68–71, 72, 86, 87, 88
Rio+20 69n, 76–78, 79, 87
Stockholm Declaration 62–65, 66, 68,
 69, 70
Sustainable Development Goals (SDGs)
 10, 12, 32, 50, 76, 78–81, 94, 104, 180
UN Mineral Resource Governance
 Resolution 79, 80, 81, 88
Washington Consensus 70, 94
International Resource Panel 50, 88
International Seabed Authority (ISA) 126,
 128, 129, 130, 131–133
**International Study Group for the Review
 of African Mining Regimes** 77
**International Union for the Conservation
 of Nature (IUCN)** 62, 65
investment
arbitration 47, 48, 58
Bilateral Investment Treaties (BITs) 97, 102
capital costs 38–39
capital-intensive nature of mining 39–41
concession agreements 46
costs assessment 38–39
developing countries, in 67, 96–97
financial value of mine, calculation 39
foreign, regulation and protection 13,
 57–59, 94, 96–105
ICSID 98
insurance schemes 40
internal rate of return 39
international law *see* international investment
 law
legal protection 40
legitimate expectations 100–102, 104, 175
MIGA 40, 116
negotiating capacity of developing
 countries 67
pre-production activities 38–40
Principles for Responsible Investment 121
protection 47, 48, 96–105
PSONR principle 57–58, 99
recovery time 37, 40
risk exposure 39–41
social license to operate 41, 70–72
transport infrastructure 39–40
UN Resolutions 57
World Bank Extractive Industries
 Review 73, 74
investment promotion agreements 157
iron 28
Iron Rhine Arbitration 84
Island of Palmas (*Miangas*) **case** 52

206 *Index*

J
Jessup, PC   13
Johannesburg Declaration and PoI   71–76, 79
joint ventures   157
JORC   103
Joyner, C   135

K
Kanetake, M   169
kaolin   30
Kimberley Process Certification Scheme
(KPCS)   75, 117

L
land
access to   82, 138, 150, 172–174
compulsory acquisition   162, 163
consultation in planning process   172–174
contamination   35
culturally or spiritually significant   3, 6, 92,
108, 173, 178
expropriation   162, 163
indigenous rights *see* indigenous peoples
land use planning   17, 140, 165, 171–174
ownership *see* ownership
peasant communities   6, 165, 178, 180
Latin America
American Declaration of the Rights and
Duties of Man   107
constitutional reforms   77–78
debt crisis   67
ECLAC   15–16
mineral rights   143, 156–157
mining precedence challenged   166–167
Mining Strategy for Latin America and the
Caribbean   47
regional governance   16
lead   28
recycled   32
licensing/permitting
allocation of mineral rights   152, 154–156,
175–176
anti-corruption measures   175–176
Berlin Guidelines   71
breach by investor, where   102
contract-based   155
custom-based regimes   155
duration and cost   38
exploration and extraction rights   138
Fair and Equitable Treatment
standard   100–102
generally   44, 152, 154–156

integrated decision-making   89
national laws   170–172
national sovereignty, principle of   57, 138,
181
non-renewal   99
obligations of licence-holder   152
reconnaissance licences   152
retention licences   152
social license to operate   41, 70–72
Sustainable Development License to
Operate   80
lithium   28, 42
Lowe, V   85
Luxembourg   137

M
Madrid Protocol   134, 135
magnesium   32, 123
Malawian Act   59
manganese   28
marine mining
Arctic Ocean   125–126
benefit sharing rule   129
beyond national jurisdiction   32, 54, 60, 123
Clarion-Clipperton Zone   132, 133
common heritage of mankind   54, 58, 60,
124, 127, 128–130, 134
continental shelves   125–126
deep seabed   123–124
developing countries   126, 128, 129, 133
the Enterprise   128, 129, 131–132
environmental impact   32, 123
environmental protection   133–134
equitable sharing   126
exclusive economic zones (EEZs)   124–125
exploration rights   132–133
generally   12, 31–32, 54, 124–134
high seas   125, 126, 128
International Seabed Authority (ISA)   126,
128, 129, 130, 131–133
landlocked states   129
mineral extraction, generally   22
Mining Code   130
non-appropriation rule   127, 129
ownership of seabed   124–134
the parallel system   131–132
payments or contributions in kind   126
peaceful purposes rule   130
pioneer investor regime   132
pollution   71, 134
precautionary principle   134
prospecting   132

Index 207

resource allocation 128
sea-bed subsoil 129
sovereign rights of coastal states 124–125
Sustainable Development Goals 123
territorial sea 123, 124–126
UNCLOS 12, 124–134, 139
mercury
Minamata Convention 83
metals
coupled elements 30
generally 30
major and minor 30
property/tenure systems 139
rare earths 28, 30
recycling 32
shift to 1–2
Mexico 154
Millennium Development Goals 76–77
Minamata Convention on Mercury 83
mineral rights
see also licensing/permitting
allocation or acquisition 47, 53, 140, 150, 152–161, 164–165, 174–176
bid or tender processes 18, 160–161
cancellation 173
contractual regimes 152, 156–159
discretionary allocation processes 160–161
exploration, transition to extraction 169–170, 175–176
free mining customs 4–5, 152–154, 160
licensing systems 152, 154–156
national laws 4, 138, 150, 151
open access processes 160–161
ownership *see* ownership
possessory systems 152–154
prior appropriation rule 160
sovereignty and 53, 181
surface rights holders and 161–163
mineral tenure
traditional patterns 6
minerals
see also metals; natural resources
construction materials 30
coupled elements 30
critical 18, 32–33, 164
depletion, minimising 68
development minerals 20, 43, 51, 56, 164, 167
disciplinary framing 29
energy minerals 30
illegal exploitation 60

industrial 30
non-metallic 30
odds of discovering 37, 161
ownership *see* ownership
recycling *see* recycling
reserves 29, 33, 37
resources 29
rights to *see* mineral rights
strategic 32–33
mining
see also exploration; extraction; mineral rights
alluvial 34
automation 39
capital-intensive nature 39–41
development agreements 157
energy usage 35
Environmental Guidelines for Mining Operations 71
environmental impact 34–35
financial value of mine, calculation 39
global nature of industry 179
governance, impact on 36
illegal 60
industry structure 41–43
Intergovernmental Forum (IGF) 50, 75
lifecycle stages 36–41, 151
precedence of, in land use 4, 138, 154, 161–163, 166, 172, 174
process, generally 33–34, 151
risk profile 39–41
social impacts *see* social impacts of mining operations
solution mining 34
surface 34, 36
underground 34, 36
water-based 34
Mining Certification Evaluation Project (MCEP) 120
mining law
see also national laws
access to land and resources 138, 150, 172–174
accountability 7
aspects of 4
community agreements 9
consultation and consent 172–173, 183
contractual turn 19
customary 4–5, 9, 102–103
distributional justice and 24, 183
domanial doctrine 140, 145–148
economic criteria 167–168

208   *Index*

exploration and extraction rights   138, 169–170, 175–176
fragmented system   7
generally   25–26
global perspective   6, 7–20, 178–183
international *see* international law
international scholarship   20–24
landownership doctrine (accession system)   140, 141–143
Latin America   16
licensing systems *see* licensing/permitting
local peoples' rights   19
mineral rights *see* mineral rights
national *see* national laws
origins   139
ownership and rights, generally   4, 138–139, 140–150
public purpose, regulation in   4, 18, 138, 139, 140, 146, 151
regalian doctrine   4–5, 140, 144–145, 146
res nullius doctrine   128, 144, 148–149
spatial planning   172–174
surface rights holders   4, 138, 141–143, 161–163
sustainability as objective   9–10, 176–177
terminology   6, 22, 29, 178
transnational *see* transnational governance
transparency   7, 23, 149, 175–176
Mining and Metals Sustainable Development Project (MMSD)   73, 87, 119
Mirabeau, H-G Riqueti comte de   148–149, 163
Mitsubishi   42
Monterrey Consensus on Financing for Development   72
Moon Agreement   12, 127, 136
Most-Favoured Nation (MFN) principle   95–96, 98–99
Multilateral Investment Guarantee Agency (MIGA)   40, 116
multinational companies *see* **transnational companies**

N
Namibia   31, 123
nation states
laws *see* national laws
PSONR principle   12, 13, 21, 46, 54–61, 64, 68–69, 92, 99, 166, 180
sovereignty *see* sovereignty
national interest principle
control by nationals, calls for   50

critical minerals lists   18, 32–33, 164
national laws and   4, 162–164, 165
national minerals policies   18–19
public interest and   165
national laws
access to land and resources   138, 150, 172–174
accountability   149
administrative   151, 165, 175–176
compulsory acquisition of land   162, 163
consultation and consent   16, 18, 19–20, 172–174, 183
developing countries   166
dispute settlement   151
domanial doctrine   140, 145–148
exploration and extraction rights   138, 169–170, 175–176
extra-territorial application   14, 121–122
free mining customs   4–5, 152–154
generally   3–5, 17–19, 44, 138–140, 150–152, 165–167
governance paradigm   166
human rights law and   106
impact assessments *see* impact assessments
international investment law and   103–105
international law interfaces   13, 168–176, 180–183
international treaties   13, 18
landownership doctrine (accession system)   140, 141–143
licensing systems *see* licensing/permitting
limits to state powers   174–175
mineral rights *see* mineral rights
national interest principle   4, 162–164, 165
national sovereignty, principle of   55–61, 138, 166, 181
ownership and rights, generally   3–4, 53, 138–139, 140–150
planning law   4, 17, 165, 171–174
precedence of mining in land use   4, 138, 154, 161–163, 166, 172, 174
protection of local populations   19
public purpose, regulation in   4, 18, 138, 139, 140, 146, 151, 163–164, 165
public trust doctrine   165, 166
regalian doctrine   4–5, 140, 144–145, 146
res nullius doctrine   128, 144, 148–149
restricting rights of foreign companies   57–59
royalties   140, 143
rule of law   149, 174–175, 181
security of supply, ensuring   151, 164

Index 209

states' duty to manage resources 149–150
subnational levels 19–20, 140
surface rights holders 4, 138, 141–143,
   161–163
taxation powers 17, 140
territorial sovereignty 52–53, 61, 123–126,
   138
title registration 150
transnational enterprises 57, 112
transparency 7, 23, 149, 175–176
national minerals policies
critical minerals lists 18, 32–33, 164
generally 18–19
state control over resources and
   mining 57–59
national treatment principle 95–96, 98–99
nationalisation
customary international law 103
generally 58–59
transnational enterprises 57, 58
**Natural Resource Governance Institute
   (NRGI)** 50, 75
natural resources
see also minerals
Agenda 21 70–71, 72
Agenda 2030 78–81, 104
Berlin Guidelines 71, 79
biological 86; *see also* biodiversity
Brundtland Report 65–68
critical minerals 18, 32–33, 164
demand resulting in armed conflict 14,
   54, 62
depletion, minimising 68
environmental protection 63
Global Resource Outlook 2019 79
integrated decision-making 86, 87, 88–91
International Resource Panel reports 88
management 65, 83–91, 96
New Delhi Declaration 86–87
non-renewable 68
ownership *see* ownership
PSONR principle 54–61, 64, 68–69, 92,
   123, 166, 180
recycling *see* recycling
sharing benefits derived from 65, 129
state control 57–59, 144
state revenue from 149–150
states' duty to manage 149–150
Stockholm Declaration 62–65, 69, 70
sustainable use *see* sustainability
territorial sovereignty 52–53, 61, 123–126,
   138, 181

transboundary *see* transboundary resources
wasteful exploitation 62, 63, 64–65, 67
World Charter for Nature 64–65, 79, 88
Nef, JU 164
neoliberalism 75, 94
New Delhi Declaration 86–87
**New International Economic Order
   (NIEO)** 12, 54, 56–57, 60, 67, 94,
   113, 127
New Zealand 156, 160
nickel 28

O
OK Tedi Agreement 59
Open Government Partnership 118
**Organisation for Economic Co-operation
   and Development (OECD)**
anti-corruption instruments 111
Due Diligence Guidelines 116
Guidelines for Multinational
   Enterprises 76, 104, 114, 115–116
National Contact Points (NCPs) 115
Recommendation on Public
   Procurement 111
Otto, J and Cordes, J 45
Outer Space Treaty 12, 127, 135–137
ownership
see also global commons
Anglo-American legal systems 141–142
civil law systems 140, 141, 146, 148
compulsory acquisition of land 162, 163
customary landholders 44
discovery, rule of 148–149, 154
domanial doctrine 140, 145–148
dominium 53, 140, 150
extracted minerals 4
foreign property, expropriation or
   transfer 57, 58, 99–102, 103
free mining customs 4–5, 152–154
identifying 164
landownership doctrine (accession
   system) 140, 141–143
minerals in situ 140–150, 164, 165, 166
mining and, generally 138, 140, 141–143
national laws 3–4, 57, 138–139
nationalisation of transnational
   enterprises 57, 58
occupation theory 148
possessory 152–154
primary 4, 138, 139, 140, 150
property rights 4, 18, 57
public or state ownership 141, 145–150

210 Index

regalian doctrine   4–5, 140, 144–145, 146
res communis doctrine   128, 165
res nullius doctrine   128, 144, 148–149
right to own property   107
rights, precedence   4, 138, 154, 161–163, 166, 172, 174
seabed and resources   124–134
state control over resources   57–59, 144–145, 146, 148–149
states' duty to manage resources   149–150
subsoil   138, 148, 150, 165
surface rights holders   4, 138, 141–143, 148, 161–163
Washington Consensus   94
water entitlement rights   4, 138

P
Papua New Guinea   59, 143, 174
Pardo, A   127
Permanent Sovereignty over Natural Resources (PSONR)   12, 13, 21, 46, 54–61, 64, 92, 99, 123, 166, 180
permitting *see* **licensing/permitting**
Peru   154
Philippines   120
planning law
  see also impact assessments; indigenous peoples
  anti-corruption measures   176
  consultation and consent   16, 18, 19–20, 172–174, 183
  generally   4, 17, 165, 171
  peasant communities   6, 165, 178, 180
  transparency   176
platinum   28, 30
political considerations
  political risk   40
  social impacts of mining operations   35–36
pollution
  see also climate change; environmental protection
  Agenda 21   71
  air   35
  Brundtland Report   67
  chemical   35
  Exxon Valdez oil spill   135
  land   35
  marine   71
  Minamata Convention on Mercury   83
  polluter-pays principle   134
  product controls or bans   82–83
  radioactive waste   64

Stockholm Declaration   63, 69
water   35
potash   30, 34
poverty
  cosmopolitan legal thought   179
  distributional justice   24, 53, 55, 70, 72, 85, 86–87, 182–183
  Johannesburg Declaration and PoI   74–75
  New Delhi Declaration   86–87
  Sustainable Development Goals   79
precious stones   30
Principles for Responsible Investment   121
privatisation
  generally   42, 47, 94, 158
  Washington Consensus   94
production-sharing agreements   157
property ownership and rights *see* **mineral rights; ownership**
prospecting   36–37, 151
  marine mining   132
  reconnaissance licences   152
  rights   161
public consultation
  environmental issues   16, 18, 173–174
  generally   19–20, 172–174, 183
  human rights law   107
  indigenous peoples   18, 172–174
public procurement
  transparency   18
  WTO Code   87
Pulp Mills **case**   84

R
radioactive waste   64
rare earth metals   28, 30
reclamation   151
  Action Plan for the Human Environment   64
  duration and costs involved   38–39
  Johannesburg Declaration and PoI   74
  Sustainable Development Goals   80
reconnaissance licences   152
recycling
  see also circular economy; sustainability
  European Union   17
  generally   3, 78
  metals   32
  new business models   50
Reddy J   149–150
regalian **doctrine**   4–5, 140, 144–145, 146
regional and subregional legal ordering
  Africa   15–16

Index 211

European Union 16–17
   generally 15–17, 44
   Latin America 16
Reliance Industries Ltd v Reliance Natural
       Resources Ltd 149–150
rentier states 49
res communis **doctrine** 128, 165
res nullius **doctrine** 128, 144, 148–149
'resource curse' 22, 48, 49, 72–73, 77, 111
resource diplomacy 17
Responsible Jewellery Council (RJC) 121
Responsible Mineral Development
       Initiative 75
ResponsibleSteel 121
retention licences 152
Rio Declaration 68–71, 72, 86, 87, 88
Rio+20 69n, 76–78, 79, 87
risk
   climate-related 120
   contractual allocation 157
   environmental 41
   ESG risks 121
   financial 39–41
   geological 40
   industrial mining 39–41
   planning decisions and 173
   political 40
Roman law 139, 140, 141, 144, 148, 153, 165
Roosevelt, FD 93
royalties 140, 143
Ruggie, J 113–114
Russia 31, 156

S
Salacuse, J 60
salt 30, 32, 34, 123
sand 30, 123
Sand and Sustainability 79
sapphires 34
Schill, S 181
Schlauch, P and Ireland, G 38
Schrijver, N 128
Scientific Conference on Resource
     Conservation and Utilisation 62
Scott, A 17, 138
seabed *see* **global commons; marine mining**
self-determination principle 53, 55
service contracts 157
Shrimp/Turtle **case** 84
Sierra Leone 75
silica 30
silver 28
smartphone technology 29

social impacts of mining operations
   Berlin Guidelines 71
   corporate social responsibility 73, 87, 119
   distributional justice 24, 53, 55, 70, 72, 85,
      182–183
   generally 3, 35–36
   impact assessments 19, 37, 71, 85, 86, 151,
      171–172
   integrated decision-making 88–91
   Johannesburg Declaration and PoI 72
   social planning in project development 71,
      170–171, 173
social license to operate 41, 70–72
solar energy
   metals required 28–29
South Africa 31, 123, 142
sovereignty
   allocation of property rights 53
   basic constitutional doctrine, as 52
   continental shelves 125
   dominium 53, 140
   exclusive economic zone 124–125
   foreign investment, national authority
      over 57–59
   imperium 53
   internal and an external dimensions 52–53,
      181
   international law, generally 138
   mining and minerals 3, 13, 17, 53, 181
   national laws, generally 55–61, 138, 166
   PSONR principle 12, 13, 21, 46, 54–61, 64,
      68–69, 92, 99, 123, 166, 180
   sovereign equality of states 53, 57, 58
   taxation 17
   territorial 52–53, 61, 123, 138
   territorial sea 123, 124–126
   transnational enterprises and 57
   treaties and 102
space resources
   celestial bodies 136
   common heritage of mankind 3, 54, 58,
      124, 127
   generally 22, 32, 123
   global commons 126, 126n, 127,
      135–137
   Moon Agreement 12, 127, 136
   Outer Space Treaty 12, 127, 135–137
Spain 120, 156, 160
state-owned enterprises 42
   privatisation 42, 47, 94, 158
   Washington Consensus 94
state participation or control 50
   duty to manage resources 149–150

212 Index

forms of 58–59
res nullius doctrine 128, 144, 148–149
steel 28, 42, 121
recycled 32
Stockholm Declaration 62–65, 66, 68, 69, 70
strategic minerals 32–33
sulphur 32, 123
sustainability/sustainable development
see also circular economy; recycling
Agenda 21 70–71, 72
Agenda 2030 10, 12, 50, 76, 78–81, 104
Brundtland Report 65–68
concept of sustainable development 84
core constitutive elements 86–88
cosmopolitan legal thought 179
European Union 17
Forests, Statement of Principles 68
generally 65, 83–91
Global Partnership for Sustainable
   Development Data 118
global perspective 6, 9, 54
governance system 10
IFC Sustainability Framework 116
integrated decision-making 85, 86, 87,
   88–91
integration, principle of 84–85, 86
Intergovernmental Forum (IGF) 50, 75
international law, status in 83–91
Johannesburg Declaration and PoI 71–76,
   79
Latin America 16
mining and, generally 87–88
mining law and 9–10, 176–177, 182–183
MMSD 73, 87, 119
new business models 50
New Delhi Declaration 86–87
objective 84–85
precautionary principle 71, 86–87, 134
principle 84–85, 180
procedural elements 86
Rio Declaration 68–71, 72, 86, 87, 88
Rio+20 76–78, 87
Sand and Sustainability 79
SDGs 10, 12, 32, 50, 76, 78–81, 82, 88, 94,
   104–105, 123, 180
Stockholm Declaration 62–65, 69, 70
substantive elements 86
Sustainable Development License to
   Operate 80
sustainable use of resources 65–68, 86
temporal scale of decisions 89
transnational enterprises, role 67, 116

water supply 50
World Bank Extractive Industries
   Review 73, 74
WSSD 71–76, 79, 87
Sweden 42
Szablowski, D 14

T
tailings
generation 34–35
Mine Tailings Storage 79
pollution from 35
radioactive waste 64
reworking 34
Tanzania 160
Tanzanian Act 59
taxation
international investment law 100
laws governing, generally 4, 17, 140
stabilisation policies 48
terminology, inconsistent 6, 22, 29, 178
Theodosian Code 144
Tianqi Lithium Global 42
tin 30, 31, 123
titanium 28
Towards Sustainable Mining 119–120
trade
see also international economic law
Agenda 21 70–71
arbitration 13
Bretton Woods Agreement 93–94
commodity trading firms 42
Doha Conference 72
foreign direct investment (FDI) 94
free trade agreements 97
GATS 97
GATT 93–94, 95
international treaties 13, 94
Internet era interdependency 94
liberalisation 93, 94, 95
new *lex mercatoria* 13
PSONR principle 55
trade agreements, generally 95
TRIMS 97
UNCITRAL 98, 105
WTO *see* World Trade Organisation
transboundary impacts
environmental harm 68–69
Johannesburg Declaration and PoI 74
transboundary matters
international law 68–69
transboundary resources 13, 123

Index 213

transnational enterprises
see also transnational governance
accountability   93, 112, 115–116
Africa   77
commodity trading firms   42
dominance in mining sector   112
generally   34, 41–42
home states   113, 114
human rights and   110, 114–115, 180,
    182–183
national laws   57, 112
national sovereignty and   57
nationalisation   57, 58
OECD Guidelines   76, 104, 114, 115–116
property of, expropriate or transfer   57, 58,
    99–102, 103
regulations   44
responsibility in international law   93, 111,
    112–115
self-regulation   118–122
sustainable development and   67, 116
UN Centre on Transnational
    Corporations   46
transnational governance
see also transnational enterprises
accountability mechanisms   115–116
Alliance for Responsible Mining   120
Aluminium Stewardship Initiative   121
arbitration   13, 40, 47, 48, 58, 98–102, 180–181
corporate self-regulation   118–122
EITI standard   22, 23, 75, 111, 117–118, 122
Equator Principles' Financial Institutions
    116
extra-territorial application, laws of   14,
    121–122
Fairmined Certification   120
Global Partnership for Sustainable
    Development Data   118
global supply chains   14
globalisation and   8, 9, 13–14
ICMM Principles   75, 120
IFC Sustainability Framework   116
ILO instruments   76, 114–115
institutions, generally   75
intergovernmental standards   113–115
international contracts   13
international investment   13
international law, generally   112–113
International Open Data Charter   118
IRMA   121
Kimberley Process Certification Scheme
    75, 117

MCEP   120
MIGA   40, 116
MMSD   73, 119
multi-stakeholders   116–118
National Contact Points (NCPs)   115
new *lex mercatoria*   13, 102
No Dirty Gold campaign   120–121
OECD Guidelines   76, 104, 114, 115–116
Open Government Partnership   118
Principles for Responsible Investment   121
private firms, regulation   14
responsibility of transnational enterprises
    93, 110, 112–115, 119, 180
ResponsibleSteel   121
soft law   112–113
Task Force on Climate-related Financial
    Disclosures   120
Towards Sustainable Mining   119–120
UN Code of Conduct   57, 113
UN Global Compact   76, 104, 114–115
UN Guiding Principles on Business and
    Human Rights   75–76, 110,
    113–115, 182
voluntary initiatives   75
Voluntary Principles   116–117
World Bank ESS   116
transparency
anti-corruption measures   110–111,
    175–176
bidding processes   18
Dodd-Frank Act   122
EITI   22, 23, 75, 111, 122
Escazú Agreement   16
Global Partnership for Sustainable
    Development Data   118
governance, generally   49, 73–74, 77, 122
International Open Data Charter   118
Kimberley Process Certification Scheme
    75, 117
mining law, generally   7, 23, 149,
    175–176
New Delhi Declaration   87
Open Government Partnership   118
planning decisions   176
public procurement   18
resource governance   49, 73–74
Sustainable Development Goals   79, 80
Task Force on Climate-related Financial
    Disclosures   120
transportation
cost assessment   37, 151
infrastructure   39–40

214 Index

treaties
  Bilateral Investment Treaties (BITs)   97,
    102, 105
  international investment law   96–105
  international law, as   11–12, 47, 85, 94, 97
  sovereignty and   102
Turgot   148
Twining, W   1, 10, 12, 79

U
United Kingdom
  mineral rights   141–143, 164, 165
  royal prerogative   142–143
United Nations
  Action Plan for the Human
    Environment   64–65
  agencies, influence   44, 46
  Agenda 21   70–71, 72
  Agenda 2030   10, 12, 50, 76, 78–81, 104
  Centre on Transnational Corporations   46
  Charter   55, 69, 78, 105
  Charter of Economic Rights and Duties
    of States (CERDS)   56, 57
  Code of Conduct for Transnational
    Companies   57, 113
  Commission on International Trade Law
    (UNCITRAL)   98, 105
  Conference on Environment and
    Development (UNCED)   68–71
  Conference on the Human Environment
    (UNCHE)   62–65, 79
  Conference on Sustainable Development
    76–78
  Convention against Corruption   111
  Convention on the Law of the Sea
    (UNCLOS)   12, 124–134, 139
  Declaration on the Rights of Indigenous
    Peoples   108
  Development Programme (UNDP)   50
  Economic Commission for Africa
    (UNECA)   49, 77
  Economic and Social Council (ECOSOC)
    62
  Environment and International Resource
    Panel   79
  Environment Programme (UNEP)   63,
    65, 71
  Environmental Guidelines for Mining
    Operations   71
  Framework Convention on Climate
    Change   68, 81
  Global Compact   76, 104, 114–115

  Guiding Principles on Business and Human
    Rights (UNGP)   75–76, 110,
    113–115, 171, 182
  human rights principle   53, 105
  Millennium Declaration   72, 78
  Millennium Development Goals   76–77
  Mineral Resource Governance   79, 80,
    81, 88
  mining and minerals, applicable principles
    57–59
  New International Economic Order
    (NIEO)   12, 54, 56–57, 60, 67, 94,
    113, 127
  Protocol Against the Illegal Exploitation of
    Natural Resources   60
  PSONR principle   46, 54–61, 64, 68–69, 92,
    99, 123, 180
  Resolutions   11, 46, 55
  Rio Declaration   68–71, 72, 86, 87, 88
  Rio+20   76–78, 79, 87
  SDGs   10, 12, 32, 50, 76, 78–81, 82, 88, 94,
    104, 123, 180
  self-determination principle   53, 55
  sovereign equality of states   53, 57, 58
  Stockholm Declaration   62–65, 69, 70
  sustainability, global action plans   54
  UN Environment   50, 79–81
  UNESCO   62, 63
  World Summit on Sustainable Development
    (WSSD)   71–76, 79, 87
United States
  claim-staking system   154, 155, 160
  Dodd-Frank Act   122
  mineral production   31
  mineral rights   141–142, 165
  public trust doctrine   165, 166
  space resources legislation   137
  transnational enterprises   41
Uruguay Round   95

V
value addition   68, 167

W
Washington Consensus   70, 94
waste
  Action Plan for the Human
    Environment   64–65
  generation   34–35
  pollution from   35
  radioactive   64
  waste dumps, reworking   34

Index   215

water
diversion of watercourses   67
entitlement rights   4, 138, 150, 163
marine mining _see_ marine mining
planning decisions   171
pollution   35
res communis doctrine   165
scarcity   50
social license to operate   41
supply, feasibility studies   37, 151
Sustainable Development Goals   79
water-based mining   34
Weeramantry J   84
West African Economic and Monetary Union (WAEMU)   15
wind energy
metals required   28–29
women
international human rights law   106, 109, 178
Johannesburg Declaration and PoI   74
Sustainable Development Goals   79
traditional mining rights   6, 74
World Bank
Climate-Smart Facility   82
Environmental and Social Standards (ESS)   116
establishment   54, 93–94
Extractive Industries Review   73, 74
finance for developing countries   67

financing mining industry   73
good governance concept   25–26
influence   44, 47
Mining Strategy for Latin America and the Caribbean   47
policy documents   12
Strategy for African Mining   15, 47
World Charter for Nature   64–65, 79, 88
World Commission on Environment and Development (WCED)   66
World Conservation Strategy   65–68
World Economic Forum (WEF)
Responsible Mineral Development Initiative   75
World Summit Outcome (2005)   78
World Trade Organisation (WTO)
Code on Public Procurement   87
establishment   95
law, generally   95–96
membership   95
Most-Favoured Nation principle   95–96, 98–99
national treatment principle   95–96
sustainability concept   84
World Wide Fund for Nature (WWF)   65, 120

Z
Zambian Act   59
zinc   28, 30
recycled   32

CPSIA information can be obtained
at www.ICGtesting.com
Printed in the USA
LVHW081922211022
731249LV00004B/156